Representing Women in Parliament

Written by a major international team of authors, this is the first book-length treatment of the political representation of women in countries sharing a Westminster-based political regime.

Featuring 12 chapters on new and established parliaments in Australia, Canada, New Zealand and the United Kingdom, this new book tests the latest and most broad-based theories about women's numerical and substantive political representation within the context of the commonalties and variations that have evolved from the Westminster legacy. The book is organised into three sections:

- First, the book examines the extent to which the descriptive representation of women in the 'old' Westminster parliaments has progressed in recent years, and the factors which have enhanced or impeded this progress.
- Second, the book explores the relationship between the numbers of women elected and the substantive representation of women – that is, the extent that women 'act for' women.
- Last, the volume reviews the recent experiences of four 'new' Westminster parliaments (Northern Ireland, Scotland, Wales and Nunavut) and evaluates the political opportunities for women provided by the creation of new institutions.

This comparative study will be of interest to students and researchers of legislative studies and gender politics/studies.

Marian Sawer leads the Democratic Audit of Australia at the Australian National University and chairs the Research Committee on Gender, Politics and Policy of the International Political Science Association. **Manon Tremblay** is Professor of Political Science and Head of the Research Centre on Women and Politics at the University of Ottawa. **Linda Trimble** is a Professor of Political Science at the University of Alberta.

Routledge research in comparative politics

1 **Democracy and Post-Communism**
Political change in the post-communist world
Graeme Gill

2 **Sub-State Nationalism**
A comparative analysis of institutional design
Edited by Helena Catt and Michael Murphy

3 **Reward for High Public Office**
Asian and Pacific Rim states
Edited by Christopher Hood and B. Guy Peters

4 **Social Democracy and Labour Market Policy**
Developments in Britain and Germany
Knut Roder

5 **Democratic Revolutions**
Asia and Eastern Europe
Mark R. Thompson

6 **Europeanisation and the Transformation of States**
Edited by Bengt Jacobsson, Per Lagreid and Ove K. Pedersen

7 **Democratization**
A comparative analysis of 170 countries
Tatu Vanhanen

8 **Determinants of the Death Penalty**
A comparative study of the world
Carsten Anckar

9 **How Political Parties Respond to Voters**
Interest aggregation revisited
Edited by Kay Lawson and Thomas Poguntke

10 **Women, Quotas and Politics**
Edited by Drude Dahlerup

11 **Citizenship and Ethnic Conflict**
Challenging the nation-state
Haldun Gülalp

12 **The Politics of Women's Interests**
New comparative and international perspectives
Edited by Louise Chappell and Lisa Hill

13 **Political Disaffection in Contemporary Democracies**
Social capital, institutions, and politics
Edited by Mariano Torcal and José Ramón Montero

14 **Representing Women in Parliament**
A comparative study
Edited by Marian Sawer, Manon Tremblay and Linda Trimble

Representing Women in Parliament

A comparative study

Edited by Marian Sawer, Manon Tremblay and Linda Trimble

LONDON AND NEW YORK

First published 2006
by Routledge
2 Park Square, Milton Park, Abingdon, Oxon OX14 4RN

Simultaneously published in the USA and Canada
by Routledge
711 Third Avenue, New York, NY 10017, USA

Routledge is an imprint of the Taylor & Francis Group, an informa group business

Typeset in Baskerville by Wearset Ltd, Boldon, Tyne and Wear

British Library Cataloguing in Publication Data
A catalogue record for this book is available from the British Library

Library of Congress Cataloging in Publication Data
A catalog record for this book has been requested

ISBN10: 0-415-39316-7 (hbk)
ISBN10: 0-415-47952-5 (pbk)

ISBN13: 978-0-415-39316-4 (hbk)
ISBN13: 978-0-415-47952-3 (pbk)

Contents

Figures

Tables

Contributors

Paul Chaney is a Lecturer at Cardiff University School of Social Sciences. He is author of *'An Absolute Duty': The Equality Policies of the Welsh Assembly Government* (2002) and (with Fiona Mackay and Laura McAllister) *Women, Politics and Constitutional Change* (2006, University of Wales Press).

Sarah Childs is a Lecturer in the Department of Politics at the University of Bristol. Her book *New Labour's Women MPs: Women Representing Women* was published in 2004. She is working on projects that explore the effect of women's presence – as MPs, Ministers, in the gender machinery and in civil society – on the policy agenda.

Jennifer Curtin is a Senior Lecturer in the Department of Political Studies at the University of Auckland. She has published a number of book chapters and articles in the area of gender politics and policy and is the author of *Women and Trade Unions: A Comparative Perspective* (1999, Ashgate) and co-author of *Rebels with a Cause: Independents in Australian Politics* (2004, University of New South Wales Press).

Yvonne Galligan is Reader in Politics at Queen's University, Belfast and Director of the Centre for the Advancement of Women in Politics. Her research interests cover comparative gender politics, political representation and public policy. Her recent publications include *Sharing Power: Women, Parliament, Democracy* (2005, Ashgate; co-edited with Manon Tremblay) and 'A job in politics is not for women: Analysing barriers to women's political representation in CEE' (2005, *Czech Sociological Review* 41(6), with S. Clavero). She was Fulbright Scholar and Distinguished Scholar in Residence at the School of Public Affairs, American University, Washington DC for 2005–6.

Sandra Grey is a Lecturer at Victoria University, Wellington. She has published a number of times on the topic of women and representation, including 'Does Size Matter? Critical Mass and New Zealand MPs' (*Parliamentary Affairs* 55:1, 2002) and Sawer and Grey, 'Australia and New Zealand', in Tremblay and Galligan (eds) *Sharing Power* (Ashgate,

2005). Her current research looks at the role of social movements, including the women's movement, in public policy change.

Fiona Mackay is a Senior Lecturer in Politics at the University of Edinburgh. She is author of *Love and Politics* (Continuum, 2001) and co-editor of *Women and Contemporary Scottish Politics* (EUP, 2001) and *The Changing Politics of Gender Equality in Britain* (Palgrave, 2002). Her current research explores gendered dimensions to constitutional Change Programme). Her latest book, co-authored with Paul Chaney and Laura McAllister, *Women, Politics and Constitutional Change: The First Years of the National Assembly for Wales*, is published by University of Wales Press (2006).

Ian McAllister is a professor in the Political Science Program and former Director of the Research School of Social Sciences at the Australian National University. His recent research includes Australian political parties and political behaviour; Russian electoral behaviour and democratisation; political behaviour and violence in Northern Ireland. He has worked extensively on gender patterns in voting and representation, with particular reference to Australia, Britain and the United States.

Elizabeth McLeay teaches in Political Science and International Relations Programme, Victoria University of Wellington. She has published in the following areas: constitutional change, including electoral system change and its impact on New Zealand's political system; cabinet government; the political representation of Maori and women; housing and policing policies.

Marian Sawer is an Adjunct Professor in the Political Science Program, Research School of Social Sciences at the Australian National University. Her books include *Sisters in Suits: Women and Public Policy in Australia* (1990), *A Woman's Place: Women and Politics in Australia* (with Marian Simms, 2nd edn 1993)*; Elections: Full, Free and Fair* (2001), *Speaking for the People: Representation in Australian Politics* (edited with Gianni Zappalà, 2001), *The Ethical State? Social Liberalism in Australia* (2003) and *Us and Them: Anti-elitism in Australia* (edited with Barry Hindess, 2004).

Jackie F. Steele is a doctoral candidate in Political Science at the University of Ottawa and recipient of the Canada Graduate Scholarship. Her Parliamentary Internship research paper, 'The Liberal Women's Caucus: An Effective Player in the Parliamentary Process', was awarded the 2001 Alf Hales Award. Her doctoral thesis will draw on republican and feminist theories of citizenship as a basis for contemporary representative democratic praxis. As a visiting researcher at the COE Gender, Law and Policy Centre (Tohoku University), she will interview the women elected to the Japanese House of Representatives.

Donley T. Studlar serves as the Eberly Family Distinguished Professor of

Political Science at West Virginia University and formerly as Executive Secretary of the British Politics Group. His articles on gender representation in Western democracies have appeared in journals such as the *British Journal of Political Science, Canadian Journal of Political Science, Electoral Studies, European Journal of Political Research, Governance, Journal of Legislative Studies, Journal of Politics, Legislative Studies Quarterly, Political Research Quarterly, Representation* and *Social Science Quarterly.*

Manon Tremblay is Professor of Political Science and Director of the Research Centre on Women and Politics at the University of Ottawa. She is author of *Des femmes au Parlement: une stratégie féministe?* (1999), co-author of *Questionnements féministes et méthodologie de la recherche* (2000), *Maires et mairesses: les femmes et la politique municipale* (1997) and *Que font-elles en politique?* (1995), editor of *Les Politiques publiques canadiennes* (1998) and co-editor of *Sharing Power: Women, Parliament, Democracy* (2005), *Women and Electoral Politics in Canada* (2003), *Le Parlementarisme canadien* (2nd edn 2000), *Women and Political Representation in Canada* (1998) and *Femmes et représentation politique au Québec et au Canada* (1997). She is the French co-editor of the *Canadian Journal of Political Science.*

Linda Trimble is a Professor in the Political Science Department at the University of Alberta. She is co-author with Jane Arscott of *Still Counting: Women in Politics across Canada* (2003) and co-editor of *Reinventing Canada* (with Janine Brodie, 2003), *Women and Electoral Politics in Canada* (with Manon Tremblay, 2003) and *In the Presence of Women: Representation in Canadian Governments* (with Jane Arscott, 2003). Her current research project analyses media coverage of female government leaders in Canada, Australia and New Zealand.

Lisa Young is an Associate Professor of Political Science at the University of Calgary. She is author of *Feminists and Party Politics* and co-author of *Rebuilding Canadian Party Politics* and *Advocacy Groups: A Democratic Audit* (forthcoming). Her research projects include the analysis of data from a survey of Canadian political party members, a study of youth participation in Canadian political parties and an examination of the implications of electoral finance regimes for the election of women in the United States and Canada.

Foreword

As an irony of our times, it may appear that the newer the democracy the more likely women's political participation will figure on the agenda. Local women's movements, benefiting nowadays from global networks and support, may have staked an early claim for a place at the table in peace and constitution building talks. The international community, which may be reticent about prescribing models of democracy, may nevertheless be happy to invoke the Beijing goals and press for guaranteeing some representation for women in parliament. Though progress is uneven, many countries have indeed been able to jump-start gender equality in politics recently as new democratic regimes were installed and new constitutions designed in Africa, Latin America and the Balkans in particular. Quotas, whether legislated or voluntarily imposed by political parties, are now a familiar tool for those serious about improving women's political participation in particular and democratic credentials in general.

Many politicians in parts of the developing world may now look askance at the situation of women in the parliaments of the older democracies and wonder why progress is so slow.

This volume shows that older democracies are also capable of change. Its great value lies precisely in comparing four countries which share much in terms of political culture and institutional legacy. Two of the four were among the first to grant women the right to vote, but progress towards representation was slow for a variety of reasons, well documented here. The obstacles for women created by the majoritarian electoral system (first-past-the-post), though undeniable and nowadays well documented, were perhaps overshadowed by the system's other disadvantages and distortions of political representation. They nevertheless remain significant: New Zealand with a mixed electoral system has achieved 28.3 per cent representation; Australia with an alternative vote (majority) electoral system achieves 25.3 per cent. Canada and the United Kingdom still using first-past-the-post reach 21 per cent and 20 per cent respectively.

The story told in these pages is about how reform and change came about. It shows on the one hand how important it is for older as well as newer democracies to question continuously the legitimacy of their political institutions and be ready to adjust or innovate. And on the other hand, it shows how women can capitalise on such changes. New Zealand showed that electoral reform is possible if properly managed. The United Kingdom showed that devolution and proportional representation could both be accommodated within the 'Westminster system'.

The chapters relating to the Scottish Parliament and the Welsh Assembly also highlight vital aspects of the campaign for change – the need for the sustained mobilisation of the women's movement around the unique political opportunity presented by devolution and the need to build up political will in the party leadership to ensure that positive measures are introduced. The results were historic, with the Scottish Parliament achieving 39 per cent women members and the Welsh Assembly 50 per cent after the 2003 elections, the highest representation of women in a legislative assembly.

Though the political and institutional structures provide the framework, progress in strengthening in the political inclusion of women is dependent on the strength and cohesion of the women's movement and its capacity to work with political parties or parliaments to ensure mobilisation of support both within the political system as well as outside. Women's groups can maintain constant pressure on political parties to include women on their slate of candidates for election. Then support from civil society for women candidates is particularly important, through fund raising and networking.

Political parties remain the focus. They decide on the political desirability of a renewal of candidates and the electoral wisdom of reinforcing the gender dimension. They control the nomination process. They can make policy and manifestoes, they can also set the tone of political debate on issues of participation and representation. It may well be that opposition parties are more willing to experiment and reach out to new members and sources of support. It may on the contrary be a strong reforming government party that feels it can impose change on its ranks and set a pace of change which is unbeatable by the opposition.

Women can be very effective in navigating political processes. But there is always a fear that they can become pawns and symbols, especially if quotas are used. The second part of this study makes a most important contribution to understanding what happens to the nature of politics and the perception of politics as the numbers of women increase. Improving ways by which more groups in the population can identify with their representatives and gain trust in the political system is in itself a valuable contribution to strengthening democracy. Can women parliamentarians also contribute to the accountability and responsiveness of government and make a real impact on policy?

The International Institute for Democracy and Electoral Assistance (IDEA) is an intergovernmental organisation which develops materials and policy options for political reform and democracy, drawing on comparative experience across the world. For IDEA the task of increasing the access of women to political power is fundamental to the process of building a democracy. Inclusiveness is a precondition for a sustainable democracy, though the long-established democracies discussed in these pages show that the struggle to include women has not been straightforward. IDEA's own work in this field has looked in detail at the use of quotas and other affirmative action tools within electoral and political processes, and this study gives an admirable account of how Westminster systems can adapt to that challenge.

The study will be a fascinating read for those close to the Westminster system, giving a 'close-up' and admirably clear analysis of the processes of political change. It will of course also be of great interest to those engaged in supporting women's political empowerment in other democracies. The rich variety of experience between the four countries shows there are no blueprints even within the 'Westminster system' but that insights and lessons learned may have much wider application. I hope it will be an inspiration both to those who study and those who work in the field for women in politics.

Karen Fogg
Secretary General, IDEA

Acknowledgements

This book would not have been possible without the generous support of many benefactors. In particular, the Canadian government provided Marian Sawer and Linda Trimble with a SPIRT grant that enabled the project to take off in 2003. It brought Linda Trimble, Manon Tremblay and Jennifer Curtin to the Political Science Program in the Research School of Social Sciences at the Australian National University for a forum comparing research on women's representation in Australia and Canada. The scope of the project was soon widened to include New Zealand research and Sandra Grey joined the project.

The next stage in the development of the project was the 'Women and Westminster Compared' conference, held on Parliament Hill in Ottawa in June 2004. Generous sponsorship of this conference enabled the project to be expanded to include the United Kingdom. We are grateful to the British Council in Canada, the Canadian Department of Foreign Affairs and International Trade, the Canadian Study of Parliament Group, Elections Canada, the Law Commission of Canada, the Social Sciences and Humanities Research Council of Canada and the University of Ottawa for funding for the conference. At the University of Ottawa funding was provided, in particular, by the Faculty of Social Sciences, the Institute of Women's Studies and the Research Centre on Women and Politics. Additional support came from the British High Commission in Canada, the International IDEA (Institute for Democracy and Electoral Assistance), the House of Commons of Canada and the Canadian Senate.

We wish to extend warm thanks to Francesca Binda (International IDEA), Nathalie Des Rosiers (Law Commission of Canada), Medha Nanivadekar (Shivaji University, India), Senator Lucie Pépin, Mr David Reddaway (British High Commissioner in Ottawa) and Caroline St-Hilaire MP for their special involvement in the conference, as well as to Jennifer Curtin (Monash University), Chantal Maillé (Concordia University) and Jocelyne Praud (University of Regina), who acted as panel discussants.

We would also like to thank all the participants in the 'Women and Westminster Compared' conference for their comments. Almost all the final authors presented their draft chapters at this conference and benefited from the presence of non-government organisations active in the areas of electoral reform and women's representation. The discussion became very lively at times! We would also like to thank Jackie F. Steele, who supervised the organisation and logistics of the conference. Not only did Jackie prove to be a gifted conference organiser, but she also ensured there were many happy memories. We are indebted to Jayme Pettit, Stephanie Mullen and Megan Kimber for their assistance in the preparation of the manuscript.

Abbreviations

ACTU	Australian Council of Trade Unions
ALP	Australian Labor Party
AM	Assembly Member
APNI	Alliance Party of Northern Ireland
AWP	Association of Women Parliamentarians
AWS	All Women Short-list
CEDAW	Convention on the Elimination of all Forms of Discrimination against Women
CSG	Consultative Steering Group
DUP	Democratic Unionist Party
DTI	Department of Trade and Industry
EDM	early day motion
EL	EMILY's List
FPP	first-past-the-post
GB	Great Britain
ICPR	Independent Commission to Review Britain's Experiences of PR Voting Systems
IDEA	International Institute for Democracy and Electoral Assistance
ILO	International Labour Organisation
IRA	Irish Republican Army
MEP	Member of the European Parliament
MLA	Member of the Legislative Assembly
MMP	mixed member proportional
MP	Member of Parliament
MPP	Member of the Provincial Parliament
MSP	Member of the Scottish Parliament
NAC	National Action Committee (On the Status of Women)
NDP	New Democratic Party
NGO	non-governmental organisation
NI	Northern Ireland
NIC	Nunavut Implementation Commission
NIWEP	Northern Ireland Women's European Platform

NIWC	Northern Ireland Women's Coalition
NIWRM	Northern Ireland Women's Rights Movement
NSW	New South Wales
NWT	North West Territories
NZ	New Zealand
PEI	Prince Edward Island (Canada)
PLP	Parliamentary Labour Party
PR	Proportional Representation
SCC	Scottish Constitutional Convention
SDP	Social Democratic Party
SDLP	Social Democratic and Labour Party
SNP	Scottish Nationalist Party
STV	single transferable vote
UK	United Kingdom
US	United States of America
UUP	Ulster Unionist Party
WEL	Women's Electoral Lobby

1 Introduction

Patterns and practice in the parliamentary representation of women

Marian Sawer, Manon Tremblay and Linda Trimble

'Women in parliament' became the object of increased international attention in the 1990s. In the United States the entry of an unprecedented number of women into Congress led 1992 to be dubbed the 'year of the woman'. In New Zealand, one woman Prime Minister replaced another at the end of the decade, leading to the view that 'women were on top' in that country. In the United Kingdom, 'Blair's Babes' brought colour to the House of Commons and controversy over what difference they made to politics. Women's presence in the new Scottish parliament and the Welsh Assembly reached levels previously associated only with the Nordic countries. In Australia, Labor Party quotas continued to increase women's presence in parliaments around the country. In Canada, progress was stalling, but Canada continued to boast more elected women than its neighbour to the south.

The representation of women was a priority issue for the 1995 Beijing Platform for Action adopted by 189 countries at the Fourth United Nations World Conference on Women. It was promoted by a range of multilateral bodies, including the United Nations, the European Union, the Inter-parliamentary Union and the International Institute for Democracy and Electoral Assistance (IDEA). The underrepresentation of women has become widely associated with problems of 'democratic deficit' and donor agencies have focused attention on it as part of strategies to strengthen democratic accountability and good governance. It is also a cause that has been taken up by new and existing non-government organisations, including those operating at regional or international levels.

The increased salience of the issue of women's parliamentary presence has generated a wealth of research on the factors that facilitate women's legislative recruitment. It has also stimulated exciting theoretical work on when and why we should expect the presence of women to make a difference to the substance of politics. This book draws on this new scholarship to explore the causes and meaning of women's increased presence in parliamentary politics in four Westminster regimes – the United Kingdom, Canada, Australia and New Zealand. It also looks at the opportunities that have been created by the changing architecture of politics, including devolution in the United Kingdom and the creation of Nunavut in Canada. American experience and research is drawn on to provide a complementary non-Westminster perspective.

The United Kingdom left its former colonies, Canada, Australia and New Zealand, with a legacy of 'Westminster' institutions, providing a family resemblance between our four countries. The variations that have evolved within this Westminster legacy help explain some of the differences in women's political recruitment. It is the combination of commonalities and variations that makes the comparison so useful – comparing apples and crab-apples, perhaps, rather than apples and pears. To date much analysis of women's political recruitment and representation has been either of the single-country type or of the global type although regional studies do exist.[1] There have also been a number of studies of the Nordic countries, which share a family resemblance like the Westminster countries.[2]

Our study similarly focuses on four countries with much in common in terms of political institutions, democratic traditions and level of socio-economic development. The common features provided by Westminster make it easier to focus on the variations that may explain the differing patterns in the representation of women. The differences in party and electoral systems, the path taken by women's mobilisations and the political opportunity structure provided by federalism or devolution provide some initial explanatory variables.

The patterns revealed by the four Westminster nations are further explored by means of comparison with the United States in the Introduction and Conclusion. The United States has some of the features of the nations explored in this volume – but it is marked by institutional arrangements that depart from the Westminster model. The separation of powers in the presidential system dilutes authority and renders political parties less cohesive, and the congressional system allows legislators considerable autonomy in their representative roles. The dilution of authority and the relative autonomy of legislators provide greater opportunities for lobbyists than in Westminster-based regimes.[3] Of course it is not only feminist advocacy organisations that take advantage of this opportunity structure, but also powerful and well funded pro-life and pro-business organisations.

The Westminster inheritance

Australia, Canada, New Zealand and the United Kingdom have shared the Westminster legacy of representative democracy, responsible parliamentary government and strong party discipline. In the past they also shared the British preference for plurality rule, and the kind of two-party political system and majority governments that flows from this. They are all constitutional monarchies, sharing the same monarch and, in the case of Australia, Canada and New Zealand, appointing Governors General who represent the monarch and act as head of state. The latter three countries are 'settler societies' that have unresolved issues relating to their Indigenous populations; this in turn has influenced both Indigenous and non-Indigenous women's political activism over time.

While all four countries have drawn on the British experience of responsible government, they have evolved in different ways from the nineteenth century. The two countries with a large land-mass, Australia and Canada, superimposed federal systems on that of responsible government, requiring a written Constitution and judicial interpretations of the division of powers and the constitutionality of legislation. As a result, the concept of parliamentary sovereignty was significantly modified in these two countries. The two small countries retain unitary political systems but in the case of the United Kingdom there are now federalising tendencies caused by its relationship with the European Union in one direction, and by devolution in Scotland, Wales and Northern Ireland in the other direction. Again parliamentary sovereignty has been modified by the jurisdiction of, for example, the European Court of Human Rights.

People and place

These four countries vary significantly in population as well as geography. In population the four countries range from the United Kingdom with some 60 million people to New Zealand with around four million. Canada and Australia are in the middle with 31 million and 19 million respectively. The proportion of women in parliament seems to have a negative relationship to population size in our group, with women doing best in the smallest country, New Zealand, and worst in the largest, the United Kingdom.

Australia, Canada and New Zealand share the unresolved conflicts, characteristic of settler societies, over past dispossession and the present status and rights of Indigenous peoples. New Zealand has a large Indigenous population with treaty rights dating from the Waitangi Treaty of 1840 and has official biculturalism based on the Maori/Pakeha (European-derived) populations. Australia and Canada have much smaller Indigenous populations although in both cases there are concentrations in northern territories. The United Kingdom does not have an Indigenous population in the same sense, although it has experienced Celtic minority parties.

Although Maori women obtained political rights in step with Pakeha women in New Zealand, Indigenous women in Australia and Canada had to wait much longer. The existence of Maori seats also facilitated the election of the first Maori women to parliament long before Indigenous women were elected in Canada or Australia. Canada has official bilingualism based on Anglophone and Francophone settler populations, while

New Zealand has Maori and English as its official languages. Australia and Canada have multicultural policies covering their diverse immigrant populations. In all four countries women parliamentarians have become more representative of ethnic diversity in recent years, but it has been a slow process.

Pluses and minuses of Westminster for women

As we have seen, the 'Westminster model' of representative democracy includes features such as strong political parties and single-member electoral systems that result in majority governments and executive dominance over parliament. This model stands in stark contrast to the American congressional system, which fragments power among the presidency, the Congress and the Senate, including powerful congressional committees, and features less cohesive political parties.

One advantage of the strong party discipline associated with Westminster is that once a party includes women's rights in its platform parliamentarians are largely bound to uphold them, regardless of personal views. It provides a different context for women's political representation from that of weak party systems, such as that of the United States, where legislators are not subject to a party whip and are exposed to a great deal of lobbying as to how they will cast their votes. In Westminster party systems, however, traditionally there is a free vote on issues such as abortion, so the same kind of cross-pressures occur on these issues as in candidate-centred systems.

Another advantage of strong party systems is that the cost of campaigning is carried by the party rather than by the candidate and there is not the barrier for women of having to raise large amounts of campaign finance, as in candidate-centred political systems. For instance, in the United States, where state law regulates political parties and electoral systems, rules governing electoral financing constrain the ability of parties to assist candidates financially.[4] In the United States, and to a lesser extent in Canada, the candidate has borne a large portion of the costs associated with contesting nominations and elections, a financial burden that many female political aspirants have found onerous. In Canada political finance reforms at the national level now cap nomination expenditures and provide assistance with election expenses; the government reimburses 60 per cent of the amount spent by those candidates who win at least 10 per cent of the vote in their constituencies. In Australia there are also public funding regimes at the national level and in the three largest states (and one territory). At the national level public funding is restricted to parties or independents who obtain at least 4 per cent of the vote and in 2005 each vote was worth about A$2.00. In New Zealand and the United Kingdom expenditure is limited both by overall caps and by the restriction of electronic advertising.

One of the disadvantages for women associated with Westminster is the tradition of single-member electorates. It is clear from international evidence that multimember electorates facilitate women's and minority representation – giving parties an incentive to construct tickets appealing to all sections of the community and satisfying all sections of the party. Another disadvantage for women of systems based on single-member electorates is that they militate against the representation of non-regionally based minority parties. Most notably in Australia and New Zealand, post-materialist minor parties like the Australian Democrats and the Greens have fielded the highest proportion of women candidates and have given significant leadership opportunities to women. In Canada the New Democratic Party (NDP), which has given unrivalled leadership opportunities to women, has also been disadvantaged by the electoral system.

The single-member electorate system is also the cornerstone of what political scientist Arend Lijphart identified as the 'majoritarian' model of democracy.[5] Under this model we get strong Cabinet government and classic Westminster parliaments, with government on one side and the opposition on the other, engaged in ritualised warfare. This model can be contrasted with electoral systems based on proportional representation, such as those in European countries, where parties gain representation in proportion to their support in the community. A multi-party system emerges, and governments are formed through a process of bargaining and coalition-building between parties. Lijphart terms this the 'consensus' model of democracy.

The highly confrontational game played out on the floor of the chamber in Westminster parliaments is a game at which few women MPs believe they excel: they are subject to adverse judgements on their femininity (transgressing gender codes) if they adopt the existing rules of engagement and adverse judgements on their effectiveness if they do not. When reinforced by strong party discipline, this confrontational game makes co-operation across the floor on issues of special concern to women very difficult. Committee work, on the other hand, provides some scope for cross-party co-operation.[6]

Sometimes the confrontational game played out in public masks agreement between the major parties on issues of economic ideology. In both New Zealand and the United Kingdom there has been significant discontent with the Westminster model of untrammelled executive power and women have been active in campaigning for more inclusive and consultative political institutions. In the United Kingdom devolution has led to significant gains for women in Scotland, Wales and Northern Ireland,[7] while in New Zealand the adoption of MMP, supported by groups such as Women's Electoral Lobby, has also modified Westminster majoritarianism.

For and against federalism

The advantages and disadvantages of federalism for women's political representation are complex.[8] Federalism can be seen as providing more opportunities for women's political participation and opportunities that are closer to home. On the other hand, federal systems may enshrine the power of state or provincial government at the expense of local government. Where local government has had broad responsibilities for areas such as housing and education, as in the United Kingdom, it has been an important forum for women's political participation.

In both Canada and Australia the original process of federation was one that largely excluded women, although federation did provide a window of opportunity in Australia for the extension of women's political rights, across the country. Where federalising tendencies are more recent, they can provide important opportunities for women's participation in the design of new political institutions. The creation of the new Scottish parliament and associated processes for community consultation is a good example.

The framework for the federal division of power in Australia and Canada is laid down in written constitutions. In Australia, there are no significant human rights provisions in the Constitution but in Canada the Charter of Rights and Freedoms of 1982 has greatly expanded the opportunity structure for the pursuit of women's claims. In 2001 the Charter underpinned a case claiming that the existing Canadian electoral system is unconstitutional because it limits or impedes the election of women.[9]

In Australia and Canada neo-liberalism in recent times has been associated with attempts to shed federal responsibilities for funding or service delivery in various areas of social provision and hand back responsibility to the sub-national level. Women's organisations in Australia and Anglophone Canada have mobilised against such a retreat, seeing it as a threat to equal levels of access across the country to services such as health, child care and women's services. Yet in Québec francophone women have had more confidence in the Québec government than in the federal government to provide access to such services.

Women's mobilisation

In the four Westminster countries, as in the United States, it is customary to talk of two main waves of the women's movement, the first expressed in the suffrage, temperance and social reform movements of the late nineteenth century and the second gaining momentum in the 1970s. This is an oversimplification, as women's political activity continued between the waves and patterns were also different in Anglophone and Francophone Canada. Nevertheless, definite upswings in parliamentary representation

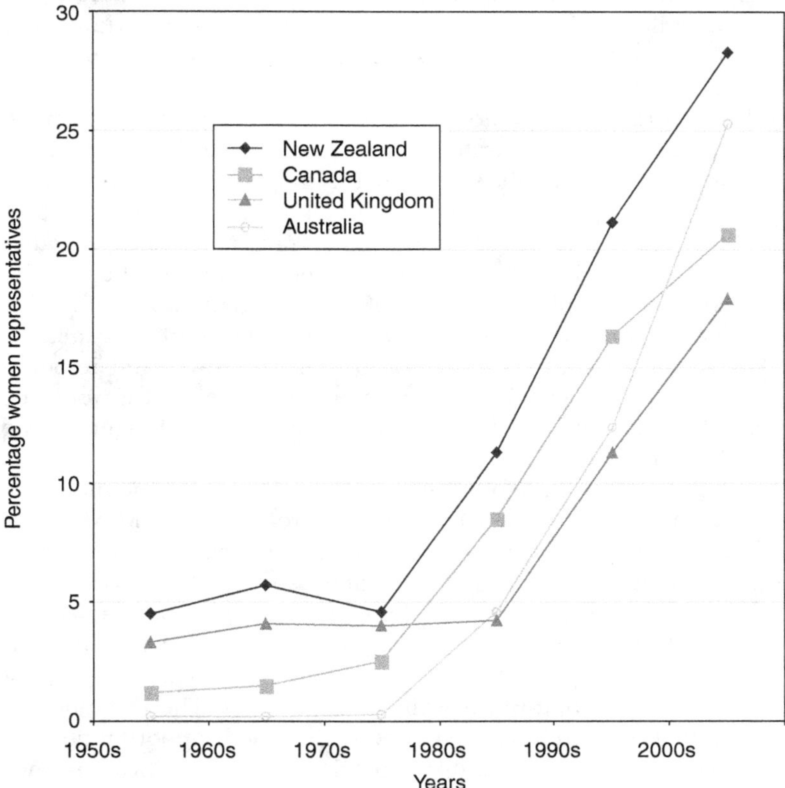

Figure 1.1 Women's parliamentary representation, 1950–2004.

can be charted for three of the countries from the 1980s as the impact of the new mobilisation flowed through to political institutions. This upswing took place significantly later in the United Kingdom, where the political opportunity structure was particularly unfavourable in the Thatcher period and where the women's movement was particularly distrustful of patriarchal institutions.

In both waves, the women's movement successfully mobilised gender identity as a basis for political action. This mobilisation of identity required a discursive strategy that played down differences between women, and played up common experiences of subordination, in order to activate a constituency for change. A 'strategic essentialism' helped create a political base for claims for gender equality. In recent years such essentialism has been much contested by postmodernist theorists who perceive the category 'woman' as privileging a white, middle-class and heterosexual identity and imposing a rigid construct on fluid and intersecting identities. An even more important source of the demobilising of gender identity has been the increased dominance of neo-liberal discourse. The latter replaces collective identities with the construct of the individual who is author of his or her own choices, unconstrained by inequalities of power or expectations.

To go back to the first wave, one puzzle is why women achieved political rights much earlier in Australia and New Zealand than in Canada or the United Kingdom. We might expect that if innovation generally occurs on the periphery, this rule would apply as much to Canada as to the other colonies. While the timing of federation in Australia presented particular opportunities at the national level (which flowed through to the remaining states), it does not explain why none of the Canadian prairie provinces achieved the early breakthroughs of New Zealand and South Australia. As for the United Kingdom, its panoply of aristocratic power and imperial status presented particular barriers to women's suffrage, and it would be true to say that electoral reform in general took much longer in the metropole than in the colonies.

The Crown. As we have seen, our four countries share the same monarch. Queen Elizabeth II of the United Kingdom of Great Britain and Northern Ireland is also Queen of Australia and of fourteen other Commonwealth countries, including Canada and New Zealand. Is there any advantage for women in the fact that the head of state for over 50 years has been a woman? Queen Elizabeth II is not on record like her predecessor, Queen Victoria, as thinking that women's rights are madness; on the other hand she has not been outspoken in her support for women's aspirations. The institution of the constitutional monarchy has, however, provided opportunities for women who are self-declared feminists to fill positions such as Governor General, Governor and Lieutenant Governor. While such positions do not involve the direct exercise of executive power, they are important in symbolic terms, giving scope to women to represent the nation, state or province, and to encourage the aspirations of other women. Current Governors General include prominent legal feminist Dame Silvia Cartwright in New Zealand and Haitian-born Michaëlle Jean in Canada.

The Commonwealth of Nations

The women's movement has always been international in character and, for example, enfranchised Australian and New Zealand women played a significant role in the struggle for women's suffrage in the United Kingdom before the First World War. The Commonwealth of Nations has provided one of a number of multilateral forums through which feminists have sought to advance issues of gender equality. The Commonwealth Secretariat has been particularly important in disseminating the principles and methods of analysing government budgets for their gender effects, and producing handbooks for this purpose. Gender budgeting was a topic for the 2002 meeting of Commonwealth Finance Ministers.

Historically the networking of women's international non-government organisations was also facilitated by the development of multilateral bodies such as the League of Nations and subsequently the United Nations (UN). Women from all four countries have played a significant role in the development of status of women agencies in such bodies. Australian, Canadian and New Zealand governments have all seen multilateral diplomacy as an important means of extending their influence as comparatively small powers, often taking lead roles, sometimes in partnership, in human rights and status of women issues. For example, Australia and Canada were co-sponsors of the UN Declaration on the Elimination of Violence against Women, while New Zealand worked closely with them. Both government and non-government representatives from these countries have helped strengthen international norms regarding the representation of women in public decision-making and mainstreaming of gender analysis into the policy process, whether through the Convention on the Elimination of All Forms of Discrimination against Women (CEDAW) or through instruments such as the Beijing Platform for Action.[10]

The reporting required under such international conventions and agreements provides leverage for claims made at the domestic level. The Inter-parliamentary Union has played its role in monitoring the presence of women in parliaments worldwide as well as sharing best practice in relation to matters such as CEDAW reporting.[11] Having said this, until 1997 the United Kingdom was the outlier among these four countries both in terms of developing machinery of government to ensure gender-based analysis within government – the so-called femocrat phenomenon found

Table 1.1 Political rights and representation at the national level

Event	*Australia*	*Canada*	*New Zealand*	*UK*
Right to vote: most women	1902	1918	1893	1918/1928
Right to stand: most women	1902	1919	1919	1918/1928
Right to vote: all Indigenous women	1962	Inuit 1950; Status Indians 1960	1893	n.a.
First woman elected	1943	1921	1933	1918
First Indigenous woman elected	–	1988	1949	n.a.
First woman cabinet minister	1949	1957	1947	1929
First woman party leader	1986	1989	1993	1975
First woman prime minister	–	1993	1997	1979

in the other three countries – and in terms of disseminating models for gender mainstreaming through multilateral institutions. British women, however, have benefited from the normative regime imposed by the European Union in relation to women's rights and social standards. During the Conservative government of Margaret Thatcher more than 40 per cent of policy decisions favourable to women's movement demands came about as a result of pressure from Europe.[12]

Part I: explaining differences in parliamentary representation

International research has generally found that where we can assume a high level of women's education and workforce participation, as in our particular Westminster family, factors that are significant in explaining variations in women's political representation include the electoral system, the existence of quotas, a 'contagion' effect where one party significantly increased its women candidates, the nature of political parties and the party system and background factors such as religion and the nature of women's movement strategies.[13] Here we briefly outline how these factors intersect with the Westminster system. The chapters in Part I of the book take these issues further in analysing the influences on women's descriptive representation in the parliaments of the four Westminster countries.

Supply and demand factors

Before we examine specific factors affecting women's legislative recruitment we need to look at the supply side of the supply and demand equation. Although candidate figures are not a pure indication of willingness of women to stand for parliament, because of the gatekeeping role of political parties discussed below and their historical disinclination to field women candidates, they do tell us something. For example, prior to the Second World War, 99.3 per cent of candidates for the Australian federal parliament were male, while between the Second World War and 1969 about 96 per cent of candidates were male. Similarly in New Zealand nearly 93 per cent of all candidates between 1946 and 1975 were male.[14] In all four Westminster countries there were strong social expectations that women would marry and that married women would not pursue careers outside the home. Indeed, in the Westminster countries, as in the United States, early women parliamentarians were often 'standing in' for a husband, whether deceased or otherwise.[15]

In addition to the small number of women standing as candidates, another reason for the failure of women to be elected was the decision by many to remain outside the existing political parties, by choice as well as by necessity. In the period up to 1940 in Australia, 75 per cent of women candidates ran as independents or for minor parties, a remarkable figure given high levels of stable party identification and voting. A number of women also stood as independent or minor-party candidates in the United Kingdom in 1918 although not in the subsequent period.[16] A distrust of the existing party system was a common legacy of the suffrage struggle.

It was the arrival of the 'second wave' of the women's movement that led to a sudden jump in the number of women candidates. Several factors combined in the 1970s to enhance the willingness of women to enter politics, including increased participation in higher education; economic changes resulting in increased workforce participation; and political mobilisation of women through the women's movement and other new social movements. Women exerted increased pressure on the political parties to become more women-friendly, for instance Labour women demonstrated outside their own party conference in New Zealand in 1974.

Supply factors continue to be important and need further exploration in the four Westminster countries under study here. Turning to the United States, research has found that women who run are as likely to win as their male counterparts, but women are still less likely to run.[17] Indeed, the primary reason for women's underrepresentation in the United States is that women do not seek elected office in sufficient numbers to achieve gender parity. Determining why women eschew political careers is key to understanding why the supply of women candidates remains low. Preliminary results from American studies show that gender role socialisation, lack of political efficacy and absence of high-profile role models deter women from seeking political candidacy.[18]

Electoral system

The four countries mostly began the twentieth century with the Westminster model of plurality rule (first-past-the-post) in single-member constituencies. As we have seen, such a system exaggerates majorities – meaning the winning party usually gains a much higher proportion of seats than of votes – and usually leads to the alternation of two parties in government. Such an electoral system makes it very difficult for minor parties to gain political representation unless they are regionally based.

Of the four countries in our study, Australia has historically been the most prone to electoral experimentation, being the first country (apart from Denmark) where proportional representation was used for parliamentary elections and developing the distinctive single transferable vote form of PR as well as adopting majority preferential voting where single-member constituencies are used. Australia now generally uses PR for one chamber of its bicameral parliaments and majority preferential for the other. Women have generally done better in houses of parliament elected by PR than in those elected from single-member constituencies. This effect, however, has been blurred by the implementation of quotas by the Labor Party.

New Zealand has shifted away much more belatedly from first-past-the-post, but in a more dramatic way. There had been drastic policy experiments in the 1980s, undertaken by governments untrammelled by the kind of brakes found in the other countries, such as upper houses, multi-party governments, federal division of powers or constitutional challenges. There was wide disillusionment in the community over the electoral system that had enabled this to happen. Two referendums were held and the popular choice was for a shift to the Mixed-Member Proportional form of proportional representation. Each voter would be able to vote both for a constituency member and for a party, and party representation within the parliament would be proportionate to the party vote, through a process of topping up from the party lists. MMP was introduced in 1996 and resulted in an increase in women parliamentarians from 21 per cent to 29 per cent. Its effect on the election of women is not as clear, however, as its effect on increasing the ethnic and political diversity of both male and female parliamentarians. More women were elected from constituency than from list seats in 2002, almost half the women in parliament being elected from Labour-held constituencies. Because Labour did so well in the constituencies it was allocated only a handful of the party-list seats used to achieve proportionality.

Canada has so far resisted reform of its electoral system although it is of increasing interest at the provincial level, with several provinces giving serious consideration to proportional or mixed electoral systems. A proposal for a multi-member single transferable vote system was narrowly defeated in a May 2005 referendum in British Columbia and the government has promised to keep electoral reform on the legislative agenda. As mentioned above, a constitutional challenge was mounted in 2001 on the grounds that first-past-the-post voting systematically discriminates against women. On the other hand, the Canadian party system is highly regionalised – a different kind of departure from the two-party model. A new party system was generated in 1993 when five parties, two of them regionally based, won representation in the House of Commons. Canada does not have the kind of strong bicameralism found in Australian parliaments, having an appointed Senate and no upper houses at provincial level. So there is not the kind of electoral architecture found in Australia, where more often a lower house will be elected using single-member constituencies (and in the expectation that one party will be able to form government with a clear majority of seats) while in the other house PR enables a broader representation of opinion within the community and a clearer mirroring of social and cultural diversity.

The United Kingdom has adopted electoral reform, but so far only for its devolved Scottish Parliament and Welsh, Northern Ireland and London Assemblies, and for European elections rather than for the House of Commons (see 'Basic Political Data on the United Kingdom'). As we shall see below, the combination of the MMP electoral system and of quota systems such as zipping and twinning has led to very high proportions of women in the Welsh Assembly (50 per cent from 2003) and the Scottish Parliament (39.5 per cent). Representation remains at a much lower level in the House of Commons (20 per cent from 2005).

Parties

As political parties effectively control legislative recruitment in the Westminster countries, the attitudes and ideology of political parties are a key factor in determining the political representation of women. The existence of a left-progressive labour party distinguishes the four Westminster nations from the United States and provides a partial explanation for their higher levels of female political representation. Australia, New Zealand and the United Kingdom all have labour parties, while Canada also has a labour party in the sense of a party with affiliated trade unions – the New Democratic Party. While the NDP has formed government at the provincial and territorial level, it is unlike the labour parties of the other countries in that it has never constituted either government or official opposition at the national level. The blue-collar unions that created the labour parties had their own fraternal traditions that emphasised the achievement of the 'family wage' sufficient to keep wives at home. In Australia these traditions were reinforced by the influence of Irish Catholicism with its conservative gender ideology and traditions of machine politics.

On the other hand, the labour parties also have historic goals of social justice, preparedness to acknowledge structural barriers and to take collective action to pursue such goals. In three of the countries they have adopted quotas for women's representation. It is in New Zealand, however, that the Labour Party has proved most effective as a conduit for the political representation of women and in this case without quotas. The party became 'feminised' in the 1980s, with women becoming the majority of party membership by the 1990s and supporting a significant increase in Labour women candidates.

By the time its new electoral system was introduced in the 1990s, New Zealand had a higher percentage of women in parliament than any other country with single-member electorates. Almost half the women in the parliament in 2004 had still entered via the Labour Party's constituency seats. The fact that the New Zealand Labour Party did not require quotas to achieve such a high level of women's parliamentary representation, despite the adverse nature of the electoral system, is a key part of the story of this book.

In all four Westminster countries the proportion of women in left parliamentary parties is much higher than the proportion of women in conservative parliamentary parties. This effect has been exacerbated as competition from populist parties in Australia, Canada and New Zealand pulls conservative and even centrist parties to the right.

Changes in the party system, such as a shift from a two-party (Westminster) system to the multi-party systems associated with PR, may significantly increase the opportunities for women's representation and leadership. In Australia and New Zealand, post-materialist parties created after the arrival of the new social movements of the 1960s and benefiting from the existence of PR have the highest proportion of women in their parliamentary parties and are most likely to have women in leadership positions. The Greens are a good example of this, as the Green Party of Canada has also had a woman leader.

Quotas

Worldwide, there has been a dramatic increase in the 1990s in the use of quotas to increase women's parliamentary representation. Quotas may be inscribed in constitutions, in ordinary statute law or in the rules of political parties. In the four Westminster countries quotas are of the latter sort and, as elsewhere, they are more likely to be adopted by parties of the left than of the right. The pattern has been as follows. In Australia the Labor Party adopted enforceable quotas in 1994 and reinforced them in 2002. An independent feminist fund-raising trust, EMILY's List, also claimed credit for helping Labor women into Australian parliaments.

In Canada the NDP adopted a target in 1985 of 50 per cent women for its federal candidates and has also adopted a policy whereby there must be at least one woman in the running at the nomination stage in each riding. While this policy has boosted the number of women candidates for the party, the fact that the goal has not yet been reached reflects the non-mandatory nature of the policy and the strength of local riding association autonomy in Canadian electoral politics. The Liberal Party of Canada also has an informal and unambitious target of 25 per cent women candidates, a goal which has been met on a couple of occasions in small part because of a rule allowing the party leader to bypass the nomination process to directly appoint candidates.

In New Zealand, as we have seen, the increasingly feminised Labour Party did not need to introduce quotas to achieve substantially increased levels of women's parliamentary representation. Provision was made, however, for women to be represented on the panels that select parliamentary candidates.

In the United Kingdom the mechanism of all-women short lists for target seats was adopted by the Labour Party in 1993. After women had been selected for 35 such seats the process was challenged under the United Kingdom Sex Discrimination Act and temporarily abandoned. In 2002 the Labour government passed the Sex Discrimination (Election Candidates) Act to ensure the future legality of such measures by political parties.

For the 1999 elections to the Scottish Parliament and the Welsh Assembly Labour used a strategy apparently less vulnerable to legal challenge, that of 'twinning', devised by political scientist Alice Brown. Twinning meant that constituencies were matched in terms of location and winnability and party preselectors had two votes, one for a man and one for a woman. The man with the highest vote was allocated one constituency and the woman with the highest vote the other. In Wales Plaid Cymru adopted the 'zipping principle' for its party list, with women in first and third positions. Northern Ireland differed from Scotland and Wales in so far as the political parties did not adopt positive measures to increase women's political representation. None the less the mobilising of women to have a greater voice in the peace process and the formation of the Northern Ireland Women's Coalition has had a catalytic effect. The introduction of the single transferable vote form of PR for the election of the Northern Ireland Assembly in 1998 enabled the election of Coalition candidates and raised the salience of gender issues. In Nunavut in Canada, a proposal to introduce two-member electorates for the new Assembly, each with a male and female representative, was defeated at referendum in 1997.

The use of party tactics ranging from active recruitment through affirmative action to quotas underlines the importance of political parties to the electoral project for women. The era of parties recruiting women merely to stand-in for deceased husbands or to serve as partisan 'sacrificial lambs' has given way to a new sensitivity to gender-based representation.

Turning to the United States, there seems to be no discernible partisan bias in fund-raising efforts for men and women candidates, and some studies suggest considerable efforts by both Democrats and Republicans to boost the presence of women in Congress and state legislatures. [19] Yet refusal by American political parties to adopt firm affirmative action strategies, coupled with evidence of discrimination against women candidates by male party chairs and the press, suggests the impact of party and media elites on women's representation requires further examination. The intersection of such factors with party competition and electoral system design demands similar attention. It is clear that the numbers game is complex, multi-faceted, and irreducible to a single feature of institutional design or political will.

Part II: beyond numbers

The second part of the book is devoted to issues of the 'substantive representation' of women, going beyond the mere presence of women (descriptive representation) to ask what difference women make in parliament and by what methods this difference can be established. Political scientist Hannah Pitkin was the first to distinguish systematically between forms of representation in terms of 'standing for' (descriptive or symbolic representation) or 'acting for' (substantive representation).[20]

The demand for the presence of women may rest simply on justice arguments, that women have equal rights and talents to men and should have equal opportunity to participate in public decision-making. The absence of women from such decision-making is ascribed to forms of direct and indirect discrimination, such as the nature of the electoral system (discussed in Part I), the failure to accommodate family responsibilities within the structure of public life or the privileging of gladiatorial parliamentary styles.

The right of women to participate in public life on an equal basis with men is inscribed in international human rights law such as Article 25 of the International Covenant on Civil and Political Rights (ICCPR) and Article 7 of the Convention on the Elimination of All Forms of Discrimination against Women (CEDAW). The justice argument does not require women to 'make a difference' to the content or style of politics.

More usually, however, justice arguments are buttressed by other kinds of argument, including those which will have greater appeal to the powerful, like partisan utility or increasing the electoral appeal of political parties. Women can provide a 'new look' for parties beset by scandal or associated with harsh economic policies. Electoral competition may be brought into play (the 'contagion' effect discussed in Part I) where one party has already significantly increased its female parliamentary representation. Some may even talk up the more general advantages of doubling the pool of talent from which to draw the nation's legislators.

Deliberative arguments

In recent years theorists such as Anne Phillips, Jane Mansbridge and Iris Marion Young have written forcefully of the need for the presence of women and minorities in legislatures, to ensure that a diverse range of life experiences, including experiences of group-based discrimination, are brought to bear on public issues.[21] These theorists stress the contribution of diversity of background and experience to the kind of inclusive deliberative process, which many now regard as a central defining feature of democracy.

However, it is not unmediated personal experience that serves to broaden debate in this way – rather it is the process of giving new collective meanings to such experience. Gender identity is not something pregiven that will automatically be brought by women into parliament. Social movements such as the women's movement mobilise new ways of interpreting everyday life, new 'cognitive frames' through which to view the world. It is the access of representatives to these collectively generated and oppositional political meanings that enables them to bring new perspectives into the political process.

It is also often assumed that women's presence will have a 'civilising' effect on parliamentary culture for two reasons. First, that the presence of those who are different will elicit at least a veneer of civility rather than the dynamics of an all-male group. Second, that women themselves will bring a less confrontational approach as a consequence of their gender socialisation and family roles. The strength of existing norms of conduct in Westminster parliaments makes it difficult, however, for women to have this desired effect. In New Zealand the increased presence of women in parliament coincided with an increase rather than a decrease in aggression, as measured by personal attacks and interjections, including those by women.[22]

Symbolic arguments

Different from either the justice, utility or the deliberative democracy arguments are the symbolic arguments for increasing women's representation. These are themselves of different kinds – one stressing effects of the presence of women inside parliament on the status of women outside, another stressing the significance of representativeness for the legitimacy of political institutions, and yet another highlighting the cultural significance of the public performance of gender.

The first symbolic argument is that the presence of women in parliament increases respect for women in society and is a form of recognition of the equal status of women, whether or not this is associated with recognition of 'difference'. This symbolic argument is also associated with a motivational or role-model argument – that the visible presence of women in public life serves to raise the aspirations of other women, the 'girls can do anything' effect. Some have suggested this is one of the most important functions that women legislators can perform.[23]

The second and very different symbolic argument wrapped up in the slogan of underrepresentation is that of institutional legitimacy – the idea that the legitimacy of political institutions will be undermined if significant sections of the community appear to be locked out of them. It assumes political mobilisation of a group identity, in this case gender identity, and a refusal to acknowledge the authority of an institution that does not reflect this identity.

The third symbolic argument is less an argument for increasing the number of women in parliament than an argument for increasing the public representation of different ways of performing gender. It is suggested that the representation of such alternatives in top-level politics increases the cultural choices available to women – they too may see that female identity does not have to be bound up with domesticity, and that women in public life do not have to emphasise the priority of wife/mother identities, although they may choose to do so.

Agency argument

Another kind of argument, different from and even more difficult than the justice, utility, deliberative democracy or symbolic arguments is the argument that the interests of women differ from those of men and that the presence of women is required for them to be taken into account. The reason this is a difficult argument is twofold. First, there is the disputed nature of 'women's interests' and the argument that intersecting identities will overpower even a collective interest in contesting gender subordination. Political ideology and affiliation, class, race or ethnicity may be better predictors of political attitudes than gender, and even where gender is significant, as on questions of equal opportunity for women, age may be a complicating factor.[24]

Second, even if we agree that shared experience of subordination does give rise to shared interests and collectively articulated demands for gender equality, the representation of such interests requires commitment and action, rather than simply presence. When trying to measure whether such substantive representation of women is occurring, we might find that men from a political party committed to women's rights are more likely actively to support such demands than are conservative women. Or we might find that, even where women politicians express their commitment to representing women and to promoting gender equality, the cross-cutting pressures and norms of parliamentary life and party and constituency responsibilities prevent their doing so. Or we might suggest that women are inhibited from identifying with feminist demands while they are only a small minority in a legislative body and are trying to earn the trust of the dominant group by not rocking the boat. Or we might try to separate the descriptive and substantive representation of women altogether and say that if we tie the substantive representation of women too closely to the physical presence of women, that lets male legislators off the hook: that it absolves them from responsibility for representing women's interests or from considering the gender implications of policy.

The different kinds of argument introduced here are summarised in Table 1.2.

Critical mass

It is sometimes argued that it is exceptionally difficult for women to engage in the critical acts required for substantive representation while they are present only in very small numbers in parliaments or other organisations. This theory was first set out by Rosabeth Moss Kanter in her classic work *Men and Women of the Corporation.*[25] Kanter explored the effects of relative proportions on group behaviour and found that enormous pressures were imposed on those who were 'tokens', or part of a very small

Table 1.2 Arguments for increasing women's political representation

Representation	*Argument*
Equal right to represent (justice arguments)	Right to participate in public decision making Right not to be discriminated against by structure of public life
Utilitarianism (utility arguments)	Increase pool of talent Partisan advantage
Improving deliberation (deliberative democracy arguments)	Debate needs to be enriched by women's perspectives or collectively mediated experience Civilising effect on debate
Representativeness (symbolic argument)	Effects on status of group Effects on aspirations Legitimacy of institution Widening cultural choices
Protection of interests (agency arguments)	Women have different interests and/or values from men that need protection

minority. There was a need to overcome the distrust associated with being visibly 'different' and to survive the additional scrutiny involved. Such pressures arising from visibility could lead to the over-assimilation of small minorities to dominant norms in the desperate attempt to be accepted as one of the group. Kanter suggested such pressures diminished as minorities grew larger, as they became useful allies for political players and able to exercise some leverage.

Danish political scientist Drude Dahlerup was the first to explore the relevance of Kanter's work to the role of women in politics. She concluded by querying the relevance of the critical mass concept, taken from physics, to the social sciences and suggesting that the willingness and ability of members of minority groups to engage in critical acts was perhaps more important than critical mass.[26] Her criticisms have been taken up by others, who have emphasised the contextual nature of gender identity and the ways in which gendered norms and expectations are reshaped over time and place, regardless of relative numbers.[27] None the less, the idea became popularised that when women moved from being a small to a large minority in parliament constraints would be lessened and they would find it easier to engage in acts of substantive representation. Some, however, found evidence of the reverse, that a perception that women were 'taking over' generated backlash and hostility.[28]

American political scientist Karen Beckwith argues that newness, defined as the 'substantial increase in the numbers and proportions of women elected for the first time', may be as important as numbers in prompting a substantive response to the presence of women.[29] Yet the evidence of the chapters comprising Part II of this volume suggests the novelty value of newly elected women may have less impact in Westminster systems than in congressional systems like that of the United States.

Others have pursued different lines of inquiry from that of numbers to try to answer the question of when we can expect women representatives to take up issues of gender equality. What political backgrounds or orientations make it more likely that women parliamentarians will engage in 'critical acts' and act as advocates for women as a group? What kinds of structures within parliament or parliamentary parties make it more likely that they will do so? How important is the mobilisation of women's organisations outside parliament and linkages with them?

Factors identified by researchers as influencing the likelihood of legislators acting as advocates for women include: the compatibility of party ideology with feminism,[30] self-identification of legislators as feminists or acknowledgement by them of a special responsibility to represent the interests of women,[31] existence of women's caucuses within parliamentary parties or within parliament,[32] links of such caucuses to strong women's councils within the organisational wing of the party,[33] membership of and association with women's movement organisations, or simply the strength of women's movement mobilisation in society at large.[34] These are not, of course, factors independent of each other and clearly the strength of women's political mobilisation in society at large influences the propensity of women parliamentarians to identify as feminists or to acknowledge a special responsibility to represent women. It is sometimes argued that such 'surrogate' representation, or acknowledgement of the responsibility to represent a group beyond a territorial constituency, is stronger when there are relatively few members of the group in question in parliament – the opposite of the critical mass argument.[35]

Some of this research also grapples with the issue of accountability. As women parliamentarians are generally elected to represent territorial constituencies rather than gender constituencies, there is an issue of how they can be held accountable for claims to be representing women as a group.[36] There may be a nexus of accountability in the relationship between parliamentarians and institutions that audit the gender impact of policy. Such institutions include women's non-government organisations that monitor performance of both men and women in advancing issues of gender equality. They also include feminist organisations that provide support for women candidates but expect some return in the form of equality initiatives.

These are the kinds of matters explored in Part II of the book. After identifying factors that might facilitate substantive representation, the authors seek to establish whether women indeed are making a difference in the four countries. Various methods are used, such as examining what women legislators are contributing to parliamentary debate and whether they are broadening the scope of deliberation to include issues identified as of special concern to women in the community.

Part III: new institutions, new opportunities

The third part of the book is devoted to the opportunities provided by 'being in at the beginning' of the development of new political institutions. New institutionalist theory suggests that timing is extremely important in explaining the trajectory of institutions. Once institutions have been established, 'path dependence' and the costs of changing direction ensure that the ideas and expectations built into them have long-term effects.[37] In the United Kingdom the timing of devolution, following the effective mobilisation of women, particularly in Scotland, provided the opportunity to design institutions that were far more gender-inclusive than those of the old Westminster parliament. Indeed, there were deliberate departures to reduce the adversarialism associated with the Westminster model and to ensure more participatory and inclusive political processes.

The case studies of institution-building in Scotland, Wales and Northern Ireland highlight the different ways in which women have organised to build their concerns into the foundations of new political institutions. They also assess the outcomes in terms of both the presence of women and the operation of new structures and processes. These new structures have been designed to create greater accountability for equality outcomes, both through formal auditing of executive proposals and through the creation of new channels for community engagement in the work of legislative bodies and government agencies.

New structures for gender equality have been established in each of the three jurisdictions, but in Northern Ireland women's political participation continues to be overshadowed by sectarian conflict. In Wales women have achieved parity in terms of political presence and in Scotland they constitute around 40 per cent of parliamentarians – leading to a new centrality for issues such as child care and domestic violence.

In Canada the development of a new legislative assembly in Nunavut produced less favourable results. A proposal for two-member seats with gender parity did not receive the support of the population at referendum. Several factors may help explain this failure, notably poor timing, regional tensions and the weak mobilisation of the women's movement on the issue of electoral politics.

This book shows that the parliamentary representation of women is an issue that has been successfully politicised within and beyond the world of Westminster. It has become a measure of democracy of universal application. The representation of women is now on the public agenda, and the creation of new political structures opens up possibilities to institutionalise gender equity in various ways. Yet although the issue is now on global agendas, the examples of Northern Ireland and Nunavut show that the development of new institutions does not guarantee the increased political representation of women. Success or otherwise in increasing the political presence of women is inextricably linked with the nature of civil society and with effective women's movement mobilisation and electoral engagement.

Notes

1 Single-country accounts of political recruitment and representation have been produced for all four Westminster countries in the present study. For examples of global comparisons see Matland, 'Women's Representation in National Legislatures'; Reynolds, 'Women in the Legislatures and Executives of the World'; Paxton, 'Women in National Legislatures'. For examples of regional studies see Craske and Molyneux, *Gender and the Politics of Rights and Democracy in Latin America*, Lee and Clark, *Democracy and the Status of Women in East Asia*.
2 See Haavio-Mannila and Skard, *Unfinished Democracy*; Bergqvist *et al.*, *Equal Democracies?*
3 Young, *Feminists and Party Politics*, 184–5; Costain and Costain, 'Strategy and Tactics of the Women's Movement in the United States'.
4 See Alexander, *Financing Politics*; Ballington, 'Gender Equality in Political Party Funding'.
5 See Lijphart, *Democracies*.
6 See, for example, Young, 'Fulfilling the Mandate of Difference'.
7 See Brown *et al.*, 'Women and Constitutional Change in Scotland and Northern Ireland'; Dobrowolsky, 'Crossing Boundaries'.
8 See Vickers, *Reinventing Political Science*.
9 Joan Russow and the Green Party of Canada *v.* The Attorney General of Canada, The Chief Electoral Officer of Canada and HM The Queen in Right of Canada, 2001.
10 See True and Mintrom, 'Transnational Networks and Policy Diffusion'.
11 United Nations and the Inter-parliamentary Union, *The Convention on the Elimination of All Forms of Discrimination against Women and its Optional Protocol*. This Handbook was produced with financial support from Canada and Sweden.
12 Bashevkin, *Women on the Defensive*, 89.
13 See for example, Rule and Zimmerman, *Electoral Systems in Comparative Perspective*; Matland and Studlar, 'The Contagion of Women Candidates in Single-member District and Proportional Representation Electoral Systems'; Caul, 'Political Parties and the Adoption of Candidate Gender Quotas'.
14 See Grey and Sawer, 'Australia and New Zealand'.
15 See Kincaid, 'Over his Dead Body'.
16 Sainsbury, 'Rights without Seats', 73.
17 See Elder, 'Why Women Don't Run'; Swers, 'Research on Women in Legislatures'.
18 See Elder, 'Why Women Don't Run'.
19 See Swers, 'Research on Women in Legislatures'.
20 See Pitkin, *The Concept of Representation*.
21 See Phillips, *The Politics of Presence*; Mansbridge, 'Should Blacks Represent Blacks and Women Represent Women?'; Young, *Inclusion and Democracy*.
22 Grey, 'Does Size Matter?', 24.
23 Burrell, *A Woman's Place is in the House*, 173.
24 See Erickson, 'Might More Women Make a Difference?'.
25 See Kanter, *Men and Women of the Corporation*.
26 See Dahlerup, 'From a Small to a Large Minority'.
27 See Towns, 'Understanding the Effects of Larger Ratios of Women in National

Legislatures'. See also Beckwith, 'The Substantive Representation of Women'; Mackay, 'Gender and Political Representation in the UK'.

28 See Yoder, 'Rethinking Tokenism'.

29 See Beckwith, 'The Substantive Representation of Women'.

30 See Tremblay and Pelletier, 'Feminist Women in Canadian Politics'.

31 See Wängnerud, 'Testing the Politics of Presence'; Waring, *Politics: Women's Insight.*

32 See Sawer, 'Parliamentary Representation of Women'; Tremblay, 'Do Female MPs Substantively Represent Women?'; Burt *et al.*, 'Women in the Ontario New Democratic Government'.

33 See Grey and Sawer, 'Australia and New Zealand'.

34 See Carroll, 'Have Women Legislators in the United States Become More Conservative?'.

35 See Mansbridge, 'The Many Faces of Representation'.

36 See Phillips, *The Politics of Presence.*

37 See Pierson, 'Increasing Returns, Path Dependence and the Study of Politics'.

Part I

The descriptive representation of women

2 Women's electoral representation in Australia

Ian McAllister

With the exception of New Zealand, Australia was at the forefront of granting political rights to women at the turn of the nineteenth century, with South Australia granting women the vote on the same basis as men in 1894. Women gained the right to vote in Commonwealth elections in 1902. However, the success of women in winning the right to stand for election has varied greatly across the states and territories, as has the success of women candidates standing for election, and there have also been significant variations in representation between upper and lower houses. Although women had the right to stand for election in Commonwealth elections from 1902, it was not until 1943 that the first woman was elected. Several state upper houses did not have their first woman member until well into the second half of the twentieth century.

What explains the long period between the granting of political rights to women and the realisation of those rights, with the election of significant numbers of women elected representatives? One possible explanation is differences in institutional arrangements, especially the type of electoral system that used. Australia is a particularly appropriate case study to examine the role of the electoral system, given the wide variations that exist across the country, notably between Commonwealth upper and lower houses. A second possible explanation is the role of public opinion, and the social context in which women have sought nomination as election candidates and contested elections. Related to this is the impact of the women's movement, which, in Australia as in many other countries, has had a significant effect on elite political opinion. And, finally, there is the role of political parties, particularly in regard to whether or not they have adopted quotas for women candidates nominating for winnable seats.

This chapter evaluates these different explanations by examining patterns of women's electoral representation in Australia, focusing particularly on national variations, and variations by upper and lower houses and by party. The analyses show that much of the variation that emerges can be attributed to institutional factors, such as the different electoral systems that have operated in the states, and between the Senate and the House of

Basic political data

Australia

Land area 7,692,030 sq. km.

Population 18,927,350 (2001 census).

Indigenous population Aboriginal and Torres Strait Islander population of 410,003 (2.2 per cent) (2001 census).

Administrative divisions Federal system with six states, two territories.

Head of state Queen Elizabeth II, represented by Governor General appointed on advice of Prime Minister.

Parliament Bicameral: House of Representatives with 150 members elected for three-year terms; Senate, 76 members, elected for six-year terms from states, three-year terms from territories.

The Australian political system is broadly based on the Westminster tradition of responsible parliamentary government, complicated by federalism and by strong upper houses that are popularly elected, largely by the single transferable vote (STV) form of PR. Characteristically minor parties and independents now hold the balance of power in such upper houses and have been able to strengthen the legislative review and executive scrutiny functions of Parliament. Lower houses, where governments are formed as in the Westminster tradition, are mainly elected by majority preferential (alternative vote) and have single-member constituencies.

Apart from the Commonwealth (federal) parliament there are six state parliaments, deriving from the nineteenth-century colonial parliaments and two Territories that became self-governing in the twentieth century. Many functions are shared across different levels of government, leading to the growth of 'executive federalism'. Local government exists as a third tier of government in all jurisdictions except the Australian Capital Territory. By international standards, local government is relatively weak and is responsible for only 5 per cent of total government expenditure. Voting is compulsory in federal and state elections and in some states for local government elections as well.

Table 2.1 Electoral systems used in Australia*

Jurisdiction (listed in order of population size)	*Chamber*	*Electoral system*
Commonwealth	House of Representatives	Alternative vote
	Senate	STV
New South Wales	Legislative Assembly	Alternative vote (optional preferences)
	Legislative Council	STV
Victoria	Legislative Assembly	Alternative vote
	Legislative Council	STV (from 2006)
Queensland	Legislative Assembly (unicameral parlt)	Alternative vote (optional preferences)
Western Australia	Legislative Assembly	Alternative vote
	Legislative Council	STV
South Australia	House of Assembly	Alternative vote
	Legislative Council	STV
Tasmania	House of Assembly	STV
	Legislative Council	Alternative vote
Australian Capital Territory	Legislative Assembly	STV
Northern Territory	Legislative Assembly	Alternative vote

*Not including systems used for municipal government.

Representatives. But differences in party strategies and policies are also shown to have been, and continue to be, important. It is also apparent that changes in voter and elite opinion in the 1980s and 1990s have also made a major contribution. Finally, the role of political parties, and the adoption of quotas by the Labor Party, has had a significant impact on the overall levels of women's electoral representation.

The extension of women's political rights

Australia's origins as a settler society and the consequent effects on the development of democracy have had a major influence on establishing women's political rights. The legacy of the settler society has been two themes, egalitarianism and utilitarianism, and these are sometimes identified as encapsulating the distinctive Australian ethos. Both have played a major role in securing political rights for women much earlier than occurred in the other Westminster democracies, with the exception of New Zealand, another settler society.[1]

The notion of equality in Australian society has its origins in the frontier tradition which emerged in the early years of white settlement, and the reliance of the early settlers on their friends and neighbours for support – what became known as 'mateship'.[2] This frontier spirit was also present in other immigrant societies, notably the United States, Canada and South Africa, but the Australian frontier experience – with fewer people and in many ways a harsher environment – fostered a degree of egalitarianism far beyond that found in the other colonial societies. Equality was also fostered by the convict heritage and since few convicts wished to return to Europe after serving their sentences, most had the goal of establishing an open, less privileged and meritocratic society very different from the one that they had left behind.

Once egalitarianism was firmly established in social relations, demands grew for it to be applied to political institutions as well. Throughout the 1850s, a range of political reforms were introduced in the colonies which were far ahead of those in any other country in the world, with the possible exception of New Zealand, which, in any event, shared many of the same characteristics as Australia. By 1859 all the colonies, with the exception of Western Australia and Tasmania, had introduced universal manhood suffrage. In Britain, by comparison, although the franchise was extended in 1884 to working men, it was not properly universal until 1918, almost 60 years after its introduction in Australia. New Zealand led the world in granting votes for women, in 1893, with most of the Australian colonies following shortly thereafter. Once again, Britain and the United States lagged behind their Australasian counterparts. The nineteenth amendment to the US constitution gave women the right to vote in 1920, while British women had to wait until 1928 in order to vote on the same basis as men.[3]

In addition to quickening the pace of democratic reform, egalitarianism was also important in providing a utilitarian expectation about the proper role of the state. Utilitarianism is the desire to see everyday problems resolved efficiently by the use of whatever methods are available and at whatever cost. As Hancock[4] put it in his famous observation, 'Australians have come to look upon the state as a vast public utility, whose duty it is to provide the greatest happiness for the greatest number.' In other words, the state exists primarily in order to resolve problems and disputes, not to preserve individual liberty. The influence of utilitarianism is seen in the system of compulsory voting, which was introduced for Commonwealth elections in 1924, and by 1941 had been adopted by all the states and territories.[5]

Egalitarianism and utilitarianism fostered women's political rights in complementary ways. The absence of an inherited political culture and inherited privilege meant that women were accepted for what they could contribute, and in the context of a settler society they were regarded as having at least as much to contribute as men. The granting of political rights to women was seen as a logical extension of their social role. In turn, once the principle of gender equality in political rights had been established, implementing them was relatively easy, since the change depended simply on the passage of the appropriate legislation. Even then, of course, there was popular opposition, but not at the level found, say, in Britain or Europe during the same period.

Once the principle of equal political rights was accepted, the pace of reform was rapid. South Australia was the first colony to grant women the vote, in 1894, one year later than New Zealand, with the legislation gaining assent in 1895. Women were first able to vote in 1896 in the election to the South Australian House of Assembly (Table 2.2). It was no accident that South Australia led the way: the colony had a strong Protestant heritage, and of all the six colonies, it had the fewest convict settlers. The granting of the vote in South Australia also proved to be important for granting the right to stand for parliament at federation. The delegates to the 1897–98 Constitutional Convention argued that women should not lose the right to vote at federation, and since federation required the

Table 2.2 The extension of women's political rights in Australia

State	*Votes for women*[a]	*First election eligible*	*Right to stand*[a]	*First woman elected*
Commonwealth				
House of Representatives	1902	1903	1902	1943
Senate	1902	1903	1902	1943
New South Wales				
Legislative Assembly	1902	1904	1918	1925
Legislative Council (to 1978)	n.a.	n.a.	1926	1931
Legislative Council (from 1978)	1978	1978	1978	1978
Victoria				
Legislative Assembly	1909	1911	1924	1933
Legislative Council[b]	1909	1924	1924	1979
South Australia				
House of Assembly	1895	1896	1895	1959
Legislative Council[b]	1895	1897	1959	1959
Western Australia				
House of Assembly	1900	1901	1920	1921
Legislative Council[b]	1900	1900	1920	1954
Queensland				
Legislative Assembly	1905	1907	1915	1929
Tasmania				
House of Assembly	1904	1906	1922	1955
Legislative Council[b]	1920	1921	1922	1948

Notes

a Date of Bill gaining assent.

b Property qualifications applied until 1950 in Victoria, 1973 in South Australia, 1963 in Western Australia and 1968 in Tasmania.

consent of a majority of the electors in each colony, this assisted the argument in favour of granting women the vote. Since the franchise and the right to stand for parliament had been linked, this too provided a lever to political change.[6]

The other colonies soon followed South Australia's example – Western Australia in 1900, New South Wales in 1902, Queensland in 1907 and Victoria in 1909. Of course, the extension of the franchise to women in Commonwealth elections in 1902 meant that it was difficult for the new states to argue against the universal franchise. However, the granting of the vote to women in the upper houses of the colonies was still a very uneven process, with Tasmania the last to do so, in 1920, with the exception of New South Wales, which did not have a directly elected upper house until 1978.[7]

In the Commonwealth and South Australia, the right to stand for election was granted simultaneously with the right to vote; in the other colonies, this right came later. Victoria and Tasmania were the slowest in extending the right, in 1924 and 1922, respectively. The right to stand for election to the upper houses was granted even later, in most cases. The right to stand for election in Australia was exercised at the national level at the earliest opportunity, and the Commonwealth was the first national parliament in the British Empire for which women stood for election, when three women nominated for the Senate and one for the House of Representatives.[8]

Women's parliamentary representation

Although women gained the right to vote and to stand for election in Australia earlier than in almost any other established democracy, women did not succeed in gaining election until some time after they gained the right to stand.[9] This pattern is common between all the states and the Commonwealth, and between the upper and lower houses. Although Australia's first female parliamentarian was Edith Cowan, who was elected to the Western Australian Legislative Assembly in 1921, just one year after the right to stand was granted, the gap was much greater in most of the other states. In South Australia, the first colony to grant women the vote in 1895, it was not until 1959 that a woman was elected. The successful candidate, Joyce Steele, had been pre-selected for a safe Liberal seat in place of the government whip, who had attracted the disapproval of the branch members, a majority of whom were women, by quickly remarrying following the death of his wife.[10] In Tasmania, the gap between the right to stand and the election of the first woman in the lower house was 33 years and ended when Mabel Miller, a barrister and deputy lord mayor of Hobart, was elected as a Liberal member.

In the case of the Commonwealth, women did not gain election to parliament until 1943 – with the election of Enid Lyons representing the seat

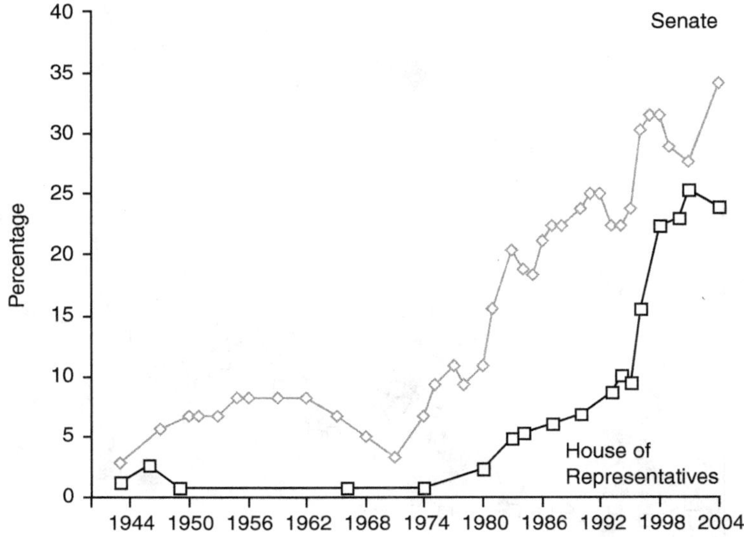

Figure 2.1 Women members of the Australian parliament, by House, 1943–2004 (%).

Note
The figures take account of changes due to by-elections.

of Darwin in Tasmania to the House of Representatives, and Dorothy Tangney representing Western Australia in the Senate. Enid Lyons, who was the widow of Joe Lyons, the prime minister between 1932 and 1939, won the seat for the United Australia Party (the forerunner of the Liberals) and was the only new member of that party to gain election.[11] Dorothy Tangney had stood for state seats for Labor in 1936 and 1939 and for the Senate in 1940, all unsuccessfully. She was elected for the Senate unexpectedly in 1943, having been placed fourth on the ticket, and held her seat continuously until 1968, when she was defeated, having been relegated to a lower position on the ticket after a change in the party's preselection rules.[12]

The patterns of parliamentary representation among women since 1943 shown in Figure 2.1 suggest two observations. First, throughout the period, women have been more successful in gaining election to the Senate than to the House of Representatives. Indeed, at no point over the period has the proportion of female representatives in the lower house exceeded the proportion in the upper house, and during an extended period the proportion in the upper house has been substantially higher. In the 1983 election, for example, six of the 125 members of the lower house (or 4.8 per cent) were female, compared with 13 of the 64 members

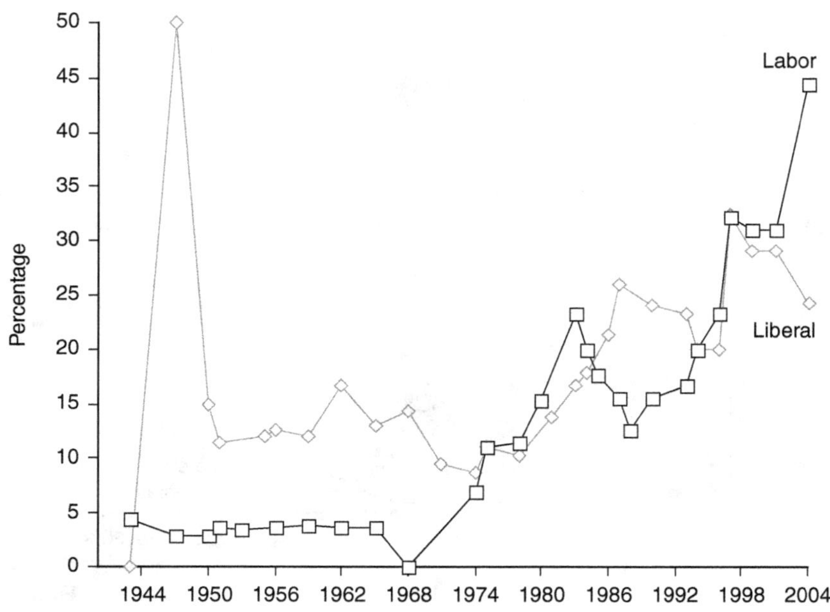

Figure 2.2 Women members of the Senate, by party, 1943–2004 (%).

Note
The figures take account of changes due to by-elections.

of the Senate (or 20.3 per cent). One of the explanations for this trend, which is examined in detail later, is the evolution of the different electoral systems between the two houses, and the strategic ways in which the major parties have used them to increase their vote. A second observation is the significantly greater increase in the proportion of women representatives since 1970 – what is sometimes referred to a 'critical mass'.[13] In this approach, increased representation in itself accelerates the likelihood that other women will stand and gain election.

The patterns of women's representation disaggregated by party between the two houses suggest a further set of observations (Figures 2.2 and 2.3). In the Senate, the Liberals have generally had higher levels of female representation than Labor, although the numbers, particularly in the years before 1970, are often small, so that relatively small shifts in numbers can translate into more significant percentage changes. This accounts for the apparent dramatic rise in 1947, when Annabelle Rankin was one of only two Liberal senators. In the period from 1987 to 1996, the Liberals, as a proportion of their representation, counted more women in their ranks than Labor. Thereafter the differences in the proportions of women senators between the two parties has been much smaller, with the

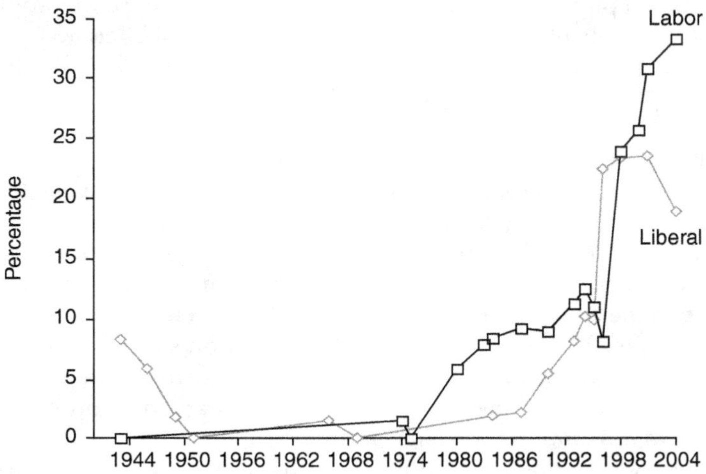

Figure 2.3 Women members of the House of Representatives, by party, 1943–2004 (%).

Note
The figures take account of changes due to by-elections.

exception of the 2004 election when Labor's proportion of women representatives was almost double the Liberal figure.

In the House of Representatives there is a reverse pattern to the Senate, and Labor has generally had more women representatives than the Liberals. This pattern is particularly notable in the late 1980s and early 1990s, and again in 2001 and 2004. Following the 2004 federal election, for example, 33.3 per cent of Labor representatives were women (20 out of a total of 60), compared with 18.9 per cent of Liberals (14 out of a total of 74). This gap between the levels of women's representation in the two parties is the largest since women were first elected, and it remains to be seen if it is a temporary deviation from the long term trend, or a more lasting feature of party representation.

These patterns suggest that there is a broadly similar pattern in women's parliamentary representation between the parties and between the upper and lower houses, with a large rise in representation occurring after 1970. That said, there are significant variations by party and house. It is clear that, historically at least, women have been more likely to gain representation in the Senate than in the House of Representatives, and to gain election for Labor in the lower house and for the Liberals in the upper house. These patterns are the result of a complex interaction between electoral system rules, the strategies adopted by the political parties to increase women's representation, and the role of external agencies such as public opinion and the lobbying activities of the women's movement. The role of each of these is examined in detail below.

The role of the electoral system

One of the most consistent and robust findings in studies of women's representation is the importance of the electoral system, especially the favourable impact of party list proportional representation (PR).[14] Other factors which relate to the operation of the electoral system include the degree of competition in a constituency, and comparative studies have shown that women have more success in gaining election if the competition for seats is less at the pre-selection or nomination stage.[15] Once nominated, a more competitive party system seems to provide more incentives for parties to search for new voters, which leads to a contagion effect for women candidates among the major parties.[16]

One factor which does not apply in Australia is turnout, since voting has been compulsory in all Commonwealth elections from 1924, and in all state lower house elections from 1942. Opinion polls show that the system is widely supported and in consequence, complied with.[17] Reduced turnout lowers women's representation, net of a wide range of other factors – including the presence or absence of compulsory voting.[18] This appears to occur because turnout and voter registration vary among social groups, as a consequence of different levels of political interest and involvement. This has had a negative influence on women's representation, especially in earlier years of the universal franchise when women tended to vote less frequently than men.[19]

Australia has used a variety of electoral systems for the House of Representatives and the Senate during the course of the twentieth century, and these are outlined in Table 2.3. This experimentation owes much to the political debates in Britain around the end of the nineteenth century, where impending mass suffrage stimulated discussion about electoral reform. Another influence on Australian experimentation was the role of electoral system activists, such as Catherine Helen Spence, Inglis Clark and Edward Nanson, all of whom had a significant influence on the arguments for and against the various systems then under consideration. And a third influence was the experiences of the states, all of which had experimented at various times with electoral system design. Indeed, the first Commonwealth elections in 1901 were conducted using the electoral systems then existing in the states, in the absence of an agreed uniform system.[20]

The House of Representatives utilised the single-member plurality electoral system from 1903 until 1918, when it was replaced by the alternative vote also based on single-member constituencies. The lower house electoral system has remained relatively unchanged since then. By contrast, the Senate has undergone three major changes during the course of

Table 2.3 House of Representatives and Senate electoral systems since 1901

Year	*State*	*Electoral system*
House of Representatives		
1901	NSW, Vic, WA	SMP
	Qld	AV (using contingent vote)
	SA	Block vote
	Tasmania	STV
1903	All states	SMP
1918	All states	AV
Senate		
1901	All states, except Tasmania in 1901	Block vote (STV in Tasmania)
1919	All states	Preferential block
1949	All states	STV
1983	All states	STV with ticket voting

Notes
SMP single-member plurality, AV alternative vote, STV single transferable vote.

the twentieth century. In 1919, preferential voting was introduced in place of block voting, but since it requires a candidate to gain an absolute majority it turned out to be as disproportional as the system it replaced. As a consequence, proportional representation using the single transferable vote method was introduced in 1949. This has remained the Senate system with the exception that the option of ticket voting was introduced in 1983, and currently about 95 per cent of the electorate use this preference rather than list their own preferences.[21]

Bearing in mind that proportional representation (and especially the party list variety) is favourable to women's representation, it is not surprising that the proportion of women elected has historically been greater in the Senate than in the House of Representatives. The marrying of STV with ticket voting has created, in all but name, a party list system, with the parties effectively sealing the fate of individual candidates by virtue of determining their order on the party ticket. On balance, this has advantaged women's representation by taking the electoral decision away from voters and putting it in the hands of parties; provided parties are minded to promote women for legislative office (as they have been in recent years) this increases women's representation. The preferential system for lower house elections has meant that, until relatively recently, parties have been less willing to select women for winnable seats unless they have had a considerable public profile.

Changing public opinion

The role of public opinion in shaping women's representation is often overlooked. While political elites are usually responsible for leading public opinion on certain major issues, elites are more likely to take their cue from voters if the issue is potentially divisive, or if it is one which is not aligned with the dominant economic dimension of party conflict. The net effect is that on the issue of women's social and economic role in society, public opinion plays a more important role than would be the case on, say, taxation or health policy. On this issue, political elites may have a view, but they are constrained by public opinion in the leadership that they can deliver.

Identifying changes in public opinion towards women is problematic, since few survey questions have been asked over an extended period, and even fewer where the question wordings are consistent. The extent of our knowledge about over-time changes in public opinion towards women comes from a question about women's job opportunities which has been asked consistently in the Australian Election Study (AES) from 1987 onwards. The question asks whether the respondents felt that the changes in women's job opportunities that have taken place had 'gone too far', 'not far enough' or were 'about right' (Figure 2.4). The results suggest that about half those interviewed felt that opportunities were 'about right'. However, the proportion believing that they had 'not gone far enough' doubled over the period, to four in ten of voters in 2004. The

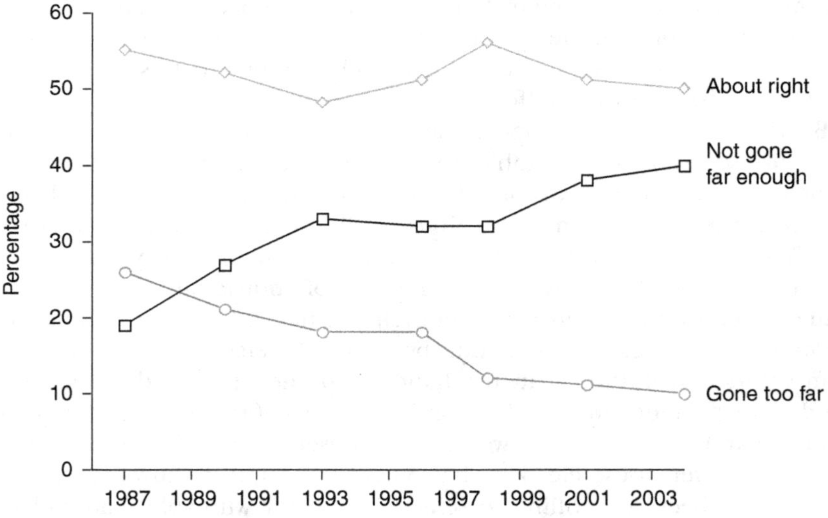

Figure 2.4 Public opinion towards equal opportunities for women, 1987–2004 (%).

Note
The question was 'The statements below indicate some of the changes that have been happening in Australia over the years. For each one, please say whether you think the change has gone too far, not gone far enough, or is about right? Equal opportunities for women'.

largest proportional increase took place between 1987 and 1993, but another notable increase took place between 1998 and 2001.

One of the explanations that is commonly advanced to account for the changes in the legislative representation of women is the events of the 1960s, and the increasing politicisation and consequent policy impact of the women's movement. These changes are examined in more detail in the next section, but we might hypothesise that they have had a significant impact on public opinion among women, with those experiencing their political socialisation in this period being more radical in their resolve to remove gender inequalities than their counterparts who were socialised before or after this period. This hypothesis can be tested by examining support for women's job opportunities by generation, in this case by the decade of the person's birth. If the hypothesis were to be confirmed, we would expect greater levels of support for these views among those who were socialised in the 1960s or 1970s, and were therefore born during the 1950s or 1960s.

Figure 2.5 shows the results of this analysis, plotting support for women's job opportunities by the decade of birth among the respondents. The analysis is conducted for two of the AES surveys, 1990 and 2004. If the

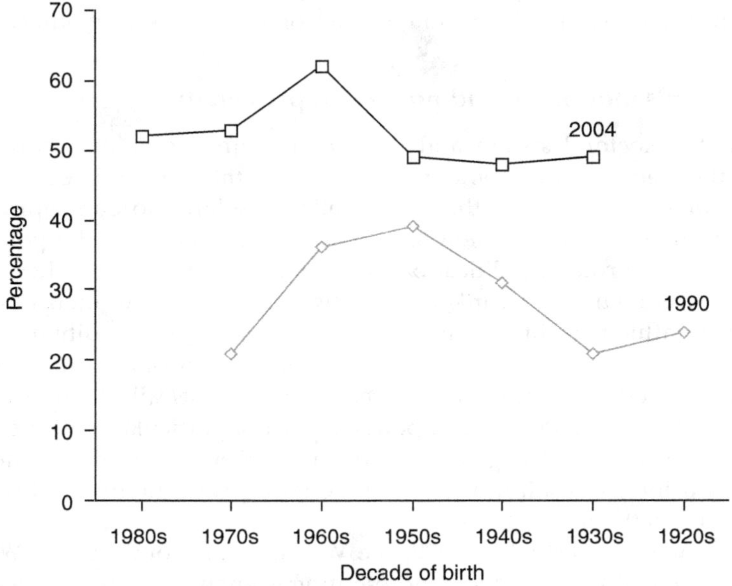

Figure 2.5 Generational views about equal opportunities for women, 1990 and 2004 (%).

Note

The figures are the percentages who said the changes had not gone far enough. For the wording of the question see Figure 2.4.

generational explanation were to be confirmed, we would expect to observe the same pattern in both surveys. The results confirm that this is the case. In 1990, there is strongest support for the proposition among those who were born in the 1950s and 1960s, and were therefore socialised a decade or more afterwards. Thus, the 39 per cent of those born in the 1950s in the 1990 survey believed that women's job opportunities had 'not gone far enough', compared with nearly half of those born in the 1970s or 1930s. The pattern is also evident among the survey respondents to the 2004 AES; here, among those born in the 1960s, no less than 62 per cent endorsed more women's job opportunities, the highest level of support among any generation.

These findings provide empirical support for the common perception that there was a 'second-wave feminist movement' (the first wave was the suffrage movement), stemming from developments on women's issues during the 1960s and early 1970s. The argument is that these changes in views among women manifested themselves in legislative representation terms starting in the 1970s, when women's representation began to increase.[22] While it is impossible to prove the link, it would appear that the activities of the women's movement in the 1960s and broader changes during that decade had a tangible effect on public opinion among women (and perhaps also among men) and that this in turn facilitated the nomination and election of greater numbers of women to legislative office.

The women's movement and political representation

Beyond the electoral system and changes in public opinion, there are many other factors which potentially influence the electoral representation of women. Two factors that are usually considered to be major ones are the degree to which women have mobilised to influence the political agenda, and the role of political parties in establishing quotas. These two factors are, of course, interlinked. An active and effective women's movement will influence elite party opinion in favour of recruiting more women for legislative office, and we might expect many of the women who become involved in the women's movement as activists will themselves be candidates for selection. In turn, political parties, particularly on the left, will welcome the mobilising activities of the women's movement, since it should in principle result in the recruitment of greater numbers of voters sympathetic to them.

Since it was established in 1972, the Women's Electoral Lobby (WEL) has been the main organisation representing women on a range of issues. WEL was very much the leader of second-wave feminism in Australia, and was composed for the most part of professional women born in the 1950s who, as we saw in the previous section, held clear views about issues of women's equality. The goal of WEL is to ensure greater participation by women in all aspects of society, and the movement's platform is based on the five demands of second-wave feminism: equal pay, equal employment opportunity, free contraception, abortion on demand and free child care.[23]

To what extent has WEL or any similar women's group played a role both in recruiting women to parliament, and influencing the opinions of those who are elected? The Australian Candidate Study (ACS), starting in 1987, has asked a range of questions about candidates' backgrounds and opinions, but has not asked a direct question about the affiliation with women's groups. The ACS has, however, asked about prior activity in women's organisations and the support that was provided by such organisations during the course of the election campaign. In the 2001 ACS, 68 per cent of Labor women candidates and 60 per cent of Liberal-National candidates said that they had been 'very active' in women's organisations in their community. Perhaps more revealingly, 59 per cent of Labor women candidates but only 31 per cent of their Liberal-National counterparts said that they had received 'very positive' support for their campaign from such groups. It would appear, then, that Labor women candidates had stronger links with women's groups than their Liberal-National competitors, as we would expect.

Do women MPs in Australia pursue a different policy agenda compared with their male counterparts? This question has generated a substantial academic literature, the answer tending to vary with the degree of party discipline that operates within the political system and the salience of the issue to voters and elites.[24] On issues of immediate party debate, such as taxation, health or education, the views of women legislators are little different from their male colleagues', net of other things, such as age, length of incumbency and constituency marginality; on issues which are less salient in partisan terms, women legislators may take a different view. From 1987 onwards (but with the exception of the 1998 election, when no candidate survey was conducted), the ACS asked the election candidates the question about women's job opportunities analysed earlier among voters; these results are shown in Figure 2.6.

The responses of male candidates to the question about women's job opportunities are generally in line with those of the voting population, as shown earlier in Figure 2.4. By contrast, women candidates are significantly more likely to hold the view that women's job opportunities have 'not gone far enough'. For example, in the 2001 survey, 38 per cent of male candidates took this view, but the same figure for women candidates was more than twice this estimate, at 81 per cent. Over the period for which data are available, women candidates are consistently and significantly more likely to display stronger support for the proposition than their male counterparts.

These results present suggestive, though not conclusive, evidence that the women's movement has been an important element in influencing elite opinion on women's issues, and in providing an activist pool for the

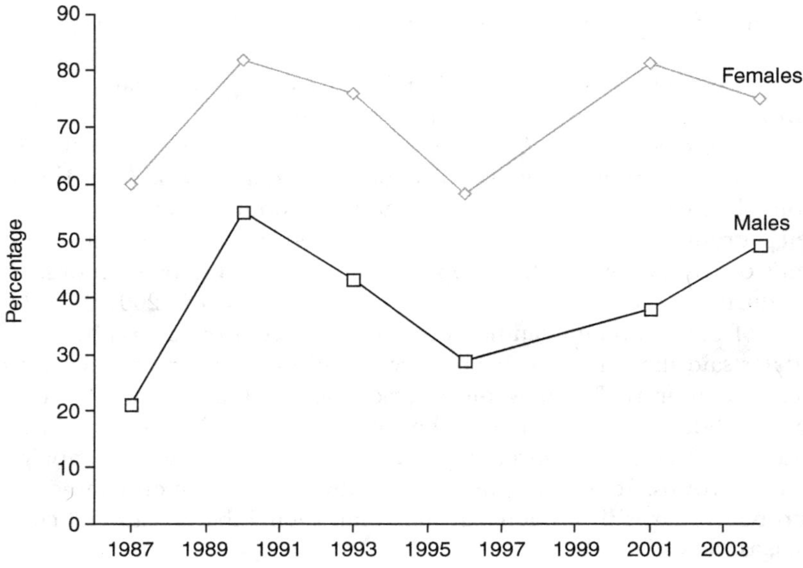

Figure 2.6 Election candidates' views on equal opportunities for women, 1987–2004 (%).

Notes
The figures are the percentages who said women's equal opportunities had not gone far enough. The estimates are for Labor and Liberal-National candidates only. For the wording of the question see Figure 2.4.

recruitment of women legislators. This is more likely to have occurred within the Labor Party than among the Liberal-National coalition.[25] Nevertheless, even if the changes originated first in Labor circles, the contagion effect is likely to have resulted in their transfer to the coalition, and to have influenced Liberal Party thinking on women's issues and on the representation of women more generally.

Political parties and gender quotas

Perhaps more than anywhere else, democracy in Australia is synonymous with party democracy. Early Australian democracy was a laboratory for electoral experiments, and the cleavage structure around which the party system coalesced was frozen during this period of experimentation. As a consequence, the party system has remained stable during the course of the century. Moreover, since the political system was embedded in a utilitarian political culture, where efficiency was and is regarded as of paramount importance, this has enhanced the role of mass political parties, which were able to provide accountability, policy choice and a ready and able elite willing to hold political office. In practical terms, however, it has been the system of compulsory voting that has ensured that Australian political parties remained dominant and relatively unchallenged during the course of the twentieth century. Each new generation identifies with and retains party loyalty, and that loyalty is reinforced by a frequent round of state and federal elections which involve 95 per cent of voters.

Once it was agreed that women candidates did not cost the parties votes, numerous studies identified the selection process within political parties as representing the major barrier to the equal political representation of women.[26] Even where political parties were prepared to nominate significant numbers of women candidates, they were often selected for unwinnable seats, and since incumbency is the major factor predicting future election, this creates a vicious circle accounting for future lack of success among women.[27] Across a range of countries, the solution to this problem has taken the form of quotas for women candidates, with a certain number of winnable seats allocated solely to nomination by women.[28]

There is little doubt that quotas are an important mechanism in their own right in increasing the political representation of women. In Norway, where they were first introduced in the 1970s, they substantially increased the number of women MPs coming from the Labour Party.[29] The use of quotas by the British Labour Party in the 1997 general election significantly increased women's representation,[30] but not without major internal dissent over the principle, which was seen as discriminatory by some branches.[31] Equally important is the influence that quotas have exerted on the party system as a whole, through emulative behaviour by other parties.[32]

The Labor Party was the first party in Australia to raise the issue of quotas, and to follow it up with concrete policies. Following an internal inquiry in the late 1970s into women's electoral representation in general, a variety of affirmative action measures were considered, including women-only shortlists. The 1981 conference set a target of 30 per cent women within the parliamentary party to be achieved by 1990, but did not establish processes to ensure that this target was met, or to monitor progress towards its achievement.[33] In the absence of an agreed process, progress was slow. In 1994 a further target of 35 per cent of women in winnable seats by 2002 was set, but this time various sanctions were put in place against the state branches if they did not meet the target.

In 2002 the target of 35 per cent was further increased to 40 per cent, to be achieved by 2012.[34] The evidence suggests that quotas – particularly the 1994 quota, which for the first time identified winnable seats – has been a major factor in increasing Labor representation in the House of Representatives. By contrast, the Liberal Party has historically rejected quotas as a matter of principle, and in the past its representation of women has exceeded Labor's. However, since 1998, largely because of the implementation of quotas, Labor has surpassed the Liberals in the numbers of women who have succeeded in winning election.

Conclusion

Although Australia was the second established democracy to grant women the vote, and one of the first to permit them to stand for national elected office, the progress of women's electoral representation has been similar to most other countries'. The first woman was not elected to the national legislature until near the middle of the century, and it was not until the 1970s that women's electoral representation began to make any significant headway. It is clear that no single explanation accounts for this pattern of representation; rather, what has been occurring is a complex interaction between a wide range of factors which impact on women's electoral representation. Certainly, political culture was important in establishing these rights earlier than in other countries, but the same political culture was perhaps also at least partly responsible for ensuring that comparatively few women were elected, at least until the 1970s.

Political institutions and public opinion and activism have played an important role, at different times, in women's electoral representation in Australia. The electoral system in the Senate has provided a facilitating mechanism for increased representation, at least compared with the preferential system that has operated in the House of Representatives. The major political parties have been mediators in this process, in the strategies they have adopted to maximise their vote in each of the two houses. It is evident that the Senate electoral system – particularly since the 1983 reform, which has allowed the parties unprecedented control over the party ticket and hence to determine who gets elected – has served to increase the representation of women across both major parties.

These institutional changes have also occurred at a time when public opinion has been particularly receptive to these changes. One component of this new climate of opinion has been the influence exercised on the political elite through the activities of the Women's Electoral Lobby. The results presented here have suggested that this has particularly resonated among women born in the 1950s, who have had – at least compared with their predecessors – unprecedented access to education, and to the labour force. Overall, as the experience of other countries has shown, women's increasing electoral representation in Australia has been a consequence less of one single change than of a complex pattern of interaction and reinforcement across a wide range of areas.

Notes

The 1987–2004 Australian Election Studies and the Australian Candidate Studies were funded by the Australian Research Council and are available from the

Australian Social Science Data Archive at the Australian National University. My thanks to the editors and contributors to the volume for their helpful suggestions on a draft of this chapter.

1 The task of understanding and explaining the origins of Australian political culture has been mainly one for historians. The most influential work is probably W. F. Hancock's *Australia*, published in 1930. In turn, the roots of Australia's political culture stretch back to the circumstances surrounding Australia's white settlement and the colonial 'fragment' that was separated from Britain and which took root in Australia in the nineteenth century.
2 See Ward, *The Australian Legend*.
3 A range of other democratic reforms were also introduced in Australia far in advance of the other English-speaking democracies. Plural voting was abolished in the colonies and states around the turn of the century, half a century before Britain. Australia was the first country in the world to introduce secret voting, and it had been introduced in all but one of the colonies by 1859. By contrast, Britain did not introduce the secret ballot until 1872 and the United States not until 1893. The principle of payment for elected representatives was also established early – in 1870 in Victoria, with most of the remaining colonies following by 1890.
4 Hancock, *Australia*, 69.
5 See McAllister and Mackerras, 'Compulsory Voting, Party Stability and Electoral Advantage in Australia'.
6 See Grey and Sawer, 'Australia and New Zealand'.
7 The extension of the franchise to women in Australia contrasts sharply with the experience in Britain, where women did not get the vote until 1918, and it was a further ten years before they were granted the vote on the same basis as men. Even in Canada, most women did not gain the vote until 1918, and in the United States, not until 1920. The Australian experience was even used to try and influence Britain into granting women the vote, and in 1910 both houses passed identical resolutions intended to persuade their British counterparts that granting women the vote had a range of positive aspects which would strengthen, not weaken, parliamentary democracy (*Commonwealth Parliamentary Debates*, 17 November 1910, p. 6300).
8 The three Senate candidates were Vida Goldstein, a feminist and suffragist; Mrs Nellie Martel, an elocutionist; and Mrs Mary Ann Moore Bentley, a journalist.
9 See Sainsbury, 'Rights without Seats'.
10 Sawer and Simms, *A Woman's Place*, 129–30.
11 Joe Lyons was originally a Labor member who split from the party in 1931 and Enid Lyons had herself contested a Tasmanian state seat for Labor, unsuccessfully, in 1925.
12 She had won the first position on the ticket in 1946, 1951, 1955 and 1961, based on a branch vote. In 1967 each candidate's position on the ticket was shifted to the male-dominated state executive, which relegated her to a lower position (Sawer and Simms, *A Woman's Place*, 120).
13 See, for example, Dahlerup, 'From a Small to Large Minority'; Davis, *Women and Power in Parliamentary Democracies*; Studlar and McAllister, 'The Recruitment of Women to the Australian Legislature'.
14 See Rule, 'Electoral Systems, Contextual Factors, and Women's Opportunities for Election to Parliament in Twenty-three Democracies'; Norris and Franklin, 'Social Representation'; Matland, 'Institutional Variables Affecting Female Representation in National Legislatures'.
15 See Darcy *et al.*, *Women, Elections and Representation*.
16 See Matland and Studlar, 'The Contagion of Women Candidates in Single-member District and Proportional Representation Electoral Systems'; Curtin and Sexton, 'Are Quotas Contagious?'

17 See McAllister and Mackerras, 'Compulsory Voting, Party Stability and Electoral Advantage in Australia'.
18 See Studlar and McAllister, 'Does a Critical Mass Exist?'
19 See Norris, 'Women's Power at the Ballot Box'.
20 See Uhr, *Rules for Representation.*
21 See Farrell and McAllister, *The Australian Electoral System*; Wright, 'Changes in Australia's Federal Electoral Laws in 1983'.
22 See Randall, *Women and Politics.*
23 Sawer and Simms, *A Woman's Place,* 244–5.
24 See McAllister and Studlar, 'Gender Representation among Legislative Candidates in Australia'.
25 Sample sizes make it problematic to further disaggregate the results by party, or by incumbent and challenger.
26 See Matland and Studlar, 'The Contagion of Women Candidates in Single-member District and Proportional Representation Electoral Systems'; Welch and Studlar, 'The Opportunity Structure for Women's Candidacies and Electability in Britain and the United States'.
27 See McAllister and Studlar, 'Gender Representation among Legislative Candidates in Australia'; Studlar and McAllister, 'The Recruitment of Women to the Australian Legislature'.
28 For a review, see Caul, 'Political Parties and the Adoption of Candidate Gender Quotas'.
29 See Matland, 'Institutional Variables Affecting Female Representation in National Legislatures'.
30 Labor had 419 candidates returned in the 1997 election, of whom 102 (or 24.3 per cent) were women.
31 See Studlar and McAllister, 'Candidate Gender and Voting in the 1997 British General Election'.
32 See Matland and Studlar, 'The Contagion of Women Candidates in Single-member District and Proportional Representation Electoral Systems'.
33 See Sawer, 'A Question of Heartland'.
34 Curtin and Sexton, 'Are Quotas Contagious?'

3 Women's representation in the Canadian House of Commons

Lisa Young

For anyone concerned about women's numerical representation in the Canadian House of Commons the past decade has been discouraging at best. After a period of sustained increases in the representation of women between 1970 and 1993, the past decade has brought virtually no improvement in the number of women in Canada's national legislature. In the Canadian provinces, the situation is almost as bleak. Women make up only 20 per cent of the membership of the country's 13 provincial and territorial legislatures, ranging from a low of just over 10 per cent of the membership of the North West Territories (NWT) and Nunavut territorial legislatures to a high of 30 per cent in the Quebec National Assembly.[1] Looking at the most recent election in each province, we find that women's representation declined in seven provinces and territories, remained constant in one and increased in only five. One bright spot in this otherwise dismal landscape is the slow but perceptible increase in the election of women from minority ethnic groups over the period since 1993. Although minority and Aboriginal women remain underrepresented, they are becoming more numerous in the country's national Parliament.[2]

The focus of this chapter will be on explaining how progress on the electoral project came to stall, or even reverse, in Canada over the past decade. The primary focus will be on the federal level. Four possible sets of explanations for the stalled progress of the electoral project will be examined: the role of the electorate, the electoral system (broadly defined), the role of political parties and the party system, and the role of organised feminism. Each of these will be evaluated with respect to the most recent Canadian federal election and, where possible, prior elections. The chapter argues that the lack of progress in women's representation can be attributed in large part to the change in the Canadian party system from 1993 to the present and to the declining role of organised feminism in advocating political engagement for Canadian women.

Basic political data

Canada

Land area 9,976,140 sq. km.

Population 29,639,030 (2001 census).

Indigenous population North American Indian, Métis and Inuit, 976,305 (3.3 per cent) (2001 census).

Administrative divisions Federal system with ten provinces, three territories.

Head of state Queen Elizabeth II, represented by Governor General appointed on advice of Prime Minister.

Parliament Bicameral: House of Commons with 308 members elected for five-year terms; Senate with some 100 members appointed until age 75.

Like Australia, the Canadian political system is broadly based on the Westminster tradition of responsible parliamentary government, complicated by federalism, but Canada has a relatively weak appointed Senate and does not have upper houses at the provincial level. In addition to the national parliament, there are ten provincial and three territorial legislatures, including the new territory of Nunavut, created in 1999. The territories began as administrative agencies of the federal government but now exercise jurisdiction over most of the areas in which provincial governments have legislative authority, including health care, education and social services. Canadian federalism, while originally endowing the federal government with more powers than was the case in Australia, has seen a shift in the other direction and the provincial governments have grown in power and autonomy since the advent of the welfare state. Federal–provincial relations in Canada are marked by centrifugal forces such as Quebec nationalism and province-building. Because of jurisdictional overlap and significant disparities in resources and wealth between the provinces, institutions and processes of executive federalism are essential to managing the complex arrangements for welfare state programme financing and service delivery.

The electorate

When we consider the role of the electorate with respect to women's representation in the Canadian House of Commons, two questions arise. First, does the electorate contribute to the underrepresentation of women by discriminating against female candidates? Second, does the electorate provide a basis of public support for measures designed to increase the demographic representativeness of the Canadian parliament?

Do Canadian voters discriminate against female candidates?

The conventional wisdom in the electoral behaviour literature holds that Canadian voters do not discriminate between male and female candidates.[3] Given that vote choice in Canada is driven largely by national, as opposed to local, considerations, this is entirely plausible. If voters are making their choice based largely on party affiliation and evaluation of the party leader, then it would be entirely reasonable to expect that the characteristics of the local candidate would have no impact on voting behaviour. That said, recent research studying the 2000 federal election suggests that some 44 per cent of voters formed a preference for a local candidate and that this preference affected vote choice.[4] The most recent examination of this question is Black and Erickson's study of voting in the 1993 federal election.[5] They found that female candidates receive fewer votes, on average, than do male candidates. However, once they controlled for constituency characteristics, they found that female candidates received more votes than similarly situated male candidates, suggesting that being female offered these candidates a slight electoral advantage.

In an admittedly crude effort to re-examine the question of whether voters discriminate against female candidates, Table 3.1 shows the mean change in a party's vote share in each electoral district from the 1997 election to the 2000 election, broken down by gender. Although imperfect, using the change in the vote share offers something of a control for the party's competitiveness in each riding. To further control for the party's competitiveness, three categories are employed: ridings in which the party did not have an incumbent, ridings in which the party had an incumbent, and ridings in which the party won the seat in 1997 but the incumbent did not run again.[6] Positive numbers indicate that the party increased its vote share; negative numbers indicate that the party's vote share dropped.

Among non-incumbent candidates we find relatively modest gender differences, with female candidates reducing their party's share of the vote in their riding by one percentage point more than male candidates. Among incumbents the gender differences in vote share change are similarly small, but once again female incumbents of all parties increased their vote share by one percentage point less than male incumbents. The most striking differences are found in the small sub-set of seats that were won by the

Table 3.1 Change in party's popular vote in riding from 1997 to 2000 (means)

Party	*Male*	*n*	*Female*	*n*	*Male–Female*
Liberal					
Not incumbent	2.81	117	1.36	30	1.45
Incumbent	3.36	119	3.77	35	**–0.41**
Other Liberal-held riding	3.79	5	–5.16	2	8.95
PC					
Not incumbent	–6.04	239	–9	37	2.96
Incumbent	3.79	13	1.96	2	1.83
Other PC-held riding	–28.16	4	–35.91	2	7.75
BQ					
Not incumbent	0.51	31	0.91	8	**–0.4**
Incumbent	3.94	26	2.37	10	1.57
Other BQ-held riding	1.31	8	1.54	1	**–0.23**
NDP					
Not incumbent	–2.68	198	–2.98	81	0.3
Incumbent	–2.35	12	–1.64	7	**–0.71**
Other NDP-held riding	–12.72	1	–31.93	1	19.21
CA					
Not incumbent	4.47	218	6.07	29	**–1.6**
Incumbent	7.21	48	6.77	3	0.44
Other REF-held riding	3.95	9	7.35	1	**–3.4**
Totals					
Not incumbent	–0.82	803	–1.89	185	1.08
Incumbent	3.99	218	2.95	57	1.03
Party held; open seat	–2.24	27	–15.03	7	12.79

Source: Calculated from 2000 candidate data set, Munroe Eagles principal investigator.

party in the 1997 election but did not have an incumbent running in 2000. Such seats are generally seen as highly desirable, winnable seats. It was only in the Canadian Alliance that we find female candidates improving vote share more than male candidates did; in this instance, the lone woman nominated in an open seat improved the party's vote share by just over seven percentage points, while her male counterparts improved their party's vote share by just under four percentage points on average. The gender differences for Liberal, Progressive Conservative (PC) and New Democratic Party (NDP), held ridings with no incumbent are striking. Male Liberal candidates in these ridings improved the party's vote by almost four percentage points on average, while female candidates lowered the party's vote by over five percentage points. PC candidates of both genders lowered their party's vote in these ridings, but by almost eight percentage points more for the female candidates. The one female NDP candidate lowered her party's vote by 32 percentage points, which was 19 percentage points more than her male counterpart.

Although by no means conclusive, these figures suggest that further research is required to determine whether the Canadian electorate does, in fact, discriminate against female candidates. That said, if there is discrimination, its magnitude is so limited that it is unlikely to decide the outcome of local contests in most cases under the current first-past-the-post electoral system. Discrimination against female candidates would have much broader significance under an electoral system that allows voters to select among candidates running under their preferred party's banner, such as the Single Transferable Vote (STV) or Mixed Member Proportional (MMP) with open lists. As such systems have been recommended by the Citizens' Assembly of British Columbia and the Law Reform Commission of Canada, the question of voter discrimination may become highly relevant in the Canadian context.

To what extent does the electorate support positive measures?

Examination of data from a survey of the Canadian public in 2000 suggests that a substantial minority of Canadian voters are concerned about the underrepresentation of women, and that there is a moderate degree of public support for measures designed to make the Canadian parliament more reflective of the country's demographic composition.[7] As Figure 3.1 illustrates, approximately one-third of respondents to this

Figure 3.1 Percentage indicating underrepresentation as a 'serious' or 'very serious' problem (source: Howe and Northrup (2000)).

survey indicated that the underrepresentation of women was a serious or very serious problem. It comes as no surprise that women were more inclined to identify this as a problem than were their male counterparts. What is somewhat surprising, however, is that women were more inclined to identify the underrepresentation of visible minorities as a problem than the underrepresentation of women. Overall, these figures suggest that there is not an overwhelming concern among either Canadian men or women regarding women's underrepresentation.

Despite this, survey respondents expressed a considerable degree of support for measures designed to increase the representativeness of the Canadian parliament. Figure 3.2 shows that a large minority of survey respondents agreed that political parties should be required to choose more women and more visible minorities. The survey split the sample, asking half of respondents whether they would favour or oppose requiring political parties to choose 'as many female as male candidates' and asking the remaining respondents whether they would favour or oppose requiring political parties to choose 'more female candidates than they do now'. Predictably, respondents were more inclined to agree with the less demanding option of requiring parties to choose more female candidates than they do now. None the less, fully 48 per cent of women and 33 per cent of men agreed with requiring gender parity in candidate selection and almost 60 per cent of women and 40 per cent of men agreed with requiring parties to choose more female candidates than they do now.

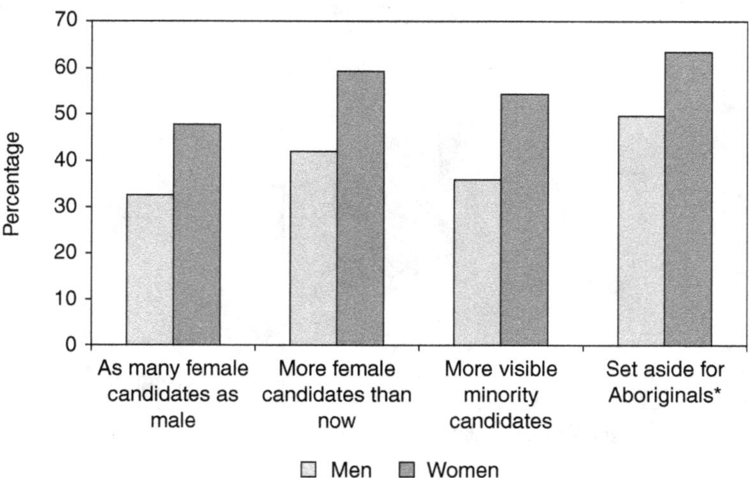

Figure 3.2 Percentage in favour of requiring parties to choose ... *This question did not mention parties. It asked, 'Would you favour or oppose setting aside a small number of seats in Parliament in Ottawa for aboriginal people?' (source: Howe and Northrup (2000)).

The greatest public support was expressed for setting aside a small number of seats for Aboriginal people.

It is, however, important to keep in mind that general support expressed in an opinion survey – particularly when it has been primed with a question asking whether the underrepresentation of women is a serious problem – could well melt away in the face of a public debate. Arguments about allowing parties to choose the 'best qualified' candidate could well move opinion on these issues should a public debate arise. None the less, these data suggest the presence of a modest reservoir of support among Canadians for positive measures, should parties or Parliament decide to implement them.

The electoral system

Canada remains one of the last holdouts clinging to a single-member plurality electoral system. As discussed in Chapter 1 of this book, a considerable body of research demonstrates that electoral systems based on single-member electorates are, for a variety of reasons, less amenable to women's representation than are variants of proportional representation (PR).[8] There is every reason to believe that adopting some variant of a PR electoral system would have at least a modest positive impact on women's representation in Canadian legislatures. If nothing else, electoral system change would probably improve the electoral fortunes of the federal NDP, which has consistently nominated more female candidates than any of the other federal parties. In anticipating the effect of some variant of PR, one must of course keep two cautions in mind. First, the form of PR and the details of the system's design are important. For instance, comparative research suggests that list PR is more likely to improve women's representation than is STV, and closed lists may be more favourable to women's representation than are open lists.[9] Second, if some form of PR is adopted without mandatory quotas for women's representation, it will affect the number of women elected only to the extent that political parties are concerned with increasing women's representation. As will be discussed below, at least one of the major Canadian political parties at the federal level would almost certainly take no affirmative measures to increase women's representation under a list system.

For many years, electoral system change has been an illusory objective for Canadian reformers. In 2004–05, however, several Canadian provinces have begun formal examinations of the possibility of electoral system change. The government of Quebec has introduced legislation implementing an MMP system modelled loosely on the German electoral system; the Citizens' Assembly of British Columbia recommended an STV electoral system that received substantial support in a province-wide referendum;[10] in Prince Edward Island a commission has recommended a move MMP and the province will hold a referendum on it; in New

Brunswick the Commission on Legislative Democracy has recommended a move to a modest region-based MMP system. At the federal level, the Law Commission of Canada in 2004 issued a report advocating adopting a PR electoral system for elections to the House of Commons.

Beyond the electoral system itself, are there aspects of the conduct of elections in Canada that have positive or negative impact on women's representation? One possibility is the regulation of political finance.

Political finance

In all industrialised democracies, including Canada, electoral competition has become a very expensive undertaking. Contemporary voters are reached not by knocking on doors but by buying television advertising. Campaigns are staffed by high-priced professionals. Media buys, polling, direct dial and a presence on the Internet are the hallmarks of modern campaigns, and all of them are expensive. If we want to understand barriers to the election of women in this era of capital-intensive politics, then it is necessary to examine the issue of whether access to money belongs on the list of impediments to women's election.

Political scientist Janine Brodie's research for the Canadian Royal Commission on Electoral Reform and Party Financing found that female candidates in the 1988 federal election reported that funding outweighed all the other factors that female candidates considered to be major barriers to nomination and candidacy.[11] It should be noted, however, that Brodie's research surveyed only female candidates, so it is possible that male candidates might have been just as likely to report similar concerns. That said, Erickson's survey of candidates in the 1993 federal election found that 85 per cent of female candidates, as compared with 77 per cent of male candidates, favoured spending limits governing nomination contests.[12] Although this is not a direct measure of perceptions of the difficulty of raising money, it may lend some support to the idea that women are somewhat more concerned about their ability to raise sufficient funds than are men.

If there are consistent gender differences in the ability to raise campaign funds, we would expect to find these differences at the nomination/primary election stage rather than in the general election. In nomination contests and primary elections, individuals are generally running without the endorsement of their political party. This forces them to rely more heavily on personal networks for soliciting campaign support, rather than drawing on their party's financial backers. If, in fact, women are disadvantaged in some way in their ability to raise funds, it would consequently be more likely to be evident at this stage.

While inconclusive, the limited Canadian evidence suggests that women do not experience substantial difficulties in fund-raising for nomination bids. In her 1993 survey of candidates, Erickson found that female candidates reported outspending their male counterparts. On average, a female candidate reported spending $2,425 to secure her nomination, while an average male candidate reported spending $2,210. Of these candidates, 55 per cent of women and 55 per cent of men reported that their nomination contest was contested. On average, a female candidate whose nomination was contested spent $3,494 and a male candidate spent $3,117.[14]

More comprehensive data are available from the 2004 election. As of January 2004, the Canada Elections Act includes provisions governing parties' nomination contests. The legislation now requires candidates for a registered political party's nomination to disclose the size and source of their contributions and to abide by spending limits. New rules governing the size and source of contributions also apply to candidates, who can now receive a maximum of $1,000 from any business or union, and a maximum of $5,000 from any individual. Spending limits for nomination contests were adopted in large part in response to concerns about female candidates' ability to raise funds and compete on a level playing field.

Analysing data from the candidates' disclosure, we find some evidence supporting the proposition that female candidates face financial obstacles. The evidence is not overwhelming, however. Women were no less likely than men to spend under $1,000 on their nomination contest: only 23 per cent of female contestants and 24 per cent of male spent more than $1,000 in pursuit of their party's nomination. Among those candidates who spent over $1,000, we find that on average women spent slightly less than their male counterparts (see Table 3.2). In the Liberal Party, the difference was just under $500, while in the Conservatives just over $600. Money appears important for women winning nominations: Liberal women who won their nomination spent $7,555 on average, exceeding the average for men who won their nomination by some $1,300. Among contenders for Conservative nominations, women who won outspent men by some $300, but men who lost outspent women who lost by over $1,800. All of this lends some credibility to the notion that money remains an obstacle for at least some women entering the political arena. For those who are successful, however, it appears not to pose a problem.

Table 3.2 Total expenditures by gender and party

	Total expenditures ($)		
Party	*Men*	*Women*	*Difference*
Liberal	6,216	5,748	468
Conservative	5,012	4,409	603
NDP	2,962	3,919	–957
BQ	4,393	2,376	2,017

The NDP presents an interesting case that defies expectations. On average, women contesting nominations outspent their male rivals by almost $1,000, and did so by incurring deficits. When we examine these numbers more closely, we find that much of the difference comes in one Saskatchewan electoral district where several women ran – by NDP standards – expensive campaigns for the nomination. The party's eventual nominee was a man.

Although it is too early to evaluate the effects of the spending limit on women's nominations, the early figures are not particularly promising: when we compare women as a percentage of their party's candidates between the 2000 and 2004 federal elections, we find only a one or two percentage point increase for each party. That said, 2004 was the first election to which these rules applied, and one might expect that it would take some time for potential candidates to become aware of the new regulatory environment.

If we do not find persistent evidence of gender differences in ability to raise funds at the nomination stage, then it is even less likely that we would find evidence of gender differences in raising funds for general elections. In the general election campaign, the candidate is the standard bearer for his or her political party. To the extent that support for a political party motivates the decision to make a contribution, women would be disadvantaged only if donors overtly discriminated against them. Moreover, to the extent that political contributions are motivated by a desire to influence or have access to an elected official, we would expect that the candidate's gender would affect contributions only if it affected potential donor's assessment of the candidate's ability to win the election. Analysis of candidates' receipts in the 2000 Canadian general election shows that in every party except the governing Liberals, total contributions to female candidates were lower than total contributions to male candidates (see Table 3.3). These differences were, however, fairly modest in scope.

While these findings suggest the existence of some modest gender-based differences in the ability to raise funds, differences may well be a

Table 3.3 Contributions received and funds spent by candidates in the 2000 Canadian general election

Party	*Total contributions to candidate (means in Cdn$)*		*% of limit spent (mean %)*	
	Men	*Women*	*Men*	*Women*
Liberal	58,085	58,606	72	74
Cdn Alliance	36,767	32,465	48	42
BQ	61,198	57,775	83	78
PC	17,833	13,471	27	22
NDP	17,827	15,927	24	24

Table 3.4 Effect of female candidate (regression)

Party	*Total contributions to candidate Cdn$*	*% of limit spent*
Liberal	–806	2
Cdn Alliance	199	–1
BQ	1,132	1
PC	–5,546*	–7
NDP	–1,831	–1

Source: Calculated from the 2000 General Election Candidate data set.

Note
*Statistically significant at $p = 0.05$.

product of women being disproportionately represented among candidates in electoral districts their party is unlikely to win. To account for this, a regression analysis of the same data was conducted, employing the following independent variables: the candidate's gender, incumbency, the candidate's party's percentage of valid votes in that electoral district in the 1997 general election, and the average employment income in the electoral district. Based on this analysis, Table 3.4 reports the effect that running a female candidate had on both campaign contributions and spending as a percentage of the limit, holding these other factors constant. The findings are broken down by party. The analysis suggests that candidate gender has only a minimal effect on ability to raise funds and rates of campaign spending.

Overall, then, there is little reason to believe that unequal access to campaign funds has posed a barrier to women's election in Canada in recent years. To the extent that it has, recent reforms that have enriched public funding to political parties and candidates and imposed spending limits on nomination contests should eliminate any residual barriers.

Experience in the provinces is, however, suggestive of the possibility that a regulatory regime that limits the size and source of contributions may have a positive effect on women's representation. In the two Canadian provinces that have adopted such legislation – Quebec and Manitoba – the mean proportion of women in the legislature is just under 26 per cent, while the mean proportion for the remaining jurisdictions is only 17 per cent. Although this suggests that such a measure somehow encourages the representation of women, the finding must be interpreted with some caution. This difference is driven in large part by the substantial number of women in Quebec politics: after the 2003 provincial election, women comprised just over 30 per cent of the members of the Quebec legislature. This may well be a partial product of the regulatory regime governing political finance in Quebec for over 25 years, but it may also reflect social and cultural differences. Moreover, it must be noted that Manitoba adopted the practice of restricting contributions to eligible electors in

2001. In the one election fought since the rule was brought in, the proportion of women in the legislature dropped by three and a half percentage points. In short, these findings are suggestive, but not conclusive.

Political parties

Women's participation in Canadian political parties

Women were involved in Canadian political parties throughout most of the twentieth century, but until the 1970s their participation tended to be channelled into supportive roles. By the late 1960s, socially prescribed gender roles came under greater scrutiny and women involved in all three of the major political parties started to challenge the character of their involvement in party affairs. Despite the activism of women within all three of the parties, women remained underrepresented in most facets of party life through the 1980s. In her study of women's participation in Canadian political parties at the federal level and in Ontario and Manitoba, Sylvia Bashevkin found that despite extensive involvement in political parties, women were substantially underrepresented in Canadian political party elites, and that pattern of underrepresentation was all the more accentuated in political parties that were highly electorally competitive.[14] In other words, the closer one came to political power, the fewer women there were to be found.

Bashevkin's research suggested the presence of a 'pink-collar ghetto' within parties, as women's participation was channelled into traditional roles like secretary of the riding association. In more influential positions like riding association president, campaign manager or candidate, however, women remained substantially underrepresented. A survey of constituency associations in 1991 found that this pattern persisted, with women making up 20 per cent of riding presidents, 32 per cent of treasurers and 69 per cent of riding secretaries.[15] Women did, however, win some modest representational gains inside each of the three major parties during this period, including guarantees of women's representation on national party executives and positions as convention delegates.

The Canadian party system was shattered in the 1993 election by the entry of two new parties – Reform and the Bloc Quebecois – and the virtual decimation of the Progressive Conservative and New Democratic parties. The advent of this new party system, coupled with growing resistance to the principle of affirmative action, had profound consequences for the participation of women in Canadian political parties. The party that has in many ways defined the new party system is the Reform Party, which later became the Canadian Alliance and has since merged with the Progressive Conservative Party.[16] This party had an ideological commitment against affirmative action programmes of any kind and, as a consequence, has not implemented any representational guarantees for women (or other groups) within the party. The Progressive Conservative Party followed suit and disbanded its women's organisation. The newly formed Conservative Party has no women's organisation. In general terms, the trend appears to be away from measures ensuring the representation of women in party affairs.

A survey of members of the five major federal parties in 2000 gives us a glimpse of the rates and patterns of women's involvement in party organisation. Broken down by party, the proportion of female respondents to the Study of Canadian Political Party Members was as follows: Liberal 47 per cent; New Democratic Party 46 per cent; Bloc Quebecois 37 per cent; Progressive Conservatives 33 per cent; Canadian Alliance 32 per cent.[17] This pattern corresponds with what one would expect, given that both the Liberal and New Democratic parties have maintained policies designed to involve women in their parties in recent years while the Bloc Quebecois, Progressive Conservatives and Canadian Alliance have eschewed such policies. It also corresponds generally with the patterns of gender difference in electoral support for the parties.[18]

Based on this survey of party members, Young and Cross conclude that although women remain somewhat less inclined than men to join political parties, they are apparently almost as active as men in all levels of party activity, Despite the pattern of general equality with respect to women's involvement in all levels of party activity, female party members still saw themselves as insufficiently influential and, with the exception of women in the Canadian Alliance, were generally supportive of measures to increase their influence and the number of women holding elected office.[19] That the women directly involved in party affairs perceived this influence deficit and supported measures to remedy it suggests that the parties should not rush to reverse representational guarantees for women. Apparently, these measures have not outlived their utility in the eyes of women active in most of the parties.

Do the 'gatekeepers' discriminate against women?

In Canada, the selection of candidates is highly decentralised, with the electoral district associations of political parties exercising considerable autonomy in candidate selection. In all of the major parties, the selection of candidates takes place through a vote of those individuals who hold a party membership in that electoral district at the time of the contest. Generally, parties require members to have held a party membership for a number of weeks prior to the vote in order to be eligible to vote in the nomination contest. For the most part, the selectorates for Canadian political party nominations are relatively small. In his study of nomination contests in the 1993 federal election, Cross found that the average attendance at a nomination meeting was just over 400 party members, and that the average attendance at a contested nomination was 574.[20] There are, however, always a number of hotly contested nomination battles in which candidates recruit thousands, or even tens of thousands, of new party members.

Initial studies identified political parties as the 'gatekeepers' preventing women from winning party nominations. Analysing patterns of nomination between 1975 and 1994 at the provincial level, Matland and Studlar conclude that there was evidence supporting the contention that parties tended to nominate women disproportionately in ridings they were unlikely to win in the 1970s, but there is no evidence that this took place systematically after the mid-1980s.[21] The exception to this is Jerome Black's finding that minority women candidates report being encouraged by party officials to run, but tended to be placed in ridings where their party was normally expected to lose.[22]

Analysis of data from the 2000 federal election supports Matland and Studlar's contention that parties no longer nominate women disproportionately in hopeless ridings. Table 3.5 lists the proportion of male and female candidates for each party in 2000, and compares them with the gender breakdown among candidates in 'no hope' ridings – those in which the party won less than 15 per cent of the popular vote in the 1997 election. The only party which fits the pattern of nominating women disproportionately in hopeless ridings is the Bloc Quebecois. For a new candidate wanting to win a seat, the best hope generally lies in a seat held by

Table 3.5 Candidates by gender and riding characteristics, 2000 general election

Party	*All candidates*		*No hope*		*Party-held open seat*	
	Male	*Female*	*Male*	*Female*	*Male*	*Female*
Liberal						
%	78	22	89	11	71	29
No.	236	65	8	1	5	2
PC						
%	87	13	91	9	67	33
No.	252	39	97	10	4	2
NDP						
%	71	29	70	30	50	50
No.	210	88	147	64	1	1
BQ						
%	76	24	60	40	89	11
No.	57	18	3	2	8	1
CA						
%	89	11	87	13	90	10
No.	266	32	119	18	9	1

Note
a Less than 15% in 1997.

their party with the incumbent retiring. There were relatively few retirements coming into the 2000 election, so such seats were quite rare. For three parties – the Liberals, Progressive Conservatives and New Democratic Party – the proportion of women nominated in these desirable seats was higher than the proportion of women running as candidates for the party overall. For the Canadian Alliance the proportion was comparable, but for the Bloc Quebecois the proportion was substantially lower – less than half.

Do parties encourage women's candidacies?

Some parties, notably the federal NDP, have undertaken explicit affirmative action campaigns for women and members of minority groups, which have yielded promising results.[23] In the run-up to the 2004 federal election, the NDP froze all nominations until the riding association could demonstrate that a thorough search for candidates from underrepresented groups had been completed. In addition, the party implemented a programme of financial assistance in which women and minority candidates are eligible for reimbursement of up to $500 for child care expenses incurred in seeking a nomination, $500 for travel costs in geographically large ridings and an additional $500 for costs incurred in seeking nomination in ridings where the NDP incumbent is retiring. The party also allows female and minority candidates to receive three times as many funds as other candidates through the party for the purposes of allowing their contributors to take advantage of the generous tax credit afforded to parties.[24] In the 2004 federal election, the NDP nominated more female candidates than any of the other major political parties, with women comprising 31 per cent of its candidates.

The Liberal Party of Canada has, on occasion, appointed female candidates, circumventing the usual nomination process. Notably, however, Liberal Party leader Paul Martin has refused to intervene in nomination contests on behalf of at least one prominent female incumbent (former Deputy Prime Minister Sheila Copps) but has used his power of appointment to appoint several male 'star' candidates in key ridings. Women comprised one-quarter of Liberal candidates in 2004, the same proportion in the BQ, and substantially less in the Conservative Party at 12 per cent.

However, the direction of change in the federal party system as a whole is away from affirmative measures. The largest opposition party, the Conservative Party of Canada, does not use any kind of internal affirmative action programme and is highly critical of other parties' efforts to do so. Its predecessor party, the Canadian Alliance, vociferously criticised other parties' efforts to promote women.[25] This view apparently informs the new Conservative Party's practices. In a letter in response to Equal Voice, a lobby group advocating election of women, the party's leader, Stephen Harper, wrote that:

> While we recognize the importance of having men and women of diverse backgrounds in our party, we are firmly committed to ensuring that the responsibility for selecting candidates in the ridings remains with our grassroots members. As a result, the women who are successful in our party owe their success to their own hard work. Moreover, many of these women have gone on to serve in key positions within our caucus, such as Diane Ablonczy, who currently serves as our Senior Citizenship and Immigration Critic.[26]

Harper's letter reflects the Reform/Alliance/Conservative view that measures undertaken to increase women's representation detract from local party autonomy and devalue the achievements of the relatively small number of women who have been elected without special measures.

This argument lies at the heart of the party-system dynamic that explains much of the decline in the rate of progress for electing women. It is no coincidence that the rate of increase in the number of women elected has declined steadily since the 1993 election, which ushered in the significant changes to the Canadian party system described above. The decimation of the NDP, the stunning defeat of the Progressive Conservative Party and the rise of the Reform Party were all negative signals for the electoral representation of women.

Unlike the old Progressive Conservative Party, which had an active women's association focused on encouraging women's participation and election, the Reform/Alliance/Conservative Party eschews any measures designed to increase women's participation in the party or in Canadian politics. Espousing an ethic of individual merit, the party nominates fewer women than did the old Progressive Conservative Party. Since its rise to official party status in 1993, the party has consistently nominated women as between 10 and 11 per cent of its candidates. Consistent with this, the new Conservative Party in 2004 nominated women in 12 per cent of electoral districts. Assuming that the Conservative Party replaces the old Progressive Conservative Party as the alternative governing party in Canada, there is reason to expect that the slow rate of change in women's representation will persist for some time.

The women's movement

The Canadian women's movement was actively engaged in advocating the election of more women to the House of Commons until the mid to late 1980s. From that time on, the peak feminist organisation, the National Action Committee on the Status of Women, adopted more oppositional tactics and downplayed the potential substantive gains for women that might arise from the election of more women to Parliament.[27] As NAC's funding from the federal government was reduced in the late 1980s, its voice on the Canadian political scene has declined commensurately.

Recent reports suggest that NAC faces bankruptcy and has become defunct. In the 1970s and 1980s, there were a number of organisations that focused specifically on the political representation of women. Most of these organisations became defunct by the early 1990s, although some have been revived in recent years.

While it is difficult to discern the effect of the women's movement on the number of women nominated and elected, Figure 3.3 lends some credence to the idea that a vibrant feminist movement focused on women's representation can have some effect. In the period since 1970, the two elections in which the number of women elected has increased at the greatest rate were the elections of 1972 and 1984. The former came one year after the Royal Commission on the Status of Women in Canada released its report, which advocated, among other things, that political parties work to encourage the election of more women. In 1984, NAC sponsored a debate among major party leaders on women's issues, and was a prominent voice pushing the parties on issues of concern to women. (It should, however, be noted that 1984 was also an election in which there was a very high rate of electoral turnover.) As the women's movement has shifted its focus away from electoral politics, and as its voice has diminished overall, the rate of change has slowed. Although not conclusive, this suggests that an active women's movement focused on electoral politics can push political parties to nominate more women and possibly

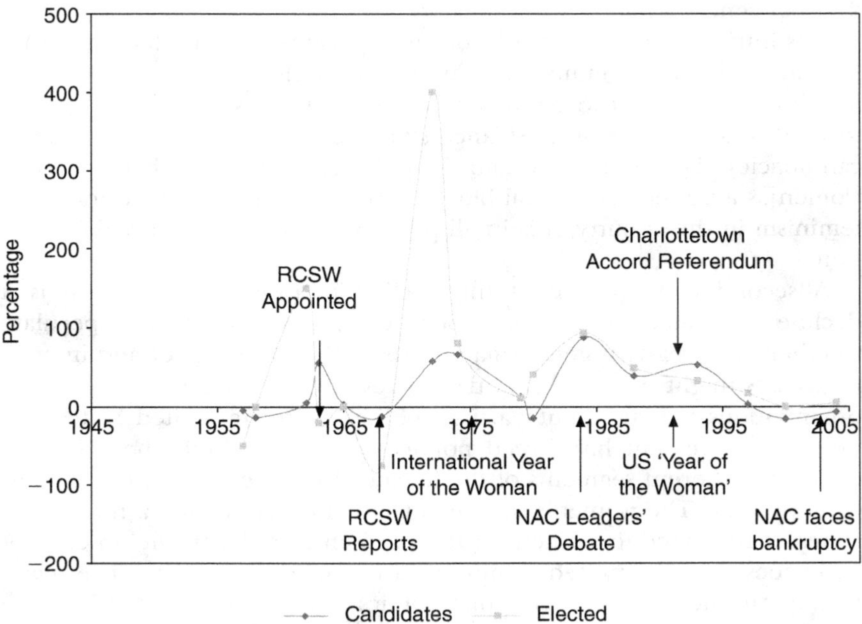

Figure 3.3 Rate of change of women's representation in the House of Commons.

may focus more women's attention on electoral politics, thereby yielding a larger candidate pool.

Conclusion

This overview of the potential explanations for the declining progress in electing women in Canada has eliminated some of the suspects. Neither the views of the electorate, the rate of turnover nor the system of political finance appear to explain the lack of progress in electing women in recent years. More likely suspects are the actions of political parties, particularly on the right of the political spectrum, the changing party system, and the apparent demise of organised feminism in Canada.

Prior to 1993, all three of the major political parties in Canada sustained some kind of commitment to the project of electing more women to the Canadian House of Commons. The decimation of the Progressive Conservative party and the rise of the Reform Party/Canadian Alliance shattered this cross-partisan consensus and ushered in an era in which parties on the right deliberately avoided taking any action to improve women's numerical representation. The newly-formed Conservative party follows in this tradition and, not coincidentally, nominated women in only 36 of its districts for the 2004 election (who represented 11.7 per cent of its candidates[28]). None the less the proportion of women in the House of Commons rose marginally after the 2004 election, from 20.9 per cent to 21.1 per cent.

It is intriguing that the newly-formed Conservative Party has chosen to portray itself as moderate on a number of policy issues, most notably avowing commitment to public health care, but does not feel compelled to modify the old Reform/Alliance stance of not encouraging women's candidacies. This is most certainly a political calculation that writes off women as a powerful electoral block. And given the decline of organised feminism in the country, it is in all probability not an inaccurate calculation.

A second consequence of the decline of organised feminism is a decline in Canadian women's focus on politics. One can speculate whether the persistent gender gap in women's knowledge of and interest in politics might be at least partially a result of the absence of women's organisations talking about partisan politics.[29] In the United States, the women's movement has forced political parties to think about how to appeal to different segments of the female electorate by pointing to their voting power. The women's movement has also maintained a number of issues of relevance to women on the partisan agenda. In the absence of such cues from organised feminism, are Canadian women once again falling into the mistaken belief that politics is the domain of men? To the extent that this is the case, the parties will feel little pressure to change their practices. Moreover, a generation of young women who believe politics does not matter to them is unlikely to yield a rich pool of potential female candidates.

If, in fact, some Canadian jurisdictions opt to change their electoral system, it will offer opportunities for women. As other chapters in this volume demonstrate, proportional representation electoral systems create opportunities for women, and not only because of their structural features. Reforming electoral democracy creates a moment during which parties must reconceive their practices for nominating candidates which opens the door to women's activism within the parties. If Canadian women have the opportunity to engage in such activism, it is the most likely route to recapturing the momentum of their electoral project.

Notes

Thanks to Munroe Eagles for making the 2000 General Election Candidate dataset available, and to Richard Matland, Donley Studlar and Lynda Erickson for making various other data available for this chapter. Portions of the chapter are adapted from several recent publications and working papers: Young, *Campaign Finance and Women's Representation in Canada and the United States*; Young, 'Women (Not) in Politics'; Young and Cross, 'Women's Involvement in Canadian Political Parties'.

1 See Still Counting at http//stillcounting.athabascau.ca.
2 See Black, 'Differences that Matter'.
3 See Hunter and Denton, 'Do Female Candidates "Lose Votes"?'; Tremblay, 'Les femmes, des candidates moins performantes que les hommes?'
4 See Blais *et al.*, 'Does the Local Candidate Matter?'
5 See Black and Erickson, 'Women Candidates and Voter Bias'.
6 Because of the structure of the data set, ridings which the party won in 1997 but the incumbent retired are included in both the 'Not incumbent' and 'Other party member held riding' categories. Because the *ns* for the latter category are so low, they do not influence the first category overly.
7 See Howe and Northrup, *Strengthening Canadian Democracy.*
8 See MacIvor, 'Women and the Canadian Electoral System'; Law Commission of Canada, *Voting Counts.*
9 See Matland, 'Enhancing Women's Political Participation'.
10 The outcome of the referendum was 57 per cent in favour of the STV system, with majority support in all but two electoral districts. The government's threshold for acting on the recommendation, however, was 60 per cent support and majority support in two thirds of electoral districts. Given the widespread support, however, it is unlikely that the issue of electoral reform will not be revisited in some way.
11 See Brodie (with Chandler), 'Women and the Electoral Process in Canada'.
12 See Erickson, 1993 candidate survey.
13 It should be noted that these figures do not represent audited or otherwise verified spending reports. They are merely based on candidates' reports of spending when asked as part of an academic survey.
14 See Bashevkin, *Toeing the Line.*
15 Carty, *Canadian Political Parties in the Constituencies*, 55.
16 For a discussion of the emerging party system and the role that reform played in shaping this system, see Carty *et al.*, *Rebuilding Canadian Party Politics*, and for a more thorough discussion of the implications of the emerging system for

women's representation, see Young, 'Representation of Women in the New Canadian Party System'.

17 Young and Cross, 'Women's Involvement in Canadian Political Parties', 93.
18 See Nevitte *et al.*, *Unsteady State*, 110, 133.
19 Young and Cross, 'Women's Involvement in Canadian Political Parties', 104.
20 Cross, *Political Parties*, 56.
21 See Studlar and Matland, 'The Dynamics of Women's Representation in the Canadian Provinces, 1975–1994'.
22 Black, 'Differences That Matter', 70.
23 See Erickson, 'Entry to the Commons'.
24 Cross, *Political Parties*, 70–1.
25 See Young, 'Representation of Women in the New Canadian Party System'.
26 Letter posted on Equal Voice website: www.equalvoice.ca/response_harper.html.
27 See Young, *Feminists and Party Politics.*
28 See www.elections.ca/content.asp?section=gen&document=part2_div5&dir=rep/re2/sta2004&lang=e&textonly=false; accessed 18 July 2005.
29 See Gidengil *et al.*, 'Gender, Knowledge and Social Capital'.

4 Climbing on

Rules, values and women's representation in the New Zealand parliament

Elizabeth McLeay

With its early enfranchisement of women, an active women's movement, a relatively sympathetic political culture and, since 1996, proportional representation, Aotearoa New Zealand would appear to be a near-ideal country for women's equal parliamentary representation. Even under plurality rules, there was a higher proportion of women MPs in New Zealand than in similar countries.[1] The adoption of a Mixed Member Proportional (MMP) electoral system initially accelerated the movement of women into Parliament, as had been expected, but then progress stalled. This chapter analyses women's achievements under an unfriendly electoral system and the subsequent mixed successes of proportionality.

The New Zealand case study provides rich longitudinal data that include the impact of radical structural change with the switch from a plurality to a proportional electoral system. That the new system was of the 'mixed' form[2] means that it offered two different career paths for women, each with its own opportunities and difficulties, illustrating the effects of contrasting district magnitudes within one political culture. The New Zealand experience also produces other internal comparisons: between two major parties of the centre-left and the centre-right, and among the range of parliamentary parties after the adoption of MMP. It shows that women's agency, party ideology and political timing played their roles, along with institutional structure and rules.

Even before the adoption of a proportional electoral system, there was only some truth in the description of New Zealand as the most typical, even the purest, example of a Westminster system.[3] It is obvious that the basic ingredients of Westminster were simply transplanted across to the other side of the world as part of the colonisation process. What is less obvious is just how much New Zealand had strayed from the British model by the time MMP was introduced. Very early on, New Zealanders began to modify aspects of their inheritance. The Maori seats (see below) were created in 1867; there was a triennial parliamentary term (except for a couple of brief periods); the ineffectual Legislative Chamber (upper house) was abolished in 1950; in 1956 Parliament employed entrenching clauses to protect part of its electoral system; and from the 1960s through

Basic political data

New Zealand

Land area 268,021 sq. km.

Population 3,792,654 (2001 census).

Indigenous population New Zealand Maori, 526,281 (2001 census).

Administrative divisions Unitary political system.

Head of state Queen Elizabeth II, represented by Governor General appointed on advice of Prime Minister.

Parliament Unicameral: House of Representatives with 120 members elected for three-year terms. The appointed upper house was abolished in 1950.

New Zealand has been regarded as the purest example of a Westminster system of government, at least until 1996. It has a unitary and unicameral political system and before 1996 had a first-past-the-post electoral system and a two-party system. The lack of checks and balances in the New Zealand system led to the bold experiment of radical state restructuring. This in turn led to popular support for change in the political system and successful referendums to introduce a form of proportional representation known as mixed-member proportional (MMP). This was first used for elections to the House of Representatives in 1996 and caused a shift towards a non-Westminster-style multi-party system and multi-party governments.

to the early 1990s a plethora of constitutional changes, especially concerning human rights, made the former Dominion even more dissimilar from its model parent. The departure from Westminster was speeded up when in 1993 New Zealanders voted to adopt a Mixed Member Proportional (MMP) electoral system.

Although never part of the written Constitution, and although never as respected by governments as by Maori, the Treaty of Waitangi influenced ideas of citizenship in ways beyond the Westminster model and ideal. In 1840 the representative of the British Crown and many Maori chiefs signed the treaty. By the twenty-first century, the treaty was playing a highly important normative and policy role, although there were deep differences between political parties on how it should be interpreted. In the

2001 census, those who identified as Maori were around 14 per cent of the population.

As far as the opportunity structure in New Zealand was concerned, the combination of political centralisation, parliamentary government and unicameralism produced one main route to political power. Although local government had important functions, the institutions that were by far the most powerful were Parliament and Cabinet. If women wanted to change the world through conventional politics they had to get themselves to the capital city, Wellington, and into the House of Representatives. Certainly some high-profile women did so. By 2003, New Zealand had an unusually high number of women in important constitutional positions: the Prime Minister, the Governor General, the Chief Justice, and the Secretary to the Cabinet. Helen Clark was actually the second female Prime Minister, Jenny Shipley having occupied that position earlier, Silvia Cartwright was the second woman to be a Governor General, and one woman succeeded another as Cabinet Secretary. These examples indicate that, to a certain extent at any rate, the political culture was not unsympathetic to women playing significant public roles.

Becoming citizens

Under the 1852 Constitution, Parliament was elected by males over the age of 21 who owned, leased or rented property of particular, not very high, value.[4] In 1867, after debates on Maori male enfranchisement ranging from the prejudiced and racist to the enlightened and liberal, Parliament created four Maori seats, giving all Maori men over 21 the vote. (Maori land was owned communally, meaning that either all or no Maori men would be enfranchised unless they owned land with individual titles, as a few did.) In 1879 all non-Maori men over the age of 21 were enfranchised. Initially temporary, the Maori seats were still in existence by the early twenty-first century. Democratisation of the seats was, however, slow: it was not until 1967 that Maori were permitted to stand for European seats and vice versa, and not until 1975 that Maori could choose whether to enrol on the Maori or non-Maori register. From 1996, under MMP, the number of Maori seats depended on the number of Maori on the Maori register so that, by the time of the 2002 election, there were seven Maori seats.

Women ratepayers could vote in local elections by 1876, and by the next year they could vote and stand for school committees and regional education boards.[5] In 1893, all women over the age of 21 gained the vote, but only after a hard-fought battle involving two nationwide petitions, the 1893 one containing 26,000 signatures.[6] Maori and non-Maori women were involved in the battle for the ballot, but Maori women were fighting also for the right to vote and stand for the Maori parliament.[7] The women suffragists had their parliamentary supporters: Bills had been introduced to grant women the vote in 1887 and 1890, defeated mainly because a clause was added allowing women to be candidates. Their opponents included the liquor industry as well as MPs. And why did New Zealand enfranchise women relatively early?[8] Certainly, and most important of all, women got the vote because they asked for it, a necessary but insufficient condition. Second, perhaps women in colonial, settler societies shared a general aspiration to start life anew in a freer, more equal society than the one they left. Third, the 1890s were one of New Zealand's 'experimental' periods. Nevertheless, although the Liberal government included liberal men sympathetic to the suffragists' arguments, it also contained men hostile to the very idea of women voting, including the Premier.[9] Fourth, that Maori men already could vote meant that there was democratic dissonance between Maori men and all women.

Unfortunately, New Zealand's shining example of early progress for women's rights was only a partial glow in the Pacific skies: women were not permitted to stand for Parliament until 1919, when, after continual agitation, the Women's Parliamentary Rights Act was passed. But women who wanted to be appointed to the upper house had to wait until 1941.[10] Despite early enfranchisement, until the 1970s the worlds of New Zealand women were as domestic and enclosed as were their sisters' in other similar countries, and until the 1980s the development of women's representation was no more rapid than elsewhere and much slower than in the Nordic countries.

After the 1919 Act, Parliament passed no legislation that directly aided women's representation. New Zealand ratified the International Convention on the Elimination of all Forms of Discrimination against Women; passed a Human Rights Act (1993); and prohibited discrimination in the Bill of Rights Act 1990. Section 19(2) stated, however, that 'Measures taken in good faith for the purpose of assisting or advancing persons or groups of persons disadvantaged because of discrimination that is unlawful by virtue of Part II of the Human Rights Act 1993 do not constitute discrimination.' This meant that parties could lawfully institute candidate quotas if they so wished, although the Greens were the only party to do so. Registered parties were instructed 'to follow democratic procedures in candidate selection' in the Electoral Act 1993 (section 71). But the principles set out were weakly specified, and there was nothing to help women.

Opportunities and constraints under two electoral systems

In 1919, three women stood unsuccessfully for election, but it was not until 1933 that a woman became an MP. Elizabeth McCombs, like many pioneer women MPs in New Zealand and elsewhere, was linked into politics through her family (she represented her former husband's Labour seat). In 1935 the first Maori woman stood for Parliament;[11] and in 1949 the first Maori woman took her seat, her husband, the sitting MP, having died. Between 1935, the beginning of two-party dominance by Labour on the centre-left and National on the centre-right, until 1975, women moved slowly indeed into Parliament. From the 1933 election (marking McComb's entry) until (and including) the 1975 election, there were only 15 women MPs, nine Labour, two of whom were Maori representing Maori seats, and six National, and there were never more than five women in the House at the one time. Of all the MPs between 1935 and 1993, the last FPP election, 7.9 per cent were women.

Supply as well as demand factors were at work. Not only did women find it difficult to leave their homes to be in Wellington, but also their lives were socially circumscribed: they lacked the business and professional contacts to propel them into a male-dominated profession such as politics, although Labour women were a little better off because some were involved in trade unions. There was little difference between the parties in terms of whether or not they chose women for winnable seats. By-elections were an important vehicle: out of the 15 early women, seven entered Parliament through by-elections, three of them contesting the seat of a deceased relative, a difference between the sexes that disappeared.

Women in New Zealand, as elsewhere, took part in the 1970s women's movement, although it rapidly became fragmented and characterised by single-issue politics, for example Women's Refuge, Rape Crisis, women's health groups, professional women's groups, and the Federation of University Women.[12] One important group was the Women's Electoral Lobby (WEL), formed in 1975 by groups that included Zonta, the Society for Research on Women, the National Organisation of Women, Labour Women and the Values Party. Like its Australian sister organisation, it lobbied for women's policies as well as supporting women candidates.[13] Several of its activists became MPs and others stood for Parliament. WEL's first major action was to survey all the candidates for the 1975 election on their policies, an action that highlighted the relative absence of women in Parliament and the interrelated problem of representing women's interests. 1975 also marked the publication of the report of the select committee on women's rights. The report spoke of the need for parties to recruit women, although it was more interested in explaining the paucity of women in public life by reference to their social situations and domestic responsibilities.[14]

From the 1978 election onwards the number of women entering Parliament gradually increased (Table 4.1). It was during these years that the representation of Labour women began to outstrip that of their National colleagues. Women involved in the women's movement and in single-issue politics moved into the Labour Party, a significant part of the explanation why, by 1993, the New Zealand parliament comprised more women than other Westminster systems (see below). 'Contagion' factors then were at work.[15] National sought women's votes, and tried (but not very hard) to

Table 4.1 Women elected to the New Zealand Parliament in the 1978–2002 general elections

Party	*1978*	*1981*	*1984*	*1987*	*1990*	*1993*	*1996*	*1999*	*2002*
ACT							3 (8)	3 (9)	4 (9)
All.						1 (2)	7 (13)	4 (10)	
Grn								3 (7)	4 (9)
Lab.	3 (51)	6 (43)	10 (56)	11 (57)	8 (29)	14 (45)	13 (37)	18 (49)	18 (52)
Nat.	1 (3)	2 (47)	2 (37)	3 (40)	8 (67)	6 (50)	8 (44)	9 (39)	6 (27)
NL					0 (1)				
NZF						0 (2)	4 (17)	0 (5)	1 (13)
PC									0 (2)
SC	0 (1)	0 (2)	0 (2)						
UF							0 (1)	0 (1)	1 (8)
Total women	4	8	12	14	16	21	35	37	34
Total no. of MPs	92	92	95	97	97	99	120	120	120
% women in Parliament	4.3	8.7	12.6	14.4	16.5	21.2	29.2	30.8	28.3

Notes

Lab. Labour, Nat. National, Grn Green, NZF New Zealand First, All. Alliance, CH Christian Heritage, PC Progressive Coalition, SC Social Credit, UF United, then United Future. The bracketed figures give the total number of MPs elected to that party. During the 1996–99 Parliament, two men and two women resigned who were replaced by two of each sex from their party lists. The list seat vacancies created by two men retiring between 1999 and 2002 were filled by men. In 2003 one Labour male MP resigned and was replaced by a woman from the list. Only one by-election was held between 1999 and 2002, when one man replaced another. These replacements are not included here.

recruit women. A further relevant factor might be the comparatively low cost of campaigning in New Zealand and the statutory constraints on electoral expenditure.

Plainly, although the supply of women aspirants was a problem, the single-member constituencies also posed a structural barrier to women's candidature. The number of women candidates rose from the end of the 1970s, but it is an indication of how difficult women found it to be nominated for winnable electorates that the proportion of women actually elected was always smaller than the proportion nominated, while it was the reverse situation for men, a difference that diminished after the introduction of MMP (Table 4.2). Anecdotal evidence from National selections suggested that many activists, including women, erroneously believed men to be more attractive candidates to electors than were women. Male incumbency was a further formidable obstacle.

Given the problems of the plurality electoral system – the absence of constraints on the political executive, the lack of minor-party parliamentary representation, as well as the underrepresentation of women and Maori[16] – it was not surprising that many women's groups supported the campaign for proportional representation. The Royal Commission on the Electoral System argued that MMP would be more likely to represent women fairly than did plurality.[17] Indeed, fair group representation was a significant criterion generally for the commission.[18] There is no doubt that major constitutional change stimulated debate about the 'gender distribution of political power', as also happened in Scotland, Wales and Northern Ireland.[19]

Table 4.2 Women candidates and MPs, 1981–2002

Election	*Female candidates % (of total number of candidates)*			*Female MPs % (of Parliament)*			*Totals*	
							Candidates	*MPs*
1981	11.8			8.7			339	92
1984	17.4			12.6			466	95
1987	19.3			14.4			424	97
1990	22.5			16.5			677	97
1993	27.7			21.2			689	99
	Electorate		*List*	*Electorate*		*List*		
1996	24.7		28.1	16.9		43.6	842	120
		26.8			29.2			
1999	29.3		34.4	23.9		39.6	965	120
		32.9			30.8			
2002	28.2		31.0	27.5		29.4	683	120
		28.7			28.3			

Source: Electoral Commission (2002), 176–7.

MMP divided parliamentary candidates into list candidates, elected from closed, nationwide party lists, and electorate candidates, elected through plurality. In order to gain parliamentary entry, parties had to win 5 per cent of the party vote. If a party did not gain that percentage but did win one electorate seat, then it could bring any other MPs into Parliament that its overall party vote entitled it to. The party vote determined the overall percentage of seats parties were awarded, with list seats added to any electorate seats won to bring them to the required total. Dual candidature was permitted. As can be seen, the system was modelled on Germany's and similar to that introduced by Scotland and Wales.

The first MMP election improved the proportion of women legislators, with women coming forward most strongly in the party lists,[20] although by the 1999 election the distinction between list and electorate percentages was less marked (Table 4.3). Thus, the first two elections appeared to confirm the significance of large electoral districts for women's candidature, since the party lists were nationwide. Because the lists were closed, the parties had every opportunity to indicate the order of their favourites, including representing groups, regions, different age cohorts, Maori, other groups, as well as women.

The difference between Labour and National in terms of women's representation continued after MMP was adopted. The smaller, newer

Table 4.3 Women's entry into the New Zealand Parliament at the 1996, 1999 and 2002 general elections, by party

Party	*1996*		*1999*		*2002*	
	Women electorate MPs (n)	*Women list MPs* (n)	*Women electorate MPs* (n)	*Women list MPs* (n)	*Women electorate MPs* (n)	*Women list MPs* (n)
ACT	0 (1)	3 (7)	0 (0)	3 (9)	0 (0)	4 (9)
Alliance	0 (1)	7 (12)	0 (1)	4 (9)	–	–
Greens	–	–	1 (1)	2 (6)	0 (0)	4 (9)
Labour	6 (26)	7 (11)	13 (41)	5 (8)	16 (45)	2 (7)
National	5 (30)	3 (14)	2 (22)	7 (17)	3 (21)	3 (6)
NZF	0 (6)	4 (11)	0 (1)	0 (4)	0 (1)	1 (12)
PC	–	–	–	–	0 (1)	0 (1)
UF	0 (1)	0 (0)	0 (1)	0 (0)	0 (1)	1 (7)
Subtotal (*n*)	11 (65)	24 (55)	16 (67)	21 (53)	19 (69)	15 (51)
Subtotal (%)	16.9	43.6	23.9	39.6	37.3	21.7
Total (%)	29.2		30.8		28.3	

Notes
PC Progressive Coalition, NZF New Zealand First, UF United Future (formerly United), NZF New Zealand First. The bracketed figures give the total number of MPs in that party in that category.

parties, relatively unencumbered with sitting male MPs and mainly dependent on the party lists, had the opportunity to place women in winnable list places. The left-wing Alliance, which until 1999 included the Greens, and ACT, at the opposite of the political spectrum, were the most open to women's candidacy, the former because of the positive discrimination and participatory beliefs of the constituent parties and the latter because it prided itself on equal opportunities and appointment through merit. (It was ironical that ACT had able women aspirants, despite its wide gender gap in voting support, with men far outweighing women supporters.) The parties of the centre-right – New Zealand First and United – were more reluctant to concede places to women.

In 2002, contrary to the usual assumptions about the significance of district magnitude, women won more electorate than list seats (Table 4.3).[21] Labour had steadily increased the number of women being nominated for electorates; and that party won so many electorates that it ended up with very few list seats. Labour women occupied 36 per cent of their party's 45 electorate seats compared with 29 per cent of their seven list seats. A second factor was that National, which polled very badly, failed to gain list seats that would have added a few more women to its caucus: they were in vulnerable places. National women took 14 per cent of their party's 21 electorate seats and half of National's six list seats.

Third, a combination of voter volatility, internal policy tensions and the heavily male lists produced by the smaller parties of the centre-right impacted on women's representation. The left-wing Alliance party, in coalition with Labour, split into two before the 2002 election, and only two of its former MPs, now running under the banner of Progressive Coalition, and both male, were returned at that election. New Zealand First had four women MPs after the 1996 election, but it split while a coalition partner with National, was reduced to five male MPs in 1999, and when it bounced back in 2002 it had a predominantly male list. United Future, spruced up with its Christian support and votes for 'common sense' and family values, also gained seats in 2002, bringing in an almost entirely male team. It was not just that these latter two parties had put their women candidates in impossible list places, for there were few women altogether among their candidates. It is difficult to tell, however, whether this was due primarily to the supply of women aspirants or to the lack of demand for them, or both.

So what happened to the shopfront approach – to party lists being constructed to represent society as a whole in order to attract voters? Little attention during the 2002 election campaign was paid to the composition of the lists of the smaller parties, although negative comment accrued to them after the election. But of course the harm had been done, since, if those parties continued to do well in subsequent elections, women aspirants would be confronting male incumbents. Plainly, party culture matters, as well as district magnitude.

MMP had a mixed impact on women's route to office. Labour and National women had two possible options, a difficult choice. Constituency seats were more expensive to campaign in, more difficult to gain nomination for, but generally safer under MMP than were list places.[22] List seats were cheaper to contest but much more insecure. For women contenders for parliamentary office through the smaller parties, however, there was only one realistic option: to find a winnable position on the party list. Except for the 'trophy' seats held by smaller party leaders, which acted as insurance policies for their parties' parliamentary entry, Labour and National MPs dominated the electorates. The smaller parties mostly depended on the list seats for their MPs. When this factor is added to the volatility of the minor-party vote, which even under proportionality had an element of the protest vote, it can be seen that choosing a minor party on which to launch a career was a risky venture. Of the 21 women representing the smaller parties who entered Parliament in the first three elections under MMP, eight lasted only one term, although it must be noted that three of them switched parties during their brief spells as list MPs. Two women in the Alliance Party, after it had split into two sections, subsequently lost their seats at the 2002 general election and two retired before it.

Overall, despite the disappointments, women's entry into politics was facilitated by electoral system change. The lists brought more women into Parliament; and the proportionality rules meant that Parliament contained new parties that were unencumbered with sitting MPs. But the parties' attitudes to women's representation varied according to their policies, structures and selection practices.

The party factor: processes and attitudes under plurality and proportionality

Of the 84 women between 1933 and 2002 (inclusive) who became MPs, 45.2 per cent (38) represented Labour, 28.6 per cent (24) represented National, and 26.2 per cent (22) women entered the House to represent the smaller parties (see Table 4.1).[23] Excluding McCombs' brief term, five out of the 37 Labour women who sat in Parliament between 1933 and 1999 (13.5 per cent) were defeated after just one parliamentary term. The equivalent figure for National was five out of 22 (22.7 per cent). So not only were National women disadvantaged at the candidate selection stage, but also they had to fight in more insecure seats than did Labour women, and this pattern continued after the introduction of MMP, in list as well as electorate selections. Why are there these differences between the two major parties? And how can the variable recruitment of women by the smaller parties be explained?[24]

Labour's selection process was committee-based and semi-centralised.[25] Selection committees comprised three delegates from the central party organisation and two or three constituency delegates (depending on membership numbers). A floor vote was also taken involving members present although the result was only equivalent to one committee member's. The process, although less participatory than either National's or the Greens', permitted a level of penetration by senior women on to the selection committees, enabling them to nominate women.[26] This selection method for constituency nominations remained in place after MMP was instituted but of course the party had to find a way to choose its list candidates. It considered but rejected the use of quotas, and instituted a two-stage process whereby delegates and leaders first voted at six regional conferences for regional lists, with candidates nominating themselves for particular list places.[27] After every five selections, there was a pause for an 'equity review', to ensure that the list represented Maori, women, ethnic groups such as Pacific Island peoples, and different age groups, including youth. A national moderating committee comprising representatives from the national and regional executives, the parliamentary party and other constituency groups (for example, Maori) then ranked the national list, also pausing after every five selections, but this time 'also in terms of geography'.[28] The leader and deputy headed the list, and in 2002 sitting MPs who wished to be on the list took the top places (thus safeguarding incumbents).

For Labour, its association with Maori, with the women's peace movement and with the trade unions, the consideration of social difference and its validity as a representative criterion, along with its somewhat greater readiness to accept positive discrimination measures, affected its relationship with women. Its belief system enveloped policy and representation. Initially as slow as National to select women candidates, Labour was more sympathetic towards gender analyses of political power, influenced by participants in the women's movement who targeted the Labour Party.[29] These activists, along with those involved in peace groups, the trade unions and neighbourhood organisations, were experienced campaigners. And they focused on three aspects for reform: policies, beyond the scope of this chapter, the party structure itself, and candidate nomination. Margaret Wilson, a party president and later a minister, wrote:

> The Labour Party was the only viable political option open to women who wished to seek change within the foreseeable future. It was viable because of its history and record of the way in which it has attempted to address the needs of women.... [T]he Labour Party supported a policy of equality for women, which provided an ideological basis from which to develop to develop a women's policy that addressed the needs of women today.[30]

Like many things in politics, the timing was crucial. After the long period in power between 1935 and 1949, by the mid-1970s, Labour had

had only two terms in government, 1957–60 and 1972–75. Its 1975 defeat was traumatic and stimulated a re-examination of itself that was occurring just when women, newly socialised by the women's movement, were considering conventional politics. The Labour Women's Council (revived in 1975) was important in bringing women to the fore of the party.[31] Elected by women at the annual conference, it brought women's issues on to the agenda and fostered women's political recruitment. Labour also had a Women's Coordinator and held a triennial Labour Women's Conference. Several women took the post of Labour Party President. Interestingly, in recent years there has been a gender gap among voters, with women more likely than men to choose Labour.[32]

In National's case, constituency candidate selection was in the hands of the local members under plurality and MMP rules. The number comprising the selectorate depended on the number of party members in a constituency, and could be as many as 60.[33] This encouraged participation in the party, but did not facilitate the creation of a balanced ticket across the country.[34] Like Labour, National chose its party lists in a two-stage process, regional then central, with delegates voting, although for this party there was no requirement to review the order of candidates at regular intervals. Indeed, rather than having a ballot for each place, as happened in Labour, there was just one vote at each of the regional and national selections.[35]

The National Party was also affected by the women's movement, but both the timing and the ideology differed markedly from that of Labour.[36] National held office between 1975 and 1984, and both party and country were dominated by the authoritarian Prime Minister, Robert Muldoon. Recalling that she was first elected as Woman Vice-president of the Party in 1977, an office she held until 1982, Sue Wood observed:

> This was a relatively new office, originally formed in 1973 as the Party's response to the impact of the women's movement here and abroad. It was essentially an advocacy role for policies affecting women and for the women's voice within the Party. In those days there was only one other woman on the Party's executive.
>
> In that role, in 1979, I was the first woman elected to the powerful policy committee . . . Rob Muldoon welcomed the role I played on that committee as a young woman and mother.[37]

Wood wrote that 'women were fine if they conformed to [Muldoon's] stereotype of how a woman should behave' and 'the very qualities he admired in men he found alarming in women'. He did not, however, oppose the advancement of women in the party.[38] These perceptive observations encapsulate the differences between Labour and National. Both contained many men who opposed women's transition from providers of cakes and scones to becoming MPs, especially among the pre-1980s generations, but the predominant ideology differed. For National, whether it was policies or group representation at issue, equal opportunities, based on the priority of individual rights, was the core belief. Despite the obstacles for National women, there were important fighters among them. Without their agitation, the Women's Vice-president (there was already a Vice-president for Youth and Maori) would not have been created. This position was lost, however, in 2003, when the party adopted a 'business model' on which to base its constitution. National women – and there have been some important ones, including a Prime Minister, Jenny Shipley, and a Minister of Finance, Ruth Richardson – accepted the equal opportunities ethos, however, so there was always going to be a limit on how far they would go to promote women as a group.[39] Nevertheless, women played an important role in the party organisation. A previous (female) president reported in 2002 that women held two out of five regional National chairs.[40]

In the case of the Greens' list selections, the selectorate comprised all those who wished to be candidates, plus members of the national executive. After this group had ranked the list, the party members, using the single transferable vote, also performed their ranking. Finally, a selection committee ranked the list again on the criteria of geographical and age spread, and gender. At least 40 per cent of the list had to be women. Note also that the Greens had co-leaders, a woman and a man. The ACT party, on the other hand, sent a list of approved candidates to all members, who then chose their 20 preferred candidates in a postal ballot. The Act Board (the central organisation) then ordered the list. 'Merit' was the sole formal criterion. The selection processes of United Future and the Progressive Coalition in 2002 were somewhat opaque, and were clearly run from Parliament, using the resources accruing to their leaders and directed by those leaders' preferences. New Zealand First candidates had first to be nominated by their electorates, using selection committees comprising local, regional and national representatives, to become eligible to stand for the list. Regional party lists were drawn up and a national committee, dominated by the leader and the national organisation but including two Maori, ranked the candidates.

It is early days to generalise about the smaller parties. After just three elections, however, a clear difference in attitudes towards women's representation had developed that was correlated with ideological differences, with the politics of presence being played out on the left but not the right: the Greens, the Alliance (no longer in Parliament) and Labour versus National, United Future and New Zealand First (although that party had a high proportion of Maori MPs, indicating an interesting attitude to representative criteria). The far-right ACT party, however, did not fit the pattern. Here an equal opportunities policy worked for women's benefit, given they had a supply of able women aspirants, no prejudices against women and a relative absence of male incumbents.

The comparison between National and Labour indicates that a degree of centralised control of candidate selection can help women's nomination: even when National wanted to nominate more women it lacked the capacity to do so. Nevertheless, centralised processes on their own do not further women's careers, as New Zealand's smaller parties demonstrated after the implementation of MMP. Attitudes towards gender relations and group rights underlie, and are reinforced by, party selection processes. Proportional representation, with its party lists, offers the opportunity to represent women fairly but does not guarantee it. Mixed systems, furthermore, can cramp the advance of women into legislatures if major parties are unwilling to nominate women for constituency seats.

Women and representation in New Zealand

The Westminster-style plurality voting rules constrained women's legislative participation. That women's representation by 1993 was comparatively high was despite the electoral system, not because of it, and can be explained by a conjuncture of forces: women's determination to access formal political power through using a particular party as the primary vehicle, Labour's readiness to accept inclusiveness and group representation in party structure and candidate selection; and fortunate timing, in that that party was out of office and searching for means of renewal. Further, the Maori seats provided opportunities for Maori women to enter Parliament long before MMP was adopted. Despite Labour's adoption of free-market policies, privatisation and commercialisation during the 1984–90 years of government, by then there were sufficient women in the parliamentary party to provide an inclusive model for the future. When out of power again, having to rethink its policies, Labour was faced with the new challenge of adapting its processes to cope with MMP. By then, women's representation was part of Labour's core identity, although equal proportions of men and women remained to be achieved.

The contagion factor during the plurality period was also an important part of the explanation for New Zealand's relative success in representing women in Parliament. National, playing adversarial politics, contested Labour over women's policies and votes, but only weakly. During the crucial period of the late 1970s and early 1980s National held office and was not therefore faced with the incentive to gain political power by expanding its attractiveness to women. When it did lose office, it moved ideologically to the free-market model that it pursued when back in power between 1990 and 1993. Thus the individualistic, equal opportunities ideal continued to shape and inhibit the political opportunities of National Party women.

MMP was intended to represent women more fairly, and it did. That its results had not fulfilled expectations after the first three elections was because party ideology influenced ideas about the nature of political representation and gender relations. Further, balancing nomination lists between women and men is complicated by other representative criteria. In New Zealand the situation is made complex by the vigorous arguments for the representation of ethnic minorities, particularly the indigenous people, the Maori.

As can be seen, descriptive representation – the number of a particular group who are represented in a political institution – and substantive representation – the representation of the views of a group by those who are members of it – overlap with one another. This is particularly the case in Westminster parliamentary systems, where there is tight party discipline. Views on party policies concerning women affect, and are affected by, their views on representative criteria, so understanding how one occurs feeds our knowledge of the other. And women's agency, which has played an essential role in furthering women's representation in New Zealand, is also expanded or constrained by party views on women's presence.

Furthermore, the importance of 'symbolic representation' should not be underestimated. When parliaments begin to contain representatives of social groups, whether ethnic, such as Maori, or female, even though their numbers may be small, they legitimise the representativeness criterion. Representativeness becomes part of the political culture. To a limited extent, this is what happened in New Zealand under the plurality electoral rules, and the representative criterion subsequently influenced the design of the new electoral system.

Notes

1 See McAllister and Studlar, 'Electoral Systems and Women's Representation'; McLeay, 'Women's Parliamentary Representation'; Rule, 'Electoral Systems, Contextual Factors and Women's Opportunity for Election to Parliament in Twenty-three Democracies', 495.
2 See Shugart and Wattenburg, 'Mixed-member Electoral Systems'.
3 See Lijphart, 'The Demise of the Last Westminster System?'
4 See Atkinson, *Adventures in Democracy.*
5 Atkinson, *Adventures in Democracy,* 84.
6 See Grimshaw, *Women's Suffrage in New Zealand.*
7 See Rei, *Maori Women and the Vote.*
8 Atkinson, *Adventures in Democracy,* 81–98; Grimshaw, *Women's Suffrage in New Zealand.*
9 King, *The Penguin History of New Zealand,* 264.
10 Atkinson, *Adventures in Democracy,* 132–3.
11 Rei, *Maori Women and the Vote,* 49–50.
12 See Dann, *Up from Under*; Devere and Scott, 'The Women's Movement'.
13 See Preddey, *The WEL Herstory.*
14 Select Committee on Women's Rights, 'Report of the Select Committee on Women's Rights: The Role of Women in New Zealand Society', 34–44.
15 See Matland and Studlar, 'The Contagion of Women Candidates in Single-member District and Proportional Electoral Systems'.

16 See Boston *et al.*, *New Zealand under MMP*; Jackson and McRobie, *New Zealand Adopts Proportional Representation*.
17 See Royal Commission on the Electoral System, *Towards Democracy*.
18 See McLeay, 'Towards a Better Democracy?'
19 Mackay *et al.*, 'Women and Constitutional Change in Scotland, Wales and Northern Ireland', 36.
20 See Catt, 'Women, Maori and Minorities'.
21 See McLeay, 'Representation, Selection, Election'.
22 See McLeay and Vowles, 'Is a Mixed Member Parliament Really "The Best of Both Worlds"?'
23 Electoral Commission, *The New Zealand Electoral Compendium*, 178–81.
24 Rae Nicholl noted a tendency for contemporary women to stay in Parliament for less time than their female predecessors a decade before, retiring earlier, mainly because they were disillusioned with their treatment as women in their parties and Parliament; 'The Revolving Door of Female Representation'.
25 See Salmond, 'Choosing Candidates'.
26 See Nicholl, 'The Woman Factor'.
27 See Salmond, 'Choosing Candidates'.
28 Salmond, 'Choosing Candidates', 96.
29 See Wilson, 'Women and the Labour Party'; Shields, 'Women in the Labour Party during the Kirk and Rowling Years'.
30 Wilson, 'Women and the Labour Party', 52.
31 Wilson, 'Women and the Labour Party', 45–7.
32 See Curtin, 'Women's Voting Patterns'.
33 Salmond, 'Choosing Candidates', 197.
34 See Nicholl, 'The Woman Factor'.
35 Salmond, 'Choosing Candidates', 197.
36 See also Sawer, 'The Representation of Women in Australia'.
37 Wood, 'Muldoon and the Party', 16.
38 Wood, 'Muldoon and the Party', 17.
39 Interestingly, however, Jenny Shipley, as Minister of Women's Affairs, successfully fought her Cabinet colleagues to retain the Ministry.
40 See Boag, 'Talking about the Women's Vote'.

5 Women and Westminster

Descriptive representation in the United Kingdom

Donley T. Studlar

Women's descriptive representation has become a significant issue within Westminster-type democracies as well as elsewhere in the world. While this issue has reached the political agenda within the past two decades, the outcomes have been variable, both over time and across jurisdictions. The mother of all parliaments, the central legislature in the United Kingdom at Westminster, has been a laggard rather than a leader in descriptive representation. This chapter offers a theoretically and comparatively informed assessment of the development, current status, and immediate future of descriptive representation in the House of Commons, the only popularly elected chamber at Westminster. In doing so, it assesses the relative impact of various factors that have been presumed to have some influence on levels of descriptive representation, including the electoral system, opinions in the electorate, political parties, and the women's movement. Recent gains for women at Westminster have largely been limited to the Labour Party. Comparatively, the United Kingdom still rates low among Western democracies. Unless the electoral system is changed into a more proportional one, this situation is likely to continue, despite efforts by parties and interest groups.

What is descriptive representation and why does it matter?

Descriptive representation refers to the socio-economic characteristics of the population and how they are reflected in representative bodies, especially legislatures. Traditionally there has been an association between demographic group characteristics and who is allowed to vote and to serve as representatives. Representation, both as legislators and voters, was only gradually extended to members of minority religions, identifiable ethnic and racial groups, agricultural and industrial workers, women, and aboriginals. By including such groups as citizens fully exercising their rights of choosing representatives, democratic regimes attempted to become more legitimate.

For a long time, it was assumed that representation of views could occur without any close resemblance between the legislature and the shares of

Basic political data

The United Kingdom

Land area 241,590 sq. km.

Population 58,789,194 (2001 census).

Indigenous population Not applicable.

Administrative divisions Unitary system but devolved legislative bodies for Scotland, Wales and Northern Ireland.

Head of State Queen Elizabeth II

Parliament Bicameral: House of Commons with 646 members elected for five-year terms; House of Lords with some 500 life peers, 92 hereditary peers (elected from among the lords) and 26 clergy.

The United Kingdom gave the world the 'Westminster' system, whereby the party that wins an election and commands a majority of seats in the lower house forms a government but remains responsible to Parliament between elections. The first-past-the-post electoral system typically produces a clear majority for the winning party and, combined with the growth of party discipline, means few brakes on executive power between elections. The constraints of federalism and a written constitution interpreted by a constitutional court are also absent. However, membership of the European Union has meant the United Kingdom has been increasingly subject to European law, for example in the economics area. Dissatisfaction with executive centralism also fuelled movements for devolution and electoral reform. The United Kingdom now has unprecedented variety in its electoral systems and legislative institutions.

Table 5.1 Electoral systems used in the United Kingdom

Arena	*System*
House of Commons	First-past-the-post
European Parliament	PR list
Scottish Parliament	MMP
Northern Ireland Assembly	STV
Welsh Assembly	MMP
London Assembly	MMP
London Mayor	Supplementary (contingent) vote

such groups in the population. In the United Kingdom, more concern was expressed about having an adequate number of legislators from the industrial working class than any other group. For most of the twentieth century this group constituted a majority of the population as well as one which was thought susceptible to Marxist appeals. Even in this case, representing this class was considered mainly the task of the party that claimed explicitly to do so, the Labour Party.[1] In recent years, however, the question of descriptive representation has become more focused on ascriptive groups such as women and ethnic minorities.

As discussed in Chapter 1 of this book, political thinkers have debated the merits and drawbacks of descriptive representation, including its relationship to issues such as justice, diversity of viewpoints, and particular policy concerns. While there was some attention to this in the United Kingdom after the first suffrage extension in 1918, especially through women's sections in the Labour Party, the revival of the women's movement in the 1960s and 1970s (second-wave feminism) reawakened concern. The disparity between women's share of the population, over half, and their share of legislative representation, below 10 per cent almost everywhere, made the arguments particularly pertinent. Were women's views systematically being excluded from legislative expression? Who was better to represent these views than women themselves? Would policies and legislative behaviour change with more women representatives? These issues achieved new prominence.

There continue to be difficulties in getting the argument for more women representatives accepted. The first is that women themselves have never been completely cohesive politically, even in pursuit of suffrage. They are divided by a variety of other socio-economic and political characteristics. Even the famed 'gender gap' involves relatively narrow differences between men and women voters in some countries, and only on some issues and behaviour.[2] Nevertheless, the general appeal of better representation for women has become politically important over the past 30 years.

The second problem is that access to the legislature in a democracy is controlled by political parties through their recruitment practices. This has proven to be malleable to some degree. Lovenduski[3] and Norris[4] argue that there are three basic strategies parties can adopt for encouraging women candidates, ranging from weak to strong: (1) rhetoric; (2) affirmative action (equal opportunities) training and monitoring programmes; (3) positive discrimination (action), usually in the form of quotas. Once the political claim was made that women voters would respond favourably to parties with more women candidates, parties in Western democracies with greater control of political recruitment through centralised mechanisms responded to these concerns by nominating more women, often through an avowed policy of quotas (or positive discrimination). Originally these parties were on the left side of the ideological spectrum, but sometimes parties on the centre and right followed in an attempt to neutralise this issue within the electorate.[5] In descriptive terms women progressively have become a larger share of members of popularly elected legislative chambers in almost all Western democracies, but more incrementally in some.

Britain traditionally has had among the lowest levels of descriptive representation for women. This has improved in recent years, both at the central (Westminster) level and especially in the devolved assemblies for Scotland and Wales. But this change in descriptive representation at Westminster is largely a function of women's improved representation within the Labour Party, which adopted a strong form of positive discrimination through all-women shortlists for targeted seats prior to the general elections of 1997 and 2005. The opposition Conservatives, and to a lesser degree the Liberal Democrats, continue to voice views that the 'best qualified candidates', regardless of demographic characteristics, should be nominated. The Liberals are even willing to have positive discrimination in requiring one woman to be on the shortlist for the nomination in those constituencies in which a woman applies. Thus increased descriptive representation for women in the United Kingdom has been slow, contested, and incomplete.

Development of descriptive representation as an issue in the United Kingdom

The issue of women's descriptive representation revolves around the question of supply and demand for candidates. The history of women's candidacy and election in the United Kingdom since the inception of suffrage for women ages 30 and over in 1918 is encapsulated in Table 5.2. Until the Second World War, women's share of candidacies was small and legislative seats were even fewer; the latter never reached 2.5 per cent. Several of the elected women first entered through by-elections, which afforded them the opportunity to stand as incumbents at the next general election.[6] In the first three decades after the Second World War, although candidacies increased substantially, those elected improved only incrementally, never more than 4.6 per cent of the total. Then, reflecting the rise of feminism, candidacies in the 1970s leaped forward and accelerated subsequently. Until 1992, however, elected women's numbers continued to be stable, only reaching 6.3 per cent in 1987. There was a 50 per cent increase to 9.2 per cent in 1992 (but also almost a 50 per cent increase in candidacies for the three major parties), and in 1997 Labour's imposition of all-women shortlists for many safe and marginal seats, plus their legislative landslide, resulted in almost a doubling of women's representation in the Commons. These overall gains largely were held in the 'stand pat' election of 2001 and increased slightly in 2005 despite Labour's decline in seats.

Table 5.2 Number of women elected (candidates) in UK general elections

Year	*Con.*	*Lab.*	*Lib.*	*Others*	*Total women*	*% total MPs*
1918	0 (7)	0 (4)	0 (4)	1 (8)	1 (17)	0.1
1922	1 (5)	0 (16)	1 (10)	0 (2)	2 (33)	0.3
1923	3 (7)	3 (12)	2 (14)	0 (1)	8 (34)	1.3
1924	3 (12)	1 (22)	0 (6)	0 (1)	4 (41)	0.7
1929	3 (10)	9 (30)	1 (25)	1 (4)	14 (69)	2.3
1931	13 (16)	0 (36)	1 (6)	0 (4)	15 (62)	2.4
1935	6 (19)	1 (35)	1 (11)	1 (2)	9 (67)	1.5
1945	1 (14)	21 (41)	1 (20)	1 (12)	24 (87)	3.8
1950	6 (28)	14 (42)	1 (45)	0 (11)	21 (126)	3.4
1951	6 (25)	11 (41)	0 (11)	0 (0)	17 (77)	2.7
1955	10 (33)	14 (43)	0 (14)	0 (2)	24 (91)	3.8
1959	12 (28)	13 (36)	0 (16)	0 (1)	25 (81)	4.0
1964	11 (24)	18 (33)	0 (24)	0 (9)	29 (90)	4.6
1966	7 (21)	19 (30)	0 (20)	0 (10)	26 (81)	4.1
1970	15 (26)	10 (29)	0 (23)	1 (21)	26 (99)	4.1
1974 (F)	9 (33)	13 (40)	0 (40)	1 (30)	23 (143)	3.6
1974 (0)	7 (30)	18 (50)	0 (49)	2 (32)	27 (161)	4.3
1979	8 (31)	11 (52)	0 (52)	0 (77)	19 (209)	3.0
1983	13 (40)	10 (78)	0 (75)	0 (82)	23 (276)	3.5
1987	17 (46)	21 (92)	2 (105)	1 (82)	41 (325)	6.3
1992	20 (63)	37 (138)	2 (143)	1 (224)	60 (568)	9.2
1997	13 (66)	101 (155)	3 (140)	3 (311)	120 (672)	18.2
2001	14 (94)	95 (150)	5 (140)	4 (259)	118 (643)	17.9
2005	17 (122)	98 (171)	10 (147)	3 (277)	128 (717)	19.8

Being a candidate in the winning party, that is, the party that gains a plurality (usually a majority) of seats in the House of Commons, helps women's chances of election. There have been fewer women candidates in the Conservative Party than in Labour at every single election since 1945, and the gap has grown larger, especially over the past two decades. Nevertheless, when the Conservatives gain office, women's numbers have risen in that party relative to Labour. As recently as 1983, there were more Conservative women MPs than Labour ones. That situation is not likely to recur in the near future, however, since the gap in legislators is now much wider, despite the Conservatives recently closing the difference in candidacies. Especially since 1974 the Liberal Democrats and other parties consistently have been willing to offer women as candidates, but most are in hopeless seats and few are ever elected to the House.

In the United Kingdom the candidate nomination procedure is normally decentralised. The selection of parliamentary candidates, one per district, traditionally lay in the hands of the local constituency party, more particularly in the local executive committee, which received applications from potential candidates, developed a shortlist, interviewed the finalists, and then chose the party standard-bearer from among them. Since the

1990s, however, all three major parties have adopted one member – one vote procedures for constituency candidate selections. But there has also been a counter-tendency of increased central intervention in the choice of candidates, especially in the Labour Party.[7] Originally this was used to combat threats from the local activists of the extreme left and in high-profile by-election contests, but the precedent proved useful when the party adopted a target list of winnable constituencies for women.

Party affiliation of the candidate and partisan voting composition in single-member constituencies is an important factor in electability in Britain. Having an opportunity to fight a safe or marginal seat for one's party is thus a key element in moving from candidate to legislator. Most minor-party and many major-party candidates simply stand no chance of election. Examples include the results from the dramatic increase of Liberal women candidates in 1950 and more women's candidacies for the Liberals and minor parties since 1974 as well as for Labour in 1983 and for the Conservatives in 2001 and 2005.

With only one member per district and increased professionalisation of MPs, individual incumbency becomes an additional barrier for an insurgent group to overcome. Most MPs desire to continue in office until age, death, or the electorate retires them, and parties try to avoid internal party disputes and to benefit from whatever 'personal vote' an MP can deliver.[8] In the United Kingdom, few incumbent MPs have been denied renomination. Even though the Labour Party, then under the influence of left-wing elements, passed a policy of 'mandatory reselection' of MPs in the early 1980s, this did not lead to wholesale party turnover of incumbents. Even during the days of mandatory reselection, the overall turnover rate for MPs was one of the smallest among Western democracies.[9] More recently, a policy of 'affirmative nomination' has been adopted, which means that it will be even harder to remove incumbents.[10]

Ironically, women traditionally have been stronger at the grass roots in the Conservative Party, but at the elite level in the Labour Party. From early days after women's enfranchisement, Labour has been willing to have women candidates and also has elected more of them. More women also have served in prominent positions within the party, including the first female cabinet minister and several other prominent ones, even when women's overall legislative numbers were low. As in many other ways, Margaret Thatcher was the great exception. With the largest number of women MPs in Conservative Party history, John Major appointed no women to his first Cabinet in 1991 and only one after his election victory in 1992. From 1918, Labour also guaranteed women five seats on the 29 member party National Executive Committee; this share has since increased to 50 per cent.

Thus, it is not surprising that Labour has been more aggressive in promoting women's descriptive representation in the party and legislature in the 1990s, eventually through a quotas policy. Nevertheless, Labour was relatively slow compared with leftist parties in other European democracies and even lagged behind the Social Democratic Party, who were the first to adopt a policy of requiring a woman to be on the constituency shortlist for nomination if one woman applied for the position.[11] As noted above, however, this did not result in substantially more women Liberal Democrat (or Social Democratic) MPs.

Eventually Labour went further. In 1989 the party adopted a similar rule as the Liberals and the SDP, that is, a woman must be shortlisted in any constituency in which one applied. At the 1990 party conference, a resolution was adopted for a goal of 50 per cent women candidates before the end of the decade or the next three general elections, whichever came first. After disappointing results on this score in the 1992 election, the 1993 party conference adopted a policy of quotas, namely that women should receive half of the nominations in Labour's top 80 non-incumbent targeted seats (safe or marginal) through the mechanism of all-women shortlists. This was to be done through regional consultations if possible, and through centralised National Executive Council imposition if necessary. Although this resolution was reaffirmed at the 1994 conference, it proved controversial in implementation in an electoral system in which there was only one possible winner in each constituency and in which party nomination was the key to victory in many seats.

For the next election women were chosen from all-women shortlists in 35 of the target seats as well as in three hopeless seats. But in 1996 an industrial tribunal, acting on an appeal from two rejected male candidates, declared all-women shortlists to be an illegal infringement on equal access to employment under the 1975 Sex Discrimination Act. The party refused to appeal the decision from fear that an affirmation of the decision at a higher level would jeopardise the position of women already selected through this method. The decision itself applied directly only to the two seats that the male applicants had sought.[12] Party leader Tony Blair already had declared the policy of all-women shortlists to be 'not ideal' and operational for this election only.[13]

Thus even the abortive quotas policy had placed Labour women candidates in more favourable seats than previously, and, with the Labour sweep in the 1997 election, women doubled their numbers in the House of Commons, becoming 24.2 per cent of the majority party. Aided by incumbency, but without a specific quotas policy, women's candidacies and winners in the Labour Party dropped slightly in the 2001 election. Buttressed by passage of the Sex Discrimination (Political Candidates) Act in 2002, all-women shortlists (AWS) were employed in 30 target seats in 2005, of which 23 were won. With a record number of women candidates (171) contesting seats, even in the face of overall Labour decline women emerged as 27.5 per cent of the party in the Commons. Nevertheless, these figures were well short of the target of 50 per cent women candidates adopted by the 1990 party conference, and the one of 35 per cent women in the parliamentary party for the 2005 election.

There is an argument about whether the relatively small share of women candidates is a result more of supply or of demand. Criddle[14] contends that, with only 28 per cent potential women candidates on its National Parliamentary Panel of candidates and 24 per cent MPs, the problem in the Labour Party, perhaps aggravated by Labour women's success in devolved assemblies, is one of supply rather than demand. In 2005 both of these figures improved, but only slightly. Others, however, claim discriminatory practices in all parties, even Labour, discourage women from becoming candidates.[15] In 2001 the Conservatives had 20 per cent women on their centrally approved list; 14 per cent nominated candidates were women, but only 8 per cent of their MPs. The latter two figures were 19 per cent and 9 per cent in 2005.

With women MPs at a plateau in 2001, there was a renewed search for ways to increase their level of representation. One demand was for the Conservatives, Liberal Democrats, and other parties to nominate more women for competitive seats. The second was to loosen the legal restraints on quotas to allow parties to take promotional action on behalf of women, including all-women shortlists. Buoyed by women's numerical success in the devolved legislatures in Scotland and Wales, most of this pressure occurred within the Labour Party.[16] In its 2001 manifesto, Labour promised: 'We are committed, through legislation, to allow each party to make positive moves to increase the representation of women.' The Liberal Democrat commitment was milder, to 'Introduce more family friendly and efficient working practices for Parliament to bring a wider range of people, particularly women, into Parliament'. The Conservative manifesto made no mention of increasing women's representation in Parliament. In 2005 only the Labour and Liberal Democrat manifestoes mentioned women specifically, and that was not in regard to representation.

Labour passed the Sex Discrimination (Political Candidates) Act through parliament in 2002 with surprisingly little controversy.[17] This Act is permissive in that it allows political parties to take actions such as all-women shortlists to promote women's candidacies and is due to expire in 2015 unless extended by a statutory instrument. For 2005, however, only the Labour Party implemented such measures by agreeing to introduce all women shortlists in at least 50 per cent of seats in which a sitting Labour MP was retiring. If insufficient constituency parties agree to all women shortlists, then the central party organisation was empowered to impose them.[18]

How does descriptive representation in Britain compare with other countries?

In order to understand the situation for descriptive representation in the United Kingdom, it is helpful to consider some comparative data, as presented in Table 5.3. As demonstrated there, the United Kingdom con-

Table 5.3 Average percentage of women's parliamentary representation by decade

Rank	*Country*	*Right to vote, stand*	*1950s*	*1960s*	*1970s*	*1980s*	*1990s*	*2000s*	*Change 1950–2005*	*Overall 1950–2005*
1	Sweden	1919	11.8	13.9	20.2	30.9	38.6	45.3	(+33.5)	26.8
2	Finland	1906	12.6	15.2	21.6	29.5	35.8	37.5	(+24.9)	25.4
3	Norway	1913, 1907	5.3	8.3	16.2	30.0	37.4	36.4	(+31.1)	22.3
4	Denmark	1915	8.5	9.9	16.4	26.3	34.1	37.0	(+28.5)	22.0
5	Netherlands	1919, 1917	7.8	9.2	10.3	18	29.9	36.7	(+28.9)	18.7
6	Germany	1918	8.4	7.7	6.6	11.1	27.1	32.2	(+23.8)	15.5
7	Austria	1918	5.1	5.5	6.7	9.7	22.1	33.9	(+28.8)	13.8
8	Iceland	1915	2.1	2.2	4.7	14.0	26.3	30.2	(+28.1)	13.3
9	New Zealand	1893, 1919	4.5	5.7	4.6	11.3	21.1[a]	28.3	(+23.8)	12.6[a]
10	Belgium	1948	3.9	4.2	5.4	7.1	11.8	35.3	(+31.4)	11.3
11	Luxembourg	1919	0	0.7	5.3	12.6	17.0	23.3	(+23.3)	9.8
12	Israel	1948	9.2	7.8	6.7	7.6	8.9	15.0	(+5.8)	9.2
13	Canada	1918, 1920	1.2	1.5	2.5	8.5	16.3	20.9	(+19.7)	8.5
14	Italy	1945	6.1	4.1	5.5	9.0	11.6[a]	11.5	(+5.4)	8.0[a]
15	United Kingdom	1918	3.3	4.1	4.0	4.2	11.3	18.9	(+15.6)	7.6
16	Australia	1902	0.2	0.2	0.3	4.6	12.4	25.0	(+24.8)	7.1
17	Ireland	1918	3.4	2.6	3.0	7.4	11.2	13.3	(+9.9)	6.8
18	United States	1920, 1919	2.9	3.2	3.6	5.0	10.5	14.5	(+11.6)	6.6
19	France	1944	3.5	1.9	2.8	6.7[a]	7.9	12.2	(+8.7)	5.8[a]
20	Japan	1945	2.1	1.5	1.5	1.5	2.6[a]	7.1	(+5.0)	2.7[a]
	Total		5.1	5.5	7.4	12.8	19.7	25.4	(+20.3)	(+12.6)

Note
a Electoral system changed.

tinues to lag behind most other democracies, not only ones with some element of proportional representation, but even other Westminster single-member systems. For 20 countries since 1950, by decades, Britain has ranked fourteenth, tied for eleventh, fourteenth, nineteenth, fifteenth, and fourteenth in women's seat share. Its overall rank for these decades is fifteenth, and its overall increase is fourteenth. Without the boost from Labour all-women shortlists, Britain would be even further down the current league table, probably around the position of France or the United States. Despite the recent infusions, in the long term Britain's position actually has declined relative to other Westminster democracies.

What has influenced Westminster descriptive representation?

There are several variables that might account for the pattern of women's descriptive representation in Westminster and its divergence from that in other countries. Possible explanations for these results include the electorate, the organisation and ideology of political parties, the women's movement, and the electoral system.

Although the British public generally has been considered a laggard among Western democracies in attitudes toward women playing unconventional roles, especially in politics, there is evidence of change.[19] Recent studies find wide support for having more women in Parliament, but this is not a major issue on which people cast their vote. As more women have become candidates over the years, there has been no demonstrable effect in either direction on voter choice. Both surveys and aggregate data analyses have failed to find a voter bias against female candidates in the electorate.[20]

The lack of voter bias even extends to those women chosen by Labour in all-women shortlists in 1997, whose support was in a similar pattern as for previous women candidates, namely based largely on the partisan and demographic makeup of their constituencies.[21] In fact, the difference between the 40 competitive seats and the actual 35 seats chosen from all-women shortlists was composed entirely of safe seats, where one might expect more resistance to the idea. Women chosen in AWS did not fare as well electorally in 2005, with one spectacular rebuff of the policy in the heretofore safely Labour constituency of Blaenau Gwent, Wales. But the larger problem was that Labour did not do nearly as well with the voters, which resulted in the loss of six out of seven marginal AWS seats but no other safely Labour ones.

Women's voting patterns have shifted since the 1980s, although not as much as Labour might have wished. Traditionally more supportive of the Conservatives, in the 1980s (when Margaret Thatcher was Prime Minister) women became evenly divided in their political support for the two major parties and in the last three general elections have favoured Labour.

Unlike some other countries, there has not been a substantial voting gender gap in the British electorate.[22] There are some opinion gaps, but not always in a conventional left–right manner.[23] In the early 1990s those favouring positive action for women candidates in the Labour Party argued that policies more appealing to women could attract their votes. Older women long have been a mainstay of the Conservative electorate, which led to the contention that a 'gender–generation gap' should benefit Labour,[24] but it is not clear that this has emerged. Although Labour held women's support in 2005 better than it did men's, both declined from 2001, with women moving more towards the Liberal Democrats.

Furthermore, some multivariate comparative studies of descriptive representation in Western democracies[25] have found long-term effects of different political cultures, as measured by when women received equal suffrage rights. See Table 5.3. These effects may not always be amenable to measurement by survey research. In summary, the general political culture in the United Kingdom does not seem especially resistant to party efforts to improve women's descriptive representation prospects. How the public would react to a government policy of mandated positive discrimination for women is less predictable. Despite the attention given to gender representation since the 1990s, there is little evidence about how the electorate views these issues. For the present, there seems to be a 'permissive consensus' in the electorate that is tolerant of party elite attempts to improve women's descriptive representation in the House of Commons.

The social movement for women's rights that arose in the 1960s has now manifested itself in the establishment of several interest groups lobbying for greater descriptive representation for women, among other issues. Among these groups are the non-partisan Fawcett Society and 300 Club. Others are specifically linked to the Labour Party, including the Fabian Society and more recent EMILY's List UK and the Labour Women's Network.[26] The Equal Opportunities Commission, a government agency, publicises differences in male/female proportions of employment, including political office. The Constitution Unit at University College, University of London, also brought women's descriptive representation into its remit, especially in regard to the Sex Discrimination (Election Candidates) Act of 2002.[27]

Non-partisan lobbying by the women's movement has been limited in its effects on descriptive representation issues. Studies of the women's movement in the United Kingdom, especially comparative ones, find it to be fragmented, localist, ideological, non-hierarchical, and schismatic; this makes consensus positions difficult to achieve and lessens any potential political effectiveness through mass mobilisation.[28] There has been no attempt to adopt laws mandating women to have a certain guaranteed share of candidacies or providing incentives for parties to do so, as has occurred in other countries with varying results.[29]

Overall, women's groups have been most successful at lobbying through the Labour Party. This was possible because of the electoral, ideological, and organisational crisis within the party in the early 1990s[30] and the decline of male-dominated trade union influence[31] as well as women's presence in significant numbers at higher levels within the party.[32] Criddle[33] credits the Labour Women's Network and EMILY's List with the greatest impact on Labour adopting all-women shortlists.

Women's movements are most effective when they can work within particular political parties to encourage policies that lead to more women being adopted as candidates, especially for winnable seats.[34] The traditional explanation for why there were not more women candidates and MPs in Britain was that political parties were the major problem, especially the constituency-level selection committees for parliamentary candidates.[35] It was at this level that the myth circulated that women candidates cost a party votes, even if there was never any convincing evidence of the phenomenon.[36] More recently, as delineated above, political parties have changed their procedures sufficiently to produce more women candidacies, even if not always more women MPs. These changes, however, ranging from training courses for potential candidates and more stringent procedures for approved candidate lists to all-women constituency shortlists, have been imposed from above, by the central organisations of the parties and, in some instances, the national conferences. In short, it has taken a sporadic and uneven movement toward centralisation of candidate selection in the parties since the 1980s to produce better descriptive representation for women.

There has been a process of macro-contagion[37] among the parties as well, at least in terms of goals and affirmative action policies. Political party changes, especially in the Labour Party but abetted by the Social Democratic Party and the Liberals, have enabled women's descriptive representation to increase. Parties tend to be more open to organisational innovations when in opposition. Labour adopted its candidate quotas policy at a time when it had suffered four consecutive general election losses and was amenable to policies that could help it become more competitive. Pressure from women's movements and change within Labour occurred just before it became the majority parliamentary party, which made this advancement for women possible.[38] In other parliamentary systems, however, including some single-member district ones, shared norms for women's political advancement are more firmly established across parties.[39]

Party ideologies also have played a role. Parties on the left first adopted quotas for candidate shortlists, both in weak form (SDP and Liberals) and stronger (Labour). But there was no small leftist 'New Politics' or 'new egalitarian' party to stimulate this process, as occurred in several continental European countries.[40] Contagion among parties has been limited.

There appear to be distinct cultures within the two major parties as to how far women's candidacies should be promoted. Data from the British Candidate/Representation Studies over several years indicate that, despite majority support among candidates of all parties for affirmative action policies, positive discrimination policies such as quotas and extra financial support for women candidates were much more popular in the Labour Party than among other parties, especially the Conservatives. Conservative candidates also were the lowest among six parties in support for affirmative action measures.[41] With the substantial increase in women's candidacies for the Conservatives over the 2001 and 2005 elections, perhaps this has abated somewhat, but no evidence has emerged that Conservative women are contesting more competitive seats.

The fourth possible explanation for women's descriptive representation at Westminster is the electoral system. For a half century comparative studies have found that a single-member district electoral system hinders women's descriptive representation in Western democracies. While not all multi-member proportional representation systems have a high percentage of women legislators, there is a marked and measurable difference across these types of electoral system.[42] See Table 5.3. Single-member plurality systems are zero-sum in that only one candidate is chosen by a party for each district and only one candidate can win the seat. Thus there is no opportunity for a 'balanced ticket' by gender or other political interests.

Furthermore, most countries employing this electoral system usually have the power of choice of candidate residing in the local constituency rather than in the central party organisation. Thus any attempt to impose a quota system involves co-ordination across local constituency parties jealous of their power of selection on the basis of whatever local criteria suit them. Even when a party in a single-member district system attempts to improve women's descriptive representation though a quota system, it encounters difficulties, as experienced by the New Democrats in Canada in 1993[43] and parties in France in 2002[44] as well as by British Labour in 1997.

Since 1997 the United Kingdom has changed its electoral systems into more proportional ones for almost all bodies except the House of Commons at Westminster. Under all of these varying arrangements, women's share of descriptive representation has grown and is larger than that under the major remaining single-member district system for the House of Commons. There are particular circumstances that apply to each of these – the lack of incumbency for the first elections of new bodies, an active women's movement, and the attempt at new institutional arrangements. Nevertheless, none of them relies exclusively on members elected in single-member districts.

Prospects for any change in the electoral system for the Westminster parliament, however, are dim. Even though Labour promised a referendum on the electoral system in its 1997 election manifesto, the 1998 Jenkins Commission report on the voting system that recommended a relatively modest change has not been pursued by the government. The disproportionate votes/seats results of the 2005 election have reignited interest in electoral system reform in some quarters, but a majority Labour government in Parliament, based on 36 per cent of the popular vote, is unlikely to pursue such a project.

The future of women's representation at Westminster

After a decade of remarkable change, the situation for women's descriptive representation in the United Kingdom today appears to have stabilised. Compared with previous levels, women's candidacies and legislative seats are at all-time records in the past three general elections, and there is a law allowing parties to take more steps in this direction. Yet compared with many other democracies, women are still lagging as a proportion of legislators. Furthermore, even in the Labour Party the goals for women candidacies and legislators are not being achieved.

Whatever the past constraints, changes in the political culture, although hardly as dramatic as Russell suggests,[45] have made it more facilitative for women becoming candidates and legislators. However fragmented women's groups may be, they do get a hearing, and, in some circumstances, especially when new institutions are being formed or when a party is desperate to improve its competitive position, they can have an impact. Parties have varied in their responses to these pressures, with Labour being most willing to accommodate them, but even Labour's responses have been limited.

What has not changed has been the single-member district electoral system for Westminster elections, and this has inhibited political parties as well. The data in Table 5.3 show that no single-member district electoral system has ever had women composing more than a quarter of its representatives. Eleven PR or mixed systems have done better, and 13 have had more women legislators than the British high. A system with a substantial element of proportional representation provides conditions more conductive to women's candidacies for *winnable* seats, including higher party magnitudes (expected number of winnable seats) within a district,[46] less reliance on individual incumbency, more centralised selection procedures for candidates, and greater willingness to implement, not only support rhetorically, women's group demands for competitive seats through a process of 'ticket balancing'.

In short, electoral systems with multi-member districts provide the optimal demand features for women's candidacies; problems in some of these systems can be more readily attributed to supply features or individual party behaviour. It is much more difficult to change party behaviour in a single-member district system. This is demonstrated by the refusal of parties to respond to financial incentives encouraging gender equality of candidates in France as well as the lagging position of women's descriptive representation in the United States, the home of a vital women's movement.

Whatever the merits of the debate about the 'supply side' versus the 'demand side' for women's candidacies, it is clear that parties have taken some measures to encourage women's candidacies and Labour has managed to get more women in winnable seats. Labour women lobbied intensively for the Sex Discrimination (Political Candidates) Act, but the hopes invested in its transforming possibilities are not likely to be realised fully in the immediate future.[47] There are limits to what can be expected from a process in which contesting a winnable seat, the first step toward not only a parliamentary but also a possible ministerial career, occurs in single-member districts in which nominations remain predominantly in local party organisations and in which individual incumbency is a major asset. The current Labour Party policy of 'affirmative nomination', which protects most incumbents from a reselection process, helps incumbent women but also makes it more difficult to replace sitting men, who remain three-quarters of the party's MPs.

Despite record increases in Conservative women candidates in the past two general elections, this had not resulted in corresponding increases in that party's MPs. For three decades Conservative Party leaders repeatedly have expressed a desire for more women candidates, and in recent years this target has been 25 per cent. But without more centralised control of party nominations, local parties, especially in competitive and safe seats, remain free to choose whom they consider the best possible candidate. Given the current imbalance among women's representation in the parties, substantial seat gains for the Conservatives and/or the Liberal Democrats at the next election could possibly even result in a decline of total women MPs, since current Labour women MPs would be defeated in the process.

Nevertheless, women usually benefit from a major change in parliamentary personnel, as occurred in 1997 when there was a post-war record of 40 per cent turnover, in contrast to an average of 25 per cent for the previous four elections.[48] If more women were to arrive in the House of Commons through substantial gains for the Conservatives and/or Liberal Democrats, they, too, would have all of the advantages of incumbency at the next election, and it would be more difficult for those parties to retreat from those levels of descriptive representation. A more volatile electorate and a more competitive party system would give women increased opportunities for winnable seats, but that is unlikely in the near future.

In summary, then, the current situation for Westminster descriptive representation for women has largely resulted from political institutions, namely political parties and the electoral system. Interest groups championing descriptive representation have had some effect, but their impact would have been greater in a PR or mixed-member electoral system and with a more receptive right-wing political party. Furthermore, they have had more influence on internal Labour Party representation issues than on the more difficult one of choosing parliamentary candidates. The general political culture for women's candidacies has never been as hostile as many political leaders assumed. Demands for positive discrimination on behalf of women candidates have not generated a backlash from the public. Nevertheless, failure to adopt such measures does not appear to have harmed the electoral prospects of the Conservatives or Liberal Democrats. The Conservatives are unlikely to move sharply towards increasing women's winnable candidacies unless its lack of women, especially in high-profile positions, evokes negative views among marginal voters, something which has not occurred.

Further tinkering under current institutional arrangements is unlikely to result in descriptive representation for women growing other than incrementally. At the next general election women's share of legislative seats might increase somewhat, remain the same, or even decline. Further improvement, especially a radical change, in women's descriptive representation in the Westminster parliament is more dependent on difficult institutional change than on cultural change. In this as in so much else in British constitutional matters, the electoral system remains the linchpin of current arrangements. Change towards a more mixed electoral system, especially one with a strong element of party list proportional representation, would enable the pressures for greater descriptive representation for women to have more effect.

Notes

Thanks to Paul Chaney, Sarah Childs, Stephanie Toth, and Rachael Rudolph for advice and data assistance.

1 See Muller, *The Kept Men?*.
2 See Studlar and McAllister, 'Candidate Gender and Voting in the 1997 British General Election'; Inglehart and Norris, *Rising Tide*.
3 See Lovenduski, 'Introduction: The Dynamics of Gender and Party'.
4 See Norris, *Electoral Engineering*.
5 See Matland and Studlar, 'Determinants of Legislative Turnover'; Caul, 'Women's Representation in Parliament'.
6 See Kohn, *Women in National Legislatures*.
7 See Criddle, 'MPs and Candidates'; Scarrow *et al.*, 'From Social Integration to Electoral Contestation'.
8 See Cain *et al.*, *The Personal Vote*; Norton and Wood, *Back from Westminster*.
9 See Matland and Studlar, 'Determinants of Legislative Turnover'.
10 See Criddle, 'MPs and Candidates'.
11 See Byrne, 'The Politics of the Women's Movement'.
12 See Russell, 'Women in Elected Office in the UK, 1992–2002'.
13 See Perrigo, 'Gender Struggles in the Labour Party from 1979 to 1995'; Studlar and McAllister, 'Candidate Gender and Voting in the 1997 British General Election'
14 See Criddle, 'MPs and Candidates'.

15 See Shepherd-Robinson and Lovenduski, *Women and Candidate Selection*; Mackay, 'Gender and Political Representation in the UK', 104.
16 See Russell, 'Women in Elected Office in the UK, 1992–2002'.
17 See Russell, 'Women in Elected Office in the UK, 1992–2002'.
18 See Childs, 'The Sex Discrimination (Election Candidates) Act 2002 and its Implications'.
19 See Gelb, *Feminism and Politics*; Byrne, 'The Politics of the Women's Movement'.
20 See Rasmussen, 'Female Career Patterns and Leadership Disabilities in Britain'; Welch and Studlar, 'British Public Opinion toward Women in Politics'; Studlar *et al.*, 'Electing Women to the British Commons'.
21 See Studlar and McAllister, 'Candidate Gender and Voting in the 1997 British General Election'.
22 See Studlar *et al.*, 'Electing Women to the British Commons'.
23 See Welch and Thomas, 'Explaining the Gender Gap in British Public Opinion'; Jelen *et al.*, 'The Gender Gap in Comparative Perspective'; Campbell, 'Gender, Ideology and Issue Preference'
24 See Norris, 'Gender: A Gender–Generation Gap?'
25 See Siaroff, 'Women's Representation in Legislatures and Cabinets in Industrial Democracies'; McAllister and Studlar, 'Electoral Systems and Women's Representation'.
26 Norris and Lovenduski, *Political Recruitment*, 242–3.
27 See Russell, *Women's Representation in UK Politics*; Russell, *The Women's Representation Bill*; Russell, 'Women in Elected Office in the UK, 1992–2002'.
28 See Gelb, *Feminism and Politics*; Lovenduski and Randall, *Contemporary Feminist Politics*; Byrne, 'The Politics of the Women's Movement'; Beckwith, 'The Gendering Ways of States'.
29 See Htun and Jones, 'Engendering the Right to Participate in Decision-making'; Dauphin and Praud, 'Debating and Implementing Gender Parity in France'; Kuhn, 'The French Presidential and Parliamentary Elections, 2002'.
30 See Perrigo, 'Gender Struggles in the Labour Party from 1979 to 1995'; Byrne, 'The Politics of the Women's Movement'.
31 See Lovenduski and Randall, *Contemporary Feminist Politics.*
32 See Caul, 'Political Parties and the Adoption of Candidate Gender Quotas'.
33 See Criddle, 'MPs and Candidates'.
34 See Caul, 'Women's Representation in Parliament'; Kaiser, 'The Rise of New Egalitarian Parties and Women's Parliamentary Participation'.
35 See Rasmussen, 'Female Career Patterns and Leadership Disabilities in Britain'; Studlar *et al.*, 'Electing Women to the British Commons'
36 See Ranney, *Pathways to Parliament*; Bochel and Denver, 'Candidate Selection in the Labour Party'.
37 See Matland and Studlar, 'The Contagion of Women Candidates in Single-member District and Proportional Representation Electoral Systems'; Caul, 'Political Parties and the Adoption of Candidate Gender Quotas'.
38 See Darcy and Beckwith, 'Political Disaster, Political Triumph'.
39 See Studlar and Matland, 'The Dynamics of Women's Representation in the Canadian Provinces, 1975–1994'.
40 See Caul, 'Women's Representation in Parliament'; Kaiser, 'The Rise of New Egalitarian Parties and Women's Parliamentary Participation'.
41 Norris and Lovenduski, *Political Recruitment*, 243; Lovenduski and Norris, 'Westminster Women'.
42 See Duverger, *The Political Role of Women*; Rule, 'Why Women Don't Run'; Rule, 'Electoral Systems, Contextual Factors, and Women's Opportunities for Election to Parliament in Twenty-three Democracies'; Norris, *Politics and Sexual*

Equality; Norris, *Electoral Engineering*; Darcy *et al.*, *Women, Elections and Representation*; Matland, 'Women's Representation in National Legislatures'; Siaroff, 'Women's Representation in Legislatures and Cabinets in Industrial Democracies'; McAllister and Studlar, 'Electoral Systems and Women's Representation'.

43 See Studlar and Matland, 'The Dynamics of Women's Representation in the Canadian Provinces, 1975–1994'.

44 See Dauphin and Praud, 'Debating and Implementing Gender Parity in France'; Kuhn, 'The French Presidential and Parliamentary Elections, 2002'.

45 See Russell, 'Women in Elected Office in the UK, 1992–2002'.

46 See Matland, 'Institutional Variables Affecting Female Representation in National Legislatures'.

47 See Russell, 'Women in Elected Office in the UK, 1992–2002'.

48 See Darcy and Beckwith, 'Political Disaster, Political Triumph'; Matland and Studlar, 'Determinants of Legislative Turnover'.

Part II

The substantive representation of women

6 When women support women . . .

EMILY's List and the substantive representation of women in Australia

Marian Sawer

In the 1990s the issue of the parliamentary representation of women became the focus of much international and national attention. The arguments for increasing women's representation often went beyond basic justice arguments to suggest that women would make a difference to politics. In particular, it was often suggested that the presence of women was essential to ensure that women's interests were represented. Nevertheless, and leaving aside the vexed notion of 'women's interests', it was soon recognised that the presence of women in legislatures does not *necessarily* result in increased attention to issues of special concern to women in the community. 'Standing for' is not the same as 'acting for' and there is a difference between the descriptive representation of women and what is termed the substantive representation of women. Indeed, the presence of women may provide an alibi for policies that are far from women-friendly.

Internationally, researchers have examined the circumstances in which women legislators do act as advocates for women as a group.[1] They have identified the importance of belief systems such as party ideology and whether the ideology of the party is compatible with promoting equality for women. They have also looked at whether legislators self-identify as feminists and at what follows from such identification in terms of feminist advocacy. Some have tested the importance of structural factors such as presence or absence of women's caucuses within parliamentary parties or within parliament.[2] It has long been argued that women's institution-building inside powerful institutions is necessary to maintain feminist identities and perspectives in the context of conflicting organisational cultures and loyalties. Others have examined the effects of membership of, and association with, women's movement organisations outside parliament.[3] A related factor is the level of women's movement activity in society at large – which may affect the propensity of politicians to identify as feminist as well as their propensity to take up women's movement issues.

Apart from the question of what prompts women to act as advocates for other women there is also the issue of accountability for this form of representation. Voters may always vote out a representative held responsible for not stopping a new flight path over a geographical electorate. In what ways can representatives be held to account for performance in achieving outcomes of specific concern to women as a group?[4] I have previously drawn attention to one light-hearted accountability tool invented in Australia in 1993 by a feminist who is now the presiding officer of the New South Wales (NSW) Legislative Council. This form of accountability involves an annual dinner at the NSW Parliament where 400 women judges decide – on the basis of the volume of booing – on awards for various categories of sexist behaviour. Prime Minister John Howard won the award, for example, for vetoing an anti-domestic violence campaign as being 'too anti-male'. There is also an 'Elaine' award, for the woman whose comments or behaviour have been least helpful to the sisterhood. The Ernies attract wide media coverage, combining as they do plenty of humour with accountability.

This chapter takes a somewhat more serious approach to the issue of accountability for the substantive representation of women. It examines the role of one extra-parliamentary feminist organisation in increasing the number of women in parliament with a feminist group perspective, in promoting the representation of issues of concern to women in the community and in providing some form of accountability. EMILY's List (EL)[5] was established in Australia in 1996 by prominent Labor women and uses the slogan 'When women support women, women win'. Its goals were first to ensure that more Labor women were elected to Australian parliaments and second that these women were committed to pro-choice positions on abortion and to gender equity issues more generally.

By April 2004 EL claimed to have helped 91 new Labor women – including Australia's first Indigenous women parliamentarians – to enter Australian parliaments. The descriptive representation of women in Australian parliaments had reached an all-time high, at 30 per cent of all parliamentarians and 35 per cent of Labor parliamentarians. EL-supported women were playing a significant role in government, with Labor holding office in all six states and both territories and being in opposition only at the federal level. Apart from its financial and mentoring support for candidates, EL played a broader role in advocating internal party reform and in achieving the renewal of commitment to quotas in 2002.

The question of the substantive representation of issues of particular concern to women is a more difficult one to track. The approach of this research is to assess substantive representation *via* the incidence in parliamentary debate of issues of particular concern to women. The hypothesis was that the significant group of EL-supported women in Australian parliaments would have some effect in ensuring such issues were represented in parliamentary debate. As noted earlier, international research suggests that membership of women's movement organisations helps women parliamentarians maintain collective identity and awareness of gender implications of policy. EL is an example of a women's movement organisation that provides woman-centred policy space and opportunity for feminist discourse but which is also specifically adapted to an era of professionalised party politics.

The research covered the two federal parliaments elected before EL was created and the subsequent two parliaments.[6] It disaggregates between the House of Representatives and the Senate, as the chambers are elected by different electoral systems and have a differing partisan and gender composition. The full version of Parlinfo, available to federal parliamentarians and used here, provides the number of documents in which the search term appears, and can provide breakdowns by party or member's name but not, unfortunately, by gender. It should be noted that there may be repeated references to the term within any given document, whether it is a speech or a parliamentary question, but what is recorded in this analysis is simply the number of documents in which the term appears.

The search was limited to debate on the floor of the chambers and does not extend to parliamentary committees. While some would argue that women parliamentarians are at their most effective in the less adversarial forums of parliamentary committees, or in behind-the-scenes lobbying in their own parties, it remains valid to examine the extent to which the representation of women is refracted through the most public form of parliamentary discourse.

The particular issues selected for the purposes of this chapter were those of paid maternity leave and domestic violence/violence against women.[7] As explained in greater detail further on, the terms were selected because of their significance to the substantive representation of women, variously understood. That is, this study explores whether the presence in parliament of a bloc of women supported by and belonging to a feminist organisation helped raise the salience of issues identified as significant by women in the community as well as by the organisation itself. The use of gender-inclusive language was also analysed for these parliaments.

Origins and attitudes of EMILY's List

Feminists within the Australian Labor Party had campaigned energetically from the 1970s to make the party less of a male bastion and more woman-friendly. The results of a voluntary affirmative action policy adopted in 1981 had been patchy and in 1994 the party adopted a new target that women should be 35 per cent of all those representing Labor in winnable seats by 2002. This time the sanction of national intervention in pre-selections was to be applied if the target was not achieved.

Meanwhile, the defeat of the federal Labor government in 1996 led to two distinct outcomes, both of which contributed to the creation of EL. On the one hand the proportion of women among federal Labor MPs fell from 13 per cent to 8 per cent, a function of the marginality of their seats. On the other hand an anti-feminist backlash emerged, with prominent

Labor identities blaming feminists and other 'special interests' for the defeat. The new conservative government, which included a significant influx of conservative women MPs, promised to end the era of political correctness and proceeded to impose heavy funding cuts in areas such as the status of women, human rights and child care.

The founding of EL involved a prolonged struggle with the National Executive of the party over issues of control. Those setting up the new organisation, led by former state premier Joan Kirner, argued that EL could never hope to attract financial and other support from women in the community if it were perceived to be under the thumb of the men in the party. The question of whether the National Executive would control the new body was related to the issue of how it fitted into the formal factional structure of the party. While EL aspired to be a non-factional body, the dominant right faction saw it as a tool of the left and largely prevented its members joining. More generally, the need to make commitments on abortion presented difficulties for the Catholic-based right.

Hostility by party power-brokers towards EL was expressed in a number of ways, including a decision in 1997 to create a rival Labor Women's Network under the control of the National Executive.[8] Meanwhile EL had been launched around Australia in 1996 with its independence intact. By 2004 it had around 2,000 members. Although EL is regarded by the Australian Electoral Commission as an 'associated entity' of the ALP in terms of disclosure requirements, its membership is by no means confined to the party. Over 40 per cent of its members are not party members, although some (about 13 per cent) are ex-members. It has a 'corporate' look and draws on a constituency of high-earning feminist women supportive of putting more feminists into parliament as well as on the experience of former parliamentarians.

To become eligible for EL funding, candidates need both to be endorsed Labor candidates and to demonstrate their commitment to women's rights. They have to satisfy an interview panel on issues such as child care, equal pay and abortion. In return for support they are expected to advocate 'EL principles' when elected.

Data from the Australian Candidate Study of 2001 shows a significant difference between the attitudes of EL and other federal women candidates on a range of issues. Not only was there a 20 point difference on the right to choose, but also a 20 point difference in strongly favouring social spending over cuts in taxation, and a 14 per cent difference in believing Aboriginal land rights had not gone 'nearly far enough'. On the central question of equal opportunities for women, EL-supported candidates were almost twice as likely as other women candidates to believe that equal opportunities had not gone 'nearly far enough'.[9] In other words, EL candidates exhibited consistent attitudes towards equal opportunity and the macro-economic policy needed to support it.

Persuading Labor to target women voters

During its first year of operation EL also embarked on research and advocacy on the electoral advantages of targeting women voters and brought over US Democrat pollster Celinda Lake for this purpose. Lake achieved saturation media coverage for a National Press Club address on how President Clinton's re-election had been achieved. Democrat gender gap strategists had found that women voters were more likely than male voters to perceive themselves as economically and socially vulnerable and could be mobilised to vote against the 'small government' policies of the Republicans.

Lake pointed out that the ALP was failing to target those juggling work and family responsibilities and suggested it was the only social democratic party in the Western world to be supported more by men than by women. The Australian Election Study in the 1990s showed a persistent if fluctuating shortfall in female support for Labor of between two and six points. By contrast in New Zealand women were nine points more likely to support Labor than men by the end of the decade. While party research showed that Australian women also placed more importance on government intervention than did men, particularly in areas such as health, unemployment and child care, the ALP had not mobilised support from women on this basis.[10]

EL proceeded to commission gender-gap research for use in the 1998 federal campaign, as it has done for subsequent campaigns.[11] It was particularly pleased with the outcomes of gender-gap research undertaken for a Victorian state election in 2002. As a result of the research the Labor Party's election platform emphasised work–life–family balance and made a number of specific commitments, including the highly popular $1,000 're-entry to the work force' grants to help women with retraining and updating of skills.

Substantive representation of women in parliamentary debate

By April 2004 there were 23 EL supported women in the federal parliament and they constituted 71 per cent of Labor women. The increased presence of women in the federal parliament in the period since 1996, and changing partisan composition, can be seen in Figures 6.1 and 6.2.

To test whether the EL women in the federal parliament made a difference to the substantive representation of Australian women I explored parliamentary debate for the incidence of key terms. The terms analysed here are 'paid maternity leave' and 'domestic violence/violence against women'. These have been major issues for the women's movement and have been selected because of their differing political connotations and constituencies. 'Paid maternity leave' is generally regarded as central to

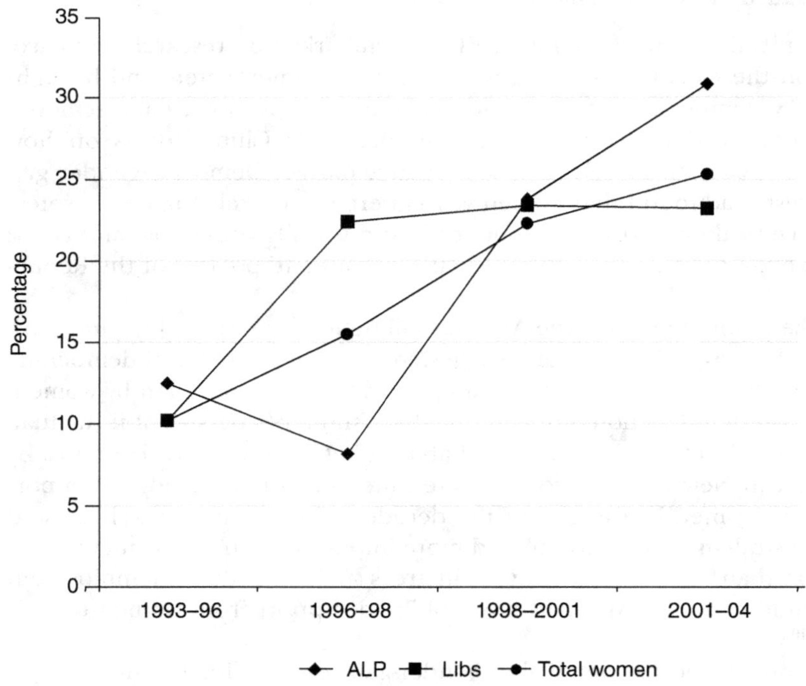

Figure 6.1 Percentage of women members of the House of Representatives.

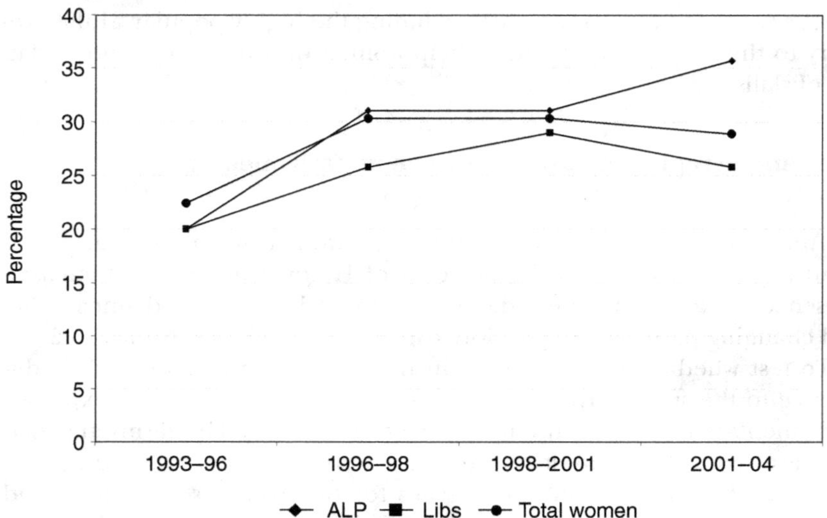

Figure 6.2 Percentage of women in the Senate.

equal opportunity for women, to the combining of work and family and to maternal and infant health. For all these reasons it is the kind of issue we would expect to form part of the 'substantive representation' of women. But it is also a redistributional issue, particularly in the context of a non-contributory social security system such as that in Australia. This means it is less likely to be supported by conservative or free-market politicians. Another possible issue of this type would have been equal pay or pay equity.

The issues of domestic violence and violence against women were also issues put on the public agenda by the women's movement. However they are issues that conservative governments have generally been more comfortable with than directly redistributional issues, in part because of their congruence with law-and-order themes. Hence we might expect that conservative governments wishing to demonstrate credentials in relation to the status of women would place considerable emphasis on this issue area.

Apart from examining the incidence of these substantive issues I decided to explore the use of inclusive language in parliamentary debate, as indicating awareness of the gendered nature of the electorate. Sensitivity to the impact of language and the effects of linguistically erasing women had been strongly promoted by feminists inside and outside government in the 1970s and 1980s. The use of the terms 'woman' or 'women' by politicians appeared to be a useful indicator of awareness of such issues. It could not be assumed that women would be 'represented' in parliamentary debate even at this level.

Paid maternity leave

Australia is one of only two OECD countries that do not provide paid maternity leave on a comprehensive basis and this has been a long-standing issue for the women's movement. When the Whitlam government introduced paid maternity leave for public servants in 1973 it was intended to be the first step in its extension to all women workers. One problem was that, like New Zealand, Australia does not have a contributory social insurance system. Moreover women workers are very unevenly spread across industries and it would have discriminated against employers of women for them to be obliged to pay maternity leave. So unlike other conditions included in industrial awards, such as paid sick leave, it was clear from early on that maternity leave would need to be funded out of general revenue. There never seemed to be a good time to do this, particularly for belt-tightening governments. As an issue it barely featured in parliamentary debate. For example, it was mentioned only once in the thirty-second parliament (1980–83) – by a feminist senator asking how far it had been made available in statutory authorities.

Even when a new Labor government was elected in 1983 and Australia ratified the UN Convention on the Elimination of all Forms of Discrimination against Women (CEDAW), it did so with a reservation on the provision of paid maternity leave. While most public-sector employees had gained access to paid maternity leave, the majority in the private sector had not, particularly lower-paid workers. Organisations such as Women's Electoral Lobby (WEL) and the National Women's Consultative Council continued to raise the issue under the Labor government, but it barely registered on the public agenda.

Instead three months' paid maternity leave was finally included in an 'Accord' negotiated between the Keating Labor government and Australia's peak union body, the Australian Council of Trade Unions (ACTU), before the 1993 federal election. The ACTU president, however, was happy for it to be dropped two years later when budget savings were required, seeing it as an example of 'middle-class welfare'. Instead a much smaller baby bonus was introduced, means-tested on 'family' income. Despite these raised and dashed expectations, paid maternity leave was still barely visible in parliamentary debate (Table 6.1).

The arrival of the first women ACTU presidents in the second half of the 1990s was to change the attitude of the peak union body. Paid maternity leave became more clearly seen as a core industrial issue. The two-year review of the International Labour Organisation (ILO) Convention on Maternity Protection, leading to the adoption of the new Convention 183 in 2000, was also a significant international influence. The new standard included 14 weeks' paid leave and guaranteed right of return with

Table 6.1 Documents mentioning paid maternity leave in the thirty-seventh and thirty-eight Parliaments (1993–98) and the thirty-ninth and fortieth Parliaments (1998–2004[a])

Party	*House*	*AD*	*ALP*	*GRN*	*Lib/CLP*	*NP/Nat*	*Other*	*Total*
Parliament	37/38							
	Senate	4	10	1	1	0	1	17
	HofRep	n.a.	12	n.a.	2	0	0	14
	Total	4	22	1	3	0	1	31
Parliament	39/40							
	Senate	26	50	4	16	0	20[b]	116
	HofRep	n.a.	85	1	15	3	3	107
	Total	26	135	5	31	3	23	223

Notes

AD Australian Democrats, ALP Australian Labor Party, Grn Western Australian Greens and Australian Greens, Lib/CLP Liberal Party of Australia/Country Liberal Party, NP/Nat National Party of Australia/Nationals, HofRep House of Representatives.

a In Tables 6.1–6.3 the record for the fortieth Parliament concludes 23 April 2004, so is incomplete.

b Includes many 'procedural' documents relating to the Democrats' private member's Bill on paid maternity leave.

reduced hours or breaks for breastfeeding. ACTU president Sharan Burrow announced that signing up to the ILO convention and the removal of Australia's reservation to the CEDAW Convention would be priority issues for the union movement.

Paid maternity leave finally began to feature in a substantial way on the parliamentary agenda in the fortieth parliament. This was in part because the Clark Labour government in New Zealand moved on the issue in 2001, leaving Australia as an outrider along with the United States. It should be noted that in New Zealand it was a minor party (the Alliance) that put paid parental leave on the parliamentary agenda. Laila Harré had promoted paid parental leave since her election in 1996 and introduced a private member's Bill on the subject. The Alliance joined the Labour Party in a coalition government in 1999 and Harré introduced paid parental leave legislation as a government minister in 2001.

In Australia it was also a minor party, the Australian Democrats, that played an agenda-setting role. The leader of the Australian Democrats, Senator Natasha Stott Despoja, campaigned on paid maternity leave in the 2001 federal election and introduced a private senator's Bill on the subject the following year. In 2002 the ALP also announced a new commitment to paid maternity leave, although as we shall see it was to be short-lived.

Even more important in terms of the public agenda was the campaign undertaken by the Australian Sex Discrimination Commissioner, Pru Goward. This came as a surprise to many, as Goward was previously known as a close friend and biographer of the Prime Minister and as a conservative appointment to head the federal Office of the Status of Women. After taking up her new position as Sex Discrimination Commissioner in 2001 she turned her considerable media skills to the cause of paid maternity leave. She issued a final report, 'A Time to Value', in December 2002 and took to the airwaves, with strong support from the ACTU and women's organisations. She adopted an effective discursive strategy, focusing on the bodily welfare of women, and physical after-effects of giving birth, to ward off claims of discrimination against men in the work-force.[12] At the Commonwealth/State Ministers' Council on the Status of Women in August 2003, five of the six states and both territories called on the Commonwealth government to introduce paid maternity leave fully funded by the Commonwealth.

The Hansard data clearly show that the issue did not become salient in parliamentary debate until after the 2001 election and the initial catalyst was Stott Despoja's Workplace Relations Amendment (Paid Maternity Leave) Bill 2002. The Bill was investigated by the relevant Senate committee, which provided opportunities for public input from a range of women's organisations and unions as well as employer organisations. The Bill returned to the Senate in March 2004 for second-reading speeches and attracted cross-party support from Labor and Greens, similar to the cross-party support attracted by Harré in New Zealand.

In terms of parliamentary debate, the Australian Democrats, reduced to seven senators in the fortieth Parliament, raised the issue of paid maternity leave at twice the rate as the ALP with their 28 senators. Senator Stott Despoja raised the subject most often (19 times). Apart from her legislative activity she launched a national petition on paid maternity leave, in conjunction with WEL and other women's groups, and followed it up with a postcard campaign.

In terms of attention to the issue Stott Despoja was followed by Labor senator Trish Crossin, who made eight parliamentary interventions on the subject. Senator Crossin was Convenor of the Status of Women Committee of the Parliamentary Labor Party as well as a member of the National Committee of EL. She commissioned her own research on paid maternity leave in 2002 for the use of the Status of Women Committee. The next highest number of interventions (five) was by another EL member, Senator Sue Mackay.

Of the Labor references to paid maternity leave in the Senate, 72 per cent were made by women, although they averaged only 39 per cent of Labor senators in the fortieth parliament. In the House of Representatives 55.5 per cent of the Labor references to the subject were made by women, who constituted 31 per cent of Labor MPs. In the House the debate tended to be dominated by frontbench members, of whom Jenny Macklin, the deputy leader, had the largest number of references (eight). Green parliamentarians, whose numbers rose to three in 2002, took a position similar to the Australian Democrats in seeking at least the ILO standard of paid maternity leave with associated right of return and reduced hours to accommodate breast-feeding.

The issue never became salient for the rural-based National Party, while in general the Liberal-National Party Coalition made only hostile references to the subject. Paid maternity leave was described as a 'one size fits all' statutory solution that ran contrary to the flexible labour market policies favoured by the Coalition, whereby individual workers could negotiate such conditions with employers. Coalition members also said the key issue was choice rather than workplace entitlements, and that paid maternity leave would advantage one group of women over another. The one exception to this hostility was Liberal senator Judith Troeth, who spoke in support of the Sex Discrimination Commissioner's Report, *A Time to Value*.

The Prime Minister maintained his stance that paid maternity leave would discriminate against women in the home. Despite the momentum that had built up for paid maternity leave, in the end both government and opposition abandoned it in favour of a payment for new mothers regardless of their workforce status. As the Sex Discrimination Commissioner pointed out, this was not paid maternity leave in the accepted sense of income replacement for working women for a mandatory period of leave, with associated guarantees of return to work and other conditions. So while the issue had achieved considerable salience, the willingness of the government to depict it as a form of discrimination against women in the home encouraged Labor to abandon it (again).

While EL women undoubtedly played a significant role in the adoption of the policy in 2002, and in ensuring it was prominent in parliamentary debate, they were not able to prevent the dumping of the policy two years later. On the other hand, the issue had achieved enough salience to push a conservative government to commit to a payment of $4,000 (from 2005) to all new mothers.[13]

Domestic violence/violence against women

The second topic used the search terms 'domestic violence' and 'violence against women'. The violence issue illustrates very well the impact of women entering parliament and bringing women's movement discourses with them. Most of the early debate on domestic violence in the federal parliament was contributed by feminist Labor senators who had been active in WEL before entering parliament.

If we go back to the thirty-second parliament (1980–83), the earliest for which an electronic Hansard is available, we find only 12 documents in total (Table 6.2) on violence against women. The issue was barely registering in parliamentary debate, despite women refuge workers being camped

Table 6.2 Documents mentioning domestic violence/violence against women in the thirty-second parliament (1980–83), the thirty-seventh and thirty-eighth Parliaments (1993–98) and the thirty-ninth and fortieth Parliaments (1998–2004a)

Party	*House*	*AD*	*ALP*	*GRN*	*Lib/CLP*	*NP/Nat*	*Other*	*Total*
Parliament	32							
	Senate	0	7	n.a.	2	0	0	9
	HofRep	n.a.	3	n.a.	0	0	n.a.	3
	Total	0	10	0	2	0	0	12
Parliament	37/38							
	Senate	28	62	5	71	7	17	190
	HofRep	n.a.	113	n.a.	81	14	15	223
	Total	28	175	5	152	21	32	413
Parliament	39/40							
	Senate	41	77	16	85	1	41	261
	HofRep	n.a.	158	0	76	12	8	254
	Total	41	235	16	161	13	49	515

Notes

Electronic Hansard dates only from 1981, so some data may be missing from this table.

a Some 46 of these documents relate to the domestic violence clause in the Constitution, i.e. defence against internal threats.

outside Parliament House in protest against the devolution of federal funds for refuges, rape crisis centres and women's health centres to unsympathetic or downright hostile state governments.

Once established on the policy agenda, however, the issue of violence against women tends to attract conservative support. While paid maternity leave is a redistributional issue, likely to be favoured more by parties on the left than on the right of politics, the issue of violence against women can mesh well with conservative law-and-order themes. When conservative governments have been elected in Australia, whether at state, territory or federal level, they have generally changed the priorities of women's units to play down redistributional issues such as equal pay and to refocus on issues such as entrepreneurship. Violence against women has, however, been an issue that conservative governments have in the past been comfortable to maintain as a policy priority. The assumption that violence against women would be an issue with which conservative parties would be relatively comfortable appears to be borne out by the data from Hansard, with Liberal senators raising the issue more often than Labor senators. For most of the time since 1996 the Minister Assisting the Prime Minister for the Status of Women has been located in the Senate, which would affect these figures.

The Howard government significantly raised budget allocations for domestic violence projects, allocating $50 million to 'Partnerships against Domestic Violence' pilot projects. During the fortieth parliament, however, the inroads into conservative politics of the men's rights movement were becoming increasingly evident. The men's rights movement, which was receiving increased operational funding from the federal government, contested all approaches to domestic violence not based on the presumption that women were equally as violent as men. In 2003 a $13 million community awareness and prevention programme called 'No respect, no relationship' was cancelled ten days before it was due to start, after an adverse report from a government committee. Groups such as the Men's Rights Agency had vociferously opposed the portrayal of men as the perpetrators in this advertising.[14] This incident came on top of an earlier decision to divert $10 million from the government's Partnerships against Domestic Violence programme to pay for anti-terrorism fridge magnets telling householders to 'Be alert not alarmed'. These became issues eagerly pursued by Labor frontbenchers, as reflected in the figures for the House of Representatives.

Violence against women is also an issue raised disproportionately by Australian Democrat senators, who have raised the issue twice as often as the Liberals, taking into account relative numbers. Interestingly about half of the Democrat interventions on the subject are made by male senators. Like men representing other post-materialist parties such as the Greens, male Democrat senators have challenged gender norms in a variety of ways. While one male senator was famous for knitting in the chamber during Wool Week, other activities have included wearing the ribbons of Men Against Sexual Assault.

On the whole, the issue of violence against women has risen in salience since 1998, particularly for Labor members of the House of Representatives pursuing government slip-ups. In the Senate, women were responsible for 47 per cent of the Labor references to the subject, while they averaged 35 per cent of Labor senators over the two parliaments. As with paid maternity leave, it is Senator Trish Crossin who raised the issue with the most frequency (nine times), but other EL-supported senators have also played a prominent role. Senators Sue Mackay and Kate Lundy both raised the issue seven times.

Gender-inclusive language

Has the increase in feminist-identified women in the Australian parliament resulted in more gender-inclusive language? Since 1998 the discourse of Coalition (Liberal and National) MPs has actually tended to become less gender-inclusive in both houses, while Labor discourse in the Senate has become more gender-inclusive (Table 6.3). During this period conservative discourse has become more inflected by populist themes of 'governing for the mainstream' and disparaging the claims of elites and special interests (for example, women, Indigenous Australians and ethnic minorities). The same populist pull within the Labor Party has encountered greater resistance.

Under the Coalition government, women's policy machinery within government, intended to analyse gender-specific impacts of policy, has largely been dismantled. There has been an erosion of previous policies directing family assistance to primary carers rather than primary

Table 6.3 Mentions of a woman or women[a] in the thirty-seventh and thirty-eighth Parliaments and the thirty-ninth and fortieth Parliaments

Party	*House*	*AD*	*ALP*	*GRN*	*Lib/CLP*	*NP/Nat*	*Other*	*Total*
Parliament	37/38							
	Senate	425	1,127	115	1,348	135	496	3,646
	HofRep	n.a.	1,664	n.a.	1,346	274	309	3,593
	Total	425	2,791	115	2,694	409	805	7,239
Parliament	39/40							
	Senate	519	1,665	163	1,200	58	390	3,995
	HofRep	n.a.	1,698	17	1,268	205	482	3,670
	Total	519	3,363	180	2,468	263	872	7,665

Note

a Includes many 'procedural' documents relating to the Democrats' private member's Bill on paid maternity leave.

breadwinners and new policies have been promoted to 'strengthen' traditional families. These trends may account for the decreasing inclination on the part of conservative politicians to specify women as the objects of government policy, rather than directing appeals to families or taxpayers. It is not only in Australia that developments of this kind have been taking place in conservative parties. A survey of state legislators in the United States showed that between 1988 and 2001 the proportion of Republican women Representatives who identified themselves as feminist reduced by half.[15]

Conclusion

Can we say that EL has contributed to the substantive representation of women in the Australian parliament as well as to their increased presence? The evidence from parliamentary debate is inconclusive on its own, although it raises a number of interesting questions. The issue of paid maternity leave did take off in the fortieth parliament but its appearance on the parliamentary agenda was due to the initiative of the then leader of the Australian Democrats. Exogenous factors such as the high-profile campaign by the Sex Discrimination Commissioner were also important. EL women pursued the issue energetically, but in the end their party bowed to the populist agenda-setting of the government – that framed paid maternity leave as 'special treatment' for working women.

The issue of violence against women was even more complex, with the Coalition government at first talking up the issue, but with Labor then making the running on government failures. Labor also made commitments to wresting the issue away from the men's rights groups, whose impact was largely responsible for government policy failures. The capacity of women's services for effective advocacy was to be restored with the funding of a new peak body. At the level of the nature of parliamentary language, the increased presence of feminist women on one side of politics was having detectable partisan effects. The increased use of gender-inclusive language by Labor, particularly in the Senate, stood out in the context of the retreat from such gender-inclusive language by the Coalition.

In general Labor women, regardless of whether they are supported by EL, have to contend with historic suspicion of feminism within the party, as well as more recent populist currents and the pervasive demands of factional loyalty. This has led one leading feminist author and former Democrat to describe Labor women as 'political eunuchs' who fail to be outspoken in defence of their sex. She alleges that while EL has been able to exert some pressure on the women it supports, it is not enough to 'galvanise the women once they are elected'[16] (Summers 2003: 214–15). The more recent post-materialist minor parties present fewer obstacles to the articulation of feminist discourse, and as we have seen, this has been true of both women and men, including the two senators who are the only openly gay men in the parliament.

On the other hand, bodies such as EL have an important role in maintaining some form of feminist collectivity. In the federal parliament, EL has worked closely with the Status of Women Committee of the Parliamentary Labor Party in performing this role. Twenty years ago many of the Labor women politicians entering Australian parliaments came straight from a background in the women's movement, most notably WEL. They introduced new discourses into parliament, as we can see from their first speeches. Today new women entering parliament are more likely to come from backgrounds similar to those of their male colleagues, often having legal qualifications and a background in electorate offices or as ministerial staffers. This means that having structures connected with their professional political careers, but providing them with a mandate to work collectively with other women, becomes potentially more important to the articulation of a group perspective.

The Status of Women Committee of the federal Parliamentary Labor Party was established in 1981 and its convenors have worked hard to focus attention on the gender impact of day-to-day public policy issues, whether in government or in opposition. It has been unusual in bringing women together across factional barriers. Its post-budget breakfast briefings in Parliament House, bringing representatives of women's organisations together with Labor women parliamentarians and shadow ministers, have been remarkably successful. Detailed critiques are provided at these events of the gender impact of budget initiatives and other government policy, such as tax cuts in 2004 pitched above the level of women's earnings.

Meanwhile, the role of EL in supporting the increased entry of Labor women to parliament has been duly acknowledged in the first speeches recorded in Hansard:

> I acknowledge the support and solidarity I have experienced from EL. This organisation, formed by strong women with experience in the political system and personified by Joan Kirner, has given many of us practical help when making the decision to be involved, and guidance when taking office, in the system that our sisters organising for suffrage knew was rightfully ours.[17]

Evidence of EL's role in maintaining pressure for the preselection of women candidates also comes from the media. Between February 2000 and 23 April 2004 EL's advocacy activity was written up in 106 press articles captured by Parlinfo. In particular its success in achieving renewed ALP commitment to quotas in 2002 received wide attention.

The role of EL in providing a form of accountability is more difficult, and an issue with which the organisation has been grappling. As we have seen, candidates are interviewed as to their track record and commitments on gender equity before EL endorsement is provided and are reinterviewed prior to endorsement or support for a subsequent term of office. So far, there has not been any dedicated accountability measure for their parliamentary performance. In 2004 a proposal was being developed to have a mid-term review of EL parliamentarians with an instrument for self-assessment of activity and outcomes that would capture some quantitative data for an EL data base.[18]

There is also the 'weak' form of accountability about which Susan J. Carroll has written in the US context.[19] This is provided by regular meetings between EL and its parliamentarians, where progress of parliamentary work on EL issues is discussed. Such contact means continued exposure to group expectations and reminders of feminist values. This is important in the context of competing pressures of constituency, party, faction, government, parliament and personal priorities. It is particularly important in the context of the pull of populist discourse within Australian politics from the 1990s and the shift away from the equal opportunity agendas of the preceding decades.

EL is an adaptation of the separate institution-building long engaged in by feminists to new circumstances – the professionalisation of political careers. In other words, it provides an institutional base for feminism within professionalised party politics. This includes selective benefits for those who can demonstrate a track record and commitment to gender equity, as well as exposure to women-centred policy perspectives and a degree of accountability for performance.

Notes

My thanks to Senator Kate Lundy for providing access to the full client version of Parlinfo, to Janet Wilson and Karen Mow for generous advice, to Peter Brent for editing and to Manon Tremblay and Linda Trimble for helpful comments.

1 For an overview, including the theory of 'critical mass', see Chapter 1 of this volume.
2 For example, Burt *et al.*, Horton and Martin, 'Women in the Ontario New Democratic Government'; Steele, 'The Liberal Women's Caucus'.
3 Carroll, 'Are US Women State Legislators Accountable to Women?'; Weldon, 'Beyond Bodies'.
4 Phillips, *The Politics of Presence*; Sawer, 'The Representation of Women in Australia'.
5 EMILY is an acronym for Early Money Is Like Yeast (it makes the dough rise). The original EMILY's List was established as a fund-raising vehicle for pro-choice Democrat women candidates in the United States in 1985.
6 I decided to conduct the research on the federal parliament because the federal Hansard has been on-line for much longer than those of the state and territory parliaments and has the advantage of a better search engine. A comparable study is yet to be undertaken elsewhere. The parliaments involved are the thirty-seventh and thirty-eighth parliaments of 1993–96 and 1996–98 and the thirty-ninth and fortieth parliaments of 1998–2001 and 2001–04.
7 The original study on which this chapter is based also analysed the incidence of

the term 'unpaid work', a term taken up by organisations representing women in the home as well as by other groups. This part of the study is not included here, for reasons of space.

8 Some of these organisational tensions were defused in 2002 by party reforms that increased internal party democracy.

9 Australian Candidate Study 2001, held in the Australian Social Science Data Archive, Australian National University. My thanks to Ian McAllister for commissioning the runs showing the difference in attitudes between EL and non-EL women candidates.

10 Lawrence, 'The Gender Gap in Political Behaviour', 20–1.

11 This research has been provided at discounted rates of $40,000 for each study.

12 See Curtin, 'Representing the "Interests" of Women in the Paid Maternity Leave Debate'.

13 Labor adopted a similar scheme but proposed means-testing it on 'family' income.

14 *MRA* (Men's Rights Agency) *News*, March 2004. Subsequently the government released a modified campaign with an accompanying hot line. No women's services were permitted to tender for the hot line, despite operating domestic violence referral services in all states and territories.

15 Carroll, 'Are US Women State Legislators Accountable to Women?', 11.

16 Summers, *The End of Equality?*, 214–5.

17 Moore, First Speech, Commonwealth of Australia Parliamentary Debates, Senate, 3805.

18 Interview with Joan Kirner, Canberra, 21 April 2004.

19 See Carroll, 'Are US Women State Legislators Accountable to Women?'

7 When do women count?

Substantive representation of women in Canadian legislatures

Linda Trimble

As Chapter 1 of this book asserts, there are several convincing and compelling reasons to promote women's descriptive representation. Women ought to be represented in numbers roughly proportionate to their presence in the population regardless of how they conduct themselves as public officials or what interests they represent. Yet women are far from realising gender parity in Canada, comprising an average of 20 per cent of the elected representatives in Canada's federal, provincial and territorial legislatures. The percentage of female representatives presently ranges from a low of 10.5 in Nunavut and the North West Territories to 30.4 in Quebec, with their presence in Parliament right at the average.[1] Even if the numbers approached or surpassed 50 per cent, it would be difficult to accept the argument that descriptive representation is good enough representation, for it does not encompass the act of representing or the outcomes of the representative process. While the 'representative should not be thought of as a substitute for those he or she represents',[2] the representative *is* expected to represent something. After all, it is not just women's (racialised and sexualised) bodies that have been excluded from, and remain underrepresented in, legislatures. Women's various experiences, interests, perspectives and policy goals have been marginalised too. Feminist scholars working in this area have broadened the research agenda beyond the question of who the representatives are. Because the deliberations and judgements of legislators matter, we are legitimately interested in what they are thinking, saying and doing.

Is there a causal relationship between descriptive and substantive representation? It is hoped that electing more women will mean more legislators who are willing to articulate women's experiences in public spaces in a manner supportive of policy changes that promote independence and equality for all women. Ideas and interests compete for discursive space in representative political institutions, and we expect representatives to hear, assess and make informed choices among competing ideas. Thus 'women's ideas' (a contestable concept, to be discussed more fully in the next section) should be part of the mix. However, to argue for descriptive representation on the grounds that women will make a difference to outcomes by articulating different ideas is a risky business. If electing more women brings little or nothing in the way of concrete results, or it seems that male and female legislators don't differ very much in their attitudes and behaviours, then what is the case for electing women? If the goal is to represent certain ideas and policy goals, then ideas can, at least in theory, be divorced from bodies.[3] Men can represent policies designed to ameliorate gender-based disadvantage. If representative political deliberations are about representing ideas and interests, the fact that the representatives differ in sexual and social and other characteristics from those whose goals they seek to represent is of little consequence.

While the notion that any*body* can represent any *idea* may be theoretically persuasive, empirical evidence clearly indicates that the interests, needs and policy goals articulated by women and women's organisations have found little purchase in legislatures dominated by men.[4] Maybe men *can* represent women's diverse interests, but with some exceptions, such as extending suffrage to women, aboriginal peoples and racialised minorities, they have tended not to do so. Arguably, male legislators do not represent the interests of all men. Without representation of the needs and perspectives of oppressed and disadvantaged groups in legislatures, 'deliberations and outcomes will most likely reflect the goals of the dominant groups'.[5] Ideas cannot always be divorced from the bodies that speak them. In Phillips's terms, there is no clear dividing line between the politics of presence and the politics of ideas.[6]

Phillips is not, as some characterise her work, articulating a 'theory of presence' whereby the presence of women legislators 'standing for' women means that they will 'act for' women as a group. Rather, she is deeply suspicious of the argument that descriptive representation translates to substantive representation: 'However plausible it is to say that male-dominated assemblies will not adequately address the needs and interests of women, it cannot be claimed with equal confidence that a more balanced legislature will fill this gap.'[7] What Phillips *is* saying is that the presence of women in legislatures *may* enable the articulation of a fuller range of ideas, as well as the introduction of a different style of politics and perhaps even different types of outcomes.[8] Even in the tightly structured, hierarchical and disciplined confines of Westminster-style parliaments there are occasional opportunities for thinking through issues and making decisions somewhat independently of party positions. If what representatives actually say and do is fashioned at least in part by who they are, then the link between identities and interests must be explored.[9] However, the case for gender parity should not be based on quantifiable outcomes. It is dangerous to argue that more, and more diverse, women ought to be elected *because* they will make certain changes and achieve certain goals. As I will argue in this chapter, women cannot be regarded as a unified group with a common set of policy opinions and interests, and the institutional environment tends to work firmly against the sorts of transformations we assume women can and will make.

'Women's interests' and social perspective

Iris Marion Young argues that there are three modes through which a person can be represented: interest, opinion and perspective. *Interests* are those matters that affect the life prospects of individuals. *Opinions* are 'the principles, values and priorities held by a person as these bear on and condition his or her judgement about what policies should be pursued and ends sought'.[10] Since women share neither interests nor opinions these modes of representation will provide at best incomplete and at worst damagingly distorted representations of women's diverse political needs and claims. The very category 'women's interests' has been thoroughly interrogated and deeply contested, as it is laden with essentialist and totalising assumptions.[11] While political interests are gendered, gender is socially constructed and located, differing across class, ethnicity, sexuality and bounded physical locations, among other factors.[12] Because of their intersecting locations, individual women can bear multiple and even conflicting interests and opinions Women's various and even inconsistent experiences, needs and priorities cannot, therefore, be understood as a particular, fixed set of identifiable political goals.

The postmodern proposition that there really are no 'women's interests' *per se* confounds those of us who want to count and measure women's interests as politically articulable and salient. Young's concept of social perspective bridges the impasse, though it is admittedly difficult to operationalise.[13] *Social perspective* captures the 'experience, history and social knowledge' derived from different social positioning and manifested in narratives developed collectively.[14] It does not assume homogeneity of interest or identity or fall into essentialism. Because social perspective 'consists in a set of questions, kinds of experience, and assumptions with which reasoning begins, rather than the conclusions drawn', people who share a social perspective may not agree on interests or opinions but they may find an affinity for the other person's way of describing their experiences and discover common starting points for discussion.[15] For oppressed or disadvantaged social groups, social perspective is particularly important because it does not attribute common interests or opinions to group members.

A social perspective provides a group of people with the latent potential to organise around a common purpose in reaction to the structural constraints or material realities experienced by the group.[16] For example, misogynist comments and a hostile working environment in the Canadian House of Commons prompted female MPs to cross party lines and form the Association of Women Parliamentarians (AWP) in 1990.[17] When Liberal MP Sheila Copps was called a 'slut' during a Commons debate in

1991 the Association sprang into action, and women from all parties, including anti-feminist Reform MP Deb Grey, condemned the remark.[18] While it only lasted as long as the thirty-fourth parliament, the AWP provided a safe and effective way for female parliamentarians to address matters of mutual concern, including the obstacles to women's participation in political life. The group allowed the female MPs to express a similar perspective about the meanings and damaging effects of sexual and gender-based harassment in the House of Commons.

Sharing a social perspective helps people understand each other, but it does not mean they will agree on political opinions, strategies and goals. So what does social perspective provide women politicians in the way of observable representational styles, ideas and activities? According to Young, from 'a particular social perspective a representative asks certain questions, reports certain kinds of experience, recalls a particular line of narrative history or expresses a certain way of regarding the positions of others'.[19] For instance, Sawer's interviews with Australian federal politicians found that female politicians were less likely to adopt Burkean positions concerning the importance of their own judgement to political decision-making, and more likely to stress processes of consultation.[20] Such processes are important to representation of social perspective because an individual legislator can give only a partial account of the group perspective. Representation of social perspective is necessarily relational. The activities and context of representation are important because representatives do not act in isolation from each other; rather their attitudes and behaviours are structured by party opinions, parliamentary processes and institutional norms. Thus social perspective must be seen as situated within complex representational processes. The nature of these processes and their effects on the capacity of individual legislators to speak from their social locations can be revealed in a number of ways, for instance by interviewing female politicians about their views of representation, their interests and opinions, and their representational goals and strategies.[21] As well, content and discourse analyses of legislative debates may reveal the extent to which legislators articulate women's opinions, interests and differently situated identities.[22]

Canadian research shows that most women politicians see their sex as posing unique representational responsibilities. When interviewed about their perceived representational roles in the late 1980s and early 1990s, the majority of women in the Quebec National Assembly and the Canadian House of Commons agreed they held a special mandate to represent women.[23] Yet few of the female MPs Tremblay interviewed in 1994 mentioned gender-based representation when asked a more general question about the meaning of representation.[24] As Lovenduski and Norris note, the validity of self-reported claims is difficult to evaluate.[25] Women politicians may express willingness to represent women without actually acting on gender-based interests or opinions. Indeed, studies conducted in

Canada indicate a weak and heavily mediated relationship between the presence of women in legislatures and the articulation of various women's interests and opinions.

Burt and Lorenzin[26] looked for discussion of 'women's issues', defined as policy areas of concern to or affecting women, such as child care, employment equity and abortion rights, in members' statements and question periods during the first and third sessions of the New Democrat (NDP) government in Ontario (1990–95). A number of factors led Burt and Lorenzin to expect women in the governing party in particular to discuss these types of issues. The Ontario NDP and its leader, Bob Rae, had a clear record of support for feminist policy initiatives; women comprised 22 per cent of the members of the provincial parliament (MPPs), 24 per cent of the government caucus and 40 per cent of the Cabinet; many of the women in the NDP caucus and Cabinet had been active in women's organisations. Members of the governing party were, as predicted, more likely to talk about these issues, but 'in both sessions, with the exception of the Liberal party, women's concerns were voiced primarily by men'.[27] Female MPPs were proportionally more likely to raise these policy matters in their statements and questions, except for women in the governing party during the first session of the Rae government. Cabinet members interviewed for the study explained this finding by saying they refused to let their male colleagues deflect responsibility for these key policy issues by deferring to their female colleagues on 'women's issues'.[28] This study illustrates that male legislators can, and do, articulate some women's interests, and that party can be a better predictor of willingness to raise these types of interests than the sex of the legislator. Similarly, Tremblay and Boivin's[29] analysis of a 1988 debate leading to a free vote on abortion in the House of Commons discovered that while female MPs were more likely than male MPs to adopt a pro-choice stance, party affiliation helped determine opinions on the issue.

Trimble and Tremblay have also examined legislative discussions, in the Alberta legislature and in the House of Commons respectively. Both scholars conceptualised 'women's issues' quite broadly to include a wide range of interests, opinions and policy stances. Tremblay's[30] content analysis of the first session of the thirty-fifth parliament tabulated all indexed references to women, women's themes and issues in all contexts (debates, motions, question period, private members' Bills). Trimble's[31] longitudinal analyses of the Alberta legislature from 1972 to 1995 offer content and discourse analyses of references to women in all debates, questions and motions. For Trimble, any reference to women's experiences, identities, policy issues and opinions in the Alberta Hansard index was counted as representing women.[32] Both scholars found a relationship between the presence of women as legislators and the discussion of women's experiences and policy interests. In the House of Commons, female parliamentarians spoke twice as often as their male colleagues about women's perspectives, but these matters were raised infrequently enough by both sexes for Tremblay to conclude that the effects of female MPs' interventions were 'extremely limited'.[33] Similarly, Trimble noted scant attention to women's perspectives over the 23 year period she studied. While the increased numbers of women, especially opposition party women, in the Alberta legislature did amplify discussion of women in the context of heightened party competition and an electorally vulnerable government, the election of the Klein Conservatives in 1993 shut most of the windows of opportunity for legislative representations of women's interests and opinions.[34] Party affiliation, ideological context and legislative role were found to be at least as influential as the election of more women in Alberta. Overall, analyses of debates in Ontario, Alberta and the House of Commons confirm that the diverse experiences and policy needs of women have hardly been a matter of great concern to legislators, even in the presence of a 'critical mass' of women.[35]

Substantive representation, social perspective and the critical mass hypothesis

These Canadian case studies provide good reason to challenge the utility of the critical mass hypothesis on both conceptual and empirical grounds. First, conceptualising the substantive representation of women as the representation of social perspective provides a theoretical challenge to the critical mass hypothesis. The critical mass schema assumes women's predetermined gender identities are carried with them into legislatures where, if the individuals combine in sufficient number, the identity-based differences can be expressed. However, that social perspective is necessarily a collective endeavour means that individuals cannot represent it *as* individuals. If 'women do not share a set of similar experiences, in what sense do women in office represent women?'[36] Thus measuring the attitudes, opinions and behaviours of individual legislators will not be sufficient to assess the substantive representation of women's social perspectives in legislatures. The additive and cumulative impact of 'more women' will likewise be insufficient to represent social perspective because 'group perspective can be thought of as a puzzle of which each member of the group has a piece'.[37] It is impossible to include all the pieces of the puzzle in any given legislative body.

Trimble's[38] longitudinal study of legislative debates in Alberta supports this point. Discourse analysis of legislative discussions between 1972 and 1995 found that while 'the white, able-bodied, heterosexual woman, in the guise of "generic woman," has at times been represented in the Alberta legislature, most of her real-life sisters have not'.[39] Even during the phase when women MLAs on the opposition benches were most vocal about the politics of gender (1986–93), the vast majority of their questions, statements and speeches illustrated a view of women as undifferentiated; that is, unmarked by class, ethnicity, sexual orientation, citizenship status or disability. Of the 2,600 remarks or speeches made about women during this time period, only 80 (3 per cent) made reference to women's diversity, and half of these were voiced by one New Democrat MLA, a woman who had been active in various feminist organisations before her election win.[40] Theoretical and empirical literature alike indicates we cannot expect a few women, or even a 'critical mass' of women, to stand for all women, given the complex, overlapping, sometimes contradictory and often internally contested nature of their identities, needs, strategies and goals.

The second challenge to the critical mass hypothesis is that empirical evidence does not support it. What we know about women in legislatures, even where they are elected in numbers close to gender parity, is that their impact is more subtle, indirect and gradual than the term 'critical mass' implies.[41] As well, change can occur even below the 10 per cent threshold. Women legislators have been able to make modest changes to legislative style, discourse and policy outcomes by engaging in critical acts even when they are not part of a critical mass.[42] Trimble[43] found this to be the case in the Alberta legislature, where during the 1970s and 80s women comprised between 3 per cent and 16 per cent of the legislators, and most of the (rare and sporadic) discussions of policy matters concerning women were dominated by male MLAs. The ideological and partisan opportunity structure was incredibly hostile to the articulation of women's perspectives prior to 1986, yet women in the governing Conservative Party caucus did use safe discursive spaces, such as debates on motions that had no chance of reaching a vote, to mention the policy needs of rural women, low-income women and battered women.[44] The election of a handful of women to the opposition benches in 1986 and 1989 brought the total proportion of women to only 12 per cent and 16 per cent respectively. Discourse analysis of the debates found that the entry of a few opposition women had a discernible impact on both the content and the style of legislative discussions.[45] For instance, female members of the opposition parties co-operated during question period by following up on each other's lines of questioning, complimenting women in Cabinet for pursuing certain issues, and even sending each other notes of encouragement across party lines.[46] Female representatives have, therefore, voiced gender-based discursive styles and feminist opinions even in skewed groups. Clearly the ideological and procedural context plays a large part in shaping women's behaviour in legislatures.

This suggests a third problem with the critical mass hypothesis: it decontextualises the relationship between numbers and impact. The critical mass approach implies that once women reach the requisite threshold of 15, or 20, or 30 per cent, they can begin to stimulate the chain reaction leading to more woman-friendly processes and outcomes. It is not clear exactly why the increasing proportion of women should have an effect on parliamentary norms and processes.[47] Critical mass theory places undue responsibility on the shoulders of female legislators. If nothing happens, or if there are few discernible changes, then the women are seen to be in dereliction of their representational duties when in fact the explanation may lie elsewhere. As Childs notes, 'because critical mass simply counts the numbers of biological males and females present it fails to acknowledge the importance of party differences'.[48] Moreover the critical mass hypothesis does not account for the possibility of a backlash or negative reaction to the increased proportion of women with the potential to negate the impact of their greater numbers.[49] Canadian studies show that the institutional, partisan and ideological milieu within which female legislators work is largely determinative of their actions.

Westminster-style parliaments can in theory provide opportunities for the types of autonomous discourse and decision-making practices that allow women's diverse interests and opinions to count for something.[50] But in Canada legislative procedures are very tightly controlled.[51] With the exception of the legislatures in the Northwest Territories and Nunavut, where parties structure neither the electoral nor the legislative systems, Canadian federal and provincial legislatures feature very strong party discipline. There are few free votes, and a firm party line is maintained, especially for the governing party, thus it is not possible to evaluate a representative's commitment to articulating women's various interests based on her voting record. Tremblay notes that private members' Bills, private members' notices of motion and MPs' statements allow some escape from the confines of party discipline but these rhetorical strategies may be considered to have little substance and negligible impact on the activities of the House.[52]

For example, committee work offers MPs and MLAs opportunities for voice and influence on matters of particular concern to them, but party discipline remains paramount, especially for members of the governing party. Failure to follow the party line in committee votes can result in sanctions such as the member's removal from the committee. In Alberta opposition members are banned from standing policy committees, thus have no opportunity so shape legislation as it works its way through the parliamentary process. Still, committees do on rare occasions present strategic opportunities for the substantive representation of women because they can facilitate collective deliberations by holding hearings and/or inviting interested parties to offer views on policy matters. Lisa Young has documented the example of the subcommittee on the status of women, formed in 1989 by the House of Commons Standing Committee on Health and Welfare, Social Affairs, Seniors and the Status of Women. Cross-party co-operation of women from three parties on the subcommittee facilitated concentration of committee efforts on issues of violence against women and health care, and prompted new policy initiatives, including firearms regulation, sexual assault legislation and breast cancer screening protocols.[53]

Canadian women MPs perceive the norms and practices of the parliamentary system as significant obstacles to the substantive representation of women. The MPs interviewed by Tremblay in 1994 identified the following types of structural barriers: parliamentary rules and procedures; party discipline and ideology; informal conventions like the importance of seniority and networking within the context of the 'old boy's network'; and performative values such as long hours and a frenetic pace.[54] On the other hand, MPs identified both formal and informal means of representing women's interests and opinions, including group-based strategies such as women's caucuses, parliamentary committees, solidarity among political women, and women's machinery within the civil service.[55] In general, the strict party discipline evident in Canadian legislatures means that opportunities for voicing interests are controlled by the parliamentary parties and how they choose to define, organise and position themselves.

Institutionalised masculinity in parliamentary spaces

I have argued that Young's[56] notion of social perspective should guide investigations of the substantive representation of women in legislatures. Social perspective is necessarily fluid, plural and mediated by a wide range of intersecting identities, opinions and interests; 'individuals should be understood as positioned in social group structures rather than having their identity determined by them'.[57] Social perspective is neither fixed nor pre-political; it can be reinforced, refashioned or even called into consciousness by social and institutional organisations and practices. Likewise, ethno-racial perspectives are historically variable, socially constructed and shaped by political struggles.[58] The representation of social perspective cannot be disentangled from the act of representation itself or from the representational context, both of which play a role in constructing social and political understandings of gender, ethnicity, sexuality, etc. Young sees representation as 'a *differentiated relationship* among political actors engaged in a process extending over space and time'.[59] The nature of the relationship between political actors, and between actors and their institutional environment, must, therefore, be explored.

Representation of social perspective calls for a plural process, requiring, in Yeatman's words, a 'complexity of dialogue that arises between subjects who understand themselves to be complexly like and different from each other'.[60] In legislatures there are few opportunities for elected women to get together and deliberate as a group. That many aspects of the representative role are profoundly isolating is not surprising given the hierarchically organised and tightly controlled nature of parliamentary activities. Moreover, the very meanings, practices and assumptions of the formal political realm have been developed and consolidated through the exclusion of women and other groups. The memoirs of Canadian women politicians relate their discomfort and sense of alienation in the institutional environment, remarking in particular on the masculine and warlike symbols and rituals of Parliament.[61] Indeed, journalist Sydney Sharpe labelled the House of Commons a 'testosterone tabernacle'.[62] The institutionalised masculinity of Canada's legislatures is nicely illustrated by a 5 May 2004 article in the *Edmonton Journal* entitled 'Duelling MPs take it outside'.[63] It tells the tale of two antagonists, Liberal Treasury Board president Reg Alcock, 'a towering man', and Conservative MP Peter MacKay, 'a trim middleweight', who 'stepped out of the Commons on Tuesday to settle a heated debate *like men*' (emphasis mine). But, to the implied disappointment of the journalist, the altercation did not 'come to blows'. As Puwar notes, 'these are not scripts that can be read by anyone'.[64]

Women's bodies are highly visible in male-dominated legislatures, and the female self is intensely scrutinised and even mocked.[65] In their memoirs and in interviews women politicians recount stories about gender-based harassment, much of it focusing on their bodies (clothes, weight, hair, even bra size) and sexuality.[66] It is important to grapple with the fact that Westminster-style parliaments remain very difficult places for women and other 'othered' persons to work. To be marked as an interloper from the moment one enters the chamber must have profound effects on the psyche of the legislator and on the representative relationships she undertakes both inside and outside the House. Indeed, Alberta New Democrat MLA Marie Laing, who served from 1986 to 1993 and persistently spoke about women's experiences and policy demands from a feminist perspective, recalled often feeling emotionally battered when she left the chamber.[67] It is not difficult to find evidence of the sexist, hostile and even physically dangerous nature of Canadian legislatures. According to an Angus Reid/CBC survey of 102 female legislators across Canada conducted in 1997, the vast majority (81 per cent) characterised politics as an 'old boys' club', more than half (60 per cent) had been subjected to inappropriate or demeaning gender-based remarks, and 31 per cent reported unwanted sexual advances.[68] The Canadian MPs interviewed by Tremblay in 1994 also pointed to the 'old boys' network' in Parliament as a barrier to women's full participation.[69]

Political institutions such as parties and legislatures replicate gendered meanings such as the sexual division of labour, meanings that can be reinforced or contested. Ladies' clubs or auxiliaries in the Liberal and Conservative parties created to provide support to men in the mainstream party organisation were transformed in the 1970s and early 1980s into women's organisations interested in promoting women's power and influence within party structures and hierarchies.[70] Similarly, the social construction of gender is evidenced when women are assigned to 'nurturing' portfolios in Cabinet or to committees dealing with stereotypically 'feminine' policy issues such as health and child care. These assumptions and practices can limit the capacity of female legislators to voice women's interests and opinions when what they want to say is interpreted as falling outside women's experiential boundaries or epistemological frameworks. On the other hand, the sexual division of labour in parliamentary structures can create opportunities for social perspective to be reflected in the representational relationship. The subcommittee on the status of women in the House of Commons, discussed above, offers a good illustration of Sawer's contention that women parliamentarians 'tend to feel more "at home" in more intimate forums such as provided by parliamentary committees'.[71]

Women's caucuses within party caucuses also provide opportunities for articulation of social perspective because of their collective and deliberative nature. Almost 60 per cent of the female MPs interviewed by Tremblay in 1994, all of whom were Liberals, identified the women's caucus as an important official avenue for representing women.[72] Jackie Steele's work provides a rare glimpse into the workings of the federal Liberal Women's Caucus, founded in 1993.[73] On the basis of a questionnaire, interviews with caucus members and attendance of caucus meetings over a five-month period in 2001, Steele determined that the weekly meetings provide a personal support network for the regular attendees, many of whom find the parliamentary environment stressful, unwelcoming and unduly competitive. The caucus also lobbies for gender parity in the distribution of parliamentary positions, promotes party measures to nominate and elect more women, works to raise awareness among the larger Liberal caucus of a wide variety of policy issues affecting women and introduces a feminist perspective on policy development. Unfortunately, women's caucuses are rare and, when they do exist, can have this sort of policy impact only when they are organised within (receptive) governing parties.

Given the masculinist, partisan, hierarchical and regimented nature of parliamentary politics, why should we expect the admission of a few more women into the club to change a socially constructed, historically constituted and deeply embedded set of gendered norms and practices? Such change is unlikely without fundamental alterations to the institutions themselves. Yet politics practised in the presence of women and other formerly excluded groups can be a different kind of politics. According to Puwar, women and racialised minority representatives disrupt the taken-for-granted world of parliamentary politics simply by being out of place in this milieu.[74] In an institutional context originally designed to keep them out, their presence is profoundly disorienting to the traditional power-holders.[75] Also, overtly sexist behaviour can call a gendered perspective into consciousness for individual legislators and can prompt representatives to join forces across party lines, to challenge aggressive and mean-spirited types of behaviour, and to model a more consensual discursive style. Yeatman argues that all 'forms of self-advocacy, in contesting the established representational dynamics of reciprocal recognition of selves, change the ways in which the . . . participants understand themselves'.[76]

Conclusion: substantive representation as process and relationship

It is important to insist on gender parity in legislatures. Given that descriptive representation is a marker of justice, political equality, and the democratic legitimacy of electoral and deliberative political institutions, its parameters must be extended to make a case for the political representation of more diverse women. However, the case for the entry of more, and more diverse, women into Canada's parliament and legislatures should not be based on their ability to represent 'women's interests', defined as women's difference from men, feminist opinions or particular policy goals. There is no single will, or set of interests, of the category 'woman' that can be intelligibly represented. The social construction of gender situates women within patriarchal norms and practices but does not necessarily lead women to share opinions, agree on political strategies or wish for a particular set of policy outcomes. Thus individual legislators do not and cannot embody the experiences, needs and often complex identities of the entire group of women, nor should they be expected to do so.

Young's concept of social perspective provides a holistic way of viewing the substantive representation of women in legislatures because it encompasses women's diversity and rejects false assumptions of homogeneity of interest. Social perspective cannot be represented by individual legislators speaking for themselves and/or whatever constellation of interests they embrace; articulation of social perspective requires collective processes, meaningful deliberations and fully developed relationships between legislators and between representatives and constituents. Conceptualising the act of representation as a complex and differentiated relationship among plural actors allows the representation of social perspective because it 'dissolves the paradox of how one person can stand for the experience and opinions of many'.[77] Moreover, seeing representation as a series of situated and highly contextualised relationships brings institutional norms and processes into focus, revealing the gendered structures and assumptions shaping legislative behaviour and calling the causal relationship between numbers and impact (the critical mass hypothesis) into question. Because social perspective is neither fixed nor pre-political, its articulation and development are conditioned by the shifting institutional context. Future research on the substantive representation of women should, therefore, examine the collective practices that might allow politically marginalised social perspectives to be voiced and debated both inside and outside parliamentary spaces.

Notes

1 See Still Counting at http://stillcounting.athabascau.ca.
2 Young, *Inclusion and Democracy*, 133.
3 Phillips, *The Politics of Presence*, 6.

4 Phillips, *The Politics of Presence*, 15.
5 Young, *Justice and the Politics of Difference*, 184.
6 Phillips, *The Politics of Presence*, 24–5.
7 Phillips, *The Politics of Presence*, 71.
8 Phillips, *The Politics of Presence*, 43, 78.
9 Trimble and Tremblay, 'Women Politicians in Canada's Parliament and Legislatures, 1917–2000', 40.
10 Young, *Inclusion and Democracy*, 135.
11 See Butler, *Gender Trouble*; Spelman, *Inessential Women*; Young, *Justice and the Politics of Difference*; Young, 'Gender as Seriality'.
12 Towns, 'Understanding the Effects of Larger Ratios of Women in National Legislatures', 5.
13 See Young, *Inclusion and Democracy*; Young, 'Gender as Seriality'.
14 Young, *Inclusion and Democracy*, 136.
15 Young, *Inclusion and Democracy*, 137.
16 See Young, 'Gender as Seriality'.
17 Young, 'Fulfilling the Mandate of Difference', 92–3.
18 Trimble and Arscott, *Still Counting*, 118–9.
19 Young, *Inclusion and Democracy*, 140.
20 Sawer, 'Representing Trees, Acres, Voters and Non-voters', 40.
21 See Childs, 'A Feminised Style of Politics?'; Tremblay, 'Women's Representational Role in Australia and Canada'.
22 See Grey, 'Does Size Matter?'; Tremblay, 'Do Female MPs Substantively Represent Women?'; Trimble, 'A Few Good Women'; Trimble, 'Feminist Politics in the Alberta Legislature, 1972–1994'; Trimble, 'Who's Represented?'
23 See Tremblay, 'Quand les femmes se distinguent'; Tremblay, 'Women's Representational Role in Australia and Canada'.
24 Tremblay, 'Women's Representational Role in Australia and Canada', 224.
25 Lovenduski and Norris, 'Westminster Women', 91.
26 See Burt and Lorenzin, 'Taking the Women's Movement to Queen's Park'.
27 Burt and Lorenzin, 'Taking the Women's Movement to Queen's Park', 213.
28 Burt and Lorenzin, 'Taking the Women's Movement to Queen's Park', 212.
29 See Tremblay and Boivin, 'La question de l'avortement au Parlement canadien'.
30 See Tremblay, 'Do Female MPs Substantively Represent Women?'
31 See Trimble, 'A Few Good Women'; Trimble, 'Feminist Politics in the Alberta Legislature, 1972–1994'; Trimble, 'Who's Represented?'
32 Trimble, 'A Few Good Women', 115–18.
33 Tremblay, 'Do Female MPs Substantively Represent Women?', 457.
34 See Trimble, 'Feminist Politics in the Alberta Legislature, 1972–1994'; Trimble, 'Who's Represented?'
35 Trimble and Arscott, *Still Counting*, 139.
36 Weldon, 'Beyond Bodies', 1155.
37 Weldon, 'Beyond Bodies', 1156.
38 See Trimble, 'Who's Represented?'
39 Trimble, 'Who's Represented?', 258.
40 Trimble, 'Who's Represented?', 272–3.
41 See Childs, 'A Feminised Style of Politics?'; Grey, 'Does Size Matter?'; Towns, 'Understanding the Effects of Larger Ratios of Women in National Legislatures'.
42 See Dahlerup, 'From a Small to a Large Minority'.
43 See Trimble, 'A Few Good Women'.
44 Trimble, 'A Few Good Women', 98–9.
45 See Trimble, 'A Few Good Women'; Trimble, 'Feminist Politics in the Alberta Legislature, 1972–1994'.

46 Trimble, 'Feminist Politics in the Alberta Legislature, 1972–1994', 146.
47 Grey, 'Does Size Matter?', 19.
48 Childs, 'A Feminised Style of Politics?', 5.
49 See Yoder, 'Rethinking Tokenism'.
50 See Phillips, *The Politics of Presence.*
51 Trimble and Arscott, *Still Counting*, 132–38.
52 Tremblay, 'Do Female MPs Substantively Represent Women?', 442.
53 Young, 'Fulfilling the Mandate of Difference', 93–8.
54 Tremblay, 'Women's Representational Role in Australia and Canada', 228–9.
55 Tremblay, 'Women's Representational Role in Australia and Canada', 232.
56 See Young, *Inclusion and Democracy.*
57 Young, *Inclusion and Democracy*, 136.
58 Ship, 'Problematizing Ethnicity and Race"in Feminist Scholarship on Women and Politics', 329.
59 Young, *Inclusion and Democracy*, 123.
60 Yeatman, 'Voice and Representation in the Politics of Difference', 241.
61 Trimble and Arscott, *Still Counting*, 113–5.
62 Sharpe, *The Gilded Ghetto*, 34–52.
63 Edmonton Journal, A7.
64 Puwar, 'Thinking about Making a Difference', 75.
65 Puwar, 'Thinking about Making a Difference', 76.
66 Trimble and Arscott, *Still Counting*, 117–20.
67 Trimble and Arscott, *Still Counting*, 120.
68 Trimble and Arscott, *Still Counting*, 112.
69 Tremblay, 'Women's Representational Role in Australia and Canada', 229.
70 Bashevkin, *Toeing the Line*, 114–32.
71 Sawer, 'Parliamentary Representation of Women', 370.
72 Tremblay, 'Women's Representational Role in Australia and Canada', 232.
73 See Steele, *An Effective Player in the Parliamentary Process.*
74 Puwar, 'Thinking About Making a Difference', 66.
75 Puwar, 'Thinking About Making a Difference', 71–2.
76 Yeatman, 'Voice and Representation in the Politics of Difference', 243.
77 Young, *Inclusion and Democracy*, 127–8.

8 The 'new world'?

The substantive representation of women in New Zealand

Sandra Grey

> Since winning the vote in 1893, New Zealand women have made slow but steady progress along the pathway to power, so much so, they're now running the country.
>
> New Zealand's Prime Minister; the Leader of the Opposition; a third of Cabinet; the Chief Justice of the High Court; the Governor-General and the CEO of the country's largest company are all women. The Maori Chief is a Queen. Even the nation's macho rugby reputation is under threat with the success of the All Black Ferns, New Zealand's world champion female football team.
>
> So what does this New World look like? How has the feminine touch transformed New Zealand society and are the women proving to be any better than men?[1]

There is an expectation expressed in the media that politics in New Zealand is substantively different at the start of the twenty-first century because the nation's legislature is under the leadership and 'control' of women. This claim is not unique to New Zealand, neither is it new. The belief that the presence of women in legislatures will make politics a kinder and gentler place has been the subject of a growing amount of research. There has also been growing interest in whether female MPs substantively represent women – will female politicians 'act for women' once elected? How different is this 'New World' being ushered in by the women of the New Zealand parliament?

An analysis of parliamentary debates on the topics of parental leave and pay equity over the past 15 years shows that gender identity has been important to many women in the New Zealand House of Representatives. Women politicians have been more likely to note the importance of gender identity than their male colleagues and this overt recognition of identity impacts upon the way they discuss 'women-centred' legislation. But the increased presence of women in New Zealand national politics to almost a third of the legislature, and their positions at the top of this domain, have not automatically guaranteed strong representation on behalf of women. Both institutional structures and the processes of political debate have constrained the substantive representation of New Zealand women by female politicians. In particular, increased diversity in the New Zealand House of Representatives over the past decade as regards political parties, ethnicity and political ideologies has complicated the 'strategic essentialism' that had in past provided a base for women-centred political claims.

The politics of presence and substantive representation

The belief that women politicians will have a substantive effect on political decision-making has its origins in debates about the 'politics of presence'.[2] It has been argued that it is not just that women politicians are 'standing as' women but also 'acting for' women as a group once elected.[3] As Melissa Williams puts it:

> The representative who is capable of acting as an advocate for women's interest must have some understanding of the ways in which the lives of her constituents are shaped by the privilege of men, and the most effective starting-point for that knowledge is the fact of her own experience of exclusion and subordination.[4]

New Zealand women politicians themselves have noted the importance of gender identity. For example, in an interview in 1999 former MP Deborah Morris stated: 'I have witnessed some very good, strong advocacy coming from some women in the New Zealand parliament ... because they are women they are able to do much more justice to some of these issues.'[5] And during debates on parental tax credits MP Christine Fletcher noted:

> I think the fact that we are debating this is a measure of the success of MMP. A lot of people would criticise it, but there is a greater number of women in Parliament, and that allows us – as we approach the new millennium – to finally begin to debate some of the issues, which I see as the hard issues.[6]

What political theory and women politicians are asserting is that women speak in a 'different voice' and we should therefore expect women in decision-making to change the political landscape and political decisions.[7]

The expectation that female MPs will represent women in political debates and decision-making is not without problems. As Drude Dahlerup noted, women politicians are caught between two conflicting expectations. They have to prove they are just like male politicians and that they will make a difference when elected.[8] Even without this double bind there are problems if women politicians are seen to represent only 'women's interests' (or perhaps more accurately 'feminist interests'). For example, New Zealand Prime Minister Helen Clark noted of her first political campaign in 1981: 'It was a difficult campaign.... If you elect Helen Clark, my political opponents said, she's for abortion and your whole society will change overnight.'[9] The substantive representation of women is further complicated, as women are by no means a coherent group, with cross-cutting identity characteristics affecting their worldviews, including age, class, and ethnicity. Despite these concerns, it is important to ascertain whether women have a 'voice' in the national legislature and whether this 'voice' comes via female MPs.

Research into the substantive representation of women in politics has focused on the changes in the culture of the legislature[10] and on the political outcomes.[11] The way politicians vote in national legislatures is often presented as the ultimate act of representing women (and other constituencies). It is implied that female politicians committed to substantively representing women will vote in favour of policies advancing the autonomy of women. However, New Zealand's system of parliamentary rule is based on the 'democratic party' model of government. In this model the essential role of political parties is acknowledged and MPs are elected primarily as representatives expected either to support or oppose the party or parties that are in power.[12] The centrality of political parties in parliamentary systems hinders the ability of women politicians to express their support of 'women's issues' in the form of a vote. Where party constraints on backbench MPs are common, legislative votes are a limited and too strict test of political effectiveness.[13]

One way to sidestep the effects of political party influence during legislative votes is to look at conscience issues.[14] However, few issues debated in the New Zealand parliament are decided by conscience votes. And given that the formal political structures of New Zealand acknowledge political parties, it is important to gauge the interaction of gender and party membership in shaping the political representation of women.

Another way to investigate the substantive impact of female MPs in national legislatures is to look for a gender gap in the values and beliefs of politicians. Numerous studies have provided evidence that on issues particularly close to women (such as abortion, child care and equality debates) female MPs will hold substantially different views from their male colleagues.[15] While it is important to discuss politicians' motivations, surveys gauge the subjective attitudes of MPs rather than objective behaviour within the bounds of legislative assemblies. As Joni Lovenduski and Pippa Norris note in their study of the 'politics of presence' in Great Britain:

> without independent verification, self-reported claims expressed during interviews that women politicians will prioritise women's interest and concerns more than men cannot be accepted at face value, any more than we would accept without demonstrable evidence any claims that Labour MPs speak for and defend the interest of the poor, or that Conservative MPs represent the business community.[16]

This chapter focuses on changes in political discourses in order to gauge the substantive representation of women in the New Zealand House of Representatives. A discourse analysis of parliamentary debates will be used to provide demonstrable evidence of the substantive representation of women in the New Zealand House of Representatives (or the lack thereof). Investigations into the language used in debating chamber will indicate the extent to which MPs are prepared to represent and advocate for women during parliamentary debates. Given that political and governmental processes are substantively linguistic processes there is a clear general rationale for using the resources of language and discourse analysis in researching politics and government.[17] However, the analysis goes beyond exploration of the content of speeches to look at the political and social context of debates and to investigate the interplay between politicians, the institutions in which they work and the broader society they are elected to represent.

Discourse analysis does have its limitations. Actors in Westminster-style parliaments are bound by standing orders (written rules) and by unwritten conventions. Also much of the activity of MPs is performed outside the debating chamber, in parliamentary committees, in their geographical constituencies, in the community. However, a discourse analysis does provide a window into the political realm.

The discourse analysis carried out in this chapter focuses on parliamentary debates held on two issues over the last 15 years: paid parental leave and the question of pay equity in the labour force. Since 1989 the topic of paid parental leave has come before the New Zealand House of Representatives three times: in 1998 when Alliance MP Laila Harré put forward a private member's Bill; in 1999 during discussions of tax credits for parents; and then in 2002 when paid parental leave legislation was passed. The second set of speeches selected focus on attempts to legislate for equal employment opportunities or pay equity, including: the debates on the Employment Equity Act 1990; the 1990 debates of the Employment Equity Bill No. 2; the discussions of the Employment Opportunity Bill 1990; and the section of the Human Rights Amendment debates in 2002 to establish the role of Equal Employment Opportunities Commissioner.

As the interest of this chapter was to gauge whether female politicians substantively represent women in the New Zealand House of Representatives, two questions were asked of each of the speeches analysed:

- How do speakers represent themselves and their roles in Parliament?
- How do speakers represent women and their roles in society?

As has been discussed, literature on a politics of presence expects women MPs to more readily speak 'for women' and to advance 'women-friendly' discourses than their male colleagues. Following Lovenduski and

Norris, I looked for a process of politicisation in which (1) women are recognised as a social category, that is, the gender neutrality of politics is contested; (2) the inequalities of power between the sexes are acknowledged; (3) policies to increase the autonomy of women are made.[18] In all 205 individual speeches on the topics of parental leave and pay equity were analysed to establish how politicians represented themselves in parliamentary debates and whether they asserted that they are 'acting for' New Zealand women.

New Zealand's changing political institutions

New Zealand provides a good testing ground for investigating the substantive representation of women in politics due to a number of distinctive features. The first is the relatively high number of women in the legislature since the late 1980s (see Figure 8.1). The high number of women in the New Zealand House of Representatives makes it possible to investigate whether substantive representation by women politicians hinges on the number of women in the House or the achievement of a 'critical mass'. The critical mass hypothesis comes out of the work of Rosabeth Moss Kanter, who presented a typology outlining the impact of groups upon organisational culture. Kanter's typology sets out four group types: *uniform* groups which have only one significant social group and its culture dominates the organisation; the *skewed* group, where the minority constitute a maximum of 15 per cent and are 'tokens'; the *tilted* group, in which the minority has between 15 per cent and 40 per cent membership and is 'becoming strong enough to begin to influence the culture of the group'; and the *balanced* group with ratios of 60:40 or 50:50.[19] From these figures one in particular has taken hold in investigations into the impact of critical mass on substantive representation of women, and that is 30 per cent.[20] This figure has even moved into the world of international politics, with the UN Economic and Social Council endorsing 30 per cent as the target for women's representation in national legislatures.[21]

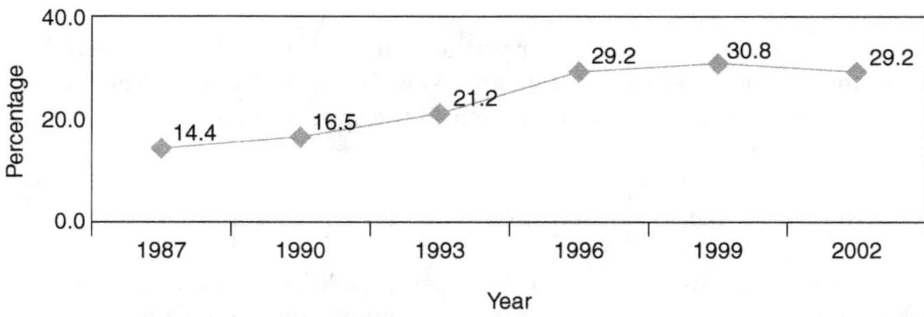

Figure 8.1 Women in the New Zealand parliament, 1987–2002.

There have been a number of challenges to the critical mass hypothesis in which researchers have looked to alternative concepts to explain how and when women politicians bring about substantive change in legislatures. Drude Dahlerup argued for the need to look for 'critical acts' as the basis for women politicians making a difference in politics.[22] Sarah Childs has argued that it is more useful, when conceptualising the relationship between women's presence and women making a difference, to think of different kinds of women acting in different gendered environments and to explore whether particular political contexts are 'safe' for women to act like (and for) women.[23] This chapter will explore whether numbers alter the willingness and ability of female MPs to represent women in New Zealand politics, or whether other factors intersect with the ratio of women and men in the debating chamber in order to encourage female MPs to 'act for women'.

It is not just the number of women in the House of Representatives that makes New Zealand a good case study for investigating substantive representation. New Zealand provides an opportunity to test whether the proportion of women in the executive of a government aids the advancement of women's issues, as Cabinet proportions in New Zealand have been at or above 30 per cent since the 1999 election (see Figure 8.2).

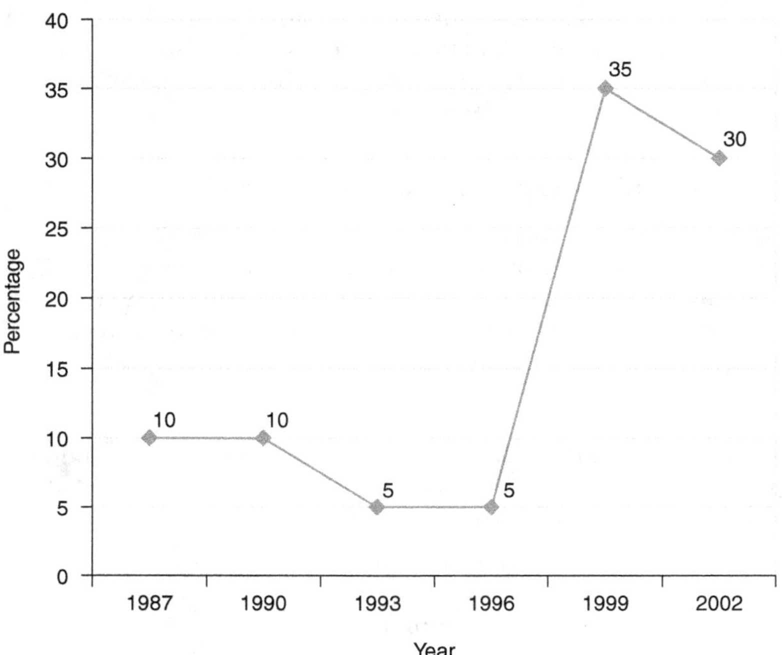

Figure 8.2 Women in the New Zealand Cabinet, 1987–2002.

The time frame used in this chapter also provides the opportunity to examine the effect that government leadership has on substantive representation by New Zealand's female politicians. The parliamentary debates analysed can be blocked into three broad time frames according to which political party/parties were in power at the time. The first time frame looks at debates that took place in 1989 and 1990 when the Labour Party was in government. The next time frame covers 1990 to 1999 with the focus on debates that took place under National rule (first National on its own, then from 1996 when the National Party formed ruling coalitions with various other political parties). Finally, the analysis centres on debates under a Labour-led coalition government from 1999 to 2002 inclusive.

Further analysis of the impact of institutional structures on the substantive representation by women politicians is possible in New Zealand owing to the change in electoral systems in 1996 from first-past-the-post (FPP) to mixed-member-proportional (MMP) representation.[24] Since the move to MMP, New Zealand's governments have been formed through coalition between one of the major parties and a minor party (or parties). The change in electoral systems and subsequent government formation makes it possible to investigate the effect that electoral systems and patterns of government formation have on the willingness and ability of women politicians to 'act for women'.

Before moving to discuss conditions that aid (or hinder) the substantive representation of women in the New Zealand House of Representatives, it is necessary to gauge whether gender advocacy is occurring. Do women politicians in New Zealand assert that they are speaking 'as a woman' or that they would 'act for women' as a group?

'Acting for women' in the New Zealand legislature

In the seven debates analysed, 'gender' was a more significant issue for New Zealand women politicians than for their male counterparts. Only four of the 91 speeches made by male MPs contained claims that they were 'representing men' or 'speaking as a man'. In contrast in the 114 speeches made by women politicians, female MPs overtly speak of their own gender in 35 of those speeches.

> *Ann Batten* (*Independent*). As a woman, and as one who for a number of years has supported paid parental leave, I did not feel that tax credit supported all women adequately.[25]

> *Anne Tolley* (*National*). I have to say that, as a woman and a mother, I was delighted and grateful to see that recognition so widely spread amongst a wide range of the community.[26]

Women politicians from both left- and right-leaning political parties made speeches in which they claimed to speak 'as a woman' or 'on behalf of women', though women of the left make more gendered claims than their conservative colleagues. In three of the seven parliamentary debates analysed it was only women of left-leaning political parties that referred to the importance of gender. The higher rate of gender recognition among left-leaning women is likely to be due to the links that some left-wing women politicians had with feminist organisations in New Zealand. This is in line with the assertions of Donley Studlar and Ian McAllister that substantive representation by female politicians requires an increase in feminist attitudes in the legislature.[27]

While the focus of the chapter is on whether female MPs 'act for women', the discourse analysis highlighted that a number of allegiances were discussed in parliamentary speeches. For example, politicians claimed that they represented geographical constituencies, asserted they spoke on behalf of the poor, and claimed they were protectors of democratic processes. But the allegiance most frequently noted by MPs was to their link to political parties, with 60 per cent of the 205 speeches analysed containing a partisan reference. For example, the allegiance to party was seen in speeches by ACT's Owen Jennings, National's Ruth Richardson and Labour's Margaret Shields:

> I wish to take a short call on behalf of the ACT party on the Parental Leave and Employment Protection (Paid Parental Leave) Amendment Bill...[28]
>
> I am proud to be a member of a party that has such an excellent record in dealing with discrimination against women. The National Party stands for the economic advancement of women.[29]
>
> The Labour Government has a record of which it is justly proud. Women can recognise the advances made.[30]

For the most part, male and female politicians were equally likely to note their allegiance to party during the speeches analysed. Though references to a political party in a speech did not preclude a politician making claims about gender representation (or other identities) with many politicians noting several allegiances within a single speech. For example, during the Employment Equity Bill debates National MP Katherine O'Regan discusses both her allegiance to her party and to women:

> We [National] would give workers more say in their choice of employment and union relationships.
>
> We [women] not only try to produce children for the next generation, but we also try to contribute to the productivity of the land in an economic sense.[31]

Evidence of the multiple allegiances of politicians in parliamentary speeches highlights the complex and competing roles of politicians in Westminster parliaments. As well as speaking 'as a woman' or 'for women' in the New Zealand House of Representatives, female politicians presented women-centred arguments more often than their male counterparts. For example, New Zealand's female MPs frequently noted that women were a group with unique needs; claimed that greater choice was needed for women; asserted that responses to policy problems are gendered; or argued that government needed to actively help women attain equity in society.

> *Sue Kedgley* (*Green*). If men gave birth to babies, paid parental leave would have been introduced into New Zealand decades ago.[32]
>
> *Margaret Shields* (*Labour*). It is a milestone for women and a milestone for the Government.[33]
>
> *Anne Collins* (*National*). First, the Bill asks employers to stop discriminating against women, the disabled, and ethnic minorities.[34]

More women, more feminist advocacy?

Given that the discourse analysis provides evidence that gender was a significant issue for New Zealand's female politicians, it seems natural to assert that the rise in the number of women in the New Zealand House of Representatives will lead to an increase in 'women-friendly' speeches and policy. In an earlier study of the impact of a critical mass in New Zealand politics, I found evidence of increased feminisation of the political agenda at a time when the number of women in the New Zealand parliament reached 14.4 per cent.[35] Similarly Sue Thomas notes that in the US congress, women are more likely to introduce and pass distinctive legislation in situations in which they find support. That support can mean increased numbers or where women's caucuses exist.[36] And in a study of the European Parliament, Jane Freedman states that MEP's were certain that the 30 per cent membership of women within the Parliament helped ensure women's rights issues were put on to the political agenda.[37]

An analysis of the debates around paid parental leave and equity Bills in New Zealand showed that the claims of substantive representation of women were at their height in the 1990s, when women held 16.5 per cent of the seats in the debating chamber. At this time 80 per cent of the speeches made by women MPs contained claims about gender representation. In contrast, during the paid parental leave debates of 2001 and 2002 – when women occupied almost a third of the seats in the New Zealand parliament – mentions of gender by women politicians were found in only 22.7 per cent of the speeches analysed. The analysis confirms that numbers on their own do not increase the overt recognition of gender by women politicians, nor do they lead to an increase in the number of times women politicians claim they are 'acting for women' in parliamentary debates. A number of cross-cutting factors influence the ability of women politicians to 'act for women' in the New Zealand House of Representatives. In particular, institutional structures influenced the substantive representation of New Zealand women by female politicians. Linda Trimble found a similar result in a study of Canadian politics where legislative discourses were seen to be shaped by larger political and societal factors, not just the number of women in a legislative assembly.[38]

New Zealand's political parties and gender representation

As has already been noted, political party affiliations impacted upon the substantive representation by women politicians in New Zealand, with left-leaning politicians more likely to note their own gender during parliamentary speeches or claim to speak 'on behalf of women'. Ideologies linked to the political parties in the New Zealand House of Representatives also affected the way female MPs talked about women in society. In the debates analysed, women politicians on the left of the political spectrum were twice as likely as female MPs from right-leaning parties to discuss women as a collective or group. This result seems unsurprising given the importance of party allegiance to New Zealand politicians and the underlying philosophies of the enduring major parties in the House of Representatives. The Labour Party has traditionally been aligned with social democratic principles and with New Zealand's labour unions (although this relationship was strained in the 1980s when the fourth Labour government pursued neo-liberal reforms of the economy and state sector). The National Party is, on the other hand, historically associated with liberal ideals and with the business and farming sectors. And as National MP (and former Prime Minister) Jenny Shipley noted during the debate of the Human Rights Amendment Bill in 2001: 'we [National] do not believe in collectivism.'[39]

This division across the political spectrum leads to the expectation that there will be more women-friendly claims and assertions in the debating chamber when left-leaning parties are in power. However, when the debates analysed were divided according to which major political party was in government, an interesting disjunction is found between the actions of the Labour Party and the voices of its women MPs. While in government from 2000 Labour's female politicians made fewer overt references to their own gender and to the needs of women than were made when the party was in opposition between 1990 and 1999.

Despite the drop in overt claims to represented women after 2000, over the last 20 years the advancement of women-friendly policy outcomes has occurred predominantly when the Labour Party is in government. It was a Labour government that passed the Employment Equity Act in 1990 and a

Table 8.1 Representations of gender in selected parliamentary debates, New Zealand House of Representatives, 1989–2002

Government	*Sex of MPs*	*No. of speeches analysed*	*No. of speeches analysed (% of speeches)*		*All statements advancing women's position*
			claiming to represent women	*advancing women-friendly policy*	
Labour 1989–90	Female	25	11 (44)	16 (64)	27
	Male	14	0 (0)	1 (7.1)	1
	All	39	11 (28.2)	17 (43)	28
National-led coalition 1990–99	Female	42	17 (40.5)	28 (66.7)	45
	Male	26	0 (0)	11 (42.3)	11
	All	68	17 (25)	39 (57.4)	56
Labour-led coalition 2000–02	Female	47	7 (15)	19 (38.3)	26
	Male	51	4 (7.8)	5 (9.8)	9
	All	98	11 (11.2)	24 (24.5)	35

Note
In total 205 'speeches' were analysed.

Labour–Alliance coalition that put in place paid parental leave in 2002 and the establishment of an Equal Employment Commissioner. In contrast, a National government repealed the 1990 equity legislation shortly after being elected that same year. Two further Bills relating to the position of women in employment were debated under National-led coalition government, the Employment Equity Bill (No. 2) and the Equal Employment Bill, but neither made it through the full parliamentary process. And the first attempt to bring in paid parental leave into New Zealand faltered under a National-led coalition.

While the acceptance of women-friendly legislation has been more likely under a Labour government than a National government, there is a caveat on the adoption of the Paid Parental Leave Act in 2002. It is unlikely that the paid parental leave legislation (which was unpopular with the New Zealand business sector) would have made it on to the books as quickly as it did if it had not been for the Alliance presence in the Cabinet. The passage of this legislation confirms expectations that MMP will provide an opportunity for small parties to influence governments.[40]

The need to garner electoral support appears to be one factor that impacted upon the substantive representation of women in politics. In 1989 and 1990, when Labour politicians were actively debating for the rights of women in the House of Representatives, the party was seeking to improve its electoral position and reinvent itself after leading six years of neo-liberal reforms that had impacted harshly on women.[41] The need to regain electoral support from women voters may explain the Labour Party's moves to pursue the Employment Equity Act at this time. Certainly other parties noted the Labour attempt to woo women voters.

> *Ruth Richardson* (*National*). The Bill should be seen for what it is – crude electoral politics – and I find it astounding that women Government members should so devalue the feminist currency by peddling crude politics rather than engaging in strategies that will work.[42]

While the Labour Party in 1990 was lagging in the polls, Labour-led coalitions between 1999 and early 2003 had very comfortable positions in the polls. The high poll ratings for Labour over these four years may have made it unnecessary for women members to continually assert their role as representatives of New Zealand women.

New Zealand's political structures and substantive representation

While the ideologies and the partisan structure of New Zealand politics help in part to explain the ebb and flow of substantive representation of women in the New Zealand parliament, not all the changes centred on party politics. Another structural factor that has impacted upon the overt claims of substantive representation of women has been the change in the electoral system and the subsequent change in the composition of the debating chamber. The change from FPP to MMP for the 1996 election resulted in a substantial rise in the women in the House (as can be seen in Figure 8.1). The effect of MMP on the number of women in the house has been noted by politicians in the New Zealand House of Representatives. For example, during the 2001 Paid Parental Leave Act debates Alliance MP Liz Gordon noted:

> I was going to start by celebrating MMP and saying how great it was that MMP had brought more women into the House, and that in particular in this instance it has brought in the Hon. Laila Harre, who is herself the mother of young children.[43]

While the increased number of female MPs on its own has not changed the substantive representation of women in New Zealand parliamentary debates, the change in the composition of the parliament after MMP has impacted on parliamentary debates and claims by women politicians that they were 'acting for women'. The analysis of the debates that had occurred under FPP showed how these were dominated by adversarial speeches from MPs from the two major parties, National and Labour. In the post-MMP environment there has been a rise in the number of small parties in the New Zealand parliament and this has meant that debates (while still adversarial) include a greater range of voices. The height of the claims about party allegiances came during the 1989 and 1990 debates on employment equity, when 80 per cent of the politicians' speeches contained references to party. The lowest number of statements about party allegiance came in 1998 and 1999 during the term of the first coalition government elected under MMP. The discourse analysis shows that post-MMP there were fewer speeches in which politicians overtly mention their own party.

Along with the increased representation of minor parties, MMP has also brought with it a rise in lobbying from MPs actively claiming to represent a wide range of constituencies, such as Maori, Pacific Island communities, other ethnic groups, the queer community, and a conservative 'traditional family' lobby. As had been noted earlier, politicians often claim multiple allegiances during political debates, for example as a Labour woman MP representing Pacific communities. Gender and other identities are not mutually exclusive. However, the diversity in voices found in the New Zealand House of Representatives post-1996 and the broad range of group issues raised by the diverse range of politicians in the legislature may have acted to drown out any united voice for women-friendly legislation. Female MPs may choose to represent a minority ethnic group rather than women during a parliamentary debate. For example, National MP Pansy Wong is best known for her advocacy on behalf of Asian minorities. And, Labour MP Winnie Laban (New Zealand's first Pacific Island woman in Parliament) has been seen as a strong advocate for Pacific Island communities and Pacific women.

The impact of diversity in the post-MMP environment was found in the way politicians discuss women as a group. The analysis of debates carried out under the FPP electoral system included twelve speeches where politicians present women as a diverse group. In the 2002 debates analysed, 34 speeches by women MPs included discussion of the diversity of women and divisions between groups of women. For example, National MP Anne Tolley noted this diversity in the debates around paid parental leave in 2002:

> Women are involved in the workplace in a wholly diverse range of ways. The Minister has not recognised that, and it shows through this legislation that she has no concept of how women work in the workplace.[44]

The rise in diversity (of political parties, ethnic and other identities) in the New Zealand debating chamber occurs at a time when the claims by female MPs that they were speaking 'for women' or advocating for 'women's needs' dropped substantially (see Table 8.2).

Another impact of the changing composition of the New Zealand House of Representatives is an increase in 'conservative' MPs (including conservative women politicians). The conservatism was evident in the 2002 Paid Parental Leave Bill debates, when a number of politicians made clear their dislike of both homosexual parents and single parents.

> *Peter Brown* (*New Zealand First*). New Zealand First generally believes that the bill should apply only to the natural parents of a child – not adopted parents, not same-sex parents, not to anybody but the natural

Table 8.2 Representations of gender in selected parliamentary debates, New Zealand House of Representatives, 1989–2002

Party	*MPs*	*No. of speeches analysed*	*(% of speeches)*		*All statements advancing women's position*
			claiming to represent women	*advancing women-friendly policy*	
FPP (1989–96)	Female	38	16 (42.1)	27 (71.1)	43
	Male	22	0 (0)	3 (13.6)	3
	All	60	16 (26.6)	30 (50)	46
MMP (1996–2002)	Female	76	19 (25)	27 (35.5)	46
	Male	69	4 (5.8)	12 (17.4)	16
	All	145	23 (15.8)	39 (26.9)	62

> parents of a child. That is our view. If it were left to me, I would go one step further and have it apply only to married couples, but I do not believe that the House would support me on that.[45]
>
> *Dr Lynda Scott* (*National*). [supporting a suggestion from New Zealand First that paid parental leave go only to married people] . . . I think that is excellent. Statistics show that one of the biggest causes of poverty in New Zealand today is single parents. It has become that way.[46]

Such claims are just one indication of the 'unfriendly' discursive terrain faced by female MPs seeking to advance the autonomy of women in the New Zealand House of Representatives.

Further evidence of the impact of the discursive terrain on overt claims about the representation of women is found in New Zealand parliamentary debates. As has been noted, women in the Labour Party were strong advocates for women in the 1980s and 1990s, but this advocacy waned in the early twenty-first century. A drop in the overt discussion of substantive representation of women in 2001 and 2002 correlates with a rise in attacks on feminist agendas and ideas:

> *Lynda Scott* (*National*). Laila Harre is stuck in the feminist ideology of the 1970s, and the language of this bill shows that feminist ideology.... Males have been expunged from this legislation by the politically correct language of the feminists.[47]
>
> *Anne Tolley* (*National*). This bill discriminates quite deliberately against a large number of women. I said at the introduction of this bill into the House that the Minister was stuck with 1970s feminist dogma.[48]
>
> *Bob Simcock* (*National*). That is the sort of politically correct, feminist nonsense that underpins this legislation.[49]

This backlash against feminism in New Zealand parliamentary debates may have made Labour politicians reluctant to make feminist claims and speak 'for women'.

Influences from outside the legislature

The level of substantive representation of women in New Zealand politics has also been influenced by the lack of a visible women's movement in New Zealand. The waning of the overt claims by female politicians that they were 'acting for women' came at a time when there is little evidence in New Zealand of a coherent women's movement, though lots of single-issue groups or service providers have been at work in New Zealand. Feminist Sandra Coney discusses this waning of feminist activity in the 1990s: 'The movement was silent because there is no movement – only isolated groups working on specific issues'.[50]

While the lack of an active feminist movement leaves a void for New Zealand women politicians seeking reinforcement for moves to debate and implement women-friendly legislation, there is evidence that the existence of an active feminist movement in the 1970s and 1980s has impacted directly on national politics. A number of women politicians in the New Zealand House of Representatives have links with women's organisations and the feminist movement of the 1970s and 1980s. Many of these women now lead the Labour Party and have been actively putting in place policies to improve the autonomy of women. Though, as had been noted, this 'feminist' influence has been criticised by right-wing politicians in recent years.

What is seen in New Zealand is how the speeches of politicians in the debating chamber and the policies pursued by governments are impacted upon by populist rhetoric. For women MPs aiming to substantively represent women, a rise in hostility to women's rights both inside and outside Parliament makes overt claims about gender representation difficult to articulate.

Conclusion

The analysis of selected New Zealand parliamentary debates since 1989 provided clear evidence that female MPs have been strong advocates for women and women's issues. New Zealand women have benefited from women-centred decision-making and advocacy owing to the values held by women in the House of Representatives. Left-leaning political parties in particular have advanced women-friendly legislation in New Zealand. However, a number of interrelated factors have impacted upon the willingness and ability of women politicians to 'speak and act for women' in the House of Representatives. The three most significant have been the lack of support outside the House for 'feminist' initiatives, the rise in diversity in the House of Representatives that has overshadowed 'strategic essentialism' in gender representation, and the resurgence of conservatism and a backlash against feminism in the debating chambers of the New Zealand parliament since 2000. Further negative impact on the substantive representation by women politicians is likely in the near future in New Zealand owing to public support for political leaders who decry any form of 'special rights' in society.[51] The popularity of this anti-group rhetoric and the drive for electoral popularity may lead to the avoidance of any overt representation of women as a group.

Notes

1 See Maher, 'New Zealand: Women on Top'.
2 See Phillips, *The Politics of Presence.*
3 See Phillips, *The Politics of Presence*; Lovenduski and Norris, 'Westminster Women'.
4 Williams, 'Memory, History and Membership', 106.

5 Deborah Morris, personal interview, Wellington, 1999.
6 Fletcher, 'Taxation (Parental Tax Credit) Bill', 16695.
7 Henig and Henig, *Women and Political Power*, 106.
8 Dahlerup, 'From a Small to a Large Minority', 279.
9 Clark, 'Helen Clark: Politician', 158.
10 See Childs, 'A Feminised Style of Politics?'; Henig and Henig, *Women and Political Power*; Thomas, 'The Impact of Women in State Legislative Policies'; Grey 'Does Size Matter?'; Lovenduski 'Women and Politics: Minority Representation or Critical Mass?'; Dahlerup, 'From a Small to a Large Minority'.
11 See Lovenduski and Norris, 'Westminster Women'; Thomas and Welch, 'The Impact of Gender on Activities and Priorities of State Legislators'; Grey 'Does Size Matter?'; Norris, 'Women Politicians'; Arscott and Trimble, *In the Presence of Women*; Kathlene, 'Power and Influence in State Legislative Policymaking'.
12 See Mulgan, *Politics in New Zealand*.
13 Lovenduski and Norris, 'Westminster Women', 90.
14 See Broughton 'Gendered Treatment of Ministers in the Australian Federal Parliament'.
15 See Studlar and McAllister, 'Does a Critical Mass Exist?'; Lovenduski and Norris, 'Westminster Women'; Norris, 'Women Politicians'; Reingold, 'Concepts of Representation among Female and Male State Legislators'.
16 Lovenduski and Norris, 'Westminster Women'. 97.
17 Fairclough, 'Discourse, Social Theory, and Social Research', 167.
18 Lovenduski and Norris, 'Westminster Women', 88.
19 Kanter, 'Some Effects of Proportions on Group Life', 966–7.
20 See Grey 'Does Size Matter?'; Studlar and McAllister, 'Does a Critical Mass Exist?'; Lovenduski, 'Women and Politics: Minority Representation or Critical Mass?'; Dahlerup, 'From a Small to a Large Minority'.
21 For discussions of this target endorsed by the UN' Economic and Social Council see the FWCW Platform for Action, www.un.org/womenwatch/daw/beijing/platform/decision.htm, and Themes for progress on gender, www.un.org/ecosocdev/geninfo/afrec/vol12no1/eca2.htm, accessed 31 August 2004.
22 Dahlerup, 'From a Small to a Large Minority', 296.
23 Childs, 'A Feminised Style of Politics?', 14.
24 For more details see McLeay, Chapter 4 in this book; Levine, 'Parliamentary Democracy in New Zealand'.
25 Batten, 'Paid Parental Leave Bill', 18995.
26 Tolley, 'Parental Leave and Employment Protection (Paid Parental Leave) Amendment Bill', 15439.
27 Studlar and McAllister, 'Does a Critical Mass Exist?', 248.
28 Jennings, 'Parental Leave and Employment Protection (Paid Parental Leave) Amendment Bill', 15250.
29 Richardson, 'Employment Equity Bill', 14341.
30 Shields, 'Employment Equity Bill', 3538.
31 O'Regan, 'Employment Equity Bill', 2078.
32 Kedgley, 'Parental Leave and Employment Protection (Paid Parental Leave) Amendment Bill', 13902.
33 Shields, 'Employment Equity Bill', 14340.
34 Collins, 'Employment Equity Bill', 2824.
35 See Grey, 'Does Size Matter?'.
36 Thomas, 'The Impact of Women in State Legislative Policies', 974.
37 Freedman, 'Women in the European Parliament', 186.
38 See Trimble, 'A Few Good Women'.
39 Shipley, 'Human Rights Amendment Act', 12996.

40 Boston *et al.*, *New Zealand under MMP*, 31; Vowles, 'Introducing Proportional Representation', 692.
41 For more on neo-liberal effects on women and other minorities see Kelsey, *The New Zealand Experiment;* Julian, 'Women: How Significant a Force?'.
42 Richardson, 'Employment Equity Bill', 2832.
43 Gordon, 'Parental Leave and Employment Protection Amendment Bill', 13901.
44 Tolley, 'Parental Leave and Employment Protection (Paid Parental Leave) Amendment Bill', 15439.
45 Brown, 'Parental Leave and Employment Protection (Paid Parental Leave) Amendment Bill', 15252.
46 Scott, 'Parental Leave and Employment Protection (Paid Parental Leave) Amendment Bill', 15254.
47 Scott, 'Parental Leave and Employment Protection Amendment Bill', 15443.
48 Tolley, 'Parental Leave and Employment Protection Amendment Bill', 15439.
49 Simcock, 'Parental Leave and Employment Protection Amendment Bill', 15346.
50 Coney, 'Why the Women's Movement Ran out of Steam', 54.
51 See Young, 'Brash drops Women's Affairs Role'; Brash, 'Nationhood: Orewa Speech'.

9 The House turned upside down?

The difference Labour's women MPs made

Sarah Childs

The unprecedented number of women MPs elected to the British House of Commons in 1997 provided an opportunity to examine the long-standing expectation that women would make a difference to Parliament once they were present in significant numbers. In both the 1997 and 2001 parliaments women MPs constituted 18 per cent of all MPs.[1] Yet, as we have seen in Chapter 1, the concept of critical mass has been increasingly questioned, theoretically and empirically. So the story of women's substantive representation by women MPs since 1997 was always likely to be more complicated than a straightforward and direct relationship between women's descriptive and substantive representation.

The focus in this chapter is predominantly on the substantive representation of women by Labour women MPs in the House of Commons.[2] In part, this reflects the imbalance of women's numerical representation in the Commons.[3] The 120 women MPs elected in 1997 comprised 101 Labour women, 13 Conservative, three Liberal Democrat, two Scottish Nationalist Party (SNP) women MPs, along with the Speaker of the House, Betty Boothroyd.[4] In the 2001 Parliament the 118 women MPs comprised 95 Labour, 14 Conservative, five Liberal Democrats and four women MPs from the nationalist parties (the SNP, the Democratic Unionist Party, the Ulster Unionist Party and Sinn Fein).[5] Of the total number of women MPs present in both parliaments Labour's women MPs constituted more than 80 per cent. Within the Labour Party they constituted first 24 per cent and then 23 per cent, making them a bigger minority there than in the House overall.[6]

In the years since 1997 Labour's women MPs have been routinely represented in the British media as having failed women.[7] Expectations that their arrival would turn the House upside down were well and truly dampened as they gained a reputation for loyalty and for putting their own careers before the needs of women.[8] Yet, far from the failures that they have been so regularly depicted as, there is increasing evidence of Labour's women MPs acting for women. Studies that examine their behaviour suggest that Labour's women MPs have not only sought, but have been able on occasions, to make a difference for women. Moreover, through reconsidering the research on the substantive representation of women by Labour's women MPs, this chapter raises questions about the conceptual and analytical frameworks used to understand the impact of women's political presence more generally. In particular, it argues that the concept of critical mass is of limited use.

Critical mass: a problematic basis for the substantive representation of women?

The concept of critical mass relies on two first-order assumptions: first, that women representatives want to act for women and, second, that the percentage of women present is the key determinant of women representatives' behaviour and effects. If the second assumption is reliant on the first – and without it there would no reason to count the numbers of women present – both are problematic.

The contention that women representatives seek the substantive representation of women is too often simply 'read' off from their bodies in a manner that is both essentialist and reductive. This assumption – that women representatives want to act for women – is itself underpinned by two unfortunate elisions: first, between sex and gender, and second, between women's bodies and feminist minds. Unless one is happy to base the substantive representation of women on an essential understanding of women's identity or to reduce women's attitudes and behaviour back to their bodies, gender needs to replace sex as the basis upon which women representatives seek to act for women: in a gendered society, women and men have different experiences that reflect and construct their gender identity.[9] As a consequence, women are more likely than men to be concerned about 'women's concerns' – those 'issues that bear on women' for either 'biological' or 'social' reasons.[10] This concern should then translate into the substantive representation of women as women representatives voice women's concerns and perspectives (women's views on all political matters) when they are present in politics.[11]

At the same time, it is important not to elide women's bodies with feminist minds. Not all women are feminists and neither are all women representatives. Consequently, while women representatives' gendered experiences may result in empathy with women's concerns, this does not mean that they will necessarily view them through feminist spectacles.[12] Whether particular women representatives play down their gender, identify as women and draw on their gendered experiences but not in a feminist way, or identify as women and articulate explicitly feminist positions, needs to be shown.

However, even when women representatives' attitudes towards the substantive representation of women have been established, claims that they will, through acting for women, transform politics remain premised upon two further unsubstantiated assumptions. The first is the contention that representatives' attitudes directly and straightforwardly translate into behaviour. The second is that this behaviour will have a re-gendering (feminising) effect. Both of these claims are by no means certain. How women representatives might effect a feminisation of politics – and what that might mean – requires further consideration. As a number of empirical studies attest, differences that accompany the presence of women representatives have not simply reflected the achievement of a particular percentage of women.[13] Beckwith reminds us that any effect derived from women representatives acting for women might be negative if opponents contest their action.[14] Furthermore, as Dahlerup suggested back in the late 1980s (see Chapter 1) women representatives might be able to make critical acts in the absence of critical mass – a contention that implies that what is important to explore is the conditions under which women representatives are or are not able to make a difference. It may be the case that women's political presence is necessary – even if the precise percentage at which the expected effects will happen remains elusive – but not sufficient to ensure the substantive representation of women.[15]

The assumption that women representatives who want to act for women can do so in a straightforward manner – at least, as long as there are enough of them present – belies the reality of the context within which women representatives act. Yet women representatives act within particular political environments, and within those, inside particular institutions. In any such institution there is likely to be a range of spaces where representatives act and activities in which they engage. It should not be surprising that representatives who face the 'same institutional norms and expectations and share the same status' are more likely than not to act in similar ways.[16] But what if women do not experience or perceive their presence in the same way as their male colleagues? Furthermore, any constraints might be expected to vary between different spaces within a political institution or in respect of different political activities.

Identities other than gender are also likely to influence the behaviour of women representatives. In situations where party identity is strong, if not predominant (such as in Westminster political systems), the space for women representatives to act other than in line with their party is likely to be much reduced.[17] In such environments it does not seem reasonable to presume that gender identity will trump party identity. At the same time, it might be the case that party identity functions as a constraint, to a lesser or greater extent, in respect of the variety of parliamentary activities that representatives engage in within a particular political institution.[18]

As gendered institutions, political institutions are also likely to constrain women, as indirect discrimination and sexism act to police women representatives' behaviour.[19] For newly elected women representatives, especially if they arrive as a relatively large cohort, being new may similarly function as a constraint. It can take time to learn how to act effectively and gain confidence in institutions.[20] It also takes time to be recruited into government or parliamentary structures.[21]

An appreciation of the different roles and positions that representatives within their political and parliamentary institutions have is also necessary. Some women representatives may remain on the back benches, others will be promoted into government or into parliamentary structures, such as committees. A failure to identify the different positions from which women representatives act may lead to an under-appreciation of women representatives' lack of opportunity or position to act for women. Alternatively, it might miss the spaces that do exist for women representatives in parliamentary or governmental positions to voice women's concerns.[22]

Analysis of women's substantive representation of women must go beyond looking at the individual or collective actions of women representatives. Treating women representatives – whether they are members of the government or ordinary representatives – as discrete individuals seeking to act for women in isolation may be to misrepresent the networks within which women representatives, just like any other representatives, act. Furthermore, institutional mechanisms (gender machinery) may constitute an alternative or (if supported by women representatives) compounding means through which the substantive representation of women occurs.[23]

The likelihood of women representatives acting for women appears, then, to be dependent upon a multiplicity of factors that may enhance or constrain the opportunities they have to translate their attitudinal predisposition into corresponding behaviour. This being the case, a simple counting of the number of women present in the House of Commons is unlikely to tell us very much about the difference Labour's women MPs might make. A more useful approach would be to examine the opportunities and constraints faced by the women MPs when they sought to act for women in Parliament.

So what difference did they make?

That Labour's women MPs in the 1997 and 2001 parliaments would seek to act for women, and do so in a feminist fashion, was likely: findings from surveys of MPs and candidates' attitudes suggest a clear potential. The 2001 British Representation Study is only the latest in a series of surveys that find sex differences in respect of women's concerns.[24] Women are 'more likely to take a pro-woman line' than the men.[25] Interestingly, gender gaps in respect of women's concerns go 'beyond party'.[26] On the scale measuring 'liberal' gender equality (support for equal opportunities, family and work roles and women's suitability for public office) women Conservative politicians were 'slightly more positive than male Labour politicians'.[27]

Data from qualitative interviews with Labour's new women MPs undertaken in 1997 also establishes that many wanted to act for women, with some 40 per cent seeing 'representing women' as part of what they understood as representation; nearly a third discussing their sense of shared affinity with women; and a similar proportion talking explicitly about the positive way in which they interpreted the responsibility to act for women.[28] The MPs considered that they could and would act for women because of shared gendered experiences. They perceived 'common themes which touch upon the lives of many, if not most women' and believed that 'by and large women's experiences of life are different from men's'. Although there was some recognition of women's differences, particularly in respect of ethnicity, the women did not consider that this prevented them from acting for women.[29]

The interview data also suggested that the difference Labour's new women MPs would make would be a feminist one: nearly three-quarters identified themselves as feminists. Most of their understandings of feminism would be considered liberal/equal rights feminism, with the women arguing, for example, that 'women should have choice in their lives' and 'the right to equal pay for work of equal value'.

On first arriving in the House, many of Labour's new women MPs were confident that they would be able to voice women's concerns in Parliament, with half seeing this as the effect of their presence. Three years later they were even more confident. Nearly two-thirds of the MPs argued that they had articulated women's concerns (violence against women, forced marriages, sexual harassment, child care, caring, breast cancer and emergency contraception) in the House. Moreover, not only did half of them now explicitly accept the link between the presence of women and the substantive representation of women, many talked about how they considered women's concerns would not have been raised, or would not have been raised in the same form, in their absence. According to the women themselves, it seemed as if Labour's women MPs had found it easy to articulate women's concerns and perspectives in the House.

The MPs' claims, however, raise two issues. First, the methodological problem of evaluating self-reported claims, and second, the issue of what constitutes evidence of the substantive representation of women. In respect of the former Carroll and Liebowitz rightly suggest that large multi-method research projects that track changes over time (which should reduce the limitation of any single research method or technique) are necessary to prove *tout court* that women representatives act for women.[30] While it is the case that women representatives' attitudes towards the substantive representation of women can quite easily be collected through quantitative surveys and qualitative interviews, acquiring data of representatives' behaviour may be harder.[31] In the House of Commons, analysing MPs' voting in the division lobbies, whilst quite straightforward, suffers from a focus on the 'end game' and not the process. Analysing MPs' behaviour other than voting is less easy. There are particular difficulties gathering behavioural data on parliamentary activity that occurs 'behind the scenes' where representatives' actions and effects are neither observable nor measurable. While it may be possible in some instances to employ surrogate measures these can only be suggestive.

Even with a range of research methods in place, the question of what constitutes proof of the substantive representation of women remains. Are *sex differences* in representatives' behaviour all that counts?[32] While many would agree that observable and measurable sex differences in representatives' behaviour (with women being more concerned with, and acting on, women's concerns) would demonstrate that the presence of women gives rise to women's substantive representation their absence does not necessarily prove the opposite.[33] A lack of sex differences in representatives' behaviour may be caused by a number of factors: it may reflect a convergence in gender roles that is hidden because studies employ sex as a proxy for gender:[34] maybe men and women's attitudes and behaviour have converged as a result of changes in gender roles over time. Alternatively, the very presence of women in politics may cause men to become more concerned with women's concerns, leaving no observable or measurable sex differences in their attitudes or behaviour.[35] In such cases, women are having a feminising effect but not one that is visible. The absence of sex differences may also be an effect of the choice of research method adopted: for example, quantitative methods testing for sex differences might reveal similar behaviour at one level (for example, in how women and men vote in legislatures) but hide differences at another level (in women's and men's levels of support for, or feelings towards, that behaviour, for example).

It is useful to distinguish between the feminisation of the political agenda (where women's concerns and perspectives are articulated) and the feminisation of legislation (where output has been transformed). Operationalising the substantive representation of women in this dual way should help capture the articulation of women's concerns even where this has little or no effect in terms of legislative output. This approach should also address the issue that a focus on the end product of parliamentary politics is likely to miss the difference that women representatives make when they effect a re-gendering at earlier and perhaps less politically charged stages of the political process.[36]

Applying the traditional approach of studying representatives' behaviour to the United Kingdom reveals a behavioural sex difference among Labour's backbench MPs.[37] During the 1997 parliament Labour's newly elected women were less than half as likely to rebel against the party whip as the rest of the Parliamentary Labour Party (PLP); and those that did rebel did so around half as often. Importantly, this difference could not be explained away. It remained after controlling for a range of factors (sex, newness, all-women shortlists, previous political history, ideology, ambition, legislative roles, age, seat marginality, personal characteristics) although the difference was not large enough (or consistent enough) to be statistically significant.[38] This pattern seems to have continued into the

2001 parliament. There was, for example, a sex difference in the voting behaviour of Labour's MPs over Iraq, with Labour's men more likely than its women to rebel against the government.[39]

The finding of a sex difference in Labour MPs' voting, though it demonstrates that the women were acting differently from the men, does not prove that they were, at the same time, acting for women. To establish this would require research that looked at both the content of the legislation and the direction of MPs' voting. At the moment all that can be confidently said is that there is a sex difference. This is an unexpected and intriguing finding in itself, and one that defies easy explanation. As Mackay notes, '[Cowley and Childs' study] ... ended in something of a stalemate, with inconclusive statistical data ... and inoperationalisable claims as to the reasons drawn from qualitative data. . . .'[40] Indeed, it had been expected that all Labour MPs – or at least all the newly elected ones – would experience the same pressure to vote with the government.[41] The women MPs themselves (or, rather, half of them) explain their voting behaviour as a reflection of a women's style of politics – a phenomenon that two-thirds of the interviewed new Labour women MPs subscribe to. Rather than rebelling, the women claim to prefer to act in less 'macho' ways and 'behind the scenes'.[42]

Another explanation for the sex difference in voting behaviour is that Labour's new women felt that they simply could not afford to rebel.[43] Interview data capture the women's perceptions: they felt uncomfortable and alien in the House, experienced pressure to conform to parliamentary norms and perceived that a higher value was placed on the dominant adversarial 'male' style;[44] Puwar uses the terms 'infantilisation', 'super-surveillance' and 'burden of doubt'.[45] Despite appearing to inhabit the same place as their male colleagues, it seems as if, at least in respect of voting, the House of Commons is experienced by many of Labour's new women MPs as a woman-unfriendly space. Although the women MPs' reflections are liable (once again) to criticism for being self-reported claims, some of the women clearly understand their reluctance to rebel in terms of how they experience their presence in the House; they perceived themselves as members of an 'endangered species' constrained in their behaviour.[46]

While voting may be the most visible and, arguably, the most important parliamentary acts it is but one of the activities they engage in. Early Day Motions (EDMs) – parliamentary motions for which there is no debate – provide similar 'hard' behavioural data that can be subjected to quantitative techniques. Long studied as indicators of MPs' attitudes, beliefs and priorities, EDMs provide an opportunity for MPs to signal their concerns and priorities in the House and to garner support from parliamentary colleagues.[47] More important, using EDM signing as a measure of the substantive representation of women has a distinct advantage over voting: signing an EDM takes little effort and has few costs.[48] As a consequence, and unlike voting, EDMs should constitute a 'safe' parliamentary activity in which women MPs who want to act for women should feel free to sign those EDMs they support.

Analysis of the signing of EDMs in the 1997 parliament shows that Labour's women MPs were disproportionately signing 'women's' EDMs – those whose 'primary subject matter' is women and/or their concerns – and especially those motions that were also coded feminist.[49] Moreover, these sex differences are evident despite women's lesser propensity to sign EDMs in general. These are important findings: they constitute a clear example of behavioural differences between women and men MPs, with women acting for women and doing so in a feminist direction.[50] They are also suggestive of how Labour's women MPs might act if other parliamentary activities were as relatively unconstrained as EDMs.[51]

Unfortunately, and although the analysis of EDMs is evidence of Labour's women MPs feminising the political agenda, it cannot tell us whether the women MPs' actions had an effect in terms of the feminisation of legislation. Indeed, critics talk disparagingly of EDMs as parliamentary graffiti.[52] And while it is claimed that well supported EDMs may influence government most seem to disappear without trace.[53]

Case study analysis suggests that a series of three EDMs calling for the removal/reduction of VAT on sanitary products were key to the government's decision to announce a reduction from 17.5 per cent to 5 per cent in VAT on sanitary products in the 2000 budget. In total more than 250 MPs signed at least one of the EDMs, tabled by Chris McCafferty, a Labour woman MP first elected in 1997. In 1999/2000 the sanitary products EDM constituted the sixth most 'signed' EDM of that parliamentary session. While it is the case that both women and men Labour MPs supported the Sanitary Products EDMs there were some sex differences in the levels of their signing: these were significant at the 5 per cent level in 1998/99 ($p = 0.050$ chi-squared), at 10 per cent in 1999/2000 ($p = 0.090$ chi-squared) although not statistically significant in 1997/98.

McCafferty's EDM campaign was clearly successful in putting the issue of reducing VAT on sanitary products on to the parliamentary agenda and in garnering widespread parliamentary support, but was it the *critical* factor in explaining the policy change? While it is the case that there may have been instrumental reasons for the government to reduce the VAT on sanitary products – not least in winning the support of women voters and Labour women MPs – it seems that the Chancellor, Gordon Brown, in addition to accepting the principle that taxing sanitary products at 17.5 per cent was unjust, was reacting to McCafferty's EDM campaign. The story is complicated, however, as the issue had been considered, although rejected, by the Treasury immediately following the 1997 general election. At this time civil service advice was that the Treasury should stick to the orthodoxy of 'flat rates' and 'single bases' of VAT. There were also particular concerns about 'me too' claims: if VAT was reduced on sanitary products, should it be reduced on sun cream, shaving foam, razors and lawnmowers? The issue was therefore put on a back burner. In this context, McCafferty's EDMs kept the issue very much alive within Parliament and made the minister responsible – Dawn Primarolo – determined to reduce the VAT at some future point. More important, in early 2000 an interview McCafferty gave on BBC Radio 4's *Woman's Hour* appears to have been the immediate trigger that translated Brown's general support for a principle into a guaranteed budget policy. A reduction in VAT on sanitary products came into effect in January 2001.

Other case studies would likely produce different accounts of the extent to which women MPs (individually or collectively, as ordinary representatives or members of governments or parliamentary bodies) are crucial in effecting the substantive representation of women. Analysis of a piece of 'women's legislation' passed in the 2001 parliament – the Sex Discrimination (Election Candidates) Act – reveals an 'effective alliance' between women representatives, women ministers and women outside Parliament acting together for women. This legislation, introduced by the government following the decline in the number of women elected to the House of Commons in 2001, allows the use of positive discrimination for the selection of candidates to the House of Commons.[54]

Analysis of the process by which the legislation – heralded by Lovenduski as a 'critical act' – was placed before Parliament suggests that women representatives, women ministers, the Women Ministers and government officials and special advisers in the Women's Unit and Department of Transport, Local Government and the Regions, as well as women's groups and campaigning organisations outside Parliament were all working to get the Bill passed.[55]

Feminists and women MPs had been vocal in pointing out the likelihood that the number of women would decline in the 2001 general election since just after the 1997 election. In January 2000 Harriet Harman MP (more than a year after she had been sacked as Minister for Women) called explicitly for more women MPs and in July that year declared that 'clearly discrimination is going on'.[56] Within government Baroness Jay, the Women's Minister, was a late convert to the necessity of positive discrimination.[57] She was supported by senior civil servants who were experienced Whitehall operators and special advisers with legal backgrounds. From outside Parliament academic research demonstrated that legal change was possible.[58] A range of groups and organisations (Fawcett, EOC, the Fabian Society, the Constitution Unit) undertook research and/or campaigned on this issue.[59] Both the Fawcett and EOC reports recommended that political parties use rhetorical, positive action *and* positive discrimination strategies.[60]

Widely advocated outside Parliament and supported within it by women, the Bill only just made it into the Queen's speech in 2001. Harriet Harman (then Solicitor General) and Hilary Armstrong (chief whip) emphasised that any legislation had to be included so that it would come into effect in time for the elections to the devolved institutions. Patricia Hewitt (later to become Women's Minister) and Stephen Byers (Secretary of State for Transport) had to fight for its inclusion during Cabinet and Blair's support was vital 'to guarantee its inclusion'.[61]

Once brought to the House, all the main parties welcomed the Bill, in no small way a reflection of its permissive rather then prescriptive nature. Yet it was women MPs – of all parties – who took a greater interest in debating the Bill's merits.[62] In the Commons second reading 61 per cent of Labour speakers were women yet they constitute only 23 per cent of the PLP; 63 per cent of the Conservatives were women, compared with their percentage in their parliamentary party of 8 per cent; and 33 per cent of the Liberal Democrats were women, while their percentage in their parliamentary party is 10 per cent. In the Commons third reading, two of the four Labour MPs (50 per cent) and four of the five Conservative MPs (80 per cent) were women, although the lone Liberal Democrat was male.

Reasons for the men's absence from the Commons debates cannot be established on the basis of current research (qualitative content analysis of Hansard debates): it may be that they considered that the Bill, as a piece of 'women's legislation', should be debated by women, for either honourable or dishonourable reasons; alternatively, they may have been too embarrassed to speak out publicly against a Bill that was aimed at securing greater levels of women's numerical representation; or they may have thought that because the Bill was only permissive they should not waste their time, as the real battles would be held later within their parties. But whatever their reasons, the parliamentary debates constitute another clear example of women MPs acting for women. And this time, it is possible to see the role of women in the other parties acting alongside Labour women MPs and for women.

Analysis of the content of MPs' contributions shows that, although women of all parties were acting for women by speaking and (for the most part) supporting the legislation, those MPs (and members of the Lords) who were more likely to favour positive discrimination and who drew on the concept of substantive representation to support the legislation were Labour members (both male and female). In contrast, those MPs who spoke against the legislation who were hostile to positive discrimination and rejected substantive representation were mostly Conservative.[63]

This finding should not be that surprising. Notwithstanding sex differences in MPs' attitudes towards women's concerns found in surveys, the dominance of party divisions in British political life remains likely to inform women's attitudes and behaviour.[64] Interview data from Labour's new women MPs reveals that they recognise the possibility of a shared political agenda among women – a concern for women's concerns – whilst at the same time contending that women MPs' responses to women's concerns will reflect their party political position. As one MP put it: 'It's when you come to the next stage about proposed policy and solutions then

[you] get the divergence', as 'proposed solutions ... probably in the majority of cases, throw up different approaches'.[65] It would be surprising, albeit not impossible, for a woman MP whose party ideology is liberal in economic terms and who subscribes to the idea of meritocracy to advocate positive discrimination in the selection of candidates for Parliament.

Conclusion

With the problems of critical mass increasingly recognised it might be time to give up on this concept. Not only does it fail to provide a theory of why women seek to act for women, it also abstracts women representatives from the context in which they act as if numbers were everything. As this analysis demonstrates, the relationship between the number of women present and the substantive representation of women is far from certain. To be in position to theorise about, or draw conclusions on, women's substantive representation it is necessary both to establish whether women representatives are attitudinally predisposed to act for women (with their attitudes demonstrating concern for women's concerns) and whether they are attitudinally feminist (whether they are predisposed to act for women in a feminist way).[66] Once this is known it is then necessary to locate the women representatives within their wider political environments and their particular political institutions.

Moreover, the choices researchers make in terms of what is studied (attitudes and/or behaviour?) and how it is studied (which method is most suitable to capture what is going on; are sex differences the only proof of women's substantive representation?) will impact on the substantive representation that is 'found'. It might be better to be less sanguine about what any single research paper or project can demonstrate: a complex phenomenon such as the substantive representation of women may be better served by the bringing together of different analyses, exploring different aspects of the substantive representation of women using a variety of methods. Indeed, it is likely that an audit of the effect of particular women representatives – such as Labour's women MPs – will need to map the multiplicity of spaces within which women act, acknowledge the different roles that women representatives may have – as ordinary representatives, as members of a governing party or parliamentary actors – and contextualise them within the networks in which they operate, both within and outside Parliament. Finally, the opportunities and constraints that they face must also be fully examined. The question might then become: when are women representatives able to act for women?

The British parliaments of 1997 and 2001 clearly provided some opportunities for Labour's women MPs to substantively represent women; on occasion they have been able translate their attitudinal predisposition to act for women in feminist ways into behaviour. If the feminisation of the political agenda – the voicing of women's concerns in the House – is evidenced by the signing of Early Day Motions, then the feminisation of legislation/policy can be seen through the case study research.

Advocates of critical mass might interpret these findings as proof that critical mass has been achieved – otherwise how could the women MPs act for women? However, critical mass reveals nothing more than the percentage of women in the House or Labour Party. It hides the nature of the opportunities that the women MPs grasped or created. As the analysis of the Sex Discrimination (Election Candidates) Act and the 2000 budget announcement to reduce VAT on sanitary products revealed, the substantive representation of women in these instances was the result not merely of the actions of women representatives *qua* women representatives, but of backbench women MPs, women ministers, Ministers for Women and women in civil society working together to create opportunities and moments of feminised change. In the case of reducing VAT on sanitary products the links between Chris McCafferty and the responsible woman minister were psychological rather than practical; in respect of the Sex Discrimination (Election Candidates) Act, they were organisational as well as psychological and supported by women's campaigning groups and academic research outside the House.

None the less, both cases, along with the signing of EDMs, are instances when the 'costs' of acting for women were minimal. So, while it can be concluded that given the opportunity Labour's women MPs will act for women, this does not mean that women are able to act for women and effect feminised change when the costs are higher. This qualification aside, critics of Labour's women MPs – and especially those who heaped bile on the new ones – should be convinced that there are, some seven years after their election, sufficient 'snapshots' that capture the substantive representation of women by Labour's women MPs. As one woman minister put it: *So is it women? I think so. Don't you think so?*

Notes

1 Kanter, *Men and Women of the Corporation.* Following the 2005 general election in the United Kingdom, women MPs constitute just under 20 per cent of the House of Commons. See Childs, 'Feminizing British Politics'.

2 While there are survey and interview data looking at constituency representation, there has been no study of the behaviour of women MPs in respect of constituency representation (see Childs, *New Labour's Women MPs*). Norris *et al.*, *Gender and Political Participation,* found a link between the sex of British MPs and women's activism at the constituency level.

3 It also reflects academic focus on the Labour women and the dearth of studies on other parties. Where there is evidence of women in other parties acting for women and/or with the Labour women MPs, even if anecdotal or derived from Labour women MPs' perceptions, this has been included. Indeed, there is case-study evidence of some cross-party women's activity in the Commons (Childs, 'Concepts of Representation and the Passage of the Sex Discrimination

(Election Candidates) Bill'; Childs, 'The Sex Discrimination (Election Candidates) Act 2002 and its Implications').

4 On election the Speaker resigns from their party.

5 There were only four Labour women MPs elected for the first time in 2001 (Lovenduski, 'Women and Politics', 186). In the 2005 Parliament there are 98 Labour women MPs, 17 Conservative, 10 Liberal Democrats, and one each for the Ulster Unionist Party, Democratic Unionist Party and Sinn Fein.

6 Labour women MPs constitute 28 per cent of all Labour MPs in the 2005 Parliament.

7 Childs, *New Labour's Women MPs*.

8 *Guardian*, 15 December 1997; *Observer*, 4 January 1998.

9 Lovenduski writes: 'gender is defined as characteristic of both women and men and is expressed in the differences between the sexes that result from the division of labour between women and men (Lovenduski, 'Women and Politics', 180).

10 Cockburn, 'Strategies for Gender Democracy', 14–15; Lovenduski, 'Gender Politics', 708.

11 Lovenduski, 'Women and Politics', 181.

12 Childs, *New Labour's Women MPs*; Dodson, *The Impact of Women in Congress*; Carroll, *The Impact of Women in Public Office*, xv.

13 Lovenduski and Norris, 'Westminster Women'; Beckwith, 'The Substantive Representation of Women'; Childs, *New Labour's Women MPs*; Carroll, *Women and American Politics*; Carroll, *The Impact of Women in Public Office*; Thomas, 'The Impact of Women in Political Leadership Positions'; Thomas, 'Women and Elective Office'; Grey, 'Does Size Matter?'; Swers, *The Difference Women Make*; Weldon, 'Beyond Bodies'; Studlar and McAllister, 'Does a Critical Mass Exist?'; Dodson, *The Impact of Women in Congress*; Reingold, *Representing Women*; Considine and Deutchman, 'Instituting Gender'.

14 Beckwith, 'The Substantive Representation of Women'.

15 This is not to say that the underrepresentation of women is not problematic. Rather the case for women's presence can be made for reasons other than the substantive representation of women (Phillips, *The Politics of Presence*) although whether the case should be made in terms of the substantive representation of women is debated (Mackay, *Love and Politics*).

16 Reingold, *Representing Women*, 116; Mackay, *Love and Politics*, 98; Carroll, *The Impact of Women in Public Office*, 24.

17 Beckwith, 'The Substantive Representation of Women'.

18 See also Mackay, 'Gender and Political Representation in the UK', 109.

19 Puwar, 'Thinking about Making a Difference'; Dodson, *The Impact of Women in Congress*; Mackay, *Love and Politics*, 97; Considine and Deutchman, 'Instituting Gender'.

20 Lovenduski, 'Women and Politics', 191.

21 Beckwith, 'The Substantive Representation of Women'.

22 Contra Beckwith ('The Substantive Representation of Women'), I argue that when women representatives are elected for the election-winning governing party this can enhance rather than reduce opportunities for the substantive representation of women. This is because some women representatives (either newly elected or, more likely, previously elected) may find themselves promoted into government. As ministers, they may be able to undertake acts 'for women' that as backbenchers or opposition representatives they would simply not be in position to do.

23 Mackay, 'Gender and Political Representation in the UK', 101; Squires and Wickham-Jones, 'New Labour, Gender Mainstreaming and the Women and Equality Unit'; Squires and Wickham-Jones, 'Mainstreaming in Westminster

and Whitehall'. Since 1997 Labour has had in place a Women's Minister (one at Cabinet and one at ministerial level) and a Women's Unit. Both have had an uncertain history – with frequent changes of name (the Unit became the Women and Equality Unit in 2001), structure and location (the Department of Social Security from 1997 to 1998, the Cabinet Office between 1998 and 2002, since then the Department of Trade and Industry) and personnel (Harriet Harman and Joan Ruddock 1997–98, Baroness Jay and Tessa Jowell 1998–2001 and from 2001 Patricia Hewitt with Sally Morgan, Barbara Roche and Jacqui Smith). The appointment of the Woman's Minister (Parliamentary Under-Secretary) following the 2005 general election was also controversial; once again the minister (Meg Munn MP) is not to be paid, just like her predecessor in 1997, Joan Ruddock (*Guardian* 16 May 2005; Childs, *New Labour's Women MPs*, 166). For new Labour women MPs' views on the women's ministers see Childs (*New Labour's Women MPs*) and Squires and Wickham Jones ('New Labour, Gender Mainstreaming and the Women and Equality Unit') for an evaluation of the Women's Unit.

24 Lovenduski and Norris, 'Westminster Women', 94–5; Norris and Lovenduski, 'Women Candidates for Parliament'; Norris and Lovenduski, *Political Recruitment*; Lovenduski, 'Gender Politics'; Lovenduski and Norris, 'Westminster Women'.

25 Norris and Lovenduski, 'Women Candidates for Parliament'; Norris and Lovenduski, *Political Recruitment*; Lovenduski, 'Gender Politics'; Lovenduski and Norris, 'Westminster Women'.

26 Norris, 'Women Politicians'.

27 Lovenduski and Norris, 'Westminster Women', 95. In the absence of recent studies on Conservative women MPs, it is difficult to examine the difference they made in any systematic way.

28 These interviews were qualitative in nature and based on an interview guide. The question of whether the interviewees saw representing women as part of their role as MPs was not directly put to them (Childs, *New Labour's Women MPs*).

29 See Childs (*New Labour's Women MPs*) for a fuller discussion of the women MPs' perceptions of women's differences and the substantive representation of women and compare with Puwar ('Thinking about Making a Difference').

30 Mackay, 'Gender and Political Representation in the UK'; Carroll and Liebowitz, 'New Challenges, New Questions, New Directions'; Swers, *The Difference Women Make*; Dodson, *The Impact of Women in Congress.*

31 This may be dependent upon the different legislatures under study.

32 Lovenduski and Norris, 'Westminster Women'; Reingold, *Representing Women.*

33 Reingold, *Representing Women.*

34 Swers, *The Difference Women Make*, 10.

35 Reingold, *Representing Women*, 50.

36 Tamerius, 'Sex, Gender, and Leadership in the Representation of Women'.

37 Cowley and Childs, 'Too Spineless to Rebel'.

38 Cowley and Childs, 'Too Spineless to Rebel'.

39 www.revolts.co.uk.

40 Mackay, 'Gender and Political Representation in the UK', 112.

41 Cowley, *Revolts and Rebellions*; Reingold, *Representing Women*, 116.

42 Cowley and Childs, 'Too Spineless to Rebel'; Childs, *New Labour's Women MPs.* Unfortunately, such claims, though rich in what they tell us about the women's perceptions and experiences, are self-reported and hence difficult to test. See Shaw ('Language, Gender and Floor Apportionment in Political Debates') for a study that looks at gendered interactions in parliamentary debates.

43 Cowley and Childs, 'Too Spineless to Rebel', 365.

44 Childs, *New Labour's Women MPs*; Puwar, 'Thinking about Making a Difference', 73–6.
45 Puwar, 'Thinking about Making a Difference', 73–6.
46 Even if the women's perceptions were misplaced they acted as if constraints on their behaviour existed. Cowley suggests that largely because they were disproportionately loyal during the 1997 Parliament Labour's new women MPs have been promoted into government at a greater rate than their male colleagues (www.revolts.co.uk): of the 1997 intake still in Parliament in 2001, 62 per cent of the women but only 54 per cent of the new men had been promoted into government (including at the PPS level) by November 2003. Once rebellion is controlled for the sex difference is very small.
47 Berrington, *Backbench Opinion in the House of Commons*; Finer *et al.*, *Backbench Opinion in the House of Commons.*
48 Compare with Dodson's analysis of roll call votes (Dodson, *The Impact of Women in Congress*; Dodson, 'Representing Women's Interests in the US House of Representatives', 147–8) and Swers's analysis of Bill co-sponsorship – a comparable activity to signing EDMs (Swers, *The Difference Women Make*).
49 Childs and Withey, 'Do Women Sign for Women?'.
50 Tremblay's study of Canadian representatives' 'notices of motion' similarly found that women presented more 'women's' motions than men ('Do Female MPs Substantively Represent Women?').
51 Self-reported claims by some of Labour's new women MPs to be acting 'behind the scenes' might also seem more justified in light of these findings. See also Tremblay ('Do Female MPs Substantively Represent Women?').
52 Flynn, *Commons Knowledge.*
53 Blackburn and Kennon, *Griffith and Ryle on Parliament*, 537; Flynn, *Commons Knowledge*, 47–9).
54 The legal situation had been unclear following the use of all-women shortlists by the Labour party in the run-up to the 1997 general election, when an industrial tribunal found the party in breach of Section 13 of Part II of the Sex Discrimination Act, which prevents sex discrimination by professional bodies in awarding qualifications. The new Act also allows positive discrimination for the European Parliament, the Scottish Parliament and National Assembly of Wales and local government elections (Childs, 'The Sex Discrimination (Election Candidates) Act 2002 and its Implications').
55 Lovenduski, 'Women and Politics', 192–3.
56 *Guardian*, 9 January 2000.
57 Evaluating the impact of the Unit on women's substantive representation is difficult. Squires and Wickham-Jones highlight the difficulties of employing performance indicators, as it is not always clear when the Unit has had a direct impact 'on any particular programme', a consequence of cross-cutting departmental units (Squires and Wickham-Jones, 'New Labour, Gender Mainstreaming and the Women and Equality Unit', 90). What they do suggest is that where it has been most successful – they highlight women and economic policy – it is a reflection of 'ideological alignment with the overall direction of the government' (Squires and Wickham-Jones, 'New Labour, Gender Mainstreaming and the Women and Equality Unit', 94). The case-study approach looks to be a more insightful approach to evaluating the impact of Labour's gender machinery and gender mainstreaming (personal correspondence between Childs, Squires and Wickham-Jones, 2004).
58 Russell, *The Women's Representation Bill*; Russell, *Women's Representation in UK Politics.*
59 Lovenduski, 'Women and Politics', 192; Squires and Wickham-Jones, 'Mainstreaming in Westminster and Whitehall'). Fawcett also undertook their own

research (in conjunction with Joni Lovenduski) and concluded that the 'problem' of women's election to the House of Commons was lack of demand by party selectorates, with Britain's political parties institutionally sexist. Fawcett's research was drawn upon by MPs and members of the Lords during the passage of the Act (Hansard, 24 October 2001: column 373; Lords, Hansard, 13 March 2002: column 914).

60 Squires and Wickham-Jones, *Women in Parliament*; Shepherd-Robinson and Lovenduski, *Women and Candidate Selection.*

61 Lovenduski, 'Women and Politics', 192.

62 Similar patterns of behaviour were also found in the Lords debates. Analysis of sex, gender and the House of Lords is limited. Anecdotal evidence suggests that a full account of the feminisation of legislation would need to look at the role of members of the House of the Lords (private information from female peer, 2003).

63 Childs, 'Concepts of Representation and the Passage of the Sex Discrimination (Election Candidates) Bill'.

64 To suggest that women representatives' party identity will influence their attitudes to women's concerns and inform their behaviour is not a reductionist argument – reducing women's propensity and direction of acting for women to their party identity. All that it suggests is that the nature of the substantive representation that women representatives might make is likely to be informed by women representatives' different conceptions of women's concerns, perspectives and feminism.

65 Many of the new Labour women MPs considered that conservative/right-wing politics (as defined by the women MPs themselves) are not compatible with the substantive representation of women.

66 Dodson, *The Impact of Women in Congress*; Carroll, *The Impact of Women in Public Office*, xv.

Part III

New institutions, new opportunities?

10 Descriptive and substantive representation in new parliamentary spaces

The case of Scotland

Fiona Mackay

The original Westminster model has been significantly modified by constitutional change in the United Kingdom in the 1990s and the creation of new parliamentary spaces in Scotland, Wales and Northern Ireland. These reform processes offered a set of opportunities and constraints for women in their struggle for equal exercise of political power and influence. It also enabled women activists and feminist ideas to play a role in building new institutions and processes that were anticipated to be more gender-inclusive and participatory.

Devolution resulted in a reconfiguration of relationships and power between the centre and the peripheral nations. It also marks a gendered redistribution of political power. The obstacles posed to women's representation and political leadership by the Westminster model have been outlined in Chapter 1 of this book. By contrast, post-devolution politics in both Scotland and Wales has a distinctly 'female face', with high proportions of women elected in successive elections. In 2005 women comprise 39.5 per cent of members of the Scottish Parliament and 50 per cent of members of the National Assembly for Wales – as compared with 20 per cent of members of the British House of Commons. Women have an unprecedented presence in electoral politics in these new spaces, together with significant positional influence as ministers and parliamentary committee convenors. Hand-in-hand with these high levels of descriptive representation has come the creation of new and multiple institutionalised channels for women as citizens and civil society actors to access the political process.

This chapter provides a case study of the dynamics and impact of institutional restructuring processes on women's descriptive and substantive representation in the new space of the Scottish Parliament. First, it assesses how and why gender was integrated into reform processes, and the relative role played by electoral systems, political parties and women's movements in the significant gains made in the descriptive representation of women. Next, it examines the extent to which the Scottish institutional blueprints depart from Westminster conventions and the ways in which gender concerns have been in-built. Third, it provides a provisional assessment of the outcomes in terms of both the presence of women and the operation of new structures and processes.

Although not systematically applying an institutional analysis, I draw upon insights from institutional theory to consider the interplay between institutional design and gender in effecting changes to 'politics as usual'. According to institutionalist commentators,[1] institutions comprise not only formal rules and structures but also informal norms and practices. Differential patterns of power and resource distribution are embedded within the design of institutions and the informal practices that evolve over time. Innovation is difficult in existing institutions, yet periods of institutional restructuring can open up spaces for the contestation of rules and underlying norms, values and ideas, including gender norms.

Opportunities for feminist interventions are created by reform processes and the chance to be in at the start of a new institution. The shaping of constitutional and institutional blueprints is, however, only the beginning of the process. Experience points to the importance of what follows afterwards; there appears to be no automatic or guaranteed translation from principles to practice. The 'constitutional moment' is followed by a longer period of institutionalisation and uncertainty as the new structures and practices outlined in constitutional settlements are either embedded and consolidated or amended, neglected and discarded.[2]

Descriptive representation: the impact of timing, rules, parties and agency

I turn first to questions of how and why gender was integrated into reform processes and with what outcomes. The electoral system departs from the Westminster model in that elections to the Scottish Parliament are conducted using the more proportional MMP. MMP (known as AMS in the United Kingdom) combines a proportion of constituency seats elected under FPP with a proportion of regional seats elected under a Party List system. Under this system, 37 per cent women were elected in 1999 and 39.5 per cent in 2003. However, the high levels of descriptive representation are better explained by the imposition of candidate gender quotas by the main political party in Scotland, Labour, and the consequent use of informal measures by its principal electoral rival, the SNP, than by the change of electoral rules. Indeed, more women were returned under FPP in constituencies than through the proportional list.

In the first elections at least, party performance with respect to women's representation was a key part of political competition and the attainment of a better gender balance was viewed as a powerful and visible symbol of 'new politics' and a shorthand for the aspirations of the Labour Party and the wider reform movement for modern, relevant and democratic politics in Scotland. As the Independent Commission to Review Britain's Experience of PR Voting Systems (ICPR) reported with respect to improved performances in gender representation: 'Evidence from devolved bodies is that changes in attitudes and rules within parties are far more important than the method of election.'[3] Furthermore pressure for candidate quotas in the Labour Party pre-dated the introduction of PR.

Twin trajectories

Timing and the framing of demands within prevailing debates are important factors in explaining the relative success or failure of reform attempts. The breakthrough of the 'electoral project' by party women and women's movement activists was made possible by the coincidence of two reform trajectories in the 1980s and 1990s: the Labour Party's internal debates at the Great Britain (GB) level, and the broader processes of devolution in Scotland. These reform trajectories are set within three wider contexts: reaction to the radical programmes of neo-liberal restructuring undertaken by successive Conservative governments over this period; the gathering pace and activism of global campaigns to tackle the chronic minority status of women in political and public life; and elite debates in advanced welfare democracies about the so-called crisis of democracy and the disengagement of citizens as evidenced by the falling electoral turn-out and rising levels of mistrust and cynicism in politicians, parties and political processes. Together these contexts provided a structure of opportunities, political, institutional and discursive, for organised women to press for improvements in political representation.

The developments in the Labour Party at GB level are described by Studlar in Chapter 5 of this volume and the twin processes of modernisation and feminisation of the Labour Party have been well documented.[4] Accounts highlight the way in which feminist activists utilised the opportunities afforded by party modernisation to push for both internal and candidate gender quotas. Whilst gains at the Scottish level were by no means an automatic flow-on from Labour Party modernisation, the Labour Party did prove to be the key 'carrying agent' for the campaign because of the congruence of women's demands and party priorities.[5]

It took, however, the strategic and creative intervention of party women, backed by a wider mobilisation of grass-roots women, to ensure that the Labour Party in Scotland maintained and delivered its promise of gender quotas in the aftermath of the UK *Jepson* ruling[6] against all-women shortlists and the resultant climate of legal uncertainty. They did this through the design and promotion of the quota-type mechanism of 'twinning',[7] which they argued would not contravene sex discrimination legislation.

Westminster critiques and 'new politics'

In tandem with internal party debates, prominent Labour women – sympathetic to gender balance – worked with grass-roots Labour Party activists and with a broad-based coalition comprising trade unionists, autonomous grass-roots women's organisations, traditional women's organisations, feminist academics and gender experts to promote 50/50 representation and to engender debates about the shape and form of constitutional change.

Women also worked through generic reform groups such as the Campaign for a Scottish Parliament and the Scottish Constitutional Convention[8] and its Women's Issues Group and, later, contributed to the Consultative Steering Group (CSG), which drafted the standing orders and procedures of the new parliament. The 50/50 campaigners successfully intervened to make specific claims about women's representation linked with wider civil society campaigns to redress the so-called 'democratic deficit' and promote the case for greater democratic participation and 'new politics'.[9]

Arguments about democratic deficit provided a new dimension to devolution debates in the 1980s and 1990s as compared with campaigns of the 1970s. In addition to long-standing aspirations to greater autonomy and self-determination, contemporary demands for devolution in Scotland were fuelled by a sense of grievance that unpopular neo-liberal Thatcherite social and economic policies could be imposed on an unwilling Scottish electorate. The ability of one party to dominate government for a long period of time and to break radically with the previous welfare consensus exposed the distorting 'winner takes all' effects of the Westminster system.

The Westminster critique and the development of ideas about 'new politics' provided discursive opportunities absent in previous decades, again highlighting the importance of timing and context. Organised women, led by feminists, integrated gender perspectives into 'new politics' debates, interweaving feminism with elements of civic nationalism and participatory democracy. It was argued that, if Scotland suffered from a democratic deficit as a peripheral nation governed from Westminster by an unpopular political party with no Scottish mandate, then women – as women – suffered a 'double democratic deficit'. Women argued that it was not enough to achieve a Scottish Parliament if it reproduced the gender inequalities and exclusions so evident at Westminster. Gender balance came to be regarded as shorthand for the wider reform movement's aspirations to a modern, relevant and democratic Scottish polity.

The main institutional opportunity was provided by the Scottish Constitutional Convention (SCC). From an early stage, women members of the SCC and their activist networks ensured that gender equality was taken into consideration during the design process. And in 1997 the incoming Labour government adopted many of the recommendations of the SCC in its devolution White Paper.[10]

High levels of descriptive representation were achieved in the first Scottish parliament, due in particular to the Labour Party's adoption of quotas and the SNP's use of informal positive action. However what made it possible was the mobilisation of women around the opportunities presented by constitutional change. The presence of well organised and well placed female party activists constituted an internal lobby, a pool of politically experienced women and a link with autonomous women's movements. The operation of dual insider and outsider strategies and coalitions enabled women to maximise their impact against a backdrop of challenges to the structures and values of the Westminster model, and debates about the need for participatory democracy, democratic renewal and 'new politics'.

The second elections in 2003 saw a modest rise in the proportion of women. Whilst the picture is far from clear on the basis of two elections, there are some positive signs that gender representation is becoming institutionalised and that the issue retains some significance as a feature of party competition. However, whilst there is some evidence of 'contagion', with respect to the adoption of quota-type mechanisms by one party leading to the adoption of formal or informal measures by other parties, overall the indications are that gains are fragile and changes in political culture slow.[11]

Institutional blueprints: a blank slate?

Next, we examine the extent to which the Scottish institutional blueprints depart from the Westminster conventions and the ways in which gender concerns have been in-built.

The Scottish Parliament and Scottish Executive (the Scottish government) were created by UK statute, the Scotland Act 1998. With primary legislative powers over most areas of domestic policy, and with limited tax varying powers, the Scottish is the most powerful settlement, created in a process of asymmetrical reform.[12] However, macro-economic policy, including taxation and benefits, remains reserved to Westminster, as do the foreign and defence policy domains. In addition, sovereignty remains formally concentrated in the Westminster parliament.

Elected under the more proportional electoral system of MMP, the new Scottish system is characterised by multi-party politics and coalition government, both significant departures from the Westminster model. A more plural party political system, with different balances of power and a relatively small chamber of 129 members, provide opportunities for backbenchers to play an active role. The key principles of the parliament (known as the CSG key principles) of power-sharing, accountability, access and participation, and equal opportunities seek to encourage a more plural and collaborative political system.

The Scottish parliament further departs from the Westminster model with regard to the role of the committee system. The committees in the Scottish parliament were designed as a check on executive dominance in a unicameral system. They are powerful and multi-functional: holding the executive to account and playing an important role in the development, scrutiny and monitoring of policy. They can hold their own inquiries and have the power to initiate legislation. The committees are also expected to promote the key principles of access and participation, for example through consultative exercises, holding meetings in other parts of the country, and through the activities of the statutory Public Petitions Committee. The membership of committees reflects the party balance in the chamber and Conveners are not always drawn from the executive parties Thus they provide another forum in which alternative political careers can be developed and in which politicians of all parties can work together to make an impact on policy.[13] Finally, the creation of a horseshoe-shaped chamber and the introduction of parliamentary codes of behaviour also encourage a less adversarial style of politics.

The 50/50 campaign was primarily concerned with descriptive representation. However as noted above, women's movement campaigners were also concerned with institutionalising women's concerns through new channels of access and through policy machinery. The institutional 'blueprints' of the parliament contained important statements and mechanisms for promoting the enhanced participation and influence of women in policy development. Key features include:

- 'Family-friendly' working hours for the parliament and the recognition of Scottish school holidays.
- A purpose-built visitors' crèhe. The crèhe provides symbolic and practical recognition of the caring responsibilities of citizens.
- A parliamentary Equal Opportunities Committee with a remit for equal opportunities issues both inside and outside the parliament.
- An Equality Unit within the Scottish Executive.
- The inclusion of equal opportunities as one of the four key principles of the parliament and a stated priority of the government.
- The commitment of both parliament and the executive to 'mainstreaming' equality – including gender equality – across all their areas of work, including legislation and policy-making.
- The power of the Scottish Parliament to encourage equal opportunities (although the power to legislate is reserved to the Westminster parliament) and to impose duties on public bodies to ensure they have due regard to equality legislation.[14]
- The requirement that memoranda accompanying executive Bills include an equal opportunities impact statement.

The designers of the Scottish Parliament, including women, had aspirations to create a new institution that would depart from the standard Westminster model and promote a different political culture. However, alongside new features are many elements of institutional and cultural continuity such as tendencies towards political centralisation, strong party discipline and executive dominance.

Great expectations? Descriptive and substantive representation in practice

The chapter turns now to provide a provisional assessment of the outcomes in terms of the presence of women and the operation of new structures and processes.

Reasons for 'being there'

Apart from demonstrating 'fair play' or justice, the presence of women in substantial numbers brings with it a set of expectations relating to deliberation, recognition, legitimacy, the 're-gendering' of politics and, finally, most controversially, expectations of female politicians as agents for the substantive representation of women.[15] Studies of the first years of the Scottish Parliament provide some evidence to support each of these contentions but the overall message is that the politics of presence in practice is complex. The relationship between descriptive representativeness and substantive representation is by no means straightforward and is mediated by other factors, most particularly in strong party parliamentary systems by party identity and partisan loyalties.[16]

Deliberative politics

Turning first to theoretical expectations that the politics of presence will increase the 'deliberativeness' of political institutions through the inclusion of previously marginalised perspectives. There is tentative evidence of links between gendered political behaviour in the Scottish Parliament and criteria suggested for improved deliberation. For example, women parliamentarians, more often than their male counterparts, draw upon personal testimony and experience and on the experiences of other women to inform debate.

In addition, female politicians, especially Labour women MSPs, are more likely to have previous and ongoing links with women's groups in the community than their male colleagues, and to draw upon these links to inform their deliberations. Unequivocally, although not universally, it was women MSPs who saw their representative role as linked with their gender, and for whom there was a sense of, if not accountability, a referring back to the views of that particular 'constituency'. In turn, women's organisations report a sense of connection with female MSPs – 'the women belong more to us' – and view them as more approachable. These perceptions of representative practices resonate with many of the elements of responsive and interactive representation advocated by democracy theorists.[17]

As noted in the previous section, the institutional blueprints of the parliament accord with many of the principles of deliberative democracy through their attention to power sharing, access and participation and the promotion of less adversarial, more collaborative values and arenas of activity. Institutionally, there are more deliberative values and more deliberative opportunities than exist at Westminster. However, to date, we just do not have the data that would systematically answer the question of whether women are more deliberative than their male colleagues nor whether the Scottish Parliament is more deliberative than the House of Commons *in practice.*

Recognition

Perhaps the clearest symbolic outcome has been the recognition of women as political actors and leaders through their concrete presence as backbenchers, committee conveners and ministers in this new parliamentary space. Women and men are equally 'at home' in the Scottish Parliament and are seen as equally equipped to exercise political authority and power. Unlike Westminster, where women are still viewed as 'space invaders',[18] the presence of women at Holyrood is seen as normal and unremarkable.

Institutional legitimacy

High levels of women parliamentarians are viewed by politicians, civil society elites, women's organisations and commentators as a signal of the parliament's progressiveness and inclusive credentials, as noted earlier. The Scottish Parliament flags its positive gender balance in press releases and its international dealings. It is a source of pride. There are no post-devolution data relating to public attitudes about the impact of high numbers of women on the perceived legitimacy of the institution, although prior to devolution the public viewed 50/50 as a positive aspect of proposed constitutional change.[19]

Civilising politics? Feminising politics?

A consensus is apparent among commentators and politicians that the culture of the Scottish Parliament is more civilised and more civil than that of Westminster. We argue that this is as a consequence, in combination, of new rules and structures, the alternative norms provided by 'new politics', and the substantial female presence. As one woman MSP remarked, 'I think some of the men have learned that to get things done you have to act in a different way.' Whilst simple assumptions about 'critical mass' have been discredited, nevertheless proportions appear to play some role. For example, The Scottish parliament with a 60/40 balance and with some apparent 'regendering' of political norms has a culture of civility and mutual respect and has largely avoided the 'yah boo' adversarial practices of Westminster. The public expression of sexualised language or sexist attitudes is rare and regarded as unparliamentary. Challenges to institutional innovations such as the statutory Equal Opportunities and Public Petitions Committees, the visitors crèhe, and the 'family-friendly' sitting hours of the parliament have to date been successfully resisted.

By contrast Westminster, with its 80/20 split and its embedded traditions, routinely doles out 'sexist insults, hostility and boorish behaviour despite the influx of female MPs' to the House of Commons.[20] MSPs have lined up to testify to the more women-friendly culture of the Scottish Parliament and even the somewhat unreconstructed Scottish media have asserted: 'It's a different story at the Scottish Parliament.'[21] These testimonials suggest significant differences in the gendered political culture of the two institutions and in the perceived legitimacy of women and their exercise of authority and leadership. The reversal of the hard-won family-friendly reform of sitting hours in the House of Commons provides another contrast.

Focusing a little closer upon style and behaviour in the Scottish Parliament, we find a picture of both differences and similarities from which it is difficult to draw firm conclusions. Quantitative measures (albeit rather crude) reveal few clear gender differences with respect to levels and types of parliamentary activities such as written and oral questions, motions and amendments and members' debates. In interviews, both male and female MSPs prioritised constituency and committee work above plenary performance. Similarly, when asked to describe, in abstract, the qualities of an effective MSP, both women and men valued similar core skills.

In terms of daily practice, some differences emerge. Men and women have different ideas of political efficacy: male politicians prize political performance more highly than do women, who in turn value low-key 'solution-oriented' activities more than men. Females MSPs perceived that they work differently from men and have been at the forefront of developing constructive working practices in the parliamentary committees and breaking down old patterns of adversarial politics. These perceptions are reinforced by some quantitative findings. Stylistically, male backbench MSPs accounted for around three-quarters of the 'critical' interventions across the three parliamentary meetings sampled in our study. Of the small number of 'hostile/aggressive' interventions a man initiated all but one. Some male MSPs preferred a low-key style and a few also reported that the strong presence of women has enabled them to reflect upon the way things are done and to think and act in less traditional or adversarial ways.

Elsewhere we have argued that instead of conceptualising gender differences as categorical it is more appropriate to consider a continuum of styles. At one pole are MSPs who might be characterised as 'background activists', seeking to achieve goals by diligence, solution-focused, more oriented towards consensus working, and using committees as the main vehicle for influence. Research to date suggests that these are mostly, but not exclusively, women. At the other pole are 'foreground activists' who seek to achieve goals by declamation, playing an active role in plenary sessions, taking a more individualist approach and employing game-playing and point-scoring strategies. These are mostly, but not exclusively, men. Behaviours are context and issue-sensitive and what is significant is the potential for overlaps and for shifts over time, or in response to specific issues, in either direction, in the characteristic patterns of men and women politicians.

Substantive representation of women

What can be drawn from the lessons elsewhere? First that, in addition to numbers, the Scottish Parliament meets many of the conditions predicted to enhance the capacity and inclination of women representatives to promote the substantive representation of women. These conditions include: significant positional power; women-friendly institutional features; the congruence of 'new politics' ideas with the substantive representation of women; a plural party system dominated by parties of the centre-left or left; and influence within party groups, particularly within Labour as the largest party. As such, the Scottish case may be viewed as a 'best-case scenario' and the expectation would be that descriptive representation should result in substantive outcomes.

However, optimism is tempered by cautionary notes. Setting aside the theoretical debates about the im/possibility of a unitary category 'woman' and a unified set of gender interests, we face at least three other sets of problems. First, empirical research demonstrates that the capacity and inclination of female representatives to 'represent' and 'act for' women are modified and constrained by numerous personal, institutional and party political factors, beyond mere numbers. Second, the capacity of parliaments and parliamentarians substantively to progress distinctive policy agendas vis-à-vis political executives is constrained. This is particularly the case with the Westminster model. Third, in multi-level polities, the capacity of any one level of governance to make policy decisions or implement programmes is constrained and interdependent upon other levels.

With these provisos in mind, we next explore the extent to which women parliamentarians might be judged substantively to represent women by raising, prioritising or supporting 'women's issues' or issues relating to gender equality.[22] Whereas female MSPs, particularly Labour women, are slightly more likely than men to raise gender/equality issues, the results are rather inconclusive in the absence of more detailed analysis of the gendered dimensions of parliamentary business. In the period studied, only a small proportion of parliamentary business in the chamber or committees related explicitly to issues about women or issues relating to gender in/equality. Most relevant interventions related to violence, health or equal opportunities.[23] Furthermore, it is a small number of MSPs, mostly but not exclusively women, who are responsible for making most of these gender-related interventions. As at Westminster,[24] gender identity and party identity are important. Labour women MSPs appear more likely to actively identify themselves with women's issues than female parliamentarians from other parties, although there are some notable identifiers across party, and some male champions.

In terms of perceptions and experience, most female and some male parliamentarians believed that women have made a substantive difference to the political agenda. Women have worked within parties and sometimes across party divides, most often on matters relating to domestic abuse, rape and sexual assault, women's health and children's rights. Female Labour backbenchers were also prominent in cross-party campaigns, which forced changes in executive policy on the issue of free personal care for the elderly. They were also prepared to maintain pressure on the executive to repeal Thatcherite 'anti-gay' legislation after the executive's resolve faltered in the face of a conservative backlash. Some female MSPs from across parties argued that they also brought gender perspectives to committee work in less traditional areas such as enterprise, transport, rural development and environment, although the outcomes of this are less evident in terms of legislative or policy outputs.

Women ministers, for the most part, have held the equalities portfolio and have actively championed equality mainstreaming and equality issues. Interview data suggest that female ministers from the 1999–2001 period saw themselves, and were seen by others, to have acted as a cohesive team on a broad equalities agenda, including some 'women's issues', as well as other social policy issues. Policy initiatives in areas such as domestic abuse, social justice, fuel poverty, teenage sexual health, improved public transport and equality mainstreaming are judged to have received a higher profile than might otherwise have been the case. However those female ministers in position since 2001 have not been seen by women activists to be highly visible 'as women' or to work as a female or feminist caucus.[25]

The presence of women MSPs was considered to have an impact by raising the priority or 'weight' accorded to issues. The difference is best understood as subtle rather than radical and relates to a 'tilting' of the political agenda. The data also suggest greater preparedness and willingness by men to raise issues traditionally reflective of women's interests and concerns, at least in part because of the certainty of receiving support from female MSPs.[26] As a result some policy areas, such as child care or domestic violence, have become reframed as mainstream issues. For example, a male non-Executive MSP headed up the cross-party parliamentary group on Men's Violence Against Women and Children

1999–2003. Similarly, in a general climate of commitment to equal opportunities and 'mainstreaming', and in response to lobbying by the feminist Scottish Women's Budget Group, successive male convenors of the parliamentary finance committee and successive male finance ministers have championed work on gender-proofing budgets.

Domestic abuse

Action against domestic violence or domestic abuse is a key achievement of the first session of the Scottish Parliament and executive and the most obvious concrete gain for a classic women's agenda. A strategic approach was taken from the start;[27] a national multi-agency partnership co-ordinates implementation and a national strategy sets out specific actions and goals, with progress to be reported every three years. Tackling domestic violence has a stated high priority of public policy in Scotland with cross party support.[28] The agenda has been driven forward as a result of sustained campaigning by women's organisations, particularly the women's refuge movement, and strong political leadership provided by women ministers and female parliamentarians, together with some key male allies.

There have been significant improvements in service provision, including a new refuge-building programme; enhanced protection through legislative developments such as the Protection from Abuse Act (Scotland) 2001, which was chosen as the parliament's first committee Bill; and prevention work through public awareness and extensive education programmes. In addition, a specialist policy unit has been established inside the Scottish Executive. Interviews confirmed that it was an issue of personal political priority for a number of the female parliamentarians and ministers. As a female former cabinet minister contended, 'Men might have got around to tackling domestic abuse eventually but women did it right away – gender does matter.' The urgency with which domestic abuse has been tackled in comparison with Westminster provides evidence of a link between descriptive and substantive representation. Gains in this policy domain were earlier and more substantial than at Westminster.

In other respects, women's issues and gender equality policy have a low profile in the parliament and in government. Women's organisations have argued that the attainment of high levels of descriptive representation has resulted in a widespread view that women's equality has now been achieved and that it is time to turn to other concerns. Whilst there is a generic equalities strategy, the lack of an action plan or strategy for gender equality has contributed to a loss of focus. Gains are not embedded and are often reliant on informal contacts and individual champions and are vulnerable to the turnover of ministers, committee conveners and civil servants. Commitments have been made to build gender into processes through gender budgeting and equality mainstreaming but gender-based analysis is far from routinised and women's lobbies need repeatedly to remind politicians and civil servants of the formal rules and policies in place.[29]

Party remains predominant. While there were strong within-party links between women, particularly within the Labour Party, cross-party links were more circumscribed and issue-specific. For example, while SNP women felt able to support the executive's position on domestic abuse on the basis that 'some issues are too important', in other areas political differences took priority over gender. Coalitions may not hold if gender interests come into direct conflict with party interests. The fragile and shifting nature of 'sisterhood' was demonstrated in responses to the proposed visit to Scotland of the US boxer and convicted rapist Mike Tyson in 2000. There was agreement among both male and female MSPs interviewed that sustained, cross-party pressure by women gave the issue a higher profile than might have been the case had there been fewer women parliamentarians. The debate was initially framed as a cross-party protest that a convicted rapist should be considered for special dispensation to enter the United Kingdom to fight in Scotland. There were concerns that the visit would undermine the public education and policy work in Scotland towards tackling violence against women as part of the national strategy. In short it would send out the 'wrong sort of signals'. Parliamentarians also saw their opposition as providing support and recognition for the work of women's anti-violence organisations. When the Labour Home Secretary in London granted a visa, the subsequent debate shifted to focus on party political constitutional politics around the issue. As a result Labour and SNP women became divided over an issue in which they were originally in agreement and each voted on party lines.[30]

The mixed fortunes and contingent nature of the politics of presence in Scotland reinforce findings elsewhere. In any event a focus on women parliamentarians, as individuals or groups, or even on parliament as a whole, does not enable a full appraisal of the complex policy process and multiple actors involved in contesting, negotiating and delivering substantive gains for women.

Conclusion: *plus ça change, plus c'est pareil*?

Devolution has presented opportunities for women, some of their own making. The Scottish case study highlights the importance of women's agency, party strategies and ideas of new politics, in the context of constitutional and institutional reform processes, in achieving significant levels of descriptive representation. The visible presence of women as backbenchers and ministers, and as lobbyists and civil society partners interacting with the new political institutions, which have been shaped in part by women and feminist ideas, has contributed to a more 'feminised' politics with some concrete policy outcomes. We have argued elsewhere that newness and gender are mutually reinforcing factors.[31]

The increased place and voice of women have influenced the politics of ideas, the traditional political agenda and political practices in the parliament, within the enabling framework of institutional innovation and discourses of 'new politics'. This impact relates not only to the agency of individual women and groups of women but also to the effect of gender balance on institutional norms and values. There is much that is promising: stated principles of equality and commitments to mainstream equality; high-profile champions; the reframing of some classic women's issues as part of the mainstream agenda; attempts at meaningful consultation and inclusiveness; important groundwork and some limited gains.

On the other hand, even within these relatively enabling institutions the capacity to effect substantive outcomes for women is circumscribed and progress has been modest rather than dramatic. It has proved difficult to turn rhetoric into reality; progress has been halting; and, without vigilance, gender equality issues can slip off the agenda. This lends support to arguments that there are too many constraints to expect a straightforward relationship between representation and concrete outcomes.

A key criterion of successful institutional innovation is the extent to which it becomes routinised and commonsense. Whilst the presence of women has become a normalised feature of post-devolution politics, many of the institutional reforms and policy developments are far from embedded. This is also the case with gender quotas and it is hard to judge the sustainability of current levels of women's representation on the basis of two elections.

The Scottish case illustrates the difficulties of embedding institutional innovation. There is a complex interplay between the politics of presence and the dynamics of institutional continuity and change. In particular, the Scottish Parliament should be understood not as a blank slate but as innovation within an existing system, an institution nested within others and with powerful institutional legacies. Whilst the Westminster model was presented as discredited during devolution debates, each design decision represented the negotiation of different normative and strategic considerations and trade-offs. The official rhetoric of the campaign was dominated by the Scottish Constitutional Convention and the Consultative Steering Group and encapsulated by the founding 'key principles' of the Scottish Parliament. Yet there were different definitions of 'new politics' at play within and outside the coalition, and very different levels of enthusiasm and commitment across and within parties, and between political parties and civil society actors.

Sections of the Labour Party were sceptical from the start about ideas of 'new politics' and concerned primarily with devolution as a means of regaining political power. Similarly, although there were champions of new politics within all the political parties, many individuals and groups remained unconvinced about the desirability or feasibility of 'new politics'. Many key elements of the Westminster model have survived or been reinstated. These include the strong party parliament, political partisanship and party loyalty, conventions constraining legislative oversight of the executive and adversarial rather than collaborative political styles. They are viewed by many as the core of 'real' politics rather than 'idealist' or 'naive' politics. As Barry Winetrobe argued in his review of the first year of the parliament, not withstanding the parliament's distinctive features and different aspirations the institution it most resembles is its Westminster parent.[32]

Therefore, whilst institutional change brings opportunities, it is important not to underplay the underlying continuities. This is why we must modify our expectations of the scope and extent of change and of the politics of presence. There are no guarantees as to whether institutional gender blueprints, women's substantial politics of presence and the nascent political culture will be more influential than the legacies of Westminster and local government politics, national UK contexts, gendered party political cultures and traditional patterns of gender relations. We must expect an ongoing struggle between competing frames and norms. It is unlikely to be the case that either 'new politics' or 'politics as usual' will decisively win out but rather that they will coexist, each shaping and constraining the other.

Finally, debates about substantive representation need to be realistic and attentive to policy environments that further shape scope and capacity of political actors and institutions. Policies and processes required to promote gender equality and diversity require co-ordination within and across government. The substantive representation of women does not rest solely, or even primarily, with women representatives. Instead a broader focus is needed taking into account government performance, the institutionalised voice of women and channels of accountability. Furthermore, many of the issues of key concern for women such as low pay, equal pay, child care and work–life balance cut across both devolved (Scottish) and reserved (Westminster) responsibilities, and many relate to EU competences. Concrete conclusions about the impact of devolution in general are difficult to draw, in part because it is still early days in terms of the life course of policies and, in part, because much of the Scottish policy agenda is shared in common with the Labour government at UK level.[33] This is compounded in the case of gender equality, which requires institutions to operate across multiple levels, and where reform in one institutional domain may be offset by resistance in another.

Notes

This chapter draws upon a project funded by the UK Economic and Social Research Council under its Devolution and Constitutional Change programme (L219252023). See www.pol.ed.ac.uk/gcc for more details.

1 See Steinmo *et al.*, *Structuring Politics.*

2 See Banaszak *et al.*, 'When Power Relocates'; Dobrowolsky and Hart, *Women Making Constitutions.*
3 Independent Commission on Proportional Representation, *Changed Voting, Changed Politics*, 124.
4 See Eagle and Lovenduski, 'High Time or High Tide for Labour Women?'; Lovenduski, *Feminizing Politics*; Lovenduski, 'Sexing Political Behaviour in Britain'; Russell, 'Women in Elected Office in the UK'; Russell *et al.*, 'Women's Representation in the Scottish Parliament and National Assembly for Wales'.
5 Bradbury *et al.*, 'Devolution and Party Change'.
6 See Russell *et al.*, 'Women's Representation in the Scottish Parliament and National Assembly for Wales'.
7 Under this scheme, constituencies are matched as far as possible in terms of a variety of indicators, including winnability. Both men and women could stand for selection for a pair of constituencies. The woman applicant with the highest number of votes was selected as the Labour candidate for one of the twinned seats, at the same time as the man with the highest number of votes was selected for the other.
8 The Scottish Constitutional Convention was an unofficial but highly influential body established by key groups in civil society, together with some political parties, which debated and considered potential blueprints for a Scottish parliament, including electoral systems (1989–95).
9 See Breitenbach and Mackay, *Women and Contemporary Scottish Politics.*
10 See Scottish Constitutional Convention, *Scotland's Parliament, Scotland's Right*; Scottish Office, *Scotland's Parliament.*
11 See Mackay, 'Women and the 2003 Elections'.
12 For details of the asymmetrical devolution geometry of the United Kingdom, see Hazell, *The State and the Nations.*
13 Brown, 'Designing the Scottish Parliament'; Arter, 'On Assessing Strength and Weakness in Parliamentary Committee Systems'.
14 Scotland Act, Schedule 5, para. L.2.
15 See Chapter 1 of this book.
16 This section draws upon a small-scale study undertaken by the author together with Fiona Myers and Alice Brown, University of Edinburgh (2000–03) and funded by the United Kingdom Economic and Social Research Council (R00223281). See Mackay *et al.*, 'Making a Difference?'; Mackay *et al.*, 'Towards a New Politics?'.
17 See Young, *Inclusion and Democracy.*
18 See Puwar, *Space Invaders.*
19 Mitchell, 'Scotland: Expectations, Policy Types and Devolution', fig. 2.2.
20 See Ashley 'Bullied, Patronised and Abused: Women MPs Reveal the Truth about Life Inside Westminster'.
21 Williams, 'Sexist Attitudes still a Problem in the Commons'.
22 Defined as issues that explicitly affect women or are traditionally seen to be of prime concern to women. Arguably too crude a typology; more nuanced analysis might well have produced more conclusive results.
23 This early finding was reinforced by the parliament's internal research, Scottish Parliament Information Centre, *Gender in the Scottish Parliament.*
24 See Childs, *New Labour's Women MPs.*
25 Mackay, 'Women and Devolution in Scotland'.
26 See Mackay *et al.*, 'Towards a New Politics?'.
27 See Scottish Partnership on Domestic Abuse, *National Strategy to Address Domestic Abuse in Scotland.*
28 Scottish Executive, *Preventing Domestic Abuse*, 5.
29 Mackay *et al.*, *Access, Voice . . . and Influence?.*

30 Immigration is a reserved matter. Therefore the decision, about whether or not a person convicted of a serious criminal offence should be given permission to enter the United Kingdom is taken by the UK Home Secretary. Attention therefore shifted to party political constitutional politicking about whether or not a decision should have been made at UK level about a matter that affected Scotland. Thus divisions arose between pro-unionist parties who wished to defend the constitutional settlement and pro-independence parties who portrayed the incident as another illustration of the flawed constitutional settlement and the need for independence.

31 Mackay *et al.*, 'Towards a New Politics?'.

32 See Winetrobe, *Realising the Vision.*

33 See Keating, *The Government of Scotland.*

11 Women and constitutional reform

Gender parity in the National Assembly for Wales

Paul Chaney

> The weight of history is against us, against women being represented in political institutions.[1]

Constitutional reform in the United Kingdom and the creation of national-regional assemblies in Wales and Scotland has seen significant progress made towards ending the earlier marginalisation of women in politics. The first elections to the National Assembly in 1999 resulted in Wales's swift progression from a country with a lamentably poor record of electing women as political representatives to being the UK polity with the highest proportion of women parliamentarians. Following elections in 2003, further progress was made when the Welsh Assembly became the first national government body in the world to achieve gender parity among its elected representatives. A recent UK government report summarised recent developments:

> devolution has provided a new political settlement in Scotland and Wales, creating new contexts within which work on equality and human rights must operate. The different political, social and cultural environments, and the provisions for promoting equality of opportunity within the Scotland Act and the Government of Wales Act will have important implications for these nations.[2]

The move to quasi-federal government in the United Kingdom and the resulting outcomes in Wales are worthy of attention for at least three key reasons. First and foremost, it is an opportunity to apply the broad body of social and political theory about women's political representation to a case where significant levels of women's representation have been achieved. Second, this chapter presents research findings from a regional legislature at time when multi-level governance is becoming increasingly important both in the development of the European Union and in achieving the aims of international bodies that advocate gender equality within such a multi-level framework of governance.[3] Lastly, the current findings add to existing knowledge about the promotion of gender equality and the future trajectory of equal opportunities policies. This is significant, for as Forbes[4] states, 'the question of the capacity of the modern state and the division over the consequences of strategies to introduce such change is a crucial aspect of contemporary politics across Europe and America'.

The origins of the recent progress towards gender balance in regional government reported on here lie in the (re-)establishment of directly elected legislatures[5] in two of the constituent countries of the United Kingdom and in the province of Northern Ireland. This was largely in answer to growing criticism about the over-centralised and undemocratic nature of the pre-existing system of governance. Research examining the arrangements for governing Wales prior to 1999 concluded that it was male-dominated, exclusive, 'centralising and anti-democratic' – or as one study dubbed it, a 'raj' style of administration.[6] An official report revealed that during this period a 'significant number' of government employees in the Welsh Office – the former territorial ministry of the UK government that served the country – 'ha[d] received no training or awareness raising at all on equality matters'.[7] Moreover, the chronic and long-standing underrepresentation of women in Welsh politics before and during the period of administrative devolution (1964–99) served to undermine both the accountability and the legitimacy of the prevailing mode of governance.

Recent constitutional change has begun a process of rapid change. From the outset, the opportunities afforded by the modernisation of government in the latter half of the 1990s allowed women equality campaigners to lobby successfully for the new Welsh Assembly to be bound by a unique and innovative statutory equality duty. In addition, the reprioritisation of equality matters that accompanied the post-1997 government reforms and associated positive action by some political parties saw significant progress towards gender balance in national politics for the first time.

The combination of these factors has effectively transformed the role of women in post-devolution politics in Wales. Furthermore, a new and distinctive equality agenda has emerged. The latter has been driven by key women Assembly Members (AMs) and has resulted in ongoing and wide-ranging reforms to promote gender and other strands of equality of opportunity both in government and the public sector.

This chapter presents an analysis of how women entered political debates and influenced the processes of constitutional change in Wales; and of the impact of the post-1999 structures, institutions and practices on women and women's political roles. The chapter begins with an outline of the research methodology and of the social and political theory associated with this study.

Research methodology

Data was gathered for this chapter between 1999 and 2004. The findings are based on an analysis of 150 semi-structured interviews and focus group meetings with politicians and officials in the Welsh Assembly government, managers of public sector agencies, representatives of the UK statutory equality commissions in Wales, and members of groups representing women and other, so-called 'minority' groups.[8] These were selected in a theoretical sample designed to reflect the size, everyday language (Welsh or English), nature and geographical location of such organisations. In addition, an extensive examination has been undertaken of the 'grey literature', minutes of meetings and internal unpublished strategy documents of women's organisations. Moreover, this research draws upon the following official sources: the 'Official Record' – and videos of committee proceedings – of the National Assembly, the analysis of key policy documents; transcripts of political debates; minutes of Assembly government Cabinet meetings; as well as participant observation of Assembly committee meetings and plenary sessions of the Welsh legislature.

Conceptual context

The principal arguments as to why women's presence matters in contemporary politics are summarised in Chapter 1 of this book. In sum, when considering women's role in contemporary systems of governance we are concerned with core political science debates about the nature of social justice, democratic legitimacy and deliberative democracy. Accordingly, given the centrality of these issues to the successful functioning of contemporary society, it is, perhaps, useful to pause and consider these key arguments before exploring their salience in relation to developments in Wales.

Descriptive representation refers to the situation whereby elected representatives are typical of the broader class of people whom they represent, such that women represent women, disabled people represent disabled people, and so on. Among the benefits of this arrangement is the ability of elected representatives to draw directly upon life experiences inextricably linked to the ascriptive characteristics of the individual, in this case derived from gender. As we have seen in Chapter 1, there are a number of dimensions to descriptive (or symbolic) representation, including equal opportunity, utility and deliberative considerations as well as recognition, role model and legitimacy factors.

Descriptive representation has been central to both women's redefined role in contemporary politics and the development of a 'new politics' following devolution in the United Kingdom. It also supports the arguments of those advocating the merits of a pluralist conception of 'deliberative democracy'. Two such exponents, Gutmann and Thompson,[9] summarise this idea. They assert that problems arise in democratic systems, such as in the male-dominated politics prior to constitutional change, when participants represent the interests of fundamentally different groups from themselves. In a similar vein, Gargarella[10] explains that full representation of all groups in civil society, including women, is necessary because otherwise elected representatives will fail to put themselves in the position of those they are supposed to represent, they will not be sufficiently motivated to advance others' causes and, moreover, they cannot be trusted to do so.

Norris and Lovenduski assert with reference to critical mass theory (see Chapter 1) that in legislatures and government bodies, women need to be present in sufficient numbers before significant changes in, and benefits to, the nature of politicking – such as those identified by proponents of deliberative democracy – become evident. Whilst such a focus places emphasis on women's *presence* in government bodies as elected politicians, an alternative, distinct – albeit related – body of literature is principally concerned with the subject matter – or *substance* – of politicking, namely the substantive representation of women. Mackay *et al.*[11] describe how this concept differs from descriptive representation in that it refers to 'the opportunities for the concerns and interests of women to be heard and taken into account in the policy-making process – through the institutionalisation of channels and mechanisms'. Lovenduski[12] offers an alternative framework, suggesting that substantive representation is most usefully examined in terms of whether distinct women's issues and perspectives can be identified and whether women parliamentarians share – and promote – these in a decisive manner.

In exploring the impact on gender and politics stemming from recent constitutional change in the United Kingdom this chapter is concerned not only with concepts of descriptive and substantive representation but also with a number of other theoretical literatures. In particular, this case study relates to the difference between representative democracy and participative democracy.[13] Often, for the former, voting is the limit of wider participation in a democratic system. Yet, as proponents of participatory democracy observe, if legitimacy is derived from the people, for a purportedly democratic institution to be truly representative it must secure the participation of all groups in society as citizens, employees and as elected representatives. In this sense democratic – or elected – devolution in Wales has increased democratic legitimacy over the earlier mode of administrative devolution, not least because in contrast to the pre-1999 situation, women – as well as men – have been given a vote to decide who exercises the devolved functions of government in Wales, and ultimately, they have attained an equal role as elected representatives.

As the following discussion will show, 'devolution' in Wales provides new empirical evidence that tests the applicability of the foregoing theoretical arguments to an understanding of contemporary politics. It has also presented an unprecedented opportunity for reprioritising the promotion of equality by government. According to Mackay and Bilton[14] 'constitutional change and the government's modernisation agenda are an important enabling context within which equalities work can develop'. Subsequent work concurs with this view and asserts that 'the political climate for equalities has undoubtedly improved and new structural spaces have opened up'. This analysis continued, 'the question is . . . about the extent to which there is continuity and to what degree different priorities and agenda can be discerned'.[15] The remainder of this chapter is principally concerned with these issues.

Women's influence on the process of constitutional change in Wales

Women in Wales have long been underrepresented and marginalised in politics. In the early 1990s, it was observed that women's inequality in Wales 'comes together in an underlying alienation of women from legislative institutions, in particular what can be perceived as male institutions, male agenda, male political methods . . .'.[17] This view is borne out by the fact that, prior to 1997, only four women had represented Welsh constituencies in the UK parliament. The post-1997 programme of constitutional reforms represented a 'window of opportunity which appeared for gender mainstreaming advocates in the context of devolution'.[17]

Despite the fact that women were largely marginalised in 'formal' party politics in Wales during the last decades of the twentieth century, they shaped and led the equality agenda through a strong tradition of civic and political activism culminating in the pro-devolution campaign group Women Say Yes. This group was a cross-party, multi-interest alliance that included a broad range of women's organisations. In the words of one member: 'one of our mantras was that "devolution is too important to be left to the politicians" – which brought in people who hadn't been involved in mainstream political parties'. Women Say Yes succeeded in raising the profile of gender equality by holding a series of events such as a major women's rally in west Wales and, later, a well publicised meeting to present the Secretary of State for Wales with a written copy of the campaigners' demands.

Reflecting on this period, participants describe 'an enormous feeling of optimism and hope and a tremendous feeling that we were actually about to change things'. According to those involved, this confidence was based on the belief that constitutional reform would mean that

> there would be somewhere where we could count on, in a way that hadn't happened in Westminster – that women would actually have a say in a way that they haven't had before in Wales. That was a sort of feeling really that you were carving your own destiny and you actually

> had the power to do that, which probably had been lacking in formal politics before. I think that the devolution movement bought in women to be active in that sort of way and that was very, very important.

According to another participant, 'it was one of those "can do" moments, empowering moments, when you knew you couldn't go backwards'.

Whilst women's role in influencing the initial process of constitutional change in Wales leading up to the 1997 devolution referendum may have differed from the broad-based mobilisation and engagement witnessed in Scotland and Northern Ireland[18] the outcomes were no less striking. Operating in the context of a traditionally fissiparous society and beset by a background of deep mistrust between the pro-devolution political parties, the small network of influential gender equality activists in the left-of-centre political parties and individuals in gender equality organisations seized the prevailing political opportunities to influence the process of devolution. Such lobbying centred on the idea that gender balance among those elected to a future Welsh legislature needed to be addressed within a wider 'commitment that the Assembly should have a responsibility to drive forward equality issues'.[19]

Such a view prevailed and these demands ultimately found their way into the Government of Wales Act. The principal equality clause in the Act is an example of a 'fourth generation' equality duty[20] and is unique among the devolution statutes, for it requires government to take a proactive stance and promote equality for *all* persons and in respect of *all* Welsh Assembly Government functions.[21] As Squires notes, 'this approach has a series of significant benefits ... it gives citizens legally enforceable rights in relation to elected representatives' actions thereby empowering citizens *vis-à-vis* the state'.[22] Overall, Welsh gender equality activists can be seen to have promulgated a 'technical approach' to 'constitution building' – or the framing of legal and procedural matters – in order to achieve an equal role for women politicians and, importantly, to *compel* the devolved Assembly to promote equality of opportunity. Reflecting upon this process, one participant, the late Val Feld AM, said:

> I think that we have succeeded in putting in place every structural measure that we could reasonably expect to try to create a new framework and ethos that means equality has a good chance of flourishing in the way that the Assembly carries out its business and in the way that it works internally and externally.

Whilst the foregoing actions of gender equality activists in shaping the institutional blueprint of the new legislature are central to an understanding of changes associated with constitutional reform in Wales, they do not fully explain the transformation in women's role in politics that has occurred in since 1999. For this it is essential to also focus on the 'positive action' adopted in the candidate selection procedures of the political parties.

Achieving a 'critical mass'

Equality activists ensured that gender equality was encouraged in the 1997 devolution White Paper, the UK government's legislative proposals for constitutional reform in Wales. Under the heading 'Representing all the people of Wales', the paper stated that: 'the Government attaches great importance to equal opportunities for all...' It believes that greater participation by women is essential to the health of our democracy. The United Kingdom Government also urges all political parties offering candidates for election to the Assembly to have this in mind in their internal selection processes.'[23] Such calls were heeded by three of the four main political parties in their preparations for the first elections to the Welsh Assembly in 1999. However, the process was far from trouble-free, for bitter infighting ensued when the Welsh Labour Party adopted 'twinning' in its candidate selection procedures. Under this process pairs of electoral constituencies were identified. These were determined on the basis of similarities of population, geographical proximity and 'winnability'. Each pair was then required to select one male and one female candidate. Ultimately, this secured a 15:13 majority of women among the party's AMs.[24]

Elsewhere the principal opposition party, Plaid Cymru, used 'zipping' as a positive action method. In other words party officials managed the order of candidates appearing on the ballot papers for regional Assembly seats elected by proportional representation in order to maximise the chance of having a female candidate elected.[25] This gave the party six women out of a total of 17 AMs. This too provoked internal party strife involving 'threats of resignation and accusations of blackmail'.[26] The Welsh Liberal Democrats were less forthright in their actions and 'offered training days for women only and emphasised an informal route in order to encourage female applications'.[27] As Table 11.1 reveals, the combination of the various measures taken by the three parties led to substantial gains in respect of women's symbolic representation, with the Assembly having the second highest proportion of women elected to a national government body in Europe (41.7 per cent).[28] Four years later, during campaigning for the second Assembly elections in 2003, party activists ensured that gender balance remained an issue for electoral competition between the two main parties. As a result earlier progress was consolidated and the Welsh Assembly became the first example of a national government body in the world to achieve gender parity (see Table 11.2).

The emerging evidence suggests that during the Assembly's first years the 'critical mass' of 42 per cent – and, subsequently 50 per cent – of

Table 11.1 National Assembly for Wales elected representatives by gender, party, and type of seat, 1999

Political party	*Constituency seats*		*Total constituency seats (% women)*	*Regional 'list' seats*[a]		*Total list seats (% women)*	*Total AMs*	*Total women*	*Total men*	*% women*
	Female	*Male*		*Female*	*Male*					
Welsh Labour	15	12	27 (55.5)	0	1	1 (0.0)	28	15	13	53.6
Plaid Cymru – The Party of Wales	2	7	9 (22.2)	4	4	8 (50)	17	6	11	29.4
Welsh Liberal Democrats	2	1	3 (66.7)	1	2	3 (33.3)	6	3	3	50.0
Welsh Conservatives	0	1	1 (0.0)	0	8	8 (0.0)	9	0	9	0.0
Total	19	21	40 (47.5)	5	15	20 (25)	60	24	36	40

The sets describe the results of the first National Assembly elections in May 1999. In February 2000 a male Assembly Member (the First Minister) resigned and was replaced by a woman AM. Thus women then totalled 25 out of the 60 AMs – or 42% – for the remainder of the Assembly's first term.

a Twenty of the National Assembly's 60 seats are based upon regional constituencies. Assembly Members are elected to represent these seats by a version of proportional representation. The remaining 40 seats are elected by a simple 'first-past-the-post' majority.

Table 11.2 National Assembly for Wales elected representatives by gender, party and type of seat, 2003

Political party	*Constituency seats*		*Total constituency seats (% women)*	*Regional 'list' seats*		*Total list seats (% women)*	*Total AMs*	*Total women*	*Total men*	*% women (% women 1999)*
	Female	*Male*		*Female*	*Male*					
Welsh Labour	19	11	30 (63.0)	0	0	0	30	19	11	63.0 (53.6)
Plaid Cymru – The Party of Wales	1	4	5 (20.0)	5	2	7 (71.4)	12	6	6	50.0 (29.4)
Welsh Liberal Democrats	2	1	3 (66.6)	1	2	3 (33.3)	6	3	3	50.0 (50.0)
Welsh Conservatives	0	1	1 (0.0)	2	8	10 (20)	11	2	9	18.2 (0.00)
Others	0	1	1 (0.0)	n.a.	n.a.	n.a.	1	0	1	0.0 (n.a.)
Totals	22	18	40 (55.0)	8	12	20 (40)	60	30	30	50.0

women AMs has had a significant impact. For as Ward[29] noted, 'in the devolved institutions of Wales and Scotland the proportion of women is substantially greater, and their ability to determine the agenda correspondingly more effective'. Although it is too early in the Assembly's history to gain a full understanding of this effect, woman AMs concur with this assessment. According to one: 'having a critical mass of women parliamentarians has made a difference to what we talk about, what we prioritise, what we do, and it's made a big difference about how we do it'. A male AM described the effect of women's increased representation in the following way:

> the Assembly's gender make-up is a crucial start. In this Chamber, I am aware of the palpable difference that a strong representation of women makes. It is the Assembly's most distinctive feature. In due course, it will inform every aspect of Welsh life. A fairer representation of women in this institution makes it more representative of the society that we wish to serve, and therefore, better able to reflect the needs and aspirations of that society in our policy priorities.[30]

It is, perhaps, surprising that, whilst there was often acrimonious politicking between the parties during the Assembly's first term, some AMs are reluctant to dismiss the notion of a 'cross-party sisterhood' that was expressed during the Assembly's initial months.[31] One noted: 'it's not nonsense . . . if you look at the committees that have succeeded in working in an inclusive way; they are predominantly committees where women are ministers and feminist women that make a difference'. Yet some women AMs are cautious about the idea that the new gender settlement is, in any way, becoming 'normalised'. Referring to the way that male colleagues have returned to the issue of abandoning family-friendly working hours[32] and resisted the introduction of equality training,[33] one observed that 'there is a big risk that people get complacent about this.' However, the virtual attainment of gender equality among elected representatives *from the outset* of the new legislature, and the way that equality was built into the original legal and constitutional blueprint of the Assembly, means there is no 'institutional memory' of significant gender imbalance among representatives thereby giving credence to the idea that gender equality *has* effectively been 'normalised' in the Assembly.

Women's representation and the 'style' of politics

The experience of the Assembly supports the findings of other chapters in this book that there are differences in ways of working that are at least partly attributable to gender. However, a cautionary note is necessary here for it is hard to separate the influence of the institutional design of the Assembly with its emphasis on committee work from the way that women have influenced the style of politicking. Nevertheless, women AMs do support a link between gender, constitutional change and putative 'consensual politics'. For example, referring to the committee's gender dynamics, the chair of the Assembly's Health and Social Services Committee concluded that: 'it is true – we have worked really, really hard in my committee to work in a way that is consensual. And I think that in the three and a half years that we have been running we have only failed to come to a consensus twice.' Other women AMs spoke of their 'determination to break down tribal, confrontational politics'.

Reflecting upon this development, managers of women's groups that are participating in the new post-devolution equality agenda have pointed to the ideological background of a number of women AMs as underpinning the emergence of a new style of politics. In the words of one: 'quite a lot of the women in the Assembly have come up through feminism'. According to another interviewee: this has 'made a difference because they're more "people-centred" ... because compared to male AMs – they're more used to working with consensus'. Despite such views, a significant minority of AMs spoke of how initial progress in establishing a new, more consensual style of politics has sometimes been held back and undermined by party politics. As one interviewee put it: 'you have got seasoned politicians ... acting in such a traditional "male way" that it makes change very, very difficult and can sabotage very positive initiatives within the Assembly'.

Descriptive representation of women and deliberative democracy

The way in which descriptive representation of women strengthens the deliberative aspects of democracy has been evident during the Assembly's first term. Women AMs have brought a direct female perspective to political debate; this was not previously possible in the male-dominated Welsh Office – the former territorial ministry of the UK government that served Wales. It was also difficult to achieve in Westminster with the small number of women representing Welsh constituencies. This aspect of gender and constitutional change has been highlighted by a number of AMs. As one put it:

> the Health Minister was the first ever national co-ordinator of Welsh Women's Aid the body that campaigns to counter domestic violence – I was one of its first national chairs – now you don't bring that shared experience of twenty years working on women's issues together into an institution and then instantly drop it as soon as one of us is elected with a green rosette and one of us is elected with a red one.

Analysis of the Official Record, the daily transcript of the plenary debates of the National Assembly, reveals numerous examples of how women AMs draw upon their direct personal gendered life experiences – including accounts of prejudice, male chauvinism and sex discrimination – in order to inform political debate, and accordingly, in turn, influence public policy. Specific examples include women AMs referring to the following experiences in debate: fighting a sex discrimination case against an employer;[34] setting up an organisation to tackle domestic violence;[35] the challenges of being a woman working in agriculture;[36] difficulties facing mothers in obtaining appropriate child care facilities;[37] the provision of information on parenting skills to new mothers;[38] challenges facing women managers;[39] and equality issues facing female schoolteachers and school governors.[40] One woman AM summarised the transformation in the qualitative nature of political debate arising from the descriptive representation of women by highlighting an incontrovertible fact, male politicians are unable to inform debate in such a way. She stated:

> without women taking part in decision-making, their views and needs are bound to be overlooked to a certain extent. It means that the life circumstances and perspective of 52 per cent of the population are inevitably ignored, played down or tackled inappropriately. This does not assume that all male politicians are chauvinist pigs ... It simply recognises that one sex, however sympathetic, cannot fully and fairly represent the interests of the other.[41]

The substantive representation of women

The opportunities for the concerns and interests of women to be heard and taken into account in the policy-making process in post-devolution Wales are in part due to the fact that, in addition to constituting a critical mass, women hold key positions in the new legislature. For example, they continue to form a majority in the Assembly government's Cabinet (five out of nine ministers), something that, according to Feld, is 'unparalleled in the Western world'.[42] In addition, women chair the majority of the Assembly's 14 subject and standing committees.[43] Typified by the publication of a separate 2003 election manifesto solely focusing on equality issues, research interviews have revealed how women have exerted a strong influence in setting the Welsh executive's policy agenda.

Evidence of women's influence is also to be found in the transcripts of political debates and policy documents during the Assembly's first years. These show how women have repeatedly been able to intervene to mainstream gender equality into proceedings across all areas of government. The following is a typical example taken from a plenary debate in the legislature:

> I note that there is no reference in the report, as far as I am aware, to the cultural contributions of the women ... The aspirations in the

> report are highly commendable, but perhaps in the spirit of equality of opportunity, to which we have a *statutory obligation*, all our reports should have a feminist eye cast over them . . . to pick out the prejudices of white, middle-aged, middle-class men in grey suits.[44]

Analysis of the published minutes and policy documents of the executive's ministerial cabinet meetings over a three-year period provide further evidence of how women government ministers have intervened repeatedly in order to mainstream gender (and other strands) of equality into the executive's policy-making. Examples include interventions in relation to: funding for a Muslim women's centre,[45] policy initiatives to achieve equal pay for women,[46] gender equality in making public appointments,[47] and securing gender equality in the work of the Cabinet's Economic Research Advisory Panel.[48]

Further numerous examples of the link between the descriptive and substantive representation of women are to be found in the transcripts of the Welsh legislature's 11 member cross-party Standing Committee on Equality of Opportunity. This is not to advance an essentialist argument, for similar examples are evident in the work of the Assembly's other committees. Nevertheless the Equality Committee stands out, for it has collectively overseen a raft of reforms shaped by the Assembly's 'internal law' or standing orders that require it to effectively prioritise – or have 'particular regard' – to gender equality (as well as promote equality for groups defined by race or disability). Latterly, the committee has begun to broaden its focus beyond these (non-discrete) groups and it has considered equality of opportunity for groups defined by language, sexuality, age and faith as well as in relation to gypsy-travellers. Notable examples of such reforms include: mandatory equality of opportunity awareness training for all civil servants; the funding of a 22 per cent increase in the Assembly's pay bill in order to move towards ending the gender pay gap; and the introduction of gender budgeting into policy development and public spending decisions. In addition, the Assembly has legislated to promote equality as in the case of a new duty placed on school governors to '*promote equal opportunities and good relations* between persons of different racial groups, and between males and females'.[49]

Whilst, as the foregoing examples indicate, significant progress has been made in the substantive representation of women, key challenges remain. Not least because the new legislature has yet to achieve a *thoroughgoing* and routinsed gender mainstreaming approach to policy-making and resource allocation. Such concerns are beginning to be addressed following the publication of the Assembly Equality Committee's *Report on Mainstreaming Equality in the Work of the Assembly*.[50]

Elsewhere, further ongoing challenges lie in ensuring that the transformative effect of constitutional reform on gender and politics extends beyond the internal practices of the National Assembly. In particular, that the new 'gender settlement' following constitutional reform achieves the sustained participation in the work of government of women drawn from across Welsh civil society. To this end the Welsh government has attempted to foster citizen engagement by funding a women's consultative policy network that has over 150,000 members.[51]

Despite such initiatives, the emerging data from an extensive, in-depth questionnaire survey of 900 grass-roots members of the network paints a worrying picture of under-funding that has contributed to neo-corporatist practices[52] – or 'the exclusive relationship between a handful of privileged groups and the state, instead of the multiplicity of relevant interest groups predicted by pluralism'.[53] This follows because the women's network has had to rely upon a managerialist solutions rather than the resource-intensive method of in-depth engagement and consultation with the entire grass-roots membership when taking part in government policy consultations and setting strategic priorities.

Conclusion

This chapter has explored a period of profound change in relation to gender and 'formal' politics in Wales. In a manner that, in several respects, contrasted with events in the United Kingdom's other devolved polities, gender equality activists successfully used the opportunities presented by constitutional change to transform the role of women in politics. A woman minister in the Welsh Assembly government summarised this shift in terms of a 'greater opportunity to scrutinise and develop policy for women, by women ... fundamentally it's about greater opportunities for democracy'. Arguably, based upon such assertions, the new gender 'settlement' may, be seen as the most significant outcome of recent constitutional reform in Wales.

Whilst the newness of the post-1999 system of governance precludes a fixed assessment, the experience of the Assembly's first years provides clear empirical evidence of discontinuity with the former, pre-devolution mode of politics – and supports the principal theoretical arguments for gender equality in contemporary politics. The evidence of this transitional period shows that constitutional change has already had a significant and positive impact on the role of women in politics, increased the legal rights afforded to citizens, and advanced the promotion of equality of opportunity.

In a manner that was hitherto impossible, the presence of a 'critical' mass of female elected representatives has enabled women to influence and manage the political agenda. This marks a major development over the earlier system of governance when gender equality was not seen as the responsibility of the territorial ministry of the UK government that served Wales. During that period in the country's history women had to rely on male politicians to represent their viewpoints. In contrast, proportional descriptive representation of women as parliamentarians has changed matters and effected an improvement in the deliberative function of democracy. Women representatives have been able to influence and shape the political debate and discourse through direct reference to gendered life experiences.

Whilst the achievements should not be understated, further significant challenges remain. Not least in applying the mainstreaming concept of promoting equality to all aspects of devolved government, securing gender equality at a local level within political parties and developing the policy process in order to fully engage with, and serve the needs of, women throughout Welsh civil society. While such formidable challenges remain, it is clear that, to date, constitutional reform has redefined gender relations in national-regional government in a way that is likely to influence and inform change in other tiers of government in Wales and beyond.

Notes

The author would like to the acknowledge research funding provided by the Economic and Social Research Council in connection with the following projects: R000239410 and L219252023 (see www.esrc.ac.uk, and www.regard.ac.uk).

1 Julie Morgan MP, Debate on the Government of Wales Bill (1997) [that led to the statute establishing the National Assembly for Wales], *Hansard – Record of the British House of Commons*, 9 December 1997: column 858.
2 Department of Trade and Industry, *Fairness for All*, 16.
3 In 1997 CEMR passed a resolution which supported the mainstreaming principle and which called upon the European bodies and institutions, national governments and local and regional authorities to take into account the application of the mainstreaming principle in their policies in order to attain a balanced participation of women and men in the decision-making process (Council of European Municipalities and Regions, *Men and Women in European Municipalities*).
4 Forbes, 'The Political Meanings of the Equal Opportunities Project', 40.
5 The National Assembly formulates and passes secondary legislation. This is overseen by the Assembly's Legislation Committee. Laws passed by the Assembly are detailed at www.wales-legislation.hmso.gov.uk/legislation/wales/wales_legislation.htm. (Over 300 statutory instruments were passed in 2003.)
6 Morgan and Rees, 'Learning by Doing', 161.
7 National Assembly of Wales, *Equality Training and Raising Awareness Strategy*, paragraph 3.1.
8 All quotations that appear in this chapter are taken from original research interviews unless otherwise attributed.
9 Gutmann and Thompson, *Democracy and Disagreement*, 55.
10 Gargarella, 'Full Representation, Deliberation and Impartiality', 124.
11 See Mackay *et al.*, 'Towards a New Politics?'.
12 Lovenduski, 'Gender Politics', 718.
13 See Pateman, *Participation and Democratic Theory*.
14 Mackay and Bilton, *Learning from Experience*, 109.
15 Breitenbach *et al.*, *The Changing Politics of Gender Equality in Britain*, 11.
16 Feld, 'Women and a Welsh Parliament', 81.

17 Beveridge, 'Mainstreaming and the Engendering of Policy-making', 401.
18 See Brown et al., 'Women and Constitutional Change in Scotland and Northern Ireland'; Dobrowolsky, 'Crossing Boundaries'.
19 See Feld, 'A New Start in Wales'.
20 See Fredman, 'Equality: A New Generation?'.
21 It should be noted that equality of opportunity is a 'reserved power' and, constitutional reforms notwithstanding, principal responsibility for equality legislation in the United Kingdom currently remains with the Westminster government. However, within this legal framework the Welsh Assembly's legal equality duty simultaneously applies to all its governmental functions and modifies UK statutes that relate to the powers that the Assembly exercises (Chaney, 'The Post-devolution Equality Agenda').
22 Squires, 'The New Equalities Agenda', 211.
23 Welsh Office, *A White Paper: A Voice for Wales*, 24.
24 See Edwards and Chapman, 'Women's Political Representation in Wales'.
25 See Squires and Wickham-Jones, *Women in Parliament.*
26 Edwards and McAllister, 'One Step Forward, Two Steps Back?', 164.
27 See Bradbury *et al.*, 'Devolution and Party Change'.
28 Inter-parliamentary Union: www.ipu.org/wmn-e/classif.htm.
29 See Ward, *The Northern Ireland Assembly and Women.*
30 R. Edwards, Official Record of Proceedings, 8 March 2000.
31 See Betts *et al.*, 'Inclusive Government for Excluded Groups'.
32 Osmond, 'Constitution Building on the Hoof', 43, 46.
33 See Committee on Equality of Opportunity Proceedings, S4C2, 31 October 2001.
34 See Alison Halford AM, Official Record, 05 July 2001.
35 See Jane Hutt AM, Official Record, 18 April 2002.
36 See Elin Jones AM, Official Record, 14 December 1999.
37 See Delyth Evans AM, Official Record, 14 February 2002, and Helen Mary Jones AM, Official Record, 11 March 2003.
38 See Kirsty Williams AM, Official Record, 23 October 02.
39 See Helen Mary Jones AM, Official Record, 11 March 2003.
40 See Christine Chapman AM, Official Record, 09 November 2000.
41 See J. Randerson, 'Debate to mark International Women's Day', Official Record, 08 March 2000.
42 Feld, 'A New Start in Wales', 76.
43 Women elected representatives chair four of the seven subject committees and four of the seven standing committees (*c.* June 2004).
44 J. Randerson, Official Record, 16 January 2001.
45 Record of Cabinet meeting, 08 October 2001.
46 Record of Cabinet meeting, 26 June 2001.
47 Record of Cabinet meeting, 15 January 2001.
48 Record of Cabinet meeting, 25 November 2002.
49 Statutory Instrument No. 3027 (W.195), The School Government (Terms of Reference) (Wales) Regulations (2000), clauses 2b, i–ii.
50 See National Assembly for Wales, *Report on Mainstreaming Equality in the Work of the Assembly.*
51 See Chaney, 'Social Capital and the Participation of Marginalized Groups in Government'.
52 See Chaney, 'Setting the Agenda?'.
53 Wilson, 'Neo-corporatism and the Rise of New Social Movements', 69.

12 Women in Northern Ireland's politics

Feminising an 'armed patriarchy'

Yvonne Galligan

The twin processes of devolution and a search for peace have had a notable impact on Northern Ireland's political arrangements since the mid-1990s. Constitutional reform in the United Kingdom gave Northern Ireland a regional political identity akin to that of Scotland and Wales, and opened up opportunities for self-government that had been absent since direct rule was imposed on the province in 1972. A parallel peace process, ongoing since the mid-1990s, delivered the stability necessary for self-administration to take root. Important shifts in Northern Ireland's customary political paradigm, then, provided a period of opportunity for the development of a new relationship between civil society, government, and the state.[1]

The devolution of power was predicated on civil-society participation in the democratic dialogue and in the process of institution-building, and it is in this context that women in Scotland and Wales mobilised to influence the constitutional and political order in their regions. Compared with their counterparts in Scotland and Wales, the environment for women's political mobilisation in the post-conflict politics of Northern Ireland was more complex and more circumscribed. None the less, the gradual evolution of a political settlement and the suspension of the ethno-national conflict created a temporary space in which women sought to shape democratic arrangements in the region.

In order to assess women's participation in building the democratic order in post-conflict Northern Ireland, this chapter will first consider the bitter sectarian history of the preceding 30 years and its impact on women's political engagement. It will then turn to women's role in negotiating the 1998 Good Friday Agreement, and finally will consider women's participation in electoral politics since the first Northern Ireland Assembly elections in 2000. The discussion concludes with an assessment of women's political future in a region of the United Kingdom that now enjoys a measure of political stability, but which, at the time of writing, has not yet resolved ethno-national issues of governance.

Women and political conflict, 1969–1994

Although male hegemony in political affairs was apparent in many liberal democracies in the 1970s, the particular circumstances of Northern Ireland's unhappy history served to reinforce women's already considerable marginalisation from political life. The Northern Ireland House of Commons, from its inception in 1921 until abolition in 1972, was a remarkably all-male institution, with only nine women (4 per cent) among the total of 242 MPs elected to the 52 member House.[2] Although the relative absence of women from political power was not an unusual feature of parliamentary life during this time, what was significant and later became relevant to modern patterns of female participation was the political dominance of the Unionist Party. Protestant/Unionist political control of the region was almost absolute and effected through a combination of a plurality electoral system and manipulation of constituency boundaries. Catholic/Nationalist representation was minimal, although the Catholics comprised over two-fifths of the population.

In the mid-1960s the anti-Catholic policies of the Unionist Party came under renewed criticism from civil rights activists and nationalist leaders. A series of peaceful civic protests against the sectarian housing and employment policies of the Unionist government met with a repressive response from the police. The situation rapidly spiralled into violence, leading to the outbreak of the 'Troubles' in 1969 and the beginning of three decades of ethno-national conflict. This turn of events militarised and further masculinised society, leading to the oft-quoted description of Northern Ireland as an 'armed patriarchy'. Women's invisibility in the public life of Northern Ireland, and the limited impact of gender politics, are attributed to this militarism, along with the dominance of the constitutional debate on Northern Ireland's relationship within the United Kingdom and with the Republic of Ireland, and the religious and socio-economic conservatism of the region. The restricted civic space for women in this period has been summed up as follows:

> The traditional link between nationalism (both orange and green) and their respective churches has ensured that the ultra-conservative view of women as both the property of, and the inferior of men remains strongly entrenched.[3]

The particular difficulties presented by conflict politics may have circumscribed the public space available to women, but did not wholly eliminate it. The Northern Ireland Women's Rights Movement (NIWRM), founded in 1975, brought together trade union women, socialist and liberal feminists, civil rights campaigners, radical and lesbian feminists and community activists in a broad coalition campaigning for women's equality. In an effort to forge a common identity and shape a common cause among women, the NIWRM campaigns focused on the gendered nature of unequal treatment in Northern Ireland. This basis for feminist action was adopted because of an acute awareness among Northern Ireland women that nationalism as an ideology held little hope for gender equality, and that historically nationalist leaders had sought to divide feminists to the advantage of the nationalist cause. However, in a society where competing nationalisms formed the basis of political, social, cultural and economic cleavages, attempts to minimise the 'national question' in the cause of feminist solidarity strained NIWRM and led to numerous splits and regroupings. From the mid-1970s, the wider discourse of competing nationalisms created parallel political and social universes, one based around unionism, loyalism and Protestantism, the other focused on Irish nationalism, republicanism and Catholicism. Both ideologies confined women's community and political activism within their respective territorial, political and cultural boundaries.

Territorial segregation became an increasing defining feature of women's civic engagement as the 'Troubles' persisted, accentuating sectarianism and making cross-community work a dangerous activity. It was not the only restriction on women's civic engagement, however. The innate conservatism of both orange and green nationalism ordained that traditional family-related roles provided their only source of socially sanctioned positions for many working-class women. Women's politics, then, was local, community-oriented and focused on supporting family and community life under the pressures of conflict. It has been observed that women's civic role as guardian of the family and community was more starkly defined when the men from their ethnic group were in prison. This 'family feminism', centring on protection of the family and the community to which they belonged, politicised women's roles without impacting on gender inequality.[4] Not surprisingly, community activists were unlikely to identify as feminist, and the different interpretations of events and experiences in a divided society led to tensions between self-identified feminists and community-based women.[5] Yet, as the conflict moved into its third decade, a multi-strand women's sector flourished. While women's scope for influencing policy and politics remained heavily conditioned and circumscribed by competing political perspectives on Northern Ireland's relationship within the United Kingdom and with the Republic of Ireland, tentative indicators of a peace process in the 1990s opened opportunities for women's groups to make their voices heard.

The emerging peace process, facilitated by the declaration of republican and loyalist cease-fires in 1994, renewed women's sense of exclusion from plans for a post-conflict polity. Mobilising their energies and resources, women's activists held a series of public discussions to press for inclusion of women in decision-making on the future of Northern Ireland.[6] Some of these events were supported and partly funded by the British government's Northern Ireland Office. A period of public dia-

Table 12.1 Northern Ireland's candidates and elected representatives, 1973–2003, by gender

Year	*Candidates*			*Elected representatives*		
	Men	*Women*	*% women*	*Men*	*Women*	*% women*
1973	194	16	7	74	4	5
1975	158	7	4	74	4	5
1982	175	9	5	75	3	4
1996	640	272	30	95	15	14
1998	247	49	17	94	14	13
2003	207	49	19	90	18	17

Note
Elections in 1973, 1982, 1998 and 2003 were to the Northern Ireland Assembly; the election in 1975 was to the Constitutional Convention, and in 1996 the election was to the Forum for All-party Dialogue.

logue between 1993 and 1995 brought about the reiteration of women's demands for inclusion in the peace process, especially in the planned constitutional, or 'peace', talks. In this regard, the lessons from other devolving regions of the United Kingdom, notably Scotland, were closely observed and discussed by women's groups and in particular women's demand for 50:50 dual-member constituencies was examined as a way of ensuring gender equality in political representation for Northern Ireland.[7]

Women and the Good Friday Agreement

On 28 February 1996, almost three weeks after the ending of the first IRA cease-fire, the Irish and British governments issued a joint communiqué proposing elections to choose delegates to a peace talks Forum, and invited parties to present their views on an inclusive electoral system that would give representation to all participants in the conflict, including the political wings of paramilitary organisations. Although the invitation was not intended for the voluntary sector, many groups responded, including the Northern Ireland Women's European Platform (NIWEP). Arguably one of the most politically skilled of women's groups in Northern Ireland at the time, NIWEP quickly pointed out the structural exclusion of women from the proposed talks, highlighted the beneficial effects of including women's perspectives and experiences in such discussions, and advocated gender-proofing of party lists. Their efforts met with little success. When plans for the electoral process leading to the peace talks were published, they revealed a two-tier electoral system consisting of 18 constituencies with five members from each elected through party lists and a regional top-up list of 20 seats, electing a total of 110 members to the Forum for Political Understanding and Dialogue.[8] The British government followed this announcement with the publication of a preliminary list of 15 parties whom it intended to endorse as entitled to nominate candidates. Women activists quickly realised that the proposals were far from woman-friendly.

In response to the absence of gender-proofing of party lists, NIWEP urged personnel in the Northern Ireland Office and officials of the Irish government to include a women's network on the list of accredited parties. Shortly thereafter, the government published a final register of 30 eligible parties, including a women's party, the Northern Ireland Women's Coalition. The sudden emergence of a women's party in the inhospitable political landscape of Northern Ireland can be attributed to the convergence of three factors: the existence of women's networks sensitive to a gendered analysis of power and their availability for mobilisation around this issue; the construction of a new political framework to determine Northern Ireland's future; and the exclusion of women's voices from the emerging decision-making processes.[9]

The formation of the Northern Ireland Women's Coalition was greeted in a rather restrained manner by some sectors of the women's movement. Activists from republican and loyalist traditions expressed strong reservations about the creation of a women's party that risked falling apart when confronted with a political settlement preferring one nationalist tradition over the other. For many of these women, the election itself was a discredited exercise, perceived as yet another process that validated British rule. Others feared that a focus on gender issues would place the new party in an isolated 'feminist' camp with little to contribute to the wider constitutional questions that affected all women's lives. None the less, the new party contested the Forum elections with 68 female candidates and campaigned on a platform of recognition of women's contribution to the future of Northern Ireland, a willingness to seek a political accommodation that was inclusive of all interests, and a commitment to equity, social justice and human rights. Although it eschewed a position on the 'national question' and thereby reduced its electoral opportunities, the novelty value of an all-woman party attracted significant media attention. Through considerable hard work, a high turnout, and the opportunity for change presented by the election, the party gained two seats at the talks, and along with 13 women elected from other party lists, brought women's representation in the Forum to just under 14 per cent.

The Forum quickly became an unworkable institution because nationalists did not consider it an appropriate arena for negotiations on the fundamental constitutional issue, and it was superseded by a new US-backed peace initiative. None the less, all parties agreed to use the results of the Forum elections as a basis for selecting their negotiating teams for the substantive inter-party talks chaired by US Senator George Mitchell. These discussions got under way in earnest in autumn 1997 following the restoration of the IRA cease-fire and the acceptance of Sinn Féin into the settlement discussions. A negotiated agreement was due for completion by

April of the following year. The Democratic Unionist Party, led by Protestant churchman Dr Ian Paisley, was highly critical of the entry of Sinn Féin into the talks and refused to participate in the inter-party negotiations. None the less, the talks on a constitutional settlement for Northern Ireland proceeded and on 10 April 1998 the Good Friday Agreement (also known as the Belfast Agreement) was signed. In the course of the negotiations, the Women's Coalition sought to achieve accommodation between the ethnonational views based on the party's core principles of justice, equity and human rights. The Women's Coalition experience of understanding, respecting and accommodating difference, developed through women's activism across the community divide, was thus brought to bear on the settlement talks. This form of interaction was aided by the basic principle underpinning the negotiations, that an agreement was not possible without compromise, countering the zero-sum politics traditionally pursued by the major parties in Northern Ireland. However, their position in the peace talks was often misrepresented by other parties in the process, with allegations from unionist supporters of the party sympathising with republicans, and charges from republicans of the Women's Coalition being too close to the unionist political agenda. Neither side openly recognised the transversal nature of the Women's Coalition's feminist politics.

The final agreement bore evidence of the influence of the Women's Coalition, with statements on equality and gender-proofing, proposals for a victims commission, and a commitment to the creation of a Civic Forum, institutionalising the principle of gender equality and bringing the voices of civil society into the political structures.[10] The party lost the argument for an electoral system similar to that proposed for the Scottish parliament, with proportional representation by single transferable vote being the preferred system of election. Once again, the possibility of representation for women in the new Assembly rested with the inclinations of the Northern Ireland parties.

A referendum on the island of Ireland saw the Good Friday Agreement, with its complex formula for Northern Irish, North and South (of Ireland) and British–Irish pan-island political relationships, was sanctioned by 71 per cent of the voters in Northern Ireland and 94 per cent of the republic's electorate. Although a majority of unionist supporters voted in favour of the agreement, a substantial minority rejected its terms, and were given political voice by Ian Paisley's Democratic Unionist Party. The first elections to the new Northern Ireland Assembly, held later in 1998, were fought around a new cleavage in Northern Irish politics – that of pro- and anti-agreement – that complicated, but did not undermine, the old ethnic divide. The PR-STV electoral system provided for 18 constituencies with six seats in each one. The Women's Coalition won two seats in this 108 seat devolved Assembly, and in total women won 14 (13 per cent) Assembly seats in this all-important first election of the devolved institution (Table 12.2).

Table 12.2 Northern Ireland's Assembly candidates 1998 and 2003, by party and gender

Party	*1998*			*2003*			*% change on 1998*
	Men	*Women*	*% women*	*Men*	*Women*	*% women*	
UUP	44	4	8	39	4	9	+1
SDLP	32	6	16	30	6	17	+1
DUP	30	4	12	36	4	10	−2
SF	29	8	22	26	12	32	+10
APNI	16	6	27	13	8	38	+11
NIWC	0	8	100	0	7	100	n.a.
Others	96	13	12	64	8	11	−1
Total	247	49	17	207	49	19	+2

Source: www.qub.ac.uk/cawp/UKhtmls/electionNInov03.htm.

Note
UUP Ulster Unionist Party, SDLP Social Democratic and Labour Party, DUP Democratic Unionist Party, SF Sinn Féin, APNI Alliance Party of Northern Ireland, NIWC Northern Ireland Women's Coalition.

The peace process, however, was not solely centred on the development of new political institutions, and the Good Friday Agreement opened policy, as well as electoral, opportunities for the gender agenda. The 1998 Northern Ireland Act, which granted devolved powers to the Assembly, also provided a highly sophisticated equality framework for the region, one that was far in advance of the equal opportunities models proposed for either the Scottish or the Welsh devolved administrations. Section 75(1) of this Act sought to mainstream equality of opportunity in public policy for gender and eight other groups. Northern Ireland's public authorities were already accustomed to implementing equity guidelines on religious background and political opinion (in the main), which over the course of the 1980s and 1990s had expanded to include other forms of discrimination, including gender. However, the context of the Good Friday Agreement provided an opportunity for further development of this agenda.

Australian political scientist Tahnya Donaghy observes the confluence of three relatively separate developments leading to an enhancement of the equality agenda – a pre-existing sophisticated communal discourse on equality issues; the mobilisation of civil society (including women's groups) around the need for a statutory obligation on public authorities to deliver on equal opportunities; and the need for the British government to comply with international commitments to mainstream equality in public policy.[11] A crucial role in shaping the 'equality duty' (or legal obligation to provide for equality of opportunity across nine grounds) was played by a loose grouping of activists, trade unionists and human rights

NGOs under the umbrella of the Equality Coalition. Perhaps even more than in Scotland and Wales, there was a view held generally by parties and governments, as well as civic groups, that civil society support for the agreement was vital to its successful adoption, and to the devolution of power. The outcome was the creation of a statutory obligation on all public bodies to provide equal opportunities on nine grounds, including equality between men and women, and for this duty to be overseen, monitored and reviewed by an Equality Commission. The value of Donaghy's work in this area is not only in charting the detail of the development of Northern Ireland's mainstreaming infrastructure, but also in drawing attention to the highly participative nature of this process, with civil society being centrally involved in framing this aspect of the legislation.

The implementation of Section 75 of the Northern Ireland Act continued this close engagement between policy-makers and civil society, opening up policy developments to previously excluded groups and, in the case of gender equality, opening channels of communication on policy between the Equality Unit and its Gender Policy section in the Office of First Minister and Deputy First Minister in the Northern Ireland Executive and civil-society groups. Even in the circumstances of a restoration of direct rule from late 2002 onwards, this bureaucratic–civil society relationship survived. Thus, in the absence of institutional devolution, the peace process, with its equality agenda, continued on a policy level. During 2004–05, the women's sector successfully lobbied direct-rule ministers for a restoration of funding to women's groups (funding was cut due to the ending of European 'peace' monies) and the reintegration of childcare provision into the funding of post-conflict reconciliation projects. Individual women MLAs facilitated the women's agenda, utilising their special access to government decision-makers to act as a conduit between the women's sector and Northern Ireland ministers. In the absence of a working Assembly offering some prospect, however slight, of the representation of women's concerns, feminist MLAs work with women's groups and women's interests are articulated through civil society, where highly politicised and effectively mobilised women's groups lobby the UK government, the European Commission and local Westminster and European MPs in pursuit of their aims. In the longer term, however, the freezing of the political institutions and the difficulties in negotiating an end to the divided politics of the last three decades have eroded the legitimacy of all Assembly representatives.

Women's space in the devolved Northern Ireland Assembly

The devolved institutions for Northern Ireland, products of the Good Friday Agreement and the devolution process across the United Kingdom, came into effect in December 1999. As with the Scottish Parliament and Welsh Assembly, the Northern Ireland Assembly at Stormont was not totally independent from Westminster, with the mother of parliaments retaining some jurisdiction over the Northern Ireland Assembly — chiefly in the areas of security, policing, taxation and foreign policy. Thus, while having less independence than Scotland, Northern Ireland's devolution project was on a par with the Welsh Assembly in terms of its relationship with Westminster. The institutional arrangements for the Northern Ireland Assembly were typical of those found in the parent parliament – plenary meetings, a committee structure with similar functions to those found in Westminster, and an Executive answerable to the Assembly.

There were, however, some important differences. For one, the Executive was composed in a manner different from the 'winner takes all' process underpinning the formation of a UK government. The political resolution of a long period of violent ethno-national conflict brought a power-sharing Executive into being, with representation from the four main ethnic parties according to their seat share in the Assembly and a joint leadership, again reflecting the ethnic divide, in the positions of First Minister and Deputy First Minister. An additional deviation from the 'normal' Westminster parliamentary rules governed the voting process of the Assembly: some critical issues, such as the election of First Minister and Deputy First Minister, required 'parallel consent' of the two ethnic blocs in the Assembly. In order to give effect to this voting rule, members were required to register their affiliation as nationalist, unionist or 'other' upon election. This requirement gave rise to difficulties for parties which had fought the election on non-nationalist grounds – the Alliance Party and the Women's Coalition – and was to put them under pressure to identify with one side or the other in moments of institutional crisis thereafter. An additional difference from the Westminster model is the absence of an effective opposition scrutiny of the Executive's policy-making, as the four major parties are represented in the power-sharing Executive. Debates in the legislature, then, remain cast along lines dictated by ethno-national identity rather than being determined by more conventional ideological positions.

This institutional background underlines the quite restricted space for gender politics in the Assembly. An analysis of women's participation, descriptive and substantive, is further hampered by the short time the Assembly actually functioned as a working body. Shortly after its empowerment on 2 December 1999, the institution faced one of many crises, and was suspended by the Secretary of State for Northern Ireland on 11 February 2000. Power was not restored to the Assembly until 29 May that year, but problems with the practicalities of power-sharing led to three further suspensions – 10–11 August 2001, 22–23 September 2001 and 15 October 2002. By mid-2005 the prospect of a restoration of devolved power to Northern Ireland was remote, and although the parties continued to engage in dialogue with the UK and Irish governments, the two main ethno-national bloc representatives – Sinn Féin and the Democratic Unionist Party – were not in negotiation with one another.

Despite the intermittent sitting of this devolved institution, there have been some opportunities to assess women's political contributions during the lifetime of the Assembly, even if the scope for examining their legislative actions is restricted by the wider challenges posed by the uncertainty around developing democratic politics in a post-conflict environment. Women's descriptive presence in the Assembly has not yet reached the level of that in other devolved institutions across the United Kingdom. Compared with Scotland's 42 per cent female MSPs and the equal gender representation among Welsh Assembly members, Northern Ireland fares badly. The 14 women elected in 1998 rose to 18 (17 per cent) in the 2003 Stormont Assembly elections, underlining the reluctance of parties to take advantage of the Westminster legislation permitting all-woman shortlists in party candidate selection processes.

The reluctance to adopt gender equity initiatives stems from a traditional perspective on women's role, more explicitly expressed in unionist politics than among nationalist parties, and among unionism the gender equality agenda has a very low priority. Table 12.3 shows that the paucity of women is not spread evenly across all parties. In general, unionist parties appear more unwilling to admit women to political office than do parties on the nationalist side. Both the Ulster Unionist Party (UUP) and the Democratic Unionist Party (DUP) indicate a serial reluctance to select women, thereby restricting unionist women's political opportunities. Shortly after the 2003 election, the collapse of the Ulster Unionist Party vote led to internal party recriminations and the defection of a number of party representatives, including the two female UUP politicians, to the more hard-line DUP.

Table 12.3 Northern Ireland's Assembly members, 1998 and 2003, by party and gender

Party	*1998*			*2003*			*% change on 1998*
	Men	*Women*	*% women*	*Men*	*Women*	*% women*	
UUP	26	2	7	25	2	7	0
SDLP	21	3	13	13	5	22	+9
DUP	19	1	5	28	2	7	+2
SF	13	5	28	17	7	29	+1
APNI	5	1	17	4	2	33	+16
NIWC	0	2	n.a.	0	0	0	n.a.
Others	10	0	0	3	0	0	n.a.
Total	94	14	13	90	18	17	+4

Source: www.qub.ac.uk/cawp/UKhtmls/MLA.htm.

Note

UUP Ulster Unionist Party, SDLP Social Democratic and Labour Party, DUP Democratic Unionist Party, SF Sinn Féin, APNI Alliance Party of Northern Ireland, NIWC Northern Ireland Women's Coalition.

The nationalist Social Democratic and Labour Party (SDLP) increased its women's representation to just over one-fifth (22 per cent) of elected members, despite its falling vote share, while the small cross-community Alliance Party of Northern Ireland (APNI) succeeded in doubling its female return to the 2003 Assembly with an increase of one woman. Sinn Féin retained the 30 per cent female composition of its representatives across both elections. The overall increase of four seats in women's membership of the Assembly in 2003 was, however, overshadowed by the Women's Coalition loss of both its seats. Party leader Monica McWilliams lost her seat by just 127 votes to a male SDLP politician in South Belfast, while Jane Morris, Deputy Speaker of the Assembly, lost her seat in North Down.

Although relatively few women make it into elected office in Northern Ireland, there is a consistent pattern since the 1990s of the nationalist/Catholic parties being more accommodating to women than unionist/Protestant parties. This behaviour is unexpected when one considers the more generally observed phenomenon of Catholic parties, and Catholicism in general, being less women-friendly than Protestantism in terms of women's political rights and representation. There are a number of reasons for Northern Ireland's apparent anomaly in this regard. Perhaps the most fundamental explanation is that both the SDLP and Sinn Fein, in challenging the hegemony of unionism, needed to mobilise support from all members of the nationalist community and in so doing were confronted with the realisation that women's political voice was a relevant part of the image and agenda of nationalist politics. Women were central figures in the Northern Ireland civil rights movement that led to the establishment of the SDLP, many of whom remained closely connected with grass-roots campaigns for social and political justice espoused by the SDLP. The republican movement could not deny women's critical role in holding nationalist working-class communities together throughout the conflict. Women were also involved in the 'armed struggle', prepared to risk and lose their lives in the cause of Irish freedom. Thus, women's active political participation in constitutional and revolutionary nationalism was a component of the pressure for political change in Northern Ireland.

Although the feminist movement was relatively weak compared with the mobilisation in Britain, feminist analyses of public and private power were readily incorporated into the perspectives of already politicised women in the Catholic community. This led to political women organising within their respective parties for gender equality in terms of representation and policy, presenting a challenge to the male-dominated party and political hierarchies within nationalism. In addition, in articulating a politics that sought to challenge the Protestant/unionist hegemony, both the SDLP and Sinn Féin positioned themselves on the liberal left dimension of the political spectrum, espousing a progressive or socialist analysis of economic and social injustices compatible with strands of liberation theology in Catholicism, and close to the social action perspective supported by many Catholic clergy in Northern Ireland.

These undercurrents of feminist political engagement, however, were strongly resisted in the highly masculinised party cultures of Sinn Féin and the SDLP until the emergence of the Women's Coalition. Both parties quickly recognised that the NIWC posed an electoral challenge to their support base. Women within nationalist parties saw the opportunity to push their demands for inclusion in party structures and electoral politics. A confluence of political and social conditions, then, led nationalism to provide a space within which women's political voice could find expression – a space that was not available to women within unionist parties preoccupied with resisting the political demands of nationalists and holding on to the *status quo* with all its innate conservatism.

The gains made by women within nationalist parties translated into ministerial power. Women's representation on the Executive stands in contrast to their paucity in the Assembly: three women (30 per cent) held ministerial posts before the suspension in late 2002 – in agriculture, health and (at a later date) employment and learning. Nor surprisingly, these positions were held by women from nationalist parties, one Sinn Féin (Bairbre de Brun in Health), and two SDLP: Bríd Rodgers (Agriculture) and Carmel Hanna (Employment and Learning). In a comment on women's post-holding in the new Assembly, Rodgers observed, 'when they were giving out the ministerial portfolios at the Assembly, the two women were given the two that nobody else wanted'.[12] However, women were less visible in the Assembly's committees, and their membership, at 15 per cent, closely matched their overall presence in Stormont and was unevenly spread among the ten policy committees. Women were strongly represented on the Health, Social Services and Public Safety Committee (45 per cent), Enterprise, Trade and Investment (27 per cent) and Higher and Further Education (27 per cent), but the important Finance and Personnel Committee was a male-only grouping, as were the significant committees of Agriculture and Rural Development, and Regional Development. There is further evidence in the allocation of committee memberships of the gender stereotyping that appeared to operate in the allocation of ministerial portfolios.

An early achievement of the Women's Coalition, supported by the SDLP, was the introduction of family-friendly hours and timetable in the new Assembly. Symbolically an important decision, it complemented efforts by some Members of the Local Assembly (MLAs), led by Eileen Bell of the Alliance Party, to form a cross-party caucus to discuss and promote women's issues, to share information and to support one another in carrying out their legislative roles. However, once again, communal identity proved stronger than gender identity, and women from the unionist parties were reluctant to participate in the group, especially when Sinn

Féin members were present. Thus, the effort to enhance the low representation of women in the Assembly by creating a supportive network did not materialise, although relations among them remained relatively cordial.

The strong party discipline typical of Westminster parliaments also carried over into the practices of the new Stormont Assembly, and was reinforced by the ethno-national cleavage structuring politics in the province. There was minimal deviation from party whip instructions in the Assembly. This fact, along with the knowledge that women and men did not differ significantly in the amount and types of parliamentary questions they posed to ministers, suggests that it is difficult to find objective evidence of gender differences in political behaviour in the Assembly. Instead, we must investigate the subjective interpretations of their legislative role held by female and male MLAs.

The literature on gender and parliamentary behaviour suggests three distinct areas in which women and men differ. On the policy front, women are generally found to raise and participate in debates on issues related to women and family more frequently than men. Studies also indicate that women legislators have a different leadership style from men, being more likely to emphasise negotiation, consensus-building and collective ownership of an outcome than men. The relationship between female representatives and their constituents is also seen to be qualitatively different from that experienced by male representatives and constituents. Women legislators are seen to be more closely connected with their constituents, place a greater priority than men on constituency work, and are more inclined to enable their constituents contribute to, and shape, their parliamentary positions.

Many of the insights of the literature on gender and parliamentary behaviour are derived from studies of US state and federal-level government, where party discipline is less confining, and women's opportunities for opening up political spaces to gender are arguably greater than in Westminster-type parliaments. Given the Westminster basis of the Northern Ireland Assembly, the absence of a critical mass of female representatives, along with the particularly complex political arrangements that inadvertently act to counter the development of conventional pluralist politics, the search for examples of women 'making a difference' is a particularly challenging one. Yet, even in the stony soil of Northern Ireland's politics, one can find some evidence of gender differences in political priorities, attitudes towards their representative role and style of decision-making. However, one must preface a discussion of these gender differences with acknowledgement of the overall similarity of views held by women and men towards these matters – if there is a difference, it is one of degree rather than a gender polarisation.

Given the highly masculinised politics of Northern Ireland, it comes as no surprise to find that the new Stormont Assembly was infused with a strongly masculinist culture. Indeed, from an early stage, many female MLAs were concerned at the lack of respect shown to them by their male colleagues during plenary sessions. Evident initially during the Forum talks, when Women's Coalition representatives were verbally abused by male representatives from the unionist community, this antipathy to female politicians carried into the Stormont debates when all women from non-unionist parties were, at some point, subjected to inappropriate sexist remarks.[13] Although women have not succumbed under the weight of coping with robust partisan politics, the persistent verbal disparaging did make one female MLA wish for 'male unionists to be sent on a course on good manners, respect and basic decency', while some male MLAs also expressed concern at the denigration of women's contributions to Assembly debates. Yet, even in this woman-unfriendly culture, female MLAs succeeded in having the institution work to family-friendly hours, similar to the innovations in the Scottish Parliament and Welsh Assembly.

In a 2001 survey of 27 MLAs, composed of 14 women and 13 men, when the Assembly had completed ten months of uninterrupted working, it became clear that there were strong similarities between male and female policy priorities – identified as education and establishing a commissioner for children, policing, the economy, environment and planning, and energy policy. This group was also more similar than different when taking a view on the tasks of being a representative, with assisting constituents and presenting their party position on the constitutional question comprising a significant part of their agenda as MLAs. Respondents also agreed that the party position on any issue was the most important influence on how they voted in the Assembly. Gender differences emerged only in relation to their attitudes towards women. Female MLAs were more conscious of gender discrimination across a range of measures, and adopted more liberal positions on women's social roles, than their male counterparts. Interestingly, the measure eliciting the strongest divergence in views asked respondents to judge whether elected women or men were the more politically astute. In contrast to the female respondents, their male colleagues held a poor view of the political judgement of women political office-holders, providing further evidence for the contention that male politicians in Northern Ireland hold stereotypical views of women's political abilities.

These findings broadly corroborate qualitative studies of the self-confidence of male members of the Assembly and lends further credence to observations regarding the male-gendered culture of this new institution. It also nuances some of the general literature findings, especially on women's construction of their representative role, gender differences in policy priorities and in political styles. The case of Northern Ireland's Assembly and its gender relationships indicates that in parliaments with devolved mandates the scope for gender differences to emerge in political priorities and in views on the role of the representative is more restricted than in sovereign or federal parliaments. In essence, backbench legislators in the Assembly cannot rely on oppositional politics to develop a profile: their contribution to policy takes place in committees, where it is more difficult to develop an individual profile. Anecdotal information suggests that while the ethno-national divide is blurred in committee work, the general conservative outlook on women's political participation carries through in attitudes towards women MLA's contributions. Unfortunately, the repeated and continued suspension of the Assembly has meant that further studies of parliamentary behaviour are not possible, therefore these tentative findings cannot be tested through observing the legislative behaviour of Northern Ireland's MLAs.

Where to for women in Northern Ireland politics?

The political opportunities for advancing a gender agenda which opened with the prospect of a peaceful settlement to Northern Ireland's sectarian conflict in the mid-1990s seemed to close with the suspension of the Assembly in 2002. In one respect, though, the future is not completely bleak. The gender equality agenda is embedded in the policy process as a result of the equality duty in Section 75, though this is to a large extent dependent on the will and commitment of bureaucrats to continue its development. None the less, the peace and devolution processes have left an equality infrastructure in place that can be utilised by civil society groups and by equality-seeking agencies to continue addressing gender concerns. The mobilisation of loose civil society–agency coalitions seen in the process leading to Section 75, can become active when the opportunity is presented, such as election time. The Equality Commission, the Women's Committee of the Irish Congress of Trade Unions and a broad NGO, the Women's Policy Group, produced a Women's Manifesto for the 2003 Assembly elections that attracted widespread endorsement from civil society and individual politicians. Yet, although women's activism in civil society is vibrant, grass-roots initiatives by women's organisations are threatened by loss of public funding and they suffer the consequences of economic and motivational disempowerment. Meanwhile, at the interfaces of Catholic and Protestant working-class communities, sectarian tensions have not diminished, and many women are as caught in this destructive dynamic as are their menfolk.

While a survey of the contemporary scene of women's civic engagement paints a mixed and multi-layered picture, the political participation of women, however, is more stark. In effect, women's political participation is in crisis, and seems set to continue in this way for the foreseeable future. This crisis is multi-dimensional: traditional perspectives on women's social roles continue to play an important part in structuring women's political opportunities; the prolonged suspension of the Assembly limits elected women's capacity to be role models for future women leaders; and the search for a resolution to the constitutional issue dominates political discourse at the expense of pluralist politics.

One outcome of the 2003 election to the Northern Ireland Assembly was the loss of the two Women's Coalition seats to other parties. This result was interpreted as disappointing for feminist voices in the province, reinforcing the suggestion that the consociational basis for the peace agreement has, ironically, had the effect of entrenching communal divisions rather than ameliorating them. Thus, while women's seat-holding in Stormont could be categorised as hovering around that of a 'tilted' group with a relatively tokenist presence, their constrained space for representing women was, and is, further restricted by the continuing dominance of constitutional political questions. This challenging environment, in the absence of a critical mass of women MLAs and the continued stereotyping of gender roles, along with the continued suspension of the regional government and legislature, offers a particularly difficult context for the emergence of gender politics. Although Northern Ireland women have begun to break into Westminster and the European Parliament, their presence in these institutions has relatively little impact on political life in the region.[14] In this unusual context, the legacy of the Westminster parliamentary tradition has deep roots, but so too has the sectarian influence on politics. Together, they present a formidable obstacle to women's representation in any future devolved Northern Ireland Assembly.

Notes

1 Meehan, 'From Government to Governance', 15–16.
2 www.qub.ac.uk/cawp/observatory.html.
3 McWilliams and McKiernan, *Bringing it out in the Open*, 81.
4 McDonough, 'Integration or Independence', www.democraticdialogue.org/report4.
5 Miller *et al.*, *Women and Political Participation in Northern Ireland*, 219–22.
6 Rooney, 'Women in Northern Irish Politics', 171–2.
7 Hinds, 'Women Working for Peace in Northern Ireland', 119.
8 This was the only occasion on which a list system was used. Elections to the new Northern Ireland Assembly have been conducted under PR-STV, as have elections to local councils since 1976.
9 This analysis draws significantly on Hinds ('Women Working for Peace in Northern Ireland', 121–2). Hinds was a founder member of the NIWC and is a long-time feminist activist.
10 Fearon and McWilliams, 'Swimming against the Mainstream', 129–30.
11 Donaghy, 'Mainstreaming: Northern Ireland's Participative–Democratic Approach', 5.
12 Ward, *The Northern Ireland Assembly and Women*, 10.
13 All commentators on gender and the institutional politics of Northern Ireland note the systematic attempts by male politicians, mainly from unionist parties, to undermine women's political agency with sexist remarks. Early comments often referred to women's reproductive roles such as the one directed at Monica McWilliams by Ian Paisley to the effect that rather than being in politics she would be better off spending her time at home 'breeding for Ulster'.

14 The 2005 UK general election saw the return of three women to Westminster from Northern Ireland – Iris Robinson (DUP), Sylvia Hermon (Unionist) and Michelle Gildernew (SF). All three women were first returned to the House of Commons in 2001. Ms Hermon is the Unionist Party's only MP. Ms Gildernew is an abstentionist MP. Bairbre de Brun (SF) was one of three MEPs returned from Northern Ireland in the 2004 elections to the European Parliament.

13 Paradise lost?

Gender parity and the Nunavut experience

Manon Tremblay and Jackie F. Steele

In 1999 Canada saw the addition of a third Territory to its political landscape, namely, the Territory of Nunavut, which means 'Our Land' or 'Our Home' in the Inuit language of Inuktitut. Situated in the Canadian Arctic, Nunavut covers over 1.9 million sq. km representing almost 20 per cent of the total area of Canada. This vast territory is inhabited by the Inuit people, whose culture and ways on the land have allowed them to live in conditions that most Canadians would consider inhospitable. Heavily dependent upon financial transfers from the federal government, the Territory of Nunavut has a mixed economy, wherein both an emergent cash economy and the relationship with the land continue to be essential. Straddling tradition and modernity, the expression of this hybrid reality can be found in the political regime of Nunavut. If the new Canadian territory maintained a privileged place for British-style parliamentary traditions, it also sought to adapt them to Inuit traditions of equality. The best example of this can be found in the proposal to retain a first-past-the-post system but to make it a two-member system that reflects the gendered duality of humanity.

An analysis of this proposal for two-member, gender-balanced representation will be the focus of this chapter. We will begin with a general profile of Nunavut, followed by an outline of the theoretical framework inspiring our analysis and the methodology employed. We will then provide a description of the proposal put forward by the Nunavut Implementation Commission. Finally, we will analyse the variables contributing to the defeat of the proposal and articulate the lessons that can be learned from this extremely rich case study.

A brief profile of Nunavut

The Territory of Nunavut resulted from the splitting of an existing northern polity, the Northwest Territories. Specifically, in 1976 the Inuit Tapirisat of Canada, a pan-Inuit organisation, put forward a proposal for the creation of the Territory of Nunavut, carved out of the centre and the eastern parts of the existing Northwest Territories. In the face of increasing tension around the sovereignist movement in Quebec, the federal government was hesitant to support the formation of what would become a second geographical jurisdiction that was defined by a cultural and linguistic community distinct from the rest of English-speaking Canada. None the less, after the election of a majority of Inuit representatives to the Legislative Assembly of the Northwest Territories in 1979, steps were taken to consult the population of the Northwest Territories about the division of the territory. In a plebiscite held on 14 April 1982 a majority voted in favour of the creation of the Territory of Nunavut. A tripartite Nunavut Implementation Commission was created to develop recommendations that would be adopted by representatives of the federal government, the government of the Northwest Territories, and of Nunavut Tunngavik; it served as the implementing body for the preparations leading up to the creation of the Territory of Nunavut on 1 April 1999.

According to the 2001 census, the Territory of Nunavut has a population of roughly 27,000 people, 85 per cent of whom are Inuit. The territory has the youngest population in Canada, with 60 per cent of Nunavummiut being under the age of 25.[1] However, the life expectancy of a baby born in Nunavut in 1996 was fully ten years lower than the Canadian average, and infant mortality rates were three times the national rate.[2] These statistics paint a reality for Nunavut families that is very different from the rest of Canada. In 2001, fully 34.5 per cent of girls/women were still citing pregnancy or child care responsibilities as the reason for not completing their elementary or high-school education.[3] The absence of quality child care services has been a serious disincentive to women's ability to enter the work force, given the isolation of communities.[4] This demographic reality persists within a societal context where basic infrastructure supports are gravely insufficient. Nunavut has virtually no roads and over half of Inuit residents live in overcrowded living conditions: an additional 3,000 housing units would be necessary to place the living conditions of the Inuit on a par with Canadian norms.[5]

With respect to its formal political institutions, Nunavut has for the most part adopted the Westminster model for its governance. The legislative branch of the state is composed of 19 Members of the Legislative Assembly (hereafter, MLAs), elected through a first-past-the-post electoral system. The Executive includes a Commissioner, who essentially assumes the role and tasks akin to the Lieutenant Governors of the Canadian Provinces, a Premier and Cabinet Ministers. The Premier and his/her Ministers are chosen from among the Members of the Legislative Assembly, who are all individually elected by universal suffrage and are enjoined by the principle of collective and individual ministerial responsibility. Unlike the Prime Minister of Canada and the Premiers of Canadian provinces, in Nunavut the Premier is elected by his/her peers in the Assembly.[6] Following the tradition adopted in the Northwest Territories, Nunavut has a non-partisan system that functions according to the principle of consensus, rather than the adversarial bipartisan system typical of the Westminster model. While this might seem like a good omen for women's representation, in fact the 2004 elections in Nunavut saw the election of only two women to the Nunavut Legislative Assembly, a proportion of merely 10.5 per cent. This has occurred despite the fact that the constitutional and institutional engineers of the new Territory of Nunavut had seriously reflected upon the issue of women's political underrepresentation.

Theoretical framework

When examining political institutions and practices, three main models of democracy come to mind: representative democracy, direct democracy and deliberative democracy. In Canada, although representative democracy predominates, the other models can also advance our understanding of political events. Representative democracy is grounded in the idea that the population delegates its sovereign authority to a restricted number of individuals who will act in their name. By contrast, a central tenet of direct democracy 'lies in recognizing that sovereignty rests with all citizens rather than exclusively with a small group of representatives, no matter how carefully chosen',[7] while deliberative democracy 'holds that decisions are best reached through public deliberation – argument, debate, exchange of ideas – among citizens'.[8]

The representative model of democracy raises the question of the selection and, moreover, of the identity of the representatives chosen, as well as their relationship with the population. An ongoing challenge for political theorists and practitioners, the question of who is to be selected is not new. Central to the debates leading up to the ratification of the American Constitution, the federalist camp argued in favour of the representation of ideas (and interests); the selection of representatives was understood to reflect the wisdom, virtue, talent or fortune of delegates, not their resemblance to the population at large. Conversely, anti-federalists pleaded in favour of representatives whose living conditions closely reflected that of the people, in order to better represent their realities or, in modern terms, to best reflect their diverse identities.

In addition to questions central to the theory and practice of political representation, in modern politics, two key institutions act as mediators between the political class and the population at large: the electoral system and political parties. The electoral system is the mechanism that serves to translate the popular vote (as expressed at election time) into seats in the legislative assembly. The principles guiding the selection of a candidate differs for each type of electoral system, be it majoritarian or proportional in nature. Under a plurality/majority system (notably, under a first-past-the-post, single-member district system), party leaders choose candidates who will maximise the party's chances of winning in a given district, irrespective of broader considerations such as the overall inclusiveness (or 'representativeness') of the assembly. By contrast, under proportional representation (notably under List PR), there is an incentive to maximise the party's collective appeal by including candidates from as many social groups as possible; the exclusion of an important demographic may be read as discriminatory, which may in turn lead to decreased support from voters. Regardless of the electoral system in place, elected representatives often feel more indebted to their political party than to the electorate, given that their election and re-election, not to mention their responsibilities, positioning and future advancement within the party and/or legislative assembly, depend upon their political party.[9]

What makes the Nunavut case of particular interest, therefore, is the absence of political parties, given that parties are often cited for their influence upon women's access to legislative assemblies. Although numerous studies point to political parties as a key obstacle to the election of women,[10] they have also served as a springboard for women's representation through the use of quotas.[11] As such, the absence of political parties in Nunavut can be interpreted positively as having removed an important barrier to the election of women; or, conversely, if understood as an opportunity structure for advancing women's representation, the absence of political parties in Nunavut can be seen as less fortunate. Our analysis will show that the election of women does not depend upon any single variable, but rather that women's representation must be understood within the context of complex circumstances relating to many political and cultural factors. Although representative democracy is often criticised for its inability to promote women's rights, our observations will serve to highlight the weaknesses that abound from deliberative and participatory democracy, especially when they are used as a last resort and without sufficient consideration given to the amount of time and preparation necessary for their successful implementation.

Methodology

In order to acquire a better grasp of the many factors influencing the gender parity plebiscite, we explored the existing literature on the creation of the Territory of Nunavut, as well as that treating the proposal of two-member, gender-balanced representation in particular. This survey of relevant primary and secondary sources was enriched with elite interviews. This approach is interesting in that it invites the perspectives of the actors who were intimately involved in the societal transformations under way. On the other hand, it is one that fails to engage the views of the general Inuit population.

Interviewees were either implicated in the events surrounding the formation of the new territory and/or are involved in Nunavut politics currently. Conducted by telephone, these interviews took place between September and December 2004 and included the following:

- An anonymous former senior official of the Status of Women Council of the Northwest Territories. This interview provided insight into the mobilising efforts of the council and the difficulties raised by virtue of having the council and its minister in opposing ideological camps.
- The Hon. Paul Okalik, Premier of Nunavut. This interview exposed the informal mechanisms that have been employed to advance women in politics since the defeat of the gender parity proposal.
- The Hon. Leona Aglukkaq, Minister of Finance and Government House Leader. Her perspectives clearly exposed the competing ideologies of representation that played out in the debates for and against gender parity.
- John Merritt, former Legal Counsel, Nunavut Implementation Commission. This interview was particularly useful in identifying the procedural and political challenges that the Nunavut Implementation Commission's gender parity recommendation faced.
- Clara Evalik, former Nunavut Implementation Commission Commissioner and a former director with Pauktuutit Inuit Women's Association. This interview highlighted the role of religion in affecting the debates for and against gender parity.
- The Hon. Ed Picco, Minister of Education. This interview illuminated the ideological and administrative concerns that motivated the campaign of the Northwest Territories Nunavut Caucus against the gender parity proposal, as well as the ideological vision of their spokesperson, Manitok Thompson.

The proposal

In December 1995, the Nunavut Implementation Commission put forward a proposal on gender parity that was ultimately brought to the representatives of the federal government, Northwest Territories and Nunavut Tunngavik for consideration. As such, the commission's proposal for a gender-balanced assembly was a few years ahead of Scotland and Wales, and of the constituency-twinning policy used in the election of 1999. The Nunavut Implementation Commission proposal argued that balanced representation in politics is more than a call for recognition of shared interest: rather, it is a call for recognition of a historically mistreated group in society.[12] Second, it proposed a model of dual-member constituencies that had been used in other provinces and arguably would be better suited to the Canadian legislative model than proportional representation.[13] According to the proposed model, the electorate of Nunavut would have two votes to choose the two representatives of their riding, one to be chosen from a list of female candidates and one to be chosen from the list of male candidates. Each electoral district would have had two representatives in the Legislative Assembly, namely the female and male candidates who received the most support in the riding. Given that each riding would have a male and female representative, the proposed model would have led to a legislative assembly with gender parity: a world first.

On 26 May 1997, the Nunavut Implementation Commission proposal was submitted to a popular plebiscite in the form of this question: 'Should the first Nunavut Legislative Assembly have equal numbers of men and women MLAs, with one man and one woman elected to represent each electoral district?' Although only 43 per cent of the voters supported the proposal, a mere 39 per cent of Nunavut residents actually cast their vote.[14] Fully 61 per cent of the Nunavut population abstained from voting. Several factors can be seen to have influenced this result. It would seem that many voters were either unsure of what choice to make, were perhaps turned off by the infighting among Inuit elites during the campaign, or were out on the land during the month when the vote was held. The vote against gender parity can hardly be understood as a clear mandate from the people. That the plebiscite would invite widespread debate on gender roles had in fact not been foreseen by political leaders and consequently there was an insufficient amount of time, energy, and resources devoted to explaining the two visions of equality being put forward.

Analysis

Given the strong support among most of the Nunavut elite, and in particular, among all of the main Inuit organisations and the vast majority of prominent Inuit leaders, what factors can be said to have contributed to the defeat of the gender parity proposal? One important factor is that it unintentionally spurred a widespread debate on the fundamentals of social organisation. First, within the discussions of the tripartite political elite, there was disagreement as to which ideal of equality should serve as the cornerstone of the new legislative assembly. Second, the move to hold a popular plebiscite led to discussions and debates as to the appropriate relationship of Inuit women and men within society.

Competing traditions of equality

At the level of ideas, the Nunavut Implementation Commission attempted to render operational, in terms of political representation, the theoretical ideal of gender equality. This ideal encompasses an understanding of gender differences as affecting the life experiences and views of both women and men, and of the value of having both groups contribute to the governance of the society. Associated by interviewees with traditional Inuit culture, the commitment to gender equality was repeatedly linked with the symbiotic relationship of women and men in society and the fact that the survival of the Inuit people had relied on their collective contributions. According to a former senior official of the Northwest Territories

Status of Women Council, it was a means of both symbolically and practically institutionalising the theoretical commitment to the equal value of the contributions and life experiences of both women and men. Indeed, the information pamphlet sent to all Nunavut homes, *Building our Future Together: Information about Gender Parity*, clearly stated, 'In traditional Inuit culture women and men were equal partners, each respected for their skills and knowledge.' Interviewees commented most often that the gender parity initiative advanced a commitment to equality grounded in the belief that the whole of Inuit society would benefit from better laws if the latter were informed by the life experiences and views of both genders. The equal representation of both groups was understood as a public good that would be upheld in each election.

Conversely, the opponents of the gender parity proposal took the universalistic view wherein 'homo politicus' is a single actor devoid of social markers. Their assumption was that equality is best ensured by ignoring gender, racial or other differences. Placed firmly at the individual level, equality was defined not in terms that relate to the collective contributions of women and men, but rather in terms that relate to the individual merit and ability of a given disembodied person to represent and advance the general interests of the population at large. Good laws and public policy were seen to result from equal opportunity of all individuals to compete for the role of representing the society at large. To that end, equal representation was to be measured in terms of both the procedural equality of competition, as well as in terms of its ability to affirm the value of the individuals that are selected in each election. Director of Community Affairs and the Women's Directorate MLA Manitok Thompson was selected by the Northwest Territories Nunavut Caucus to advance this view, and the idea that the proposal was both discriminatory (against men) by reserving seats for women who might not be the best representatives, and discriminatory against women for assuming that women could not get elected without representational guarantees.

Ultimately, given the lack of consensus among the political elite with executive decision-making power, the issue was taken outside the representative democracy model and was delegated to society at large through the vehicles of deliberative and direct democracy; this had the effect of imposing an even higher threshold on its acceptance. According to the Nunavut Implementation Commission's legal counsel, John Merritt, the Nunavut Act passed by the federal parliament in 1993 had referenced the creation of the new territory in accordance with the existing procedures used in the Northwest Territories. The decision to adopt a new form of electoral system would therefore require the federal parliament to amend the Act before the first election, and only thereafter would the new territory's executive be at liberty to amend its electoral system. Given that the Liberal Women's Commission had already taken an interest in developments in Nunavut, he suggested that the issue of gender-balanced governance might have taken on national importance, as the House of Commons would have had to specifically amend the Nunavut Act in order to support the new system of gender parity. He suggested that the federal Minister of Indian Affairs, facing strong opposition from the Nunavut Caucus, made the political decision to request a popular plebiscite in order to seek a clear mandate from Inuit society.

Competing traditions of gender relations

While the terms of the debates championed by the political elites centered around the theoretical foundations of 'gender equality' and 'equal representation', discussion among the population focused more squarely upon the practical impact the proposal might have upon the roles of women and men in society. Reflecting fears that the proposal might threaten traditional roles, proponents and opponents argued that gender parity would either strengthen or weaken the family. The former likened the Nunavut Legislative Assembly to the home and defended the equal contribution of both fathers *and mothers* in politics with the foundation of a stronger Inuit society and culture; conversely, given the central role of women in care-giving and in the maintenance of family relations, the latter group suggested that families would suffer if women were encouraged to participate in politics.[15] Women's opposition to the proposal may also reflect a deep-seated commitment to maintaining strong families, and the fear of increasing social problems that increase women's burden.[16] The practical implications of a mere 12 women being engaged in the responsibilities of territorial governance fell by the wayside in what became a more symbolic discussion around the proper sphere of women and men within Inuit society.

The maintenance of cultural identity is often a process related to symbolic control.[17] While many invoked traditional Inuit culture as having historically respected and valued the contributions of both women and men on a par without regard to their gender, others argued that women and men had distinct yet complementary spheres of influence. Increased unemployment among men and the more prominent role of women as breadwinners was such that many men saw gender parity in politics as a further encroachment upon men's traditional role in Inuit culture as the providers of income, information and power within society. While conservative groups suggested that gender parity was an 'import' from the south, the invocation of Christian beliefs to oppose the proposal went unquestioned.[18] Former Nunavut Implementation Commission Commissioner Clara Evalik criticised the role of religious groups in playing upon the fears of the communities in an attempt to defeat the proposal. The discussions that resulted from the gender parity proposal were such that the population was being asked to define which version of 'Inuit traditions' (pre-contact, post-contact or a mixture of both) should form the basis of gender relations and democratic practice in their new territory. This was not a simple question, given that the past 50 years had seen tremendous upheavals in Inuit society in terms of their connection with the land, contact with the south, the influence of Christianity and the economic restructuring of the family and society. It is not surprising that the proposal met with forward-looking optimism as well as with rampant fear if we consider that the current generation has experienced, and will likely continue to experience, a tumultuous period of social, economic and cultural transition during the first few decades of the territory's development.

Lessons from Nunavut

Six lessons can be drawn from the Nunavut experience. The first relates to the role of culture in influencing political events. More specifically, it highlights two competing ideals of equality and alternative visions of how a society and its institutions should be organised. There is no shortage of mechanisms or possibilities for guaranteeing women's representation in Westminster or other systems where there is a genuine commitment to women being equally represented. The decision not to adopt a two-member gender-balanced assembly does not point to any inherent incapacity of the Westminster model to take multiple identities into consideration in its representation of the political community. The Westminster model did not prove to be incompatible with efforts to represent geographically dispersed communities and efforts to advance women's representation. The Nunavut Implementation Commission was genuinely committed to the ideal of equal representation for women and men; the electoral mechanism best suited to institutionalising this ideal was designed accordingly.

The second lesson flows from the first. The Nunavut experience points to the force of conservatism in Canada with respect to electoral reform, as compared with other Commonwealth countries. Australia abandoned the first-past-the-post system in the early twentieth century, New Zealand in 1993, and in the contemporary United Kingdom a wide variety of electoral systems are in use. In stark contrast, during the exploration of new political structures for the Territory of Nunavut the idea of abandoning the first-past-the-post was not considered. Resistance to electoral reform was likewise present during the municipal amalgamations in Quebec; at no point was the idea of adopting proportional representation seriously addressed for the amalgamated cities of Montreal and Quebec City. The electoral reform process under way in the Province of Quebec has moved towards a mixed PR model; however, the proposed system is majoritarian not only in practice (the electorate will exercise only one vote)[19] but also in its effect, as a result of the small district magnitude. Incentives to the feminisation of the Quebec legislature are present, if very weak, in the proposed system. Conservatism has likewise expressed itself in the BC electoral reform process; despite having boasted gender parity in the composition of the Citizens' Assembly itself, gender-balanced representation in the assembly was not selected as one of the values around which to build a new electoral system.[20]

A third lesson has both conceptual and methodological implications. The Nunavut case shows that the three models of democracy (representative, participatory and deliberative) do not function in isolation from one another. Rather, their coexistence and interaction allow a more holistic interpretation of political events. Although the representative democracy model points to the fact that the political elites put forward the idea of a two-member, gender-balanced assembly, the deliberative democracy model allows us to situate the ideological framework and debates surrounding the notion of equality and gender relations that flowed from the proposal. For its part, recourse to the direct democracy model through the use of a plebiscite can be understood in the context of confirming the popular legitimacy of the proposal. The coexistence and complementary nature of these models cannot, however, be associated with their equal heuristic value. When improvised or poorly planned, the deliberative and direct democracy models can in fact prevent the realisation of the ideal of equal representation for women and men within democratic representative institutions.

The fourth lesson relates to the fact that the advent of new political institutions (and notably a legislative assembly with new electoral rules) does not necessarily produce a new 'political opportunity structure' for women. Rather, it remains crucial that actors advancing women's representation receive the support of the political elite as well as a commitment consciously to eliminate the informal mechanisms that have kept women out of politics. In short, political power must be consciously used to advance the election of women to political office by design. When examining the creation of new institutional structures within constitutional monarchies with Westminster-style governance, it is imperative that we look to the source of decision-making power, or notably to the actors exercising the executive power of the Crown.[21] In the Nunavut case, the decision-making power was ultimately exercised by the tripartite group representing Inuit civil society (Nunavut Tunngavik), incumbent MLAs (the Nunavut Caucus of the Northwest Territories government) and the interests of the federal Liberal executive (the Minister of Indian and Northern Affairs). These representatives had a mandate to decide the rules and principles according to which the new assembly would be constituted; as such, they had control over the adoption or rejection of gender equality as a foundational pillar of the new decision-making body. The failure to obtain a consensus among these individuals ultimately led to calls for a plebiscite and the 'open' competition of ideas.

A fifth lesson concerns the role of political parties in women's representation. As mentioned earlier, the absence of political parties can point to greater access for women to legislative assemblies given that a key obstacle is removed. In Nunavut the absence of political parties has not, however, translated into a sufficient number of women in the legislative assembly. The absence of political parties can also prevent the promotion of women's representation through the use of quotas or other forms of affirmative action. The Nunavut example highlights the fact that affirmative action is not limited to the actions of political parties; in his interview, the Hon. Paul Okalik, Premier of Nunavut, was very open about his commitment to seeing women serve at the highest levels of governance. He confirmed having intentionally appointed women at the deputy minister level in 1999 to provide a balance for the majority of male ministers. Moreover, since his re-election in 2004, he acknowledged having used his power as Premier to advance the two women MLAs to the most important positions in Cabinet, namely that of Deputy Premier and Minister of Finance. Albeit an effective strategy for advancing women's representation in the short term, this method is insufficient as a medium or long-term policy given that it makes a central aspect of women's citizenship (participation in decision-making institutions) subject to the goodwill of the prince, an arbitrary power that was supposedly defeated in the democratising revolutions of the modern era.

This leads us to a last important lesson, which concerns the theory and practice of women's representation. The existence of a link between descriptive and substantive representation has been increasingly questioned in light of the sheer diversity of women and/or of women's views and experiences.[22] In the case of Nunavut, the views of one prominent woman in a relatively small political community contributed to derailing the adoption of an electoral system that would have ensured an equal role for women and men in the territory's assembly. Clearly, Minister Thompson had the mandate to advance the views of the Nunavut Caucus through the political system. One may suggest that, from the perspective of the population, the fact that she, as a woman, could be so vehemently against the proposal led to confusion as to who constituted the legitimate voice of women's equality concerns. If her views worked against women's equality interests, can she be understood as substantively representing women?

In other words, does feminism have a monopoly over the substantive representation of women, and if so, what are the second-order implications concerning the ability of a society to ensure the expression of both feminine and feminist voices? Clearly, this exposes the theoretical tension inherent in assumptions about critical mass or the idea that the substantive representation of a group will necessarily flow from its descriptive representation. Dovi[23] frames the issue in terms of questions of authenticity and has advanced the idea that only those individuals who have deep and ongoing connections with their communities can claim to represent those interests. In particular, she asserts that not just any black or Latino will do. In the context of the gender parity proposal, it seems that not just any Inuit or any woman could claim to be an authentic representative of Inuit culture or of Inuit women's equality concerns.

A former Northwest Territories Status of Women Council official expressed her disappointment and discomfort with the fact that their efforts to lead an educational campaign in favour of gender parity was actively undermined by their own minister, creating confusion and making the debate seem divisive and counterproductive. While she was likely seen as a legitimate voice by the conservative segment of the population, namely those who subscribed to an individualised notion of equal competition and those who feared changes in gender roles, many interviewees felt that she had hindered the collective equality interests of women. Moreover, interviewees suggested that the arguments advanced on behalf of the Nunavut Caucus were not recognised as a legitimate voice by the vast majority of the Inuit elite involved in the creation of the territory.

For proponents of gender parity, Pauktuutit Inuit Women's Association, the Northwest Territories Status of Women Council, Nunavut Implementation Commission Commissioners and the Nunavut Tunngavik directors were seen as the authentic voices advancing Inuit women's and Inuit society's collective interests. Manitok Thompson was criticised by interviewees for having failed to understand the tenets of the gender parity proposal and for having reduced the debate to a simplistic view of democracy wherein equality is linked with each individual's ability to participate in electoral competition, rather than with a commitment to the equal participation of women and men as groups in the governance of the territory. The Minister of Finance and Government House Leader, Leona Aglukkaq, expressed her disappointment that the former minister did not address the realities affecting women such as high rates of homicide and domestic violence. Manitok Thompson was criticised for generalising from her own experience and for denying the systemic barriers to women's participation in her assertion that 'if she could get elected, any woman could'. Similarly, the Minister of Education, Ed Picco, asserted that there were no systemic barriers to women; however, he admitted the difficulties relating to strains on the family, such as frequent travel and a small political community, which strip politicians of their privacy.

Member of Parliament Nancy Karatak-Lindell[24] also observed the impact of the small size of northern communities; she felt that the ongoing hierarchies of age and gender in Inuit culture and the problems of campaigning against a male relative would discourage women from running for office if there were no proactive measures in place to validate women's equal ability to govern. Minister Picco acknowledged the degree of individual power formerly held by Ms Thompson; he suggested that had she not led the campaign against the proposal, the results of the plebiscite might have been very different. Ultimately, without a clear sense as to who had the right to speak on behalf of, or in the interests of, women's equality, the fact that there was a prominent woman speaking against the proposal only added to the other ideological positions relating to gender roles, traditional Inuit culture and the procedural barriers such as a lack of time and resources for popular education.

Conclusion

While the Nunavut Implementation Commission proposal of a two-member, gender-balanced assembly challenged the general premise of first-past-the-post parliamentary representation, it did so in such a way as to create a space for a form of political representation that can accommodate territory, as well as identities relating to gender. As such it provided one possible solution to the ongoing dilemma within feminist theory of how best to represent women as a group within electoral political practice without falling into essentialising discourses.[25]

The most ironic aspect of the Nunavut experience is the force of conservatism, and this despite the fact that the elements found in the gender parity proposal have in fact been a part of both Canadian and provincial political culture, to differing degrees, for quite some time. Not only have the House of Commons and the provincial legislatures previously used a system of two-member ridings as late as the 1980s, moreover, certain provinces (notably Nova Scotia and Quebec) have designed their electoral boundaries in order to facilitate the representation of particular identities relating to language, culture and religion.[26] Since the 1980s, proposals have been made for the representation of Aboriginal peoples, be it in the form of designated electoral ridings (the Royal Commission on the Electoral Reform and Party Financing), Aboriginal reserved seats in the Senate (the Charlottetown Accord) or the creation of an Aboriginal Parliament (the Royal Commission on Aboriginal Peoples). The most recent example is of course the creation of the new Territory of Nunavut itself.

Contrary to the position advanced by the Nunavut Caucus wherein race, creed or gender should not matter to political representation in the Assembly, the explicit recognition of Inuit 'ways of being' was the driving force behind the founding of Nunavut, as it would allow the Inuit control over their future through political institutions. Consequently, it is interesting, if disappointing, that while modern political culture in the Canadian provinces and territories has upheld the value of ensuring, to differing degrees, the descriptive representation and recognition of regional differences, religious beliefs, urban versus rural realities, ethno-cultural identities and linguistic groups, it continues to deny the relevance of the political recognition of gender differences to full citizenship for women. In the case of Nunavut, had the Inuit leaders been successful in asserting the value of what gender parity proponents termed 'traditional Inuit culture', notably the affirmation of the equal collective contributions of women and men to society, and had they secured the support of the Nunavut Caucus, the Nunavut Legislative Assembly would have become in

1999 the first living example of the modern democratic ideal of gender equality. In the absence of this unique institutional mechanism, if 'traditional Inuit culture' prevails in practice, then perhaps the paradise of gender-balanced governance is not lost, but rather, remains a collective work-in-progress.

Notes

1 See Government of Nunavut, *Nunavut at a Glance* at www.gov.nu.ca/Nunavut/French/about/fglance.shtml.
2 Hicks and White, 'Nunavut', 89.
3 See Statistics Canada, *Commonly Reported Reasons for not Completing Elementary/High School by Sex* at www.statcan.ca/english/freepub/89–595-XIE/tables/html/table2/nu2.htm.
4 Conference Board of Canada, *Nunavut Economic Outlook*, 5.
5 Government of Nunavut (Nunavut Housing Corporation) and Nunavut Tunngavik, *Nunavut Ten-year Inuit Housing Action Plan*, i.
6 White, *Cabinets and First Ministers*, 58–62.
7 LeDuc, *The Politics of Direct Democracy*, 40–1.
8 White, *Cabinets and First Ministers*, 9.
9 Cross, *Political Parties*, 53–5; Norris, *Electoral Engineering*, 230–46.
10 See, among others, Lovenduski and Norris, *Gender and Party Politics*.
11 See Global Database of Quotas for Women at www.quotaproject.org.
12 Nunavut Implementation Commission, 'Two-member Constituencies and Gender Equality', 5.
13 Young, 'Gender Equal Legislatures', 308.
14 Gombay, 'The Politics of Culture', 137.
15 Gombay, 'The Politics of Culture', 139.
16 Dahl, 'Gender Parity in Nunavut', 46–7.
17 Dybbroe, 'Questions of Identity and Issues of Self-determination', 42.
18 Gombay, 'The Politics of Culture', 139.
19 The elector would cast one vote, which will serve to elect both the constituency members of the National Assembly and list members. More precisely, 'electors would vote directly for a candidate in their division. This vote would also be used to calculate how many compensatory MNAs each party would receive for district seats'; see Ministère du Conseil exécutive (Québec) at www.institutions-democratiques.gouv.qc.ca/publications/fiche_1_chaque_vote_compte_en.pdf; accessed July 10, 2005.
20 British Columbia, Citizens' Assembly on Electoral Reform, *Making Every Vote Count*, 2.
21 See Smith, *The Invisible Crown*.
22 See Burt *et al.*, 'Women in the Ontario New Democratic Government'; Childs, *New Labour's Women MPs*, 22–7; Grey, 'Does Size Matter?'; Studlar and McAllister, 'Does a Critical Mass Exist?'; Towns, 'Understanding the Effects of Larger Ratios of Women in National Legislatures'; Tremblay, 'Women's Representational Role in Australia and Canada'; Weldon, 'Beyond Bodies'.
23 See Dovi, 'Preferable Descriptive Representatives'.
24 These views were shared on 28 February 2001 in response to a question on the gender parity proposal raised by Jackie Steele during a preparatory meeting in Ottawa leading up to the first Nunavut Legislature Study Tour of the Parliamentary Internship Programme.
25 See, among others, Campbell, 'Gender, Ideology and Issue Preference';

Diamond and Hartsock, 'Beyond Interests in Politics'; Jónasdóttir, 'On the Concept of Interest, Women's Interests, and the Limitations of Interest Theory'; Sapiro, 'When Are Interests Interesting?'; Young, 'Gender as Seriality'.

26 Courtney, *Elections*, 60–1, 108–11; Eisenberg, 'Domination and Political Representation in Canada', 46; Roach, 'One Person, One Vote?'; Royal Commission on Electoral Reform and Party Financing, *Report*, 179.

14 Conclusion

Gendering political representation in the old and new worlds of Westminster

Jennifer Curtin

Women have a long history of being excluded from consideration of what legitimately was incorporated in the study of politics, meaning that the ideas, institutions and processes constituting official politics largely ignored gender inequality in the distribution of political power. For centuries it was assumed that only men would inhabit the public arena, where 'politics' was performed. While early liberal thinkers advocated representative rather than participatory democracy, most assumed that the process of representation would be undertaken only by men. John Stuart Mill was one of the few who argued that every citizen, including women, not only ought to have a voice in the exercise of government, but at least occasionally ought to take part in government 'by the personal discharge of some public function, local or general'.[1]

In pursuit of the liberal democratic ideal, suffragists and feminist activists in the nineteenth and early twentieth centuries focused primarily on the right to enter the formal political arena as voters and representatives. This claim was often articulated in terms of an extension of women's place as citizen-mothers: many argued women's qualities as mothers and carers would enhance the practice of politics, raise the moral standards of the parliament and ultimately enrich the democratic process. While these arguments have often led to a labelling of 'conservative', in a sense these early women's rights activists were utilising a strategic essentialism.

The more radical feminist challenge of the 1960s and 1970s was important in revealing the 'artificial' public–private divide and redefining the 'political'. The catch-cry of the 'personal is political' became entrenched as one of the most famous feminist slogans, alongside calls for 'sisterhood'. The aim was a positive one, namely to 'reveal and valorize women's participation' outside formal politics.[2] It also drew attention to the way some forms of liberalism imagined public and private realms as separate rather than interconnected.[3] In contesting this separation, feminists argued that such a dichotomy undermined any possibility of substantive equality for women.

However, there were two additional and important consequences. First, the notion of women as a 'universal' category, in opposition to men, was criticised for overriding differences between women and ignoring the presence of multiple identities and therefore fluid and contingent solidarities. Second, the broadening out of what constituted the 'political' also meant that feminist engagement with formal politics became 'de-legitimised' as a practical strategy and a field of study.[4] Institutions of government were labelled as inherently male, impenetrable and where the interests of men would ultimately dominate. If women participated at all, it was seen as either tokenism or co-option. In more recent years, feminist political scientists have argued that dissolving the meaning of 'politics', to the point where formal politics is not recognised as a site of institutional power requiring feminist critique, is not in the interests of women. It is widely acknowledged by feminist thinkers and activists that, because of the diversity between women, an objective set of interests common to all women is neither real nor desirable. But the argument can still be made that one potentially 'objective' women's interest is having a political presence.[5]

It is the political presence of women that has been explored in considerable depth in this volume. More specifically, the aims have been threefold. First to examine the extent to which the descriptive representation of women in the 'old' Westminster parliaments (Australia, Canada, New Zealand and the United Kingdom) has progressed in recent years, and the factors which have enhanced or impeded this progress. Second, to explore the relationship between the numbers of women elected and the substantive representation of women – that is, the extent to which women 'act for' women. Third, to review the recent experiences of four 'new' Westminster parliaments (Northern Ireland, Scotland, Wales and Nunavut) in order to evaluate the political opportunities new institutional design has opened up for enhancing the dimensions of women's political participation.

In this chapter I revisit the historical and contemporary dimensions associated with the descriptive and substantive representation of women from an explicitly comparative perspective. The countries chosen here are similar in a number of ways, primarily as a result of their heritage as Westminster parliamentary democracies. As such they all feature an executive which is drawn from the parliament, strong party discipline, party systems which have a history of being two-party-dominated, and in the more established group this is partly a result of non-proportional electoral systems adopted over a century ago. However, these similarities are punctuated with differences: bicameralism, federalism, devolution, electoral reform, the arrival of new parties and, in some cases, the fragmentation of older ones.

While we have not included all Westminster democracies in this volume, the countries chosen here represent a useful cross-section from which to draw out some broad lessons about the various opportunities, strategies and structures that enable women's parliamentary presence.

This concluding comparative examination seeks to further expand our understandings of the political representation of women by revisiting the differing explanations that have been offered. Particular attention is given to the importance of electoral systems, the role of quotas in ameliorating the effects of the former, the continued relevance of concerted feminist action, the contested notions of critical mass, critical acts, and the vexed but relentless pursuit of a conceptual and empirical connection between the descriptive and substantive representation of women. However, in addition to providing answers, the findings from this volume also raise more questions, and remind us that understanding the dimensions of women's experiences in formal politics is an unfinished business.

Tracking trends in descriptive representation

While there is evidence to suggest that the date of women's suffrage is linked to the trajectories of women's representation, the early grant of suffrage did not necessarily herald the early election of women to parliament.[6] For example, as outlined in Chapter 1, while the United Kingdom was late in giving women the right to vote, they were the first of our four 'traditional' cases to have a woman elected to the national parliament, the first to have a woman selected for a cabinet post, and the first to have a woman party leader. By contrast, while New Zealand was the first to give women the vote, the right to become a representative took another 15 years to achieve, and another 100 years for the first woman to be appointed party leader. Thus while milestones can be viewed as an important measure of women's political achievement at a particular point in time, we cannot assume that increases in women's political power and influence will be continuous.[7]

Nevertheless, we can speculate on the extent to which the struggle for suffrage and the various political opportunities, ideologies and discourses used in the course of this struggle might act as a proxy for the gendered nature of political culture. In other words, to what extent do the first wave of demands for political representation and participation give us an insight into the openness of Westminster traditions to the presence of women?

In the case of Australia, egalitarian values were important in the process of settlement, and underpinned a number of innovative electoral initiatives pioneered in Australia, including the relatively early enfranchisement of men and the introduction of the secret ballot. Similar understandings of equality were also evident in New Zealand, with the conclusion of the Treaty of Waitangi in 1840, and the relatively early enfranchisement of, and seats reserved for, Maori. This commitment to egalitarianism provided an environment in which women's claims to political citizenship, while not universally supported, could find a legitimate discursive space. However, arguably the gender-inclusiveness of these egalitarian ideals was diluted by the different settlement patterns experienced in Australia and New Zealand, with lasting residual effects. For example, the convict settlement process in several Australian states, in combination with a large contingent of Irish Catholic among the early migrant population, had a significant impact on the structure of the trade union movement, and consequently the Labor Party, particularly after the First World War. This has ensured an entrenched masculine labourist tradition, with a history of 'conservative' views on women's interests as workers, and a factionalised Labor Party machine. By comparison, New Zealand's settlement patterns were more religiously eclectic (like those of South Australia), meaning the Labour Party in particular had less of a sectarian base. It is partly for this reason that the New Zealand Labour Party was more open to feminisation once the second wave of feminism took hold.[8]

While Canada's colonial experience came much earlier, with the arrival of the French in the seventeenth century, followed later by the British, the adoption of the Westminster model did not occur until 1867. Egalitarian values were less explicit in the Canadian settlement experience, but an active reform movement and a commitment to a treaty with indigenous people represented a challenge to the conservative notions of who might constitute a political citizen. Moreover, because some women at the municipal level were eligible to vote in the late 1800s, many women activists viewed local politics as the means of achieving reform,[9] thereby focusing less on the fight for suffrage at provincial and state level. In Quebec, women did not win the right to vote until 1940.[10]

These three colonial Westminster democracies could be considered 'new' in comparison to the original Westminster. The first UK parliament was established more than 300 years before universal male suffrage and, as such, was a place of peerage and privilege, devoid of women's presence; disrupted only when the crown was held by a woman. Once universal male suffrage was achieved, the Labour Party's focus was very much on the descriptive representation of the industrial working class (blue-collar working men). Electoral and constitutional reform has also proved difficult. Numerous attempts were made in the late nineteenth century and beyond to change the membership and effectiveness of the House of Lords. It wasn't until the 1950s that life peerages for both men and women were created, but it took until 1963 before hereditary peeresses could sit in the House of Lords. Indeed, the UK parliament has been described as 'of slow temper, essentially conservative. In our wildest periods of reform, you notice always the invincible instinct to hold fast by the Old; to admit the minimum of the New.'[11]

As already noted, the enfranchisement of British women was relatively late by comparison with their colonial counterparts (1918). Once they were allowed to vote, the fear that women would radicalise politics did not eventuate. While almost everywhere women have been identified as conservative voters in the years following suffrage, it is argued that this conservatism was greater and more deeply embedded in Britain.[12] Moreover, the representation of women in the House of Commons remained at extremely low levels between 1945 and 1987. During these 40 years, women's representation averaged only 3.7 per cent. The Labour Party consistently selected more women candidates than did the Conservatives over this time, and in most elections this translated into more Labour than Conservative women being elected. However, neither major party was particularly responsive to the idea of increasing women's representation, despite the activism of the women's movement during the 1960s and 1970s.

Thus, from a historical perspective, we see that the establishment of new parliamentary institutions has offered women an opportunity for advancing their political claims for representation, when combined with a broad cultural commitment to equality and the mobilisation by women around such claims. For example, Australian suffragists were acutely aware of the political opportunity that the establishment of the federation of Australia offered. By contrast, the UK case suggests the more entrenched the Westminster legacy the more difficult it is to reform.

The opportunity to re-gender political spaces offered up by the design and establishment of new political institutions is no doubt best demonstrated by the cases of Scotland and Wales. Not only has the representation of women surpassed that of the traditional Westminster democracies, but there have been a range of institutional rules and procedures established with the aim of entrenching equality, and gender equality in particular. However, such outcomes were possible only because there was co-ordinated and sustained feminist involvement throughout the devolution process. The importance of such a campaign is also evidenced by the counter-examples of Nunavut and Northern Ireland, where women's claims have been fragmented by 'competing' identity claims based on ethnicity, culture and nationalism.

While there is considerable diversity in the representation of women in the parliaments surveyed in this volume, several interesting features emerge. First, as we see in Table 14.1, of the four more established Westminster democracies, Australia and New Zealand are the two with the highest proportion of women parliamentarians, with both between 25 per cent and 30 per cent.[13] This compares with Canada and the United Kingdom, which are hovering around 20 per cent women. No doubt part of the explanation for this disparity is structural, with both New Zealand and Australia having a proportional component in their electoral system, compared with the plurality systems featuring in Canada and the United Kingdom. And the electoral reform experiences of Australia (1949), New Zealand (1996) and Nunavut (1999) show that electoral systems can be reinvented, if there is sufficient political support from elites alongside public desire for change.

Table 14.1 Percentage of women elected to Westminster parliaments and contextual factors

Country	*1996–98 (1)*	*1999–2001 (2)*	*2003–05 (3)*	*% change (1) – (3)*	*Electoral system*	*Party quota*	*Incumbency rate*[a]	*External feminist support*[b]
Australia[c]	22.3	25.3	24.7	+2.4	AV	Yes (1)	80	Yes
Canada	20.6	20.6	21.1	+0.5	FPP	Yes (2)	53	Fragmented
New Zealand	29.2	30.8	28.3[d]	–1	MMP	No	72.5	Fragmented
United Kingdom	18.2	17.9	19.7	+1.5	FPP	Yes (1)[e]	75.7	Yes
Northern Ireland	13	–	17	+4	STV	No[f]	n.a.	Fragmented
Scotland	n.a.	37.2	39.5	+2.3[g]	MMP	Yes (1)	n.a.	Yes
Wales	n.a.	40	50	+10[g]	MMP	Yes (2)	n.a.	Yes
Nunavut	n.a.	5.3	10.5	+5.2[g]	FPP	No	n.a.	Fragmented

Source: Chapters, supplemented with data from IPU website.

Notes

a Taken from Matland and Studlar, 'Determinants of Legislative Turnover'.

b Refers to feminist support around the issue of women's political representation.

c Figures refer to House of Representatives only. If we include the proportionally elected Senate in the calculation, the proportion of women parliamentarians is 24.6% (1998), 27% (2001) and 28.3% (2004).

d Represents the outcome of the 2002 election.

e Refers to the now defunct all-women shortlists.

f But the Women's Party gained two seats at the 1999 election.

g Refers to the percentage of change between (2) and (3).

The electoral system variable is clearly only part of the explanation for the disparity in women's parliamentary presence. Candidate gender quotas or other forms of affirmative action strategies can ameliorate the adverse consequences of a plurality or majoritarian electoral system. Five of our eight case studies have featured an initiative of this kind. For example, the UK Labour Party's women-only shortlist strategy, while short-lived, was instrumental in doubling the proportion of women elected in 1997 to 18 per cent. However, further progress has been stalled by the lack of a contagion effect, in that the Conservatives have not sought to compete with Labour in increasing their recruitment of women candidates. In the case of Australia's lower house (where a majoritarian system exists), women's representation reached 25.3 per cent in 2001 before falling back to 24.7 per cent in 2004. While primarily an effect of the adoption of a candidate gender quota by the ALP in 1994, the proportion has been enhanced by a recent contagion effect, with the Liberal Party also increasing its recruitment of women candidates, many of whom have been elected on the back of four Liberal election wins.[14] In Canada, although the representation of women has stalled over recent elections, there has been sufficient commitment to the recruitment of women candidates by the NDP in particular, and less so by the Liberals, to ensure a fifth of elected parliamentarians are women.

A critical case in this regard is New Zealand, where women's representation surpassed 20 per cent under a plurality system without either of the major parties adopting an affirmative action programme. The result is directly attributable to the fact that almost one-third of Labour MPs elected in 1993 were women (a consequence of women's persistent activism within the party organisation). However, the adoption by New Zealand of a mixed proportional system in 1996 has not resulted in the levels of female representation currently experienced in Scotland and Wales, despite their similar electoral systems. The difference between these countries is the absence/presence of quotas *and* the presence of a contagion effect. In the case of New Zealand there has been only a very minor contagion effect: there are now twice as many National women MPs compared with the 1980s, but the numbers remain low.

Alongside the importance of affirmative action strategies is the relationship between women's political recruitment (and the establishment of parliamentary careers) and turnover rates. For example, low levels of turnover have been identified as a key factor in women's inability to increase their representation in the US Congress, despite the strength of the women's movement.[15] Moreover, turnover rates are indirectly linked with the openness of a political culture to the advancement of women. If we accept that new ideas and policies are generated with changes in parliamentary representatives,[16] then the converse also holds. That is, traditional (masculine) political norms and practices remain unchallenged if incumbency equates with a lack of generational change in both parties and parliaments.

In Table 14.1 we see that Australia has only 20 per cent turnover per election, while the United Kingdom has closer to 25 per cent. By contrast, Canada's incumbency rate is considerably lower. Matland and Studlar argue that overall such rates of incumbency constitute fairly significant turnover, and in the case of Canada this has provided women with additional recruitment opportunities.[17] However, the fragmentation of Canada's party system, with the decimation of the left-wing New Democratic Party and the emergence of several new right-wing parties, has helped to undermine the opportunity structure provided by a high turnover rate. In addition, an excessively high turnover rate has the potential to thwart the accumulation of the political experience needed to enter executive government.

The turnover factor is relevant to understanding an emerging feature of women's representation in the mixed proportional Westminster systems. While proportionality allows the increased presence of minor parties, some of which are more likely to select women as candidates, the increased presence of women among the major parties is largely a result of women's election in constituency seats. For example, in both the 1999 and 2003 Scottish elections women won 10 per cent more constituency seats than list seats. A similar trend is evident in Wales. In the case of New Zealand, party lists still attract a higher percentage of women candidates than do electorate seats, where a plurality system operates. However, since the introduction of Mixed Member Proportional (MMP) electoral system in 1996 the percentage of women winning electorate seats has increased significantly. The 2002 result indicates that, like in Scotland and Wales, the proportion of electorate seats won by women was greater than the proportion of list seats won by women.

Mackay argues that this rather paradoxical result demonstrates the importance of strong gender quotas in the Scottish case, and highlights that party rules and attitudes are at least, if not more, significant than the electoral system. In the case of New Zealand, McLeay also argues that party culture and norms matter, but she adds that women candidates have recognised that because incumbency rates are higher in constituency seats compared with the party list, being elected to the former is more likely to ensure a parliamentary career. So, despite the proportional nature of the electoral system, the plurality component also features in the explanations for women's increasing representation.

The findings of this volume suggest that, almost irrespective of the electoral system in place, the adoption of candidate gender quota or alternative strategies such as twinning or zipping by one major party will result only in a partial victory. Rather, at least two major parties must make a commitment to increasing the number of women candidates selected if women are to become more than a significant minority of parliamentarians: that is, if women are to surpass the 40 per cent mark. As indicated in the literature, women's activism within and outside parties is particularly important in ensuring affirmative action strategies are implemented, institutionalised and enforced. In our analysis, external feminist support has also proved critical. In the case of Australia, the United Kingdom, Scotland and Wales, external, organised feminist support around the issue of equal political representation for women was critical to the advent of candidate gender quotas, and their implementation (see Table 14.1). In addition, it would appear that parties are most open to this kind of reform while they are in opposition and seeking to revitalise themselves in an effort to win government. However, given that women within parties on the right are increasingly being pressured into diluting their feminist interests and neutralising their gendered claims, it is easy to be pessimistic about ever reaching 40 per cent women, in the old worlds of Westminster at least.

The question of substantive representation

The issue of whether we can expect women, once elected, to act on behalf of women is a contentious one. There are clearly a range of compelling reasons why women's parliamentary presence should be encouraged, not least because it is important for parliaments to reflect the diversity of citizens they aim to represent. However, to suggest that we should have more women in parliament because it will make a difference to the representation of women's 'interests' is problematic for at least two reasons. First, sometimes quantifiable or tangible policy outcomes addressing the concerns of women constituents will not result, irrespective of the number of women elected. Second, we cannot assume that women's interests are homogeneous and therefore easily identifiable. Nevertheless, it is recognised that, without the political presence of women, the consideration of women's perspectives and experiences is unlikely. History demonstrates this. The question arises whether, in the future, the increased descriptive representation of women will in fact alter the nature, culture and legislative priorities of Westminster parliaments.

A number of scholars have spent much effort focusing on the extent to which a 'critical mass' of women parliamentarians has influenced legislative initiatives, the process of debate and the parliamentary culture.[18] However, there is a lack of uniformity in agreement as to what constitutes a critical mass. Most candidate gender quotas are set at a minimum of 30 per cent,[19] but if we take this figure as our measure, then only the new parliaments of Scotland and Wales could be considered in a study of a critical mass effect (and New Zealand in 1999). Moreover, given that most scholars have pointed out the way party loyalty complicates the relationship between gender identity and parliamentary preference, even in weak party systems like the United States', theoretically it is unlikely that any significant gender differences would be identifiable without (1) a critical mass of women elected from all the major political parties and (2) that this critical mass of women identify themselves as 'feminist' or prepared to act for women. It also seems to be the case that women are more likely to speak for women when they are a token group (as Grey on New Zealand demonstrates) while others have suggested that women's increased levels of representation may need to become entrenched over time before we see an impact, such as a change in the institutional norms of both parliament and political parties.[20]

A number of the chapters in this volume have critiqued the usefulness of the critical mass concept, primarily because of the difficulties associated with assuming that gender as a social category will override all other 'identities' not only cultural but political: that of party member and a geographically based constituency representative. Nevertheless eschewing the idea of a critical mass does not preclude the investigation of the extent to which, or the means by which, women parliamentarians perform the substantive representation of women.

There are several ways scholars have sought to identify the substantive representation of women. The first is by examining the preferences of women in parliament. That is, how do women vote on Bills that may directly impact on women? To what extent do they cross party lines and work together as women around issues perceived to be of immediate concern to women? In the United States this is an approach more commonly adopted, but, as is evident in Table 14.2, it is less applicable in the all the countries looked at here, because of the strength of party discipline, which makes it difficult for women to work across party lines or to act independently on behalf of women (the one exception is Nunavut). Private members' Bills are rare, as are conscience votes. When a conscience vote does arise an alliance among women parliamentarians may result, and can often constitute a significant 'critical act' in protecting women's rights, for example on the issue of abortion. But there is also considerable diversity among women parliamentarians on such issues even within political parties, so such alliances are not always predictable.[21] From a comparative perspective, cross-party alliances amongst women are more likely to occur, although still rarely, in the countries with proportional systems (see Table 14.2). This is primarily because the consensus politics often associated with multi-party government may provide women with negotiation opportunities not available in two-party-dominant systems.

In this volume, Childs focuses on an alternative means of measuring the preferences of women MPs. That is, instead of analysing the votes of women on the floor of the House, she examines the propensity of women parliamentarians to sign Early Day Motions dealing with issues of concern to women. While this kind of 'voting behaviour' has less direct impact on legislative outcomes, it is a 'safe' way for women to act for women. Childs reveals that women parliamentarians are more likely to sign both women-centred and feminist-focused Early Day Motions, and identifies at least two

Table 14.2 Factors affecting women's substantive representation

Country	*Party discipline*	*Cross-party alliances*	*Multi-party government*	*% women in Cabinet*[a]	*Party in government (at 2003)*	*Party groups for women*
Australia	Strong	Seldom	Partial	17.5	Conservative coalition	Yes
Canada	Strong	Seldom	Partial	30	Liberal–minority	Yes
New Zealand	Strong	Possible	Yes	30	Labour–coalition	Yes
United Kingdom	Strong	Seldom	No	27	Labour	Yes
Northern Ireland	Strong	Possible	Yes	n.a.	Coalition	Yes
Scotland	Strong	Possible	Yes	22	Labour–coalition	Yes
Wales	Strong	Possible	Yes	55	Welsh–Labour	Yes
Nunavut	Weak	Possible	No	25	Coalition	n.a.

Note

a Refers to Cabinets between 2003 and 2005.

critical cases where these Early Day Motions have resulted in a positive outcome for women.

However, all the authors in this volume argue that deciding how and what to observe and measure in an investigation of substantive representation is fraught with difficulties. In all the countries looked at here, women parliamentarians maintained an explicit interest in representing the concerns of women, but expressing this preference in mainstream political forums may equate with political suicide. And identification as feminist by non-Labour women may be on the decline. As such many of women's actions for women may be taking place behind closed doors, inside party group meetings and women's caucuses.

An alternative means of exploring substantive representation is to focus less on expressed preferences, and more on performance in parliament. For example, in her examination of the US Congress, Cramer Walsh argues that, rather than expecting to identify the distinct policy goals women hold, it is more useful to investigate the extent to which women bring distinct ways of understanding policy to the legislative process.[22] In other words, she suggests, revealing the diversity of perspectives offered by women legislators during the deliberation process is a means of understanding the quality of representation taking place. She acknowledges performance may not change preferences but she argues that through debate members can communicate to colleagues on the floor, and to constituents through televised coverage, their commitment to a range of perspectives and issues. In doing so, women can influence how others interpret a Bill, think about issues that may not have been raised in the past, and may ultimately increase the legitimacy of gendered perspectives in subsequent deliberation.

A focus on debate can reveal three dimensions of performance: the way a woman parliamentarian frames the issue; on whose behalf she makes the claim; and the testimonial component – that is, the extent to which she personally identifies with the issue.[23] In the case of Australia, Sawer's work demonstrates that women are more likely to raise the issues of paid maternity leave and domestic violence, although the latter issue received more bi-partisan attention. Similarly, in Scotland women were more likely to focus on domestic violence, gender and health and child care. In addition women politicians in Wales and Scotland have taken a lead role in seeking to inform all policy debates with a gendered perspective, both in the parliament and in the bureaucracy.

However, in the case of Australia, Sawer's analysis of the use of gender-inclusive language in the framing of parliamentary debates indicates that the increased representation of women in parliament has not resulted in the use of more gender-friendly language, although this is attributed to the presence of a conservative government. Similarly in Canada, women are more likely to talk about women's perspectives, but when a conservative party was in government this became more difficult. Thus, Trimble argues that women's attitudes and behaviours are evidently structured by party opinions and loyalty, parliamentary processes and institutional norms. And women parliamentarians themselves perceive the norms and practices of the parliamentary system as significant obstacles to the substantive representation of women.

Given this sometimes hostile environment, the support women parliamentarians gain from each other and from external women's organisations should not be underestimated. In most of the parliaments examined here, women in parties on the left/centre have established caucuses for themselves, which provide a safe discursive space in which to discuss and strategise around issues important to women constituents. And, as already demonstrated, the co-ordinated campaigns undertaken by external women's organisations and the backing they offer women parliamentarians can be crucial to the substantive representation of women. For example, EMILY's List in Australia is more than a means of holding List-sponsored women parliamentarians accountable. It also provides these women with a sense of solidarity, however contingent, thereby offering them an alternative source of support in their attempts to raise and force deliberation of the concerns of women. However, the relevance of partisanship to women's capacity to act for women is recognised by EMILY's List: it offers support only to Labor Party women, despite several Liberal Party women identifying and acting as feminists within the parliament.

Grey's New Zealand case study focuses more closely on the multiple dimensions associated with performance and reveals that, in the debates on parental leave and pay equity, women are far more likely than their male colleagues to say they are speaking for women, irrespective of party, although left-leaning women are more likely to do this than right-wing women. In addition, women are more likely than men to identify how policies were distinctly related to the lives of women. This is also the case in the Welsh Assembly. However, in attempting to quantify the performance process, Grey identifies that the proportion of interventions on behalf of women by women did not directly correlate with an increase in the number of women in the parliament – rather, Labour women were more likely to speak for women while in opposition.

Finally, what evidence is there of policy outcomes achieved by women for women? And to what extent does the proportion of women in Cabinet matter? The arguments for women's descriptive representation in parliament can be applied equally well to the executive, especially given that in the Westminster system the executive is drawn from the legislature. In other words, if we accept that the presence of women matters, if only to provide a diverse range of opinion and experience in the process of deliberation, then the representation of women in parliament needs to be complemented by an increased representation of women in Cabinet.

Table 14.2 indicates that in most of our Westminster parliaments, the proportion of women in Cabinet is at least as high as, if not higher than, the proportion of women in the parliament. Tangible policy outcomes favourable to women have clearly resulted in the case of Scotland and Wales, although this is partly attributable to the restricted policy domains that can be addressed by these devolved parliaments, and this should not detract from the activism of women parliamentarians around social policy issues in particular.

The importance of a left party in government is highlighted by the counter-example of Australia. At sub-national level, Labor governments are in power in all states and territories, and this has ensured that a range of gender policy initiatives have reached the formal agenda, including pay equity, an increase in paid maternity leave for public service workers and regulation of the conditions of clothing outworkers, among others. However, at the federal level we see that women's representation in Cabinet is comparatively low, but Australia is also the only country with a conservative government in power. Since the election of the Liberal-led Coalition there has been a considerable winding back of women's rights since 1996, with women's groups being de-funded, women's policy machinery dismantled and various attempts to dilute legislation protecting women from discrimination. Little resistance to these changes appears to have come from the women in Cabinet, although a few Liberal women backbenchers who do identify as feminist have sought to challenge their government's agenda by acting 'independently' through committees, abstaining on key votes and lobbying in the party room environment.

In direct contrast is the case of New Zealand, where the Labour Prime Minister is a committed feminist, and the Cabinet includes a number of overtly feminist parliamentarians. Partly as a consequence there have been a number of legislative reforms that have promoted the material well-being of women. However, the high profile of these explicitly 'feminist' political women has given rise to a backlash politics similar to that experienced in other countries examined here. Such a backlash is not solely a result of having women leaders (although the example of Margaret Thatcher led to a similar, albeit more generic, backlash against women in politics). Rather it is symptomatic of a general antipathy to 'special interests' expressed by parties and supporters of neo-liberalism and neo-conservatism evident in Australia, Canada the United Kingdom and the United States.[24] However, what such a backlash also suggests is that while electing more women in politics has the potential to 'neutralise' the gender factor, we have not yet reached a point where the political cultures of Westminster democracies are comfortable with the realities of equal representation. It will be interesting to see if the 'new politics' reforms underpinning the Scottish and Welsh parliaments will result in an embedded feminised political culture.

Future directions

Trimble argues that the mere presence of women can disrupt the traditional parliamentary politics. Both Margaret Thatcher and Helen Clark have done that in their own particular way, as have the many other women parliamentarians elected to the Houses of Parliament examined here. However, apart from Wales and Scotland, women still remain considerably underrepresented in the worlds of Westminster. There is no doubt that significant advances have been made, as a result of both structural and strategic factors: electoral reform, women's political mobilisation, the feminisation of party elites, candidate gender quotas, and the recent election of left-leaning governments. However, the reticence of liberal-conservative parties to actively pursue gender equality in candidate selection means that women face the possibility of declining representation in the future. But does this bode ill for the popular expectation that women's substantive representation will increase over time? The chapters in this volume highlight that women politicians do act for women, but that this is contingent on a whole range of factors, not least their partisanship, and is not necessarily related to their numerical presence.

We should not assume women will act differently from men immediately on entering parliament, if at all. Research suggests that new members, women and men, try to adapt to the norms of the institution. However, because these are male norms, it is women who have to change their behaviour, and behaving too much like a man brings its own difficulties. Complicating this is the fact that the acceptability rating differs within the electorate. The dominant cultural expectation of what it means to be female will often contrast with the expectations women's organisations have of their female representatives.[25]

Not only does it take time for women to adjust to parliamentary norms, but institutional norms and rules also take time to change. While the professionalisation of politics has demanded significant changes in both parties and parliaments, the informal norms of these institutions have been relatively slow in adjusting to the revolutionary changes in women's lives. As such, we are doomed to be disappointed if we ask our women politicians to transform parliaments immediately upon their election. Irrespective of the problems and possibilities associated with notions of a critical mass, time is an important variable in the exploration of further connections between the descriptive and substantive. Women parliamentarians need time to build a reputation, develop confidence in performance and pursue recruitment into powerful committees and the executive constituency work. These pursuits are mediated by party responsibilities, constituency work, factional alliances and election campaigns. Alongside these factors, we know that not all women are predisposed to act 'for' women, and their interpretations of what women want or need are necessarily diverse. Instead, as the previous chapters demonstrate, the impact of women's parliamentary presence is subtle, indirect and gradual. Finally, new institutions can allow the implementation of a new politics. The question now is whether a new feminised politics can become the 'norm' and the challenge is whether old institutions can embrace this new, feminised politics.

Notes

1 Mill, cited in James, 'The Good-enough Citizen', 64.
2 Squires, *Gender in Political Theory*, 195.
3 Sawer, *The Ethical State?*, 145–9.
4 See Vickers, 'The Problem with Interests'.
5 See Phillips, *The Politics of Presence*.
6 See Rule, 'Why Women Don't Run'; Siaroff, 'Women's Representation in Legislatures and Cabinets in Industrial Democracies'; Studlar and McAllister, 'Does a Critical Mass Exist?'.
7 Vickers, *Reinventing Political Science*, 128.
8 See Curtin and Sawer, 'Gender Equity in the Shrinking State'; Grey and Sawer, 'Australia and New Zealand'.
9 Although Canada was not unique in women having the vote at municipal level. For example, women ratepayers gained local government suffrage in 1861 in South Australia, 1867 in Otago and Nelson, 1869 in the United Kingdom, 1876 in Western Australia and in the other New Zealand provinces, 1879 in Queensland, 1884 in rural Tasmania, 1893 and 1894 for Hobart and Launceston City Councils.
10 See Errington, 'Pioneers and Suffragists'.
11 Carlyle, cited in Taylor, *The House of Commons at Work*, 1.
12 Short, cited in Hill, 'The Political Gender Gap'.
13 Australia has 24.7 per cent women in its lower house, but women make up 28.3 per cent of the parliament as a whole (which includes the proportionally elected Senate).
14 Curtin and Sexton, 'Selecting and Electing Women to the House of Representatives'.
15 See Matland and Studlar, 'Determinants of Legislative Turnover'.
16 See Matland and Studlar, 'Determinants of Legislative Turnover'.
17 See Young, 'Legislative Turnover and the Election of Women to the Canadian House of Commons'.
18 See Thomas, *How Women Legislate*; Childs, 'Hitting the Target'; Grey, 'Does Size Matter?'.
19 See Global Database of Quotas for Women at www.quotaproject.org.
20 See Karam and Lovenduski, 'Women in Parliament'.
21 For example, Liberal, Labor, Green and independent women parliamentarians contributed to the drafting of the successful Tasmanian abortion law reform Bill of late 2001 (which began as a private member's Bill put forward by the health minister, Judy Jackson).
22 See Cramer Walsh, 'Enlarging Representation'.
23 See Cramer Walsh, 'Enlarging Representation'.
24 See Connell, 'Change among the Gatekeepers'; Sawer, 'Women'.
25 See Cramer Walsh, 'Enlarging Representation'.

Bibliography

Alexander, Herbert (1992), *Financing Politics: Money, Elections and Political Reform*, 4th edn, Washington: Congressional Quarterly Press.

Arscott, Jane and Linda Trimble (eds) (1997), *In the Presence of Women: Representation in Canadian Governments*, Toronto: Harcourt Brace.

Arter, David (2000), 'On Assessing Strength and Weakness in Parliamentary Committee Systems: Some Preliminary Observations on the Scottish Parliament', *Legislative Studies*, 8 (2): 93–117.

Ashley, Jackie (2004), 'Bullied, Patronised and Abused: Women MPs reveal the Truth about Life inside Westminster', *Guardian*, 7 December.

Atkinson, Neill (2003), *Adventures in Democracy: A History of the Vote in New Zealand*, Dunedin: University of Otago Press and the Electoral Commission.

Ballington, Julie (2004), 'Gender Equality in Political Party Funding', in Reginald Austin and Maja Tjernström (eds), *Funding of Political Parties and Election Campaigns*, Stockholm: International Institute for Democracy and Electoral Assistance.

Banaszak, Lee Ann, Karen Beckwith and Dieter Rucht (2003), 'When Power Relocates: Interactive Changes in Women's Movements and States', in Lee Ann Banaszak, Karen Beckwith and Dieter Rucht (eds), *Women's Movements Facing the Reconfigured State*, Cambridge: Cambridge University Press.

Bashevkin, Sylvia (1998), *Women on the Defensive*, Toronto: University of Toronto Press.

Bashevkin, Sylvia (1993), *Toeing the Line: Women and Party Politics in English Canada*, 2nd edn, Toronto: Oxford University Press.

Beckwith, Karen (2003), 'The Substantive Representation of Women: Newness, Numbers and Models of Representation', paper presented at the annual meeting of the American Political Science Association, Boston.

Beckwith, Karen (2000), 'The Gendering Ways of States: Women's Representation and State Reconfiguration in France, Great Britain, and the United States', in Lee Ann Banaszak, Karen Beckwith and Dieter Rucht (eds), *Women's Movements Facing the Reconfigured State*, Cambridge: Cambridge University Press.

Bergqvist, Christina, Anette Borchorst, Ann-Dorte Christensen, Viveca Ramnstedt-Silén, Nina C. Raaum and Auður Styrkársdóttir (eds) (1999), *Equal Democracies? Gender and Politics in the Nordic Countries*, Oslo: Scandinavian University Press.

Berrington, Hugh (1973), *Backbench Opinion in the House of Commons 1945–55*, Oxford: Pergamon Press.

Betts, Sandra, John Borland and Paul Chaney (2001), 'Inclusive Government for Excluded Groups: Women and Disabled People', in Paul Chaney, Tom Hall and Andrew Pithouse (eds), *New Governance–New Democracy? Post-devolution Wales*, Cardiff: University of Wales Press.

Beveridge, Fiona (2000), 'Mainstreaming and the Engendering of Policy-making: A Means to an End?', *Journal of European Public Policy*, 7 (3): 385–405.

Black, Jerome (2003), 'Differences that Matter: Minority Women MPs, 1993–2000', in Manon Tremblay and Linda Trimble (eds), *Women and Electoral Politics in Canada*, Don Mills: Oxford University Press.

Black, Jerome and Lynda Erickson (2002), 'Women Candidates and Voter Bias: Do Women Politicians Need to be Better?', *Electoral Studies*, 22 (1): 81–100.

Blackburn, Robert and Andrew Kennon (2003), *Griffith and Ryle on Parliament: Functions, Practice and Procedures*, London: Sweet and Maxwell.

Blais, André, Elisabeth Gidengil, Agnieszka Dobyzynska, Neil Nevitte and Richard Nadeau (2003), 'Does the Local Candidate Matter? Candidate Effects in the Canadian Election of 2000', *Canadian Journal of Political Science*, 36 (3): 657–64.

Boag, Michelle (2002), 'Talking about the Women's Vote: An Interview with National Party President Michelle Boag', *Women Talking Politics*, Newsletter of the Aotearoa/New Zealand Women and Politics Network, New Issue 5: 3–5.

Bochel, John and David Denver (1983), 'Candidate Selection in the Labour Party: What the Selectors Seek', *British Journal of Political Science*, 13 (1): 45–69.

Boston, Jonathan, Stephen Levine, Elizabeth McLeay and Nigel Roberts (1996), *New Zealand under MMP: A New Politics?*, Auckland: Auckland University Press.

Bradbury, Jonathan (1998), 'The Devolution Debate in Wales during the Major Governments: The Politics of a Developing Union State?', *Regional and Federal Studies*, 8 (1): 120–39.

Bradbury, Jonathan, David Denver, James Mitchell and Lynn Bennie (2000), 'Devolution and Party Change: Candidate selection for the 1999 Scottish Parliament and Welsh Assembly', *Journal of Legislative Studies*, 6 (3): 51–72.

Brash, Don (2004), 'Nationhood: Orewa Speech', presented by Don Brash, Leader of the National Party, to the Orewa Rotary Club, Auckland.

Breitenbach, Esther and Fiona Mackay (2001), *Women and Contemporary Scottish Politics: An Anthology*, Edinburgh: Polygon at Edinburgh.

Breitenbach, Esther, Alice Brown, Fiona Mackay and Janette Webb (eds) (2002), *The Changing Politics of Gender Equality in Britain*, Basingstoke: Palgrave.

Brodie, Janine (1985), *Women and Politics in Canada*, Toronto: McGraw-Hill Ryerson.

Brodie, Janine (with Celia Chandler) (1991), 'Women and the Electoral Process in Canada', in Kathy Megyery (ed.), *Women in Canadian Politics: Toward Equity in Representation*, Toronto: Dundurn.

Broughton, Sharon (1998), 'Gendered Treatment of Ministers in the Australian Federal Parliament: A Case Study', paper presented at the Joint Conference of the Australasian Political Science Association and European Union Studies Association of New Zealand, University of Canterbury.

Brown, Alice (2000), 'Designing the Scottish Parliament', *Parliamentary Affairs*, 53 (3): 542–56.

Brown, Alice, Tahnya Barnett Donaghy, Fiona Mackay and Elizabeth Meehan (2002), 'Women and Constitutional Change in Scotland and Northern Ireland', *Parliamentary Affairs*, 55 (1): 71–84.

Burrell, Barbara (1994), *A Woman's Place is in the House: Campaigning for Congress in the Feminist Era*, Ann Arbor: University of Michigan Press.

Burt, Sandra and Elizabeth Lorenzin (1997), 'Taking the Women's Movement to Queen's Park: Women's Interests and the New Democratic Government of Ontario', in Jane Arscott and Linda Trimble (eds), *In the Presence of Women: Representation in Canadian Governments*, Toronto: Harcourt Brace.

Burt, Sandra, Alison Horton and Kathy Martin (2000), 'Women in the Ontario New Democratic Government: Revisiting the Concept of Critical Mass', *International Review of Women and Leadership*, 6 (1): 1–12.

Butler, David and Gareth Butler (2000), *Twentieth-Century British Political Facts, 1900–2000*, London: Palgrave.

Butler, Judith (1990), *Gender Trouble*, New York: Routledge.

Byrne, Paul (1996), 'The Politics of the Women's Movement', in Joni Lovenduski and Pippa Norris (eds), *Women in Politics*, Oxford: Oxford University Press.

Cain, Bruce, John Ferejohn and Morris Fiorina (1987), *The Personal Vote: Constituency Service and Electoral Independence*, Cambridge, MA: Harvard University Press.

Campbell, Rosie (2004), 'Gender, Ideology and Issue Preference: Is There Such a Thing as Women's Political Interest in Britain?', *British Journal of Politics and International Relations*, 6 (1): 20–44.

Carroll, Susan J. (2003), 'Are US Women State Legislators Accountable to Women? The Complementary Roles of Feminist Identity and Women's Organizations', paper presented to the Gender and Social Capital conference, University of Manitoba.

Carroll, Susan J. (2003), *Women and American Politics: New Questions, New Directions*, Oxford: Oxford University Press.

Carroll, Susan J. (2002), 'Have Women Legislators in the United States Become More Conservative? A Comparison of State Legislators in 2001 and 1988', *Atlantis*, 27 (2): 128–39.

Carroll, Susan J. (2001), *The Impact of Women in Public Office*, Indiana: Indiana University Press.

Carroll, Susan J. and Debra Liebowitz (2003), 'New Challenges, New Questions, New Directions', in Susan J. Carroll (ed.), *Women and American Politics: New Questions, New Directions*, Oxford: Oxford University Press.

Carty, R. Kenneth (1991), *Canadian Political Parties in the Constituencies*, Toronto: Dundurn.

Carty, R. Kenneth, William Cross and Lisa Young (2000), *Rebuilding Canadian Party Politics*, Vancouver: UBC Press.

Catt, Helena (1997), 'Women, Maori and Minorities: Micro-representation and MMP', in Jonathan Boston, Stephen Levine, Elizabeth McLeay and Nigel Roberts (eds), *From Campaign to Coalition: The 1996 MMP Election*, Palmerston North: Dunmore Press.

Caul, Miki (2001), 'Political Parties and the Adoption of Candidate Gender Quotas: A Cross-national Analysis', *Journal of Politics*, 63 (4): 1214–29.

Caul, Miki (1999), 'Women's Representation in Parliament: The Role of Political Parties', *Party Politics*, 5 (1): 79–98.

Chaney, Paul (2004), 'The Post-devolution Equality Agenda: The Case of the Welsh Assembly's Statutory Duty to Promote Equality of Opportunity', *Policy and Politics*, 32 (1): 34–56.

Chaney, Paul (2003), 'Setting the Agenda? Women and Policy-making in Post-devolution Wales', paper presented at the Seminar for Engendering Democracy Women's Organisations and their Influence on Policy Making, Queen's University of Belfast.

Chaney, Paul (2003), 'Social Capital and the Participation of Marginalized Groups in Government: A Study of the Statutory Partnership between the Third Sector and Devolved Government in Wales', *Public Policy and Administration*, 17 (4): 20–39.

Chaney, Paul and Ralph Fevre (2002), 'Is There a Demand for Descriptive Representation? Evidence from the UK's Devolution Programme', *Political Studies*, 50 (5): 897–915.

Chaney, Paul and Ralph Fevre (2002), *The Equality Policies of the Government of the National Assembly for Wales and their Implementation, July 1999 to January 2002. A Report for the Equal Opportunities Commission, Disability Rights Commission, Commission for Racial Equality, and Institute of Welsh Affairs*, Cardiff: Institute of Welsh Affairs.

Childs, Sarah (2005), 'Feminizing British Politics', in Andrew Geddes and Jon Tonge (eds), *Britain Decides: The UK General Election 2005*, Basingstoke: Palgrave.

Childs, Sarah (2004), 'A Feminised Style of Politics? Women MPs in the House of Commons', *British Journal of Politics and International Relations*, 6 (1): 3–19.

Childs, Sarah (2004), *New Labour's Women MPs: Women Representing Women*, London: Routledge.

Childs, Sarah (2003), 'The Sex Discrimination (Election Candidates) Act 2002 and its Implications', *Representation*, 39 (2): 83–92.

Childs, Sarah (2002), 'Concepts of Representation and the Passage of the Sex Discrimination (Election Candidates) Bill', *Journal of Legislative Studies*, 8 (3): 90–108.

Childs, Sarah (2002), 'Hitting the Target: Are Labour Women MPs "Acting for" Women?', in Karen Ross (ed.), *Women, Politics and Change*, Oxford: Oxford University Press.

Childs, Sarah (2001), 'Attitudinally Feminist? The New Labour Women MPs and the Substantive Representation of Women', *Politics*, 21 (3): 178–85.

Childs, Sarah and Julie Withey (2004), 'Do Women Sign for Women? Sex and the Signing of Early Day Motions in the 1997 Parliament', *Political Studies*, 52 (4): 552–64.

Clark, Helen (1986), 'Helen Clark: Politician', in Virginia Myers (ed.), *Head and Shoulders*, Auckland: Penguin Books.

Cockburn, Cynthia (1996), 'Strategies for Gender Democracy', *European Journal of Women's Studies*, 3 (7): 7–26.

Coney, Sandra (1993), 'Why the Women's Movement Ran out of Steam', in Sue Kedgley and Mary Varnham (eds), *Heading Nowhere in a Navy Blue Suit and other Tales from the Feminist Revolution*, Wellington: Daphne Brasell.

Connell, Robert W. (2005), 'Change among the Gatekeepers: Men, Masculinities and Gender Equality in the Global Arena', *Signs*, 30 (3): 1801–25.

Considine, Mark and Iva Deutchman (1996), 'Instituting Gender', *Women and Politics*, 16 (4): 1–19.

Costain, Anne and Douglas Costain (1987), 'Strategy and Tactics of the Women's Movement in the United States: The Role of Political Parties', in Mary Fainsod Katzenstein and Carol McClurg Mueller (eds), *The Women's Movements of the*

United States and Western Europe: Consciousness, Political Opportunity and Public Policy, Philadelphia: Temple University Press.

Courtney, John C. (2004), *Elections*, Vancouver: UBC Press.

Cowell-Meyers, Kimberley (2001), 'Women in Peace Building in Northern Ireland: the Effects of Gender in the New Legislative Assembly', *Women and Politics*, 23 (3): 55–88.

Cowley, Philip (2002), *Revolts and Rebellions: Parliamentary Voting under Blair*, London: Politico's.

Cowley, Philip and Sarah Childs (2003), 'Too Spineless to Rebel? New Labour's Women MPs', *British Journal of Political Science*, 33 (3): 345–65.

Cramer Walsh, Katherine (2002), 'Enlarging Representation: Women Bringing Marginalized Perspectives to Floor Debate in the House of Representatives', in Cindy Simon Rosenthal (ed.), *Women Transforming Congress*, Norman: University of Oklahoma Press.

Craske, Nikki and Maxine Molyneux (2002), *Gender and the Politics of Rights and Democracy in Latin America*, New York: Palgrave.

Criddle, Byron (2001), 'MPs and Candidates', in David Butler and Dennis Kavanagh (eds), *The British General Election of 2001*, London: Palgrave.

Criddle, Byron (1997), 'MPs and Candidates', in David Butler and Dennis Kavanagh (eds), *The British General Election of 1997*, London: Macmillan.

Cross, William (2004), *Political Parties*, Vancouver: UBC Press.

Curtin, Jennifer (2003), 'Representing the "Interests" of Women in the Paid Maternity Leave Debate', paper presented at the annual meeting of the Australasian Political Studies Association, University of Tasmania.

Curtin, Jennifer (2002), 'Women's Voting Patterns: Australia and New Zealand Compared', in *Women Talking Politics*, Newsletter of the Aotearoa/New Zealand Women and Politics Network.

Curtin, Jennifer and Marian Sawer (1996), 'Gender Equity in the Shrinking State: Women and the Great Experiment', in Francis G. Castles, Rolf Gerritsen and Jack Vowles (eds), *The Great Experiment: Labour Parties and Public Policy Transformation in Australia and New Zealand*, Sydney: Allen & Unwin.

Curtin, Jennifer and Kelly Sexton (2004), 'Are Quotas Contagious? Promoting Women's Parliamentary Presence in Australia', paper presented at the annual meeting of the Canadian Political Science Association, University of Winnipeg.

Curtin, Jennifer and Kelly Sexton (2004), 'Selecting and Electing Women to the House of Representatives: Progress at Last?', Australasian Political Studies Association Conference Refereed Proceedings, at www.adelaide.edu.au/apsa/docs_papers/Aust%20Pol/Curtin.pdf.

Dahl, Jens (1997), 'Gender Parity in Nunavut', *Indigenous Affairs*, 3 (4): 42–7.

Dahlerup, Drude (1988), 'From a Small to a Large Minority: Women in Scandinavian Politics', *Scandinavian Political Studies*, 11 (4): 275–97.

Dann, Christine (1985), *Up from Under: Women and Liberation in New Zealand, 1970–1985*, Wellington: Allen and Unwin/Port Nicholson Press.

Darcy, Robert and Karen Beckwith (1991), 'Political Disaster, Political Triumph: The Election of Women to National Parliaments', paper presented at the annual meeting of the American Political Science Association, Washington.

Darcy, Robert, Susan Welch and Janet Clark (1994), *Women, Elections and Representation*, 2nd edn, Lincoln: University of Nebraska Press.

Dauphin, Sandrine and Jocelyne Praud (2002), 'Debating and Implementing Gender Parity in France', *Modern and Contemporary France*, 10 (1): 5–11.

Davis, Rebecca Howard (1997), *Women and Power in Parliamentary Democracies*, Lincoln: University of Nebraska Press.

Devere, Heather and Jane Scott (2001), 'The Women's Movement', in Raymond Miller (ed.), *New Zealand Government and Politics*, Auckland: Oxford University Press.

Diamond, Irene and Nancy Hartsock (1981), 'Beyond Interests in Politics: A Comment on Virginia Sapiro's "When are Interests Interesting? The Problem of Political Representation of Women"', *American Political Science Review*, 75 (3): 717–21.

Dobrowolsky, Alexandra (2002), 'Crossing Boundaries: Exploring and Mapping Women's Constitutional Interventions in England, Scotland, and Northern Ireland', *Social Politics: International Studies in Gender, State and Society*, 9 (2): 293–340.

Dobrowolsky, Alexandra and Vivien Hart (2003), *Women Making Constitutions: New Politics and Comparative Perspectives*, Basingstoke: Macmillan.

Dodson, Debra (2005), *The Impact of Women in Congress*, Oxford: Oxford University Press.

Dodson, Debra (1998), 'Representing Women's Interests in the US House of Representatives', in Sue Thomas and Clyde Wilcox (eds), *Women and Elective Office*, New York: Oxford University Press.

Donaghy, Tahnya Barnett (2003), 'Mainstreaming: Northern Ireland's Participative–Democratic Approach', Belfast: Queen's University, Centre for Advancement of Women in Politics, Occasional Paper No. 2.

Dovi, Suzanne (2002), 'Preferable Descriptive Representatives: Will Just Any Woman, Black, or Latino Do?', *American Political Science Review*, 96 (4): 729–43.

Duerst-Lahti, Georgia and Rita Mae Kelly (1995), 'On Governance, Leadership and Gender', in Georgia Duerst-Lahti and Rita Mae Kelly (eds), *Gender Power, Leadership and Governance*, Ann Arbor: University of Michigan Press.

Duverger, Maurice (1955), *The Political Role of Women*, Paris: United Nations Educational Scientific and Cultural Organization.

Dybbroe, Susanne (1996), 'Questions of Identity and Issues of Self-determination', *Inuit Studies*, 20 (2): 39–53.

Eagle, Maria and Joni Lovenduski (1998), *High Time or High Tide for Labour Women?*, London: Fabian Society.

Edmonton Journal (2004), 'Duelling MPs take it outside', 5 May: A7.

Edmonton Journal (2004), [no title – Alberta news briefs], 5 May: A10.

Edwards, Julia and Christine Chapman (2000), 'Women's Political Representation in Wales: Waving or Drowning?', *Contemporary Politics*, 6 (4): 367–81.

Edwards, Julia and Laura McAllister (2002), 'One Step Forward, Two Steps Back? Women and the Two Main Political Parties in Wales', *Political Quarterly*, 21 (3): 154–66.

Eisenberg, Avigail (1998), 'Domination and Political Representation in Canada', in Veronica Strong-Boag *et al.*, *Painting the Maple: Essays on Race, Gender and the Construction of Canada*, Vancouver: UBC Press.

Elder, Laurel (2004), 'Why Women Don't Run: Explaining Women's Underrepresentation in America's Political Institutions', *Women and Politics*, 26 (2): 27–56.

Erickson, Lynda (2003), 'In the Eyes of the Beholders: Gender and Leader

Popularity in a Canadian Context', in Manon Tremblay and Linda Trimble (eds), *Women and Electoral Politics in Canada*, Don Mills: Oxford University Press.

Erickson, Lynda (1998), 'Entry to the Commons: Parties, Recruitment and the Election of Women in 1993', in Manon Tremblay and Caroline Andrew (eds), *Women and Political Representation in Canada*, Ottawa: University of Ottawa Press.

Erickson, Lynda (1997), 'Might More Women Make a Difference? Gender, Party and Ideology among Canada's Parliamentary Candidates', *Canadian Journal of Political Science*, 30 (4): 663–88.

Errington, Jane (1993), 'Pioneers and Suffragists', in Sandra Burt, Lorraine Code and Lindsay Dorney (eds), *Changing Patterns: Women in Canada*, 2nd edn, Toronto: McClelland and Stewart.

Everitt, Joanna and Elisabeth Gidengil (2003), 'Tough Talk: How Television News Covers Male and Female Leaders of Canadian Political Parties', in Manon Tremblay and Linda Trimble (eds), *Women and Electoral Politics in Canada*, Don Mills: Oxford University Press.

Fairclough, Norman (2000), 'Discourse, Social Theory, and Social Research: The Discourse of Welfare Reform', *Journal of Sociolinguistics*, 4 (2): 163–95.

Farrell, David and Ian McAllister (2005), *The Australian Electoral System*, Sydney: University of New South Wales Press.

Fearon, Kate and Monica McWilliams (2000), 'Swimming against the Mainstream: The Northern Ireland Women's Coalition', in Carmel Roulston and Celia Davies (eds), *Gender, Democracy and Inclusion in Northern Ireland*, Basingstoke: Palgrave.

Feld, Val (2000), 'A New Start in Wales: How Devolution is Making a Difference', in Anne Coote (ed.), *New Gender Agenda*, London: Institute for Public Policy Research.

Feld, Val (1994), 'Women and a Welsh Parliament', in *Wales Assembly of Women, Action for Equality, Development and Peace*, Cydweli: Wales Assembly of Women.

Finer, Samuel, Hugh Berrington and David Bartholomew (1961), *Backbench Opinion in the House of Commons, 1955–59*, Oxford: Pergamon Press.

Flynn, Paul (1997), *Commons Knowledge*, Bridgend: Seren.

Forbes, Ian (2002), 'The Political Meanings of the Equal Opportunities Project', in Esther Breitenbach, Alice Brown, Fiona Mackay and Janette Webb (eds), *The Changing Politics of Gender Equality in Britain*, Basingstoke: Palgrave.

Fredman, Sandra (2001), 'Equality: A New Generation?', *Industrial Law Journal*, 30 (2): 145–68.

Freedman, Jane (2002), 'Women in the European Parliament', *Parliamentary Affairs*, 55 (1): 179–88.

Galligan, Yvonne and Lizanne Dowds (2003), 'Women's Hour? Social Attitudes to Women's Political Participation in Northern Ireland', Research Update No. 26.

Gargarella, Roberto (1998), 'Full Representation, Deliberation and Impartiality', in Jon Elster (ed.), *Deliberative Democracy*, Cambridge: Cambridge University Press.

Gelb, Joyce (1989), *Feminism and Politics: A Comparative Perspective*, Berkeley: University of California Press.

Gidengil, Elisabeth (2003), 'Is Canada a Case of Gender Realignment?', paper presented at the annual meeting of the American Political Science Association, Philadelphia.

Gidengil, Elisabeth and Joanna Everitt, (2002), 'Damned if You Do, Damned if

You Don't: Television News Coverage of Female Party Leaders in the 1993 Federal Election', in William Cross (ed.), *Political Parties, Representation and Electoral Democracy in Canada*, Don Mills: Oxford University Press.

Gidengil, Elisabeth, Elizabeth Goodyear-Grant, Neil Nevitte, André Blais and Richard Nadeau (2003), 'Gender, Knowledge and Social Capital', paper presented to the Gender and Social Capital conference, University of Manitoba.

Gombay, Nicole (2000), 'The Politics of Culture: Gender Parity in the Legislative Assembly of Nunavut', *Inuit Studies*, 24 (1): 125–48.

Grey, Sandra (2002), 'Does Size Matter? Critical Mass and New Zealand's Women MPs', *Parliamentary Affairs*, 55 (1): 19–29.

Grey, Sandra and Marian Sawer (2005), 'Australia and New Zealand', in Yvonne Galligan and Manon Tremblay (eds), *Sharing Power: Women, Parliament, Democracy*, Aldershot: Ashgate.

Grimshaw, Patricia (1987), *Women's Suffrage in New Zealand*, 2nd edn, Auckland: Auckland University Press.

Gutmann, Amy and Dennis Thompson (1996), *Democracy and Disagreement*, Cambridge, MA: MIT Press.

Haavio-Mannila, Elina and Torild Skard (1985), *Unfinished Democracy: Women in Nordic Politics*, Oxford: Pergamon Press.

Hancock, Keith (1930), *Australia*, London: Ernest Benn.

Hanson, David (1995), *Unelected, Unaccountable and Untenable: A Study of Appointments to Public Bodies in Wales*, Cardiff: Wales Labour Party.

Hazell, Robert (2000), *The State and the Nations: The First Year of Devolution in the United Kingdom*, Throverton: Imprint Academic.

Henig, Ruth and Simon Henig (2001), *Women and Political Power: Europe since 1945*, New York: Routledge.

Hicks, Jack and Graham White (2000), 'Nunavut: Inuit Self-determination through a Land Claim and Public Government', in Jens Dahl, Jack Hicks and Peter Jull (eds), *Nunavut: Inuit Regain Control of their Lands and their Lives*, Copenhagen: International Work Group for Indigenous Affairs.

Hill, Lisa (2003), 'The Political Gender Gap: Australia, Britain and the United States', *Policy, Organisation and Society*, 22 (1): 69–96.

Hinds, Bronagh (1999), 'Women Working for Peace in Northern Ireland', in Yvonne Galligan, Eilís Ward and Rick Wilford (eds), *Contesting Politics: Women in Ireland, North and South*, Boulder: Westview Press.

Howe, Paul and David Northrup (2000), *Strengthening Canadian Democracy: The Views of Canadian*, Montreal: Institute for Research on Public Policy.

Htun, Mala and Mark Jones (2001), 'Engendering the Right to Participate in Decision-making: Electoral Quotas and Women's Leadership in Latin America', in Nikki Craske and Maxine Molyneux (eds), *Gender, Rights and Justice in Latin America*, New York: Macmillan.

Hunter, Alfred and Margaret Denton (1984), 'Do Female Candidates "Lose Votes"? The Experience of Female Candidates in the 1979 and 1980 Canadian General Elections', *Canadian Review of Sociology and Anthropology*, 21 (4): 395–406.

Inglehart, Ronald and Pippa Norris (2003), *Rising Tide: Gender Equality and Cultural Change around the World*, Cambridge: Cambridge University Press.

Jackson, Keith and Alan McRobie (1998), *New Zealand Adopts Proportional Representation*, Aldershot: Ashgate.

James, Susan (1992), 'The Good-enough Citizen: Citizenship and Independence', in Gisella Bock and Susan James (eds), *Beyond Equality and Difference: Citizenship, Feminist Politics and Female Subjectivity*, London: Routledge.

Jelen, Ted, Sue Thomas and Clyde Wilcox (1994), 'The Gender Gap in Comparative Perspective: Gender Differences in Abstract Ideology and Concrete Issues in Western Europe', *European Journal of Political Research*, 25 (1): 171–86.

Jónasdóttir, Anna G. (1988), 'On the Concept of Interest, Women's Interests, and the Limitations of Interest Theory', in Kathleen B. Jones and Anna G. Jónasdóttir (eds), *The Political Interests of Gender: Developing Theory and Research with a Feminist Face*, London: Sage.

Julian, Rae (1992), 'Women: How Significant a Force?', in Hyam Gold (ed.), *New Zealand Politics in Perspective*, 3rd edn, Auckland: Longman Paul.

Kaiser, Pia (1999), 'The Rise of New Egalitarian Parties and Women's Parliamentary Participation', paper presented at the Northeastern Political Science Association, Boston.

Kanter, Rosabeth Moss (1977), 'Some Effects of Proportions on Group Life: Skewed Sex Ratios and Reponses to Token Women', *American Journal of Sociology*, 82 (1): 965–90.

Kanter, Rosabeth Moss (1977), *Men and Women of the Corporation*, New York: Basic Books.

Karam, Azza and Joni Lovenduski (1998), 'Women in Parliament: Making a Difference', in Azza Karam (ed.), *Women in Parliament: Beyond Numbers*, Stockholm: International Institute for Democracy and Electoral Assistance.

Kathlene, Lyn (1994), 'Power and Influence in State Legislative Policymaking: The Interaction of Gender and Position in Committee Hearing Debates', *American Political Science Review*, 88 (3): 560–76.

Keating, Michael (2005), *The Government of Scotland: Public Policy Making after Devolution*, Edinburgh: Edinburgh University Press.

Kelsey, Jane (1995), *The New Zealand Experiment*, Auckland: Auckland University Press.

Kincaid, Diane (1978), 'Over his Dead Body: A Positive Perspective on Widows in the US Congress', *Western Political Quarterly*, 31 (1): 96–104.

King, Michael (2003), *The Penguin History of New Zealand*, Auckland: Penguin Books.

Kohn, Walter (1980), *Women in National Legislatures: A Comparative Study of Six Countries*, New York: Praeger.

Kuhn, Raymond (2003), 'The French Presidential and Parliamentary Elections, 2002', *Representation*, 39 (1): 44–56.

Lawrence, Carmen (2000), 'The Gender Gap in Political Behaviour', in Kate Deverall, Rebecca Huntley, Penny Sharpe and Jo Tilly (eds), *Party Girls: Labor Women Now*, Sydney: Pluto Press.

LeDuc, Lawrence (2003), *The Politics of Direct Democracy: Referendums in Global Perspective*, Peterborough: Broadview Press.

Lee, Rose and Cal Clark (2000), *Democracy and the Status of Women in East Asia*, Boulder: Lynne Rienner.

Levine, Stephen (2004), 'Parliamentary Democracy in New Zealand', *Parliamentary Affairs*, 57 (3): 646–65.

Lijphart, Arend (1987), 'The Demise of the Last Westminster System? Comments on the Report of the Royal Commission on the Electoral System', *Electoral Studies*, 6 (2): 97–103.

Lijphart, Arend (1984), *Democracies: Patterns of Majoritarian and Consensus Government in 21 Countries*, New Haven: Yale University Press.

Lipman, Beata (1973), 'Diary of a Welsh Liberationist', *Planet: The Welsh Internationalist*, 15 (1): 33–36.

Lovenduski, Joni (2005), *Feminizing Politics*, Cambridge: Polity Press.

Lovenduski, Joni (2001), 'Women and Politics', in Pippa Norris (ed.), *Britain Votes, 2001*, Oxford: Oxford University Press.

Lovenduski, Joni (2001), 'Women and Politics: Minority Representation or Critical Mass?', *Parliamentary Affairs*, 54 (4): 743–58.

Lovenduski, Joni (1999), 'Sexing Political Behaviour in Britain', in Sylvia Walby (ed.), *New Agendas for Women*, Basingstoke: Macmillan.

Lovenduski, Joni (1997), 'Gender Politics', *Parliamentary Affairs*, 50 (4): 708–19.

Lovenduski, Joni (1993), 'Introduction: The Dynamics of Gender and Party', in Joni Lovenduski and Pippa Norris (eds), *Gender and Party Politics*, London: Sage.

Lovenduski, Joni and Pippa Norris (2003), 'Westminster Women: The Politics of Presence', *Political Studies*, 51 (1): 81–102.

Lovenduski, Joni and Pippa Norris (eds) (1993), *Gender and Party Politics*, London: Sage.

Lovenduski, Joni and Vicky Randall (1993), *Contemporary Feminist Politics: Women and Power in Britain*, Oxford: Oxford University Press.

MacIvor, Heather (2002), 'Women and the Canadian Electoral System', in Manon Tremblay and Linda Trimble (eds), *Women and Electoral Politics in Canada*, Don Mills: Oxford University Press.

Mackay, Fiona (2004), 'Gender and Political Representation in the UK: The State of the "Discipline"', *British Journal of Politics and International Relations*, 6 (1): 99–120.

Mackay, Fiona (2004), 'Women and Devolution in Scotland', briefing note prepared for the Scottish Parliament Cross-party Group on Women and the Equal Opportunities Commission Scotland.

Mackay, Fiona (2003), 'Women and the 2003 Elections: Keeping up the Momentum', *Scottish Affairs*, 44 (2): 74–90.

Mackay, Fiona (2001), *Love and Politics*, London: Continuum.

Mackay, Fiona and Kate Bilton (2000), *Learning from Experience: Lessons in Mainstreaming Equal Opportunities*, Edinburgh: University of Edinburgh/The Governance of Scotland Forum.

Mackay, Fiona, Meryl Kenny and Elena Pollot-Thomson (2005), *Access, Voice . . . and Influence? Women's Organisations in Post-devolution Scotland*, Edinburgh: Engender.

Mackay, Fiona, Fiona Myers and Alice Brown (2003), 'Towards a New Politics? Women and the Constitutional Change in Scotland', in Alexandra Dobrowolsky and Vivien Hart (eds), *Women Making Constitutions: New Politics and Comparative Perspectives*, Basingstoke: Palgrave.

Mackay, Fiona, Fiona Myers and Alice Brown (2001), 'Making a Difference? Women and the Scottish Parliament: A Preliminary Analysis', paper presented at the Women and Parliaments seminar, Belfast: Queen's University, Centre for Advancement of Women in Politics.

Mackay, Fiona, Elizabeth Meehan, Tahnya Barnett-Donaghy and Alice Brown (2002), 'Women and Constitutional Change in Scotland, Wales and Northern Ireland', *Australasian Parliamentary Review*, 17 (2): 35–54.

Maher, Michael (2001), 'New Zealand: Women on Top', *Foreign Correspondent*, American Broadcasting Corporation.

Mansbridge, Jane (2003), 'Rethinking Representation', *American Political Science Review*, 97 (3): 515–28.

Mansbridge, Jane (1999), 'Should Blacks Represent Blacks and Women Represent Women? A Contingent "Yes"', *Journal of Politics*, 61 (3): 628–57.

Mansbridge, Jane (1998), 'The Many Faces of Representation', Cambridge, MA: John F. Kennedy School of Government, Harvard University, working paper.

Matland, Richard (1998), 'Enhancing Women's Political Participation: Legislative Recruitment and Electoral Systems', in Azza Karam (ed.), *Women in Parliament: Beyond Numbers*, Stockholm: International Institute for Democracy and Electoral Assistance.

Matland, Richard (1998), 'Women's Representation in National Legislatures: Developed and Developing Democracies', *Legislative Studies Quarterly*, 23 (1): 109–25.

Matland, Richard (1993), 'Institutional Variables Affecting Female Representation in National Legislatures: The Case of Norway', *Journal of Politics*, 55 (3): 737–55.

Matland, Richard and Donley Studlar (2004), 'Determinants of Legislative Turnover: A Cross-national Analysis', *British Journal of Political Science*, 34 (1): 87–108.

Matland, Richard and Donley Studlar (1996), 'The Contagion of Women Candidates in Single-member District and Proportional Representation Electoral Systems: Canada and Norway', *Journal of Politics*, 58 (3): 707–33.

McAllister, Ian and Malcolm Mackerras (1999), 'Compulsory Voting, Party Stability and Electoral Advantage in Australia', *Electoral Studies*, 18 (2): 217–33.

McAllister, Ian and Donley Studlar (2002), 'Electoral Systems and Women's Representation: A Long-term Perspective', *Representation*, 39 (1): 1–14.

McAllister, Ian and Donley Studlar (1992), 'Gender and Representation among Legislative Candidates in Australia', *Comparative Political Studies*, 25 (3): 388–411.

McDonough, Roisin, 'Integration or Independence', at: www.democraticdialogue.org/report4.

McLeay, Elizabeth (2003), 'Representation, Selection, Election: The 2002 Parliament', in Jonathan Boston, Stephen Church, Stephen Levine, Elizabeth McLeay and Nigel S. Roberts (eds), *New Zealand Votes: The General Election of 2002*, Wellington: Victoria University of Wellington Press.

McLeay, Elizabeth (1993), 'Women's Parliamentary Representation: A Comparative Perspective', in Helena Catt and Elizabeth McLeay (eds), *Women and Politics in New Zealand*, Wellington: Victoria University of Wellington Press.

McLeay, Elizabeth (1987), 'Towards a Better Democracy? Review Essay of the Report of the Royal Commission on the Electoral System', *Political Science*, 39 (1): 80–96.

McLeay, Elizabeth and Jack Vowles (2003), 'Is a Mixed Member Parliament Really "The Best of Both Worlds?" An Analysis of the Linkages between MPs and Voters in New Zealand, 1993–2002', in Dutch Ministry of Home Affairs and Kinkdom Relations (eds), *Buitenlandse voorbeelden van staatkundige vernieuwing: Vote*, The Hague: Ministerie van Binnenlandse en Koninkrijksrelaties.

McNamara, Maedhbh and Paschal Mooney (2000), *Women in Parliament: Ireland, 1918–2000*, Dublin: Wolfhound Press.

McWilliams, Monica (1995), 'Struggling for Peace and Justice: Reflections on Women's Activism in Northern Ireland', *Journal of Women's History*, 6 (4): 13–39.

McWilliams, Monica and Joan McKiernan (1993), *Bringing it out in the Open: Domestic Violence in Northern Ireland*, Belfast: HMSO.

Meehan, Elizabeth (2003), 'From Government to Governance: Civic Participation and "New Politics": the Context of Potential Opportunities for the Better Representation of Women', Belfast: Queen's University, Centre for Advancement of Women in Politics, Occasional Paper No. 5.

Miller, Robert, Rick Wilford and Freda Donoghue (1996), *Women and Political Participation in Northern Ireland*, Aldershot: Avebury.

Mitchell, James (2004), 'Scotland: Expectations, Policy Types and Devolution', in Alan Trench (ed.), *Has Devolution Made a Difference? The State of the Nations 2004*, Throverton: Imprint Academic.

Morgan, Kevin and Geoff Mungham (2000), *Redesigning Democracy: The Making of the Welsh Assembly*, Bridgend: Seren.

Morgan, Kevin and Gareth Rees (2001), 'Learning by Doing: Devolution and the Governance of Economic Development in Wales', in Paul Chaney, Tom Hall and Andrew Pithouse (eds), *New Governance: New Democracy? Post-devolution Wales*, Cardiff: University of Wales Press.

Mulgan, Richard (1994), *Politics in New Zealand*, Auckland: Auckland University Press.

Muller, William (1977), *The Kept Men? The First Century of Trade Union Representation in the House of Commons, 1874–1975*, London: Harvester Press.

Nevitte, Neil, André Blais, Elisabeth Gidengil and Richard Nadeau (2000), *Unsteady State: The 1997 Canadian Federal Election*, Toronto: Oxford University Press.

Nicholl, Rae (2002), 'The Woman Factor: Candidate Selection in the 1990s: New Zealand, Guam and South Africa', PhD thesis, Wellington: Victoria University of Wellington.

Nicholl, Rae (2000), 'The Revolving Door of Female Representation', in *Women Talking Politics*, Newsletter of the Aotearoa/New Zealand Women and Politics Network, New Issue 2: 12–16.

Norris, Pippa (2004), *Electoral Engineering: Voting Rules and Political Behavior*, Cambridge: Cambridge University Press.

Norris, Pippa (2001), 'Women's Power at the Ballot Box', in International Institute for Democracy and Electoral Assistance, *Voter Turnout from 1945 to 2000: A Global Report on Political Participation*, Stockholm: International Institute for Democracy and Electoral Assistance.

Norris, Pippa (2000), 'Gender and Contemporary British Politics', in Colin Hay (ed.), *British Politics Today*, Cambridge: Polity Press.

Norris, Pippa (1999), 'Gender: A Gender–Generation Gap?', in Geoffrey Evans and Pippa Norris (eds), *Critical Elections: British Parties and Voters in Long-term Perspective*, London: Sage.

Norris, Pippa (1996), 'Women Politicians: Transforming Westminster?', in Joni Lovenduski and Pippa Norris (eds), *Women in Politics*, Oxford: Oxford University Press.

Norris, Pippa (1987), *Politics and Sexual Equality*, Boulder: Lynne Rienner.

Norris, Pippa and Mark Franklin (1997), 'Social Representation', *European Journal of Political Research*, 32 (6): 185–210.

Norris, Pippa and Joni Lovenduski (2001), *Blair's Babes: Critical Mass Theory, Gender, and Legislative Life*, Cambridge, MA: John F. Kennedy School of

Government, Harvard University, Faculty Research Working Papers series, No. RWP01–039.

Norris, Pippa and Joni Lovenduski (1995), *Political Recruitment: Gender, Race and Class in the British Parliament*, Cambridge: Cambridge University Press.

Norris, Pippa and Joni Lovenduski (1989), 'Women Candidates for Parliament', *British Journal of Political Science*, 19 (1): 106–15.

Norris, Pippa, Joni Lovenduski and Rosie Campbell (2004), *Gender and Political Participation*, London: Electoral Commission.

Norton, Philip and David Wood (1993), *Back from Westminster*, Lexington: University Press of Kentucky.

Osmond, John (2001), 'Constitution Building on the Hoof', in *Nations and Regions: The Dynamics of Devolution*, Quarterly Monitoring Programme, Wales, May; Leverhulme Trust.

Pateman, Carole (1970), *Participation and Democratic Theory*, Cambridge: Cambridge University Press.

Paxton, Pamela (1997), 'Women in National Legislatures: A Cross-national Analysis', *Social Science Research*, 26 (2): 442–64.

Perrigo, Sarah (1995), 'Gender Struggles in the Labour Party from 1979 to 1995', *Party Politics*, 1 (3): 407–17.

Phillips, Anne (1995), *The Politics of Presence*, Oxford: Clarendon Press.

Pierson, Paul (2000), 'Increasing Returns, Path Dependence and the Study of Politics', *American Political Science Review*, 94 (2): 251–67.

Pitkin, Hannah Fenichel (1967), *The Concept of Representation*, Berkeley: University of California Press.

Porter, Elisabeth (2000), 'Participatory Democracy and the Challenge of Dialogue across Difference', in Carmel Roulston and Celia Davies (eds), *Gender, Democracy and Inclusion in Northern Ireland*, Basingstoke: Palgrave.

Porter, Elisabeth (1998), 'Identity, Location, Plurality: Women, Nationalism and Northern Ireland', in Rick Wilford and Robert L. Miller (eds), *Women, Ethnicity and Nationalism: The Politics of Transition*, London: Routledge.

Preddey, Elspeth (2003), *The WEL Herstory: The Women's Electoral Lobby in New Zealand 1975–2002*, Wellington: Women's Electoral Lobby/Fraser Books.

Puwar, Nirmal (2004), *Space Invaders: Race, Gender and Bodies out of Place*, New York: Berg.

Puwar, Nirmal (2004), 'Thinking about Making a Difference', *British Journal of Politics and International Relations*, 6 (1): 65–80.

Randall, Vicky (1987), *Women and Politics*, 2nd edn, Chicago: University of Chicago Press.

Ranney, Austin (1965), *Pathways to Parliament*, Madison: University of Wisconsin Press.

Rasmussen, Jorgen (1981), 'Female Career Patterns and Leadership Disabilities in Britain: The Crucial Role of Gatekeepers in Regulating Entry to the Political Elite', *Polity*, 13 (4): 600–20.

Rei, Tania (1993), *Maori Women and the Vote*, Wellington: Huia.

Reingold, Beth (2000), *Representing Women: Sex, Gender and Legislative Behaviour in Arizona and California*, Chapel Hill: University of North Carolina Press.

Reingold, Beth (1992), 'Concepts of Representation among Female and Male State Legislators', *Legislative Studies Quarterly*, 17 (4): 509–37.

Reynolds, Andrew (1999), 'Women in the Legislatures and Executives of the World: Knocking at the Highest Glass Ceiling', *World Politics*, 51 (4): 547–72.

Roach, Kent (1991), 'One Person, One Vote? Canadian Constitutional Standards for Electoral Distribution and Districting', in David Small (ed.), *Drawing the Map: Equality and Efficacy of the Vote in Canadian Electoral Boundary Reform*, Toronto: Dundurn Press.

Rooney, Eilish (2000), 'Women in Northern Irish Politics: Difference Matters', in Carmel Roulston and Celia Davies (eds), *Gender, Democracy and Inclusion in Northern Ireland*, Basingstoke: Palgrave.

Roulston, Carmel (2003), 'Women's Movements, Feminism and Women's Inclusion in Northern Ireland', in Esther Breitenbach (ed.), *Engendering Democracy: Women's Organisations and their Influence on Policy Making within the Devolved Administrations in Northern Ireland, Scotland, and Wales*, Belfast: Institute of Governance, Public Policy and Social Research.

Roulston, Carmel (1999), 'Feminism, Politics, and Postmodernism', in Yvonne Galligan, Eilís Ward and Rick Wilford (eds), *Contesting Politics: Women in Ireland, North and South*, Boulder: Westview Press.

Roulston, Carmel (1997), 'Women on the Margin: The Women's Movement in Northern Ireland', in Lois West (ed.), *Feminist Nationalism*, New York: Routledge.

Roulston, Carmel (1989), 'Women on the Margins: The Women's Movement in Northern Ireland 1973–1988', *Science and Society*, 53 (2): 219–36.

Rule, Wilma (1987), 'Electoral Systems, Contextual Factors, and Women's Opportunities for Election to Parliament in Twenty-three Democracies', *Western Political Quarterly*, 40 (3): 477–98.

Rule, Wilma (1981), 'Why Women Don't Run: The Critical Factors in Women's Legislative Recruitment', *Western Political Quarterly*, 34 (1): 60–77.

Rule, Wilma and Joseph Zimmerman (1994), *Electoral Systems in Comparative Perspective: Their Impact on Women and Minorities*, Westport: Greenwood Press.

Russell, Meg (2003), 'Women in Elected Office in the UK, 1992–2002: Struggles, Achievements and Possible Sea Change', in Alexandra Dobrowolsky and Vivien Hart (eds), *Women Making Constitutions. New politics and Comparative Perspectives*, Basingstoke: Palgrave.

Russell, Meg (2001), *The Women's Representation Bill: Making it Happen*, London: Constitution Unit, University College.

Russell, Meg (2000), *Women's Representation in UK Politics: What Can Be Done within the Law*, London: The Constitution Unit, University College.

Russell, Meg, Fiona Mackay and Laura McAllister (2002), 'Women's Representation in the Scottish Parliament and National Assembly for Wales: Party Dynamics for Achieving Critical Mass', *Journal of Legislative Studies*, 8 (2): 49–76.

Sainsbury, Diane (2001), 'Rights without Seats: The Puzzle of Women's Legislative Recruitment in Australia', in Marian Sawer (ed.), *Elections: Full, Free and Fair*, Sydney: Federation Press.

Salmond, Rob (2003), 'Choosing Candidates: Labour and National in 2002', in Jonathan Boston, Stephen Church, Stephen Levine, Elizabeth McLeay and Nigel Roberts (eds), *New Zealand Votes: The General Election of 2002*, Wellington: Victoria University Press.

Sapiro, Virginia (1981), 'When are Interests Interesting? The Problem of Political Representation of Women', *American Political Science Review*, 75 (3): 701–21.

Sawer, Marian (2003), *The Ethical State? Social Liberalism in Australia*, Carlton: Melbourne University Press.

Sawer, Marian (2002), 'The Representation of Women in Australia: Meaning and Make-believe', *Parliamentary Affairs*, 55 (1): 5–18.

Sawer, Marian (2001), 'Representing Trees, Acres, Voters and Non-voters: Concepts of Parliamentary Representation in Australia', in Marian Sawer and Gianni Zappalà (eds), *Speaking for the People: Representation in Australian Politics*, Melbourne: Melbourne University Press.

Sawer, Marian (2000), 'A Question of Heartland', in John Warhurst and Andrew Parkin (eds), *The Machine: Labor Confronts the Future*, Sydney: Allen & Unwin.

Sawer, Marian (2000), 'Parliamentary Representation of Women: From Discourses of Justice to Strategies of Accountability', *International Political Science Review*, 21 (4): 361–80.

Sawer, Marian (2000), 'Women: Gender Wars in the Nineties', in Marian Simms and John Warhurst (eds), *Howard's Agenda: The 1998 Australia Election*, St Lucia: University of Queensland Press.

Sawer, Marian and Marian Simms (1993), *A Woman's Place: Women and Politics in Australia*, 2nd edn, Sydney: Allen and Unwin.

Scarrow, Susan, Paul Webb and David Farrell (2000), 'From Social Integration to Electoral Contestation: The Changing Distribution of Power within Political Parties', in Russell J. Dalton and Martin Wattenberg (eds), *Parties without Partisans: Political Change in Advanced Industrial Democracies*, Oxford: Oxford University Press.

Sharpe, Sydney (1994), *The Gilded Ghetto*, Toronto: Harper Collins.

Shaw, Sylvia (2000), 'Language, Gender and Floor Apportionment in Political Debates', *Discourse and Society*, 11 (3): 401–18.

Shepherd-Robinson, Laura and Joni Lovenduski (2002), *Women and Candidate Selection*, London: Fawcett Society.

Shields, Margaret (2001), 'Women in the Labour Party during the Kirk and Rowling Years', in Margaret Clark (ed.), *Three Labour Leaders: Nordmeyer, Kirk, Rowling*, Palmerston North: Dunmore Press.

Ship, Susan Judith (1998), 'Problematizing Ethnicity and "Race" in Feminist Scholarship on Women and Politics', in Manon Tremblay and Caroline Andrew (eds), *Women and Political Representation in Canada*, Ottawa: University of Ottawa Press.

Shugart, Matthew and Martin Wattenberg (2001), 'Mixed-member Electoral Systems: A Definition and Typology', in Matthew Shugart and Martin Wattenberg (eds), *Mixed-member Systems: The Best of Both Worlds?*, Oxford: Oxford University Press.

Siaroff, Alan (2000), 'Women's Representation in Legislatures and Cabinets in Industrial Democracies', *International Political Science Review*, 21 (2): 197–216.

Smith, David E. (1995), *The Invisible Crown*, Toronto: University of Toronto Press.

Spelman, Elizabeth (1988), *Inessential Women*, Boston: Beacon Press.

Squires, Judith (2003), 'The New Equalities Agenda: Recognising Diversity and Securing Equality in Post-devolution Britain', in Alexandra Dobrowolsky and Vivien Hart (eds), *Women Making Constitutions: New Politics and Comparative Perspectives*, Basingstoke: Palgrave.

Squires, Judith (1999), *Gender in Political Theory*, Malden, MA: Polity Press.

Squires, Judith (1996), 'Quotas for Women: Fair Representation?', in Joni Lovenduski and Pippa Norris (eds), *Women in Politics*, Oxford: Oxford University Press.

Squires, Judith and Mark Wickham-Jones (2004), 'New Labour, Gender Mainstreaming and the Women and Equality Unit', *British Journal of Politics and International Relations,* 6 (1): 81–98.

Squires, Judith and Mark Wickham-Jones (2002), 'Mainstreaming in Westminster and Whitehall', *Parliamentary Affairs,* 55 (1): 57–70.

Squires, Judith and Mark Wickham-Jones (2001), *Women in Parliament: A Comparative Analysis,* Manchester: Equal Opportunities Commission.

Steele, Jackie (2002), 'The Liberal Women's Caucus', *Canadian Parliamentary Review,* 25 (2): 13–9.

Steele, Jackie (2001), *An Effective Player in the Parliamentary Process: The Liberal Women's Caucus, 1993–2001,* Ottawa: Institute on Governance.

Steinmo, Sven, Kathleen Thelen and Frank Longstreth (1992), *Structuring Politics: Historical Institutionalism in Comparative Analysis,* Cambridge: Cambridge University Press.

Studlar, Donley and Richard E. Matland (1996), 'The Dynamics of Women's Representation in the Canadian Provinces, 1975–1994', *Canadian Journal of Political Science,* 29 (2): 269–93.

Studlar, Donley and Ian McAllister (2002), 'Does a Critical Mass Exist? A Comparative Analysis of Women's Legislative Representation Since 1950', *European Journal of Political Research,* 41 (6): 233–53.

Studlar, Donley and Ian McAllister (1998), 'Candidate Gender and Voting in the 1997 British General Election: Did Labour Quotas Matter?', *Journal of Legislative Studies,* 4 (3): 72–91.

Studlar, Donley and Ian McAllister (1996), 'Constituency Activity and Representational Roles among Australian Legislators', *Journal of Politics,* 58 (1): 69–90.

Studlar, Donley and Ian McAllister (1991), 'The Recruitment of Women to the Australian Legislature: Toward an Explanation of Women's Electoral Disadvantages', *Western Political Quarterly,* 44 (3): 67–85.

Studlar, Donley, Ian McAllister and Alvaro Ascui (1988), 'Electing Women to the British Commons: Breakout from the Beleaguered Beachhead?', *Legislative Studies Quarterly,* 13 (4): 515–28.

Studlar, Donley, Ian McAllister and Bernadette Hayes (1998), 'Explaining the Gender Gap in Voting: A Cross-national Analysis', *Social Science Quarterly,* 79 (4): 779–98.

Summers, Anne (2003), *The End of Equality?,* Sydney: Random House.

Swers, Michele (2002), *The Difference Women Make: The Policy Impact of Women in Congress,* Chicago: University of Chicago Press.

Swers, Michele (2001), 'Research on Women in Legislatures: What Have We Learned? Where Are We Going?', *Women and Politics,* 23 (1–2): 167–85.

Tamerius, Karen (1995), 'Sex, Gender, and Leadership in the Representation of Women', in Georgia Duerst-Lahti and Rita Mae Kelly (eds), *Gender Power, Leadership and Governance,* Ann Arbor: University of Michigan Press.

Taylor, Eric (1979), *The House of Commons at Work,* 9th edn, London: Macmillan Press.

Thomas, Sue (2003), 'The Impact of Women in Political Leadership Positions', in Susan J. Carroll (ed.), *Women and American Politics: New Questions, New Directions,* Oxford: Oxford University Press.

Thomas, Sue (1998), 'Women and Elective Office', in Sue Thomas and Clyde Wilcox (eds), *Women and Elective Office,* New York: Oxford University Press.

Thomas, Sue (1994), *How Women Legislate,* New York: Oxford University Press.

Thomas, Sue (1991), 'The Impact of Women in State Legislative Policies', *Journal of Politics*, 53 (3): 958–76.

Thomas, Sue and Susan Welch (2001), *Times Guide to the House of Commons*, London: The Times.

Thomas, Sue and Susan Welch (1991), 'The Impact of Gender on Activities and Priorities of State Legislators', *Western Political Quarterly*, 44 (2): 445–56.

Towns, Ann (2003), 'Understanding the Effects of Larger Ratios of Women in National Legislatures: Proportions and Gender Differentiation in Sweden and Norway', *Women and Politics*, 25 (1/2): 1–29.

Tremblay, Manon (2003), 'Women's Representational Role in Australia and Canada: The Impact of Political Context', *Australian Journal of Political Science*, 38 (2): 215–38.

Tremblay, Manon (1998), 'Do Female MPs Substantively Represent Women? A Study of Legislative Behaviour in Canada's Thirty-fifth Parliament', *Canadian Journal of Political Science*, 31 (3): 435–65.

Tremblay, Manon (1995), 'Les femmes, des candidates moins performantes que les hommes? Une analyse des votes obtenus par les candidates et candidats du Québec à une élection fédérale canadienne, 1945–1993', *International Journal of Canadian Studies*, 11 (spring): 59–81.

Tremblay, Manon (1992), 'Quand les femmes se distinguent: féminisme et représentation politique au Québec', *Canadian Journal of Political Science*, 25 (1): 65–88.

Tremblay, Manon and Guylaine Boivin (1990/91), 'La question de l'avortement au Parlement canadien: de l'importance de genre dans l'orientation des débats', *Canadian Journal of Women and the Law*, 4 (2): 459–76.

Tremblay, Manon and Réjean Pelletier (2003), 'Feminist Women in Canadian Politics: A Group Ideologically Divided?', *Atlantis*, 28 (1): 80–7.

Tremblay, Manon and Réjean Pelletier (2000), 'More Feminists or More Women? Descriptive and Substantive Representation of Women in the 1997 Canadian Federal Elections', *International Political Science Review*, 21 (4): 381–405.

Trimble, Linda (1998), 'Who's Represented? Gender and Diversity in the Alberta Legislature', in Manon Tremblay and Caroline Andrew (eds), *Women and Political Representation in Canada*, Ottawa: University of Ottawa Press.

Trimble, Linda (1997), 'Feminist Politics in the Alberta Legislature, 1972–1994', in Jane Arscott and Linda Trimble (eds), *In the Presence of Women: Representation in Canadian Governments*, Toronto: Harcourt Brace.

Trimble, Linda (1993), 'A Few Good Women: Female Legislators in Alberta, 1972–1991', in Catherine Cavanaugh and Randi Warne (eds), *Standing on New Ground: Women in Alberta*, Edmonton: University of Alberta Press.

Trimble, Linda and Jane Arscott (2003), *Still Counting: Women in Politics across Canada*, Peterborough: Broadview Press.

Trimble, Linda and Manon Tremblay (2003), 'Women Politicians in Canada's Parliament and Legislatures, 1917–2000: A Socio-demographic Profile', in Manon Tremblay and Linda Trimble (eds), *Women and Electoral Politics in Canada*, Don Mills: Oxford University Press.

True, Jacqui and Michael Mintrom (2001), 'Transnational Networks and Policy Diffusion: The Case of Gender Mainstreaming', *International Studies Quarterly*, 45 (1): 29–59.

Uhr, John (2000), *Rules for Representation: Parliament and the Design of the Australian*

Electoral System, Commonwealth of Australia, Department of the Parliamentary Library, Research Paper No. 29.

Vickers, Jill (forthcoming), 'The Problem with Interests: Making Political Claims for "Women"', in Louise Chappell and Lisa Hill (eds), *The Politics of Women's Interests*, London: Routledge.

Vickers, Jill (1997), *Reinventing Political Science: A Feminist Analysis*, Halifax: Fernwood.

Vowles, Jack (2000), 'Introducing Proportional Representation: the New Zealand Experiment', *Parliamentary Affairs*, 53 (4): 680–96.

Wängnerud, Lena, 'Testing the Politics of Presence: Women's Representation in the Swedish Riksdag', *Scandinavian Political Studies*, 23 (1): 67–91.

Ward, Margaret (2000), *The Northern Ireland Assembly and Women: Assessing the Gender Deficit*, Belfast: Democratic Dialogue.

Ward, Rachel (2004), 'Gender Issues and the Representation of Women in Northern Ireland', paper presented at the annual meeting of the Political Studies Association, University of Lincoln.

Ward, Russell (1958), *The Australian Legend*, Melbourne: Oxford University Press.

Waring, Marilyn (2000), *Politics: Women's Insight*, Geneva: Inter-parliamentary Union.

Welch, Susan and Donley Studlar (1996), 'The Opportunity Structure for Women's Candidacies and Electability in Britain and the United States', *Political Research Quarterly*, 49 (4): 861–74.

Welch, Susan and Donley Studlar (1986), 'British Public Opinion toward Women in Politics: A Comparative Perspective', *Western Political Quarterly*, 39 (1): 138–52.

Welch, Susan and Sue Thomas (1988), 'Explaining the Gender Gap in British Public Opinion', *Women and Politics*, 8 (1): 25–44.

Weldon, Laurel (2002), 'Beyond Bodies: Institutional Sources of Representation for Women in Democratic Policymaking', *Journal of Politics*, 64 (4): 1153–74.

White, Graham (2005), *Cabinets and First Ministers*, Vancouver: UBC Press.

Wilford, Rick (1999), 'Women's Candidacies and Electability in a Divided Society: The Northern Ireland Women's Coalition and the 1996 Forum Election', *Women and Politics*, 20 (1): 73–93.

Wilford, Rick and Robin Wilson (2003), *A Route to Stability: The Review of the Belfast Agreement*, Belfast: Democratic Dialogue.

Williams, Melissa S. (1996), 'Memory, History and Membership: The Moral Claims of Marginalized Groups in Political Representation', in Juha Räikkä (ed.), *Do We Need Minority Rights?*, Hague: Martinus Nijhoff.

Williams, Rachel (2004), 'Sexist Attitudes still a Problem in the Commons', *Edinburgh Evening News*, 7 December.

Wilson, Frank L. (1990), 'Neo-corporatism and the Rise of New Social Movements', in Russell J. Dalton and Manfred Kuechler (eds), *Challenging the Political Order: New Social and Political Movements in Western Democracies*, Cambridge: Polity Press.

Wilson, Margaret (1992), 'Women and the Labour Party', in Margaret Clark (ed.), *The Labour Party after 75 Years*, Wellington: Department of Politics, Victoria University of Wellington.

Winetrobe, Barry (2001), *Realising the Vision: A Parliament with a Purpose*, London: Constitution Unit, University College.

Wood, Sue (2004), 'Muldoon and the Party', in Margaret Clark (ed.), *Muldoon Revisited*, Palmerston North: Dunmore Press.

Wright, Jack (1984), 'Changes in Australia's Federal Election Laws in 1983', *Representation*, 24 (1): 1–4.

Yeatman, Anna (1993), 'Voice and Representation in the Politics of Difference', in Sneja Gunew and Anna Yeatman (eds), *Feminism and the Politics of Difference*, Halifax: Fernwood.

Yoder, Janice (1991), 'Rethinking Tokenism: Looking beyond Numbers', *Gender and Society*, 5 (2): 178–92.

Young, Audrey (2003), 'Brash drops Women's Affairs Role', *New Zealand Herald Online*.

Young, Iris Marion (2000), *Inclusion and Democracy*, Oxford: Oxford University Press.

Young, Iris Marion (1994), 'Gender as Seriality: Thinking about Women as a Social Collective', *Signs*, 19 (3): 713–38.

Young, Iris Marion (1990), *Justice and the Politics of Difference*, Princeton: Princeton University Press.

Young, Iris Marion (1990), *Throwing Like a Girl and Other Essays in Feminist Philosophy and Social Theory*, Indianapolis: Indiana University Press.

Young, Lisa (2004), 'Campaign Finance and Women's Representation in Canada and the United States', unpublished paper prepared for the Organization of American States' Political Parties Program.

Young, Lisa (2004), 'Women (Not) in Politics: Women's Electoral Participation', in Alain-G. Gagnon and James Bickerton (eds), *Canadian Politics*, 4th edn, Peterborough: Broadview Press.

Young, Lisa (2002), 'Representation of Women in the New Canadian Party System', in William Cross (ed.), *Political Parties, Representation and Electoral Democracy in Canada*, Don Mills: Oxford University Press.

Young, Lisa (2000), *Feminists and Party Politics*, Vancouver: UBC Press.

Young, Lisa (1997), 'Fulfilling the Mandate of Difference: Women in the Canadian House of Commons', in Jane Arscott and Linda Trimble (eds), *In the Presence of Women: Representation in Canadian Governments*, Toronto: Harcourt Brace.

Young, Lisa (1997), 'Gender Equal Legislatures: Evaluating the Proposed Nunavut Electoral System', *Canadian Public Policy*, 32 (3): 306–15.

Young, Lisa (1991), 'Legislative Turnover and the Election of Women to the Canadian House of Commons', in Kathy Megyery (eds), *Women in Canadian Politics: Toward Equity in Representation*, Toronto: Dundurn Press.

Young, Lisa and William Cross (2003), 'Women's Involvement in Canadian Political Parties', in Manon Tremblay and Linda Trimble (eds), *Women and Electoral Politics in Canada*, Don Mills: Oxford University Press.

Official documents

British Columbia, Citizens' Assembly on Electoral Reform (2004), *Making Every Vote Count: The Case for Electoral Reform in British Columbia, Final Report*, [s. l.], [British Columbia Government] (www.citizensassembly.bc.ca/resources/final_report.pdf).

Committee on Equality of Opportunity Proceedings [Wales] (2001), S4C2, 31 October.

Conference Board of Canada (2001), *Nunavut Economic Outlook*, May, at www.gov.nu.ca/frv21.pdf.

Council of European Municipalities and Regions (1998), *Men and Women in Euro-*

pean Municipalities, Strasbourg: Council of European Municipalities and Regions.

Department of Trade and Industry (2004), *Fairness for All: A New Commission For Equality And Human Rights*, White Paper, Department of Trade and Industry in Association with the Department for Constitutional Affairs, Department for Education and Skills, Department for Work And Pensions, and the Home Office, Cm 6185.

Electoral Commission (2002), *The New Zealand Electoral Compendium*, 3rd edn, Wellington: Electoral Commission.

Government of Nunavut (2005), *Nunavut at a Glance* (www.gov.nu.ca/Nunavut/French/about/fglance.shtml).

Government of Nunavut (Nunavut Housing Corporation) and Nunavut Tunngavik (2004), *Nunavut Ten-year Inuit Housing Action Plan*, September.

Independent Commission on Proportional Representation (ICPR) (2004) *Changed Voting, Changed Politics: Lessons of Britain's Experience of PR since 1997. Final Report of the Independent Commission to Review Britain's Experience of PR Voting Systems*, London: University College.

Law Commission of Canada (2004), *Voting Counts: Electoral Reform for Canada*, Ottawa: Minister of Public Works and Government Services.

Ministère du Conseil exécutif (Québec) (www.institutions-democratiques.gouv.qc.ca/publications/fiche_1_chaque_vote_compte_en.pdf).

National Assembly for Wales (2001), *Equality Training and Raising Awareness Strategy: ETAARS*, Cardiff: National Assembly for Wales.

National Assembly for Wales (2004), *Report on Mainstreaming Equality in the Work of the Assembly*, Cardiff: Assembly Committee on Equality of Opportunity.

Nunavut Implementation Commission (1994), 'Two-member Constituencies and Gender Equality: A "Made in Nunavut" Solution for an Effective and Representative Legislature', discussion paper.

Royal Commission on Electoral Reform and Party Financing [Canada] (1991), *Report: Reforming Electoral Democracy*, Volume 1, Ottawa: Supply and Services.

Royal Commission on the Electoral System [New Zealand] (1986), *Towards Democracy: Report of the Royal Commission on the Electoral System*, Wellington: Government Printer.

Scottish Constitutional Convention (1995), *Scotland's Parliament, Scotland's Right*, Edinburgh.

Scottish Executive (2003), *Preventing Domestic Abuse*, Edinburgh: Scottish Executive.

Scottish Office (1997), *Scotland's Parliament*, Edinburgh: HMSO.

Scottish Parliament Information Centre (2002), *Gender in the Scottish Parliament*, Edinburgh: SPIC.

Scottish Partnership on Domestic Abuse (2000), *National Strategy to Address Domestic Abuse in Scotland*, Edinburgh: Scottish Executive.

Select Committee on Women's Rights (1975), 'Report of the Select Committee on Women's Rights: The Role of Women in New Zealand Society', *Appendices to the Journals of the House of Representatives*, Wellington.

Statistics Canada (2005), *Commonly reported Reasons for not completing Elementary/High School by Sex, Aboriginal Identity Population aged 15 to 34, Nunavut, 2001* (www.statcan.ca/english/freepub/89–595-XIE/tables/html/table2/nu2.htm).

United Nations' Economic and Social Council (2004), 'FWCW Platform for Action', Themes for progress on gender (www.un.org/ecosocdev/geninfo/afrec/vol12no1/eca2.htm).

United Nations and the Inter-parliamentary Union (2003), *The Convention on the Elimination of all Forms of Discrimination against Women and its Optional Protocol: Handbook for Parliamentarians*, Geneva: United Nations and the Inter-parliamentary Union.

Welsh Office (1997), *A White Paper: A Voice for Wales/Papur Gwyn: Llais dros Gymru*, Cm3718, London: Stationery Office.

Web sites

Africa Recovery On Line. A United Nations Publication: www.un.org/ecosocdev/geninfo/afrec/vol12no1/eca2.htm.

Centre for Advancement of Women in Politics: www.qub.ac.uk/cawp/observatory.html.

Elections Canada: www.elections.ca.

Equal Voice: www.equalvoice.ca/response_harper.html.

ESRC Society Today: www.esrc.ac.uk, and www.regard.ac.uk.

Gender and Constitutional Change: transforming politics in the UK: www.pol.ed.ac.uk/gcc.

Global Database of Quotas for Women: http://www.quotaproject.org.

Inter-parliamentary Union: www.ipu.org/wmn-e/classif.htm.

Still Counting. Women in politics across Canada: http//stillcounting.athabascau.ca.

Revolts.co.uk. The definitive source for academic analysis of backbench behaviour in Britain: www.revolts.co.uk.

Index

For Product Safety Concerns and Information please contact our EU representative GPSR@taylorandfrancis.com
Taylor & Francis Verlag GmbH, Kaufingerstraße 24, 80331 München, Germany

www.ingramcontent.com/pod-product-compliance
Lightning Source LLC
Chambersburg PA
CBHW050703280326
41926CB00088B/2432

* 9 7 8 0 4 1 5 4 7 9 5 2 3 *